Educational Communications and Technology: Issues and Innovations

Series Editors

J. Michael Spector, Department of Learning Technologies
University of North Texas
Denton, TX, USA

M. J. Bishop, College of Education, Lehigh University
University System of Maryland
Bethlehem, PA, USA

Dirk Ifenthaler, Learning, Design and Technology
University of Mannheim
Mannheim, Baden-Württemberg, Germany

Allan Yuen, Faculty of Education, University of Hong Kong
Hong Kong, Hong Kong

This book series, published collaboratively between the AECT (Association for Educational Communications and Technology) and Springer, represents the best and most cutting edge research in the field of educational communications and technology. The mission of the series is to document scholarship and best practices in the creation, use, and management of technologies for effective teaching and learning in a wide range of settings. The publication goal is the rapid dissemination of the latest and best research and development findings in the broad area of educational information science and technology. As such, the volumes will be representative of the latest research findings and developments in the field. Volumes will be published on a variety of topics, including: • Learning Analytics • Distance Education • Mobile Learning Technologies • Formative Feedback for Complex Learning • Personalized Learning and Instruction • Instructional Design • Virtual tutoring Additionally, the series will publish the bi-annual AECT symposium volumes, the Educational Media and Technology Yearbooks, and the extremely prestigious and well known, Handbook of Research on Educational Communications and Technology. Currently in its 4th volume, this large and well respected Handbook will serve as an anchor for the series and a completely updated version is anticipated to publish once every 5 years. The intended audience for Educational Communications and Technology: Issues and Innovations is researchers, graduate students and professional practitioners working in the general area of educational information science and technology; this includes but is not limited to academics in colleges of education and information studies, educational researchers, instructional designers, media specialists, teachers, technology coordinators and integrators, and training professionals.

Deborah Cockerham
Regina Kaplan-Rakowski
Wellesley Foshay • Michael J. Spector
Editors

Reimagining Education: Studies and Stories for Effective Learning in an Evolving Digital Environment

Editors
Deborah Cockerham
University of North Texas
Denton, TX, USA

Regina Kaplan-Rakowski
University of North Texas
Denton, TX, USA

Wellesley Foshay
University of North Texas
Denton, TX, USA

Michael J. Spector
University of North Texas
Denton, TX, USA

ISSN 2625-0004   ISSN 2625-0012   (electronic)
Educational Communications and Technology: Issues and Innovations
ISBN 978-3-031-25104-7   ISBN 978-3-031-25102-3   (eBook)
https://doi.org/10.1007/978-3-031-25102-3

This Springer imprint is published by the registered company Springer Nature Switzerland AG
The registered company address is: Gewerbestrasse 11, 6330 Cham, Switzerland

Foreword

The title of this collection of thought-provoking essays is "spot on"! In the 23 stories and studies, the reader will be carried on a journey of *Reimagining K-20 Education*. From exploring how to better address students with special needs to investigating how to form communities of practice to facilitate the design of effective learning experiences, the articles in this volume paint vivid pictures of how education can be transformed. But wait. Why do we need to "reimagine education?" Because, in the words of Mulvey and Novak, "the COVID-19 pandemic changed everything."

Early in 2020, K-12 schools around the world shuttered their schools and classrooms. Students sat at their kitchen tables and learned for the three months remaining in the 2019–2020 school year. And, for many of America's K-12 children, the 2020–2021 school year was just a continuation of remote learning, while the challenges to carry on in-class learning—from masks, to rotating absences of students and teachers, to the shot-gun marriage of technology into the classroom—made the 2020–2021 school year less than successful. That understatement is not contentious: both scholars and the media have carefully documented the studies that found losses in teaching and learning experienced by America's K-12 students and teachers.

Yes, there is ample reason to reimagine education. And it is no surprise that computing and telecommunications technologies will play a crucial role as we engage in that reimagining education effort. Indeed, over the past 30 years, Planet Earth has been undergoing a digital transformation. In virtually all human endeavors, technologies have brought about rapid and often disruptive change. The way people do things—pay bills, watch movies, consult with a physician, manufacture computers—has dramatically changed. In her landmark book, *In the Age of the Smart Machine,* Harvard Business School Professor Shoshana Zuboff (1988) points out two types of technological change: *automate*, or simply replicate a pencil-and-paper process on the computer; and *informate,* or take advantage of the technology to do something paper-and-pencil simply couldn't do. Blockbuster Video automated as they transferred movies from movie theater tape reels to smaller VHS tape reels for distribution to the public. On the other hand, Netflix *informated*: they digitized the movies and then sent digital streams over the Internet to computer screens, a.k.a. TVs. No more going to store to rent a videocassette!

It is fair to say that, by and large, over the past 30 years, education, from prekindergarten to higher education, has only been automating, e.g., taking curricular resources that started life on paper and digitizing those materials onto the computer, maybe adding some online videos, and providing teachers with educational software that more or less mimicked what the teachers were already doing in their classrooms. While electronic whiteboards were replacing chalkboards in classrooms, the pedagogy in those electronic whiteboard classrooms still looked a lot like the pedagogy in the chalkboard classrooms. Teachers were instructed to "integrate the technology" into their classrooms. On what basis? With what training? Schaffhauser (2015) shows that, even before the pandemic, K-12 teachers were spending two to five hours every week searching the Internet for relevant resources. Taken together, this is not a recipe for effective change.

But then COVID-19 appeared and "changed everything." Teachers in some districts made copies of their paper materials and drove around distributing them to their students. Giving students feedback on the worksheets in the packet was problematic. In some schools, which were already 1-to-1 and had purchased an online curricula service, the transition to remote learning was smoother, but not necessarily all that successful. By and large, the online curricula were digitized materials, and teachers were not able to personalize the materials to better accommodate struggling or accelerated learners. The interface to the systems posed significant challenges to struggling learners as well.

During the 2020–2021 school year, truckloads of personal computers (e.g., Chromebooks, iPads, laptops) were purchased by schools, along with many, many "educational software tools," which were typically provided free during the 2020–2021 school year (Rauf, 2020; Schaffhauser,2020). Was there professional development to help teachers use all this gear successfully? Not so much. And, again, the media has well documented the challenges and failings of the "shot-gun marriage" of technology into the K-12 classroom. Again, this is not a recipe for effective change!

So, yes, there is ample reason to reimagine education!

In painting a vision of next-generation education, this volume is organized into three parts.

- In Part I, *Experiences with Digital Changes*, the authors describe, often quite graphically, their personal journeys as they transition to using technology extensively in their classrooms. For example, in the first chapter of the volume, Strawn's descriptions of her fears, challenges, starts, and stops, in recounting her return to the classroom in 2020 had a visceral impact on us. In the 4th article, Norton provides another graphical account of a 1st-year teacher struggling mightily to cope with the transition from in-class to remote learning during the COVID disruption. Her account, too, had a deep impact on us. Indeed, in Part I, the seven essentially first-person narratives of classroom teachers and other education professionals attempting to educate their charges during the two COVID years clearly portray the teachers grappling, sometimes successfully and some-times less so, with novel situations for which they were unprepared.

- While the articles in Part I were teachers' personal accounts of dealing with the COVID disruption, the articles in Part II, *Research Studies Highlighting Innovative Strategies and Technologies*, use quantitative and qualitative research methods to better understand how educators addressed the myriad of issues dur-ing the 2019–2020 and 2020–2021 school years. While less visceral, the findings in Part II are no less compelling. For example, in their 2022 study of sixteen K-12 teachers, Mulvey and Novak found that "teachers considered mobile devices to bring new opportunities for learning, able to improve twenty-first-century skills, enhance learning in more flexible ways, with an aim to improve student-to-student communication." Yes! In their spring 2021 study of kindergar-ten teachers, Ndolo and Cockerham found that "all participants agreed that the kindergarteners acquired independent learning skills and technological skills online that would not have been achieved in face-to-face classroom settings." Can five-year-olds really learn independently through the use of technology? Of course, they can! The ten chapters in Part II explore the impact of technology-enhanced classrooms on different populations (e.g., kindergartners, blind/visu-ally impaired learners) and on different subject areas (e.g., literacy instruction, counseling). The breadth of coverage in this part demonstrates that technology, when done correctly, can truly have a broad impact across various subpopula-tions and across various content areas.
- As the title of Part III, *Reflections on Reimagining Education in an Evolving Digital Environment*, indicates, authors in this part reimagine education where change is of the informate sort. Let's leave automating *existing* educational prac-tices behind. Let's envision teaching and learning opportunities and experiences that research suggests are effective but require extensive technologies that simply haven't been *readily* available. For example, as explored in Knox's article, inte-grating game-based concepts, e.g., competition, scores, rewards, and levels, can lead to learners, especially the Alpha Generation learners, being more engaged and becoming more successful in their learning. But gamifying a year-long, third grade math curricula, for instance, where the needs of struggling learners and accelerated learners are addressed, as explored in Bollinger et al.'s article, requires significant software development and hardware support, both of which are only now coming to be widely available. Special education, envisioned in the Edyburn article, also describes changes of the informate sort: the article envi-sions "a future that is very different from the present."

Candidly, it is very exciting to have a volume of papers that truly challenges the status quo and truly reimagines education.

While each paper in this volume provides a specific provocative vision for how education needs to be, we can extract two themes that permeate virtually all the articles in the book.

- First, while computing and telecommunications technologies are at the core of the various visions, there is a clear consensus that technologies alone are not "the answer." Rather, the articles build on the African proverb "It takes a village to educate a child." For example, in Jordan et al.'s aptly titled chapter, "Behind the Scenes Action Makes Shift to Online Possible," the authors note that the staff in the Office of Academic Affairs at their university pitched in to support the transition to online learning during the COVID years. The Belgium researchers Torbeyns et al. found that the ICT coordinator played an important role in providing teachers and students with support for the transition. And, as Ndolo and Cockerham report, teachers and parents, too, stepped up and provided considerable support for the transition. Education requires a complex ecology!

- A second cross-cutting theme expands on the idea of education requiring a complex ecology. Virtually every paper documents some challenges and/or barriers that had to be dealt with in order to effectively provide students with a positive educational experience during the COVID years. Note that the singular version of "challenges" and "barriers" did not appear in any of the papers, only the plural version. For example, Kaiser, Strawn, and Cockerham document numerous challenges and barriers that secondary school teachers faced with respect to adopting technology during the COVID disruption. Similarly, Norton and Hernandez document numerous challenges and barriers with respect to engagement, technology fatigue, and Internet connectivity in secondary school during the COVID disruption. And on and on, each paper documents various challenges and barriers experienced by educators and students during the COVID disruption. Interestingly, while Norton and Hernandez search various databases in researching their chapter, there is not a database of challenges and barriers to technology use during the COVID disruption available. Cataloging each of the challenges and barriers identified in this volume would be a good start on just such a database.

Stepping back, the reason for this volume, the reason why it is so important that we "Reimagine Education" is this: we must prepare now *before* the next disruption occurs. We can't be scrambling as we did during the COVID disruption of 2020. The costs to students, to teachers, to society, of the scrambling have been duly documented in the media. And, whether the next one is again a viral pandemic or simply extended snow days due to impassable roads in the upper peninsula of Michigan, the notion that learning only takes place in a school building can no longer be entertained. Teaching and learning need to be seamless whether learners and teachers are co-located or not. We must envision how we can build an educational ecology that will be able to withstand disruption.

Envisioning such a supportive, flexible, and effective educational ecology is one thing; implementing it is quite another! As the current educational ecology gobbles up enormous resources, where will America find the resources to informate in K-20 education? Great question! As the present volume provides more than enough to think about, we leave that question for another time and another volume.

Ann Arbor, MI, USA   Elliot Soloway
Denton, TX, USA   Cathie Norris

References

Rauf, D. (2020). Coronavirus squeezes supply of Chromebooks, iPads, and other digital learning devices. *Education Week*.

Schaffhauser, D. (2015). *Research: Move to digital curriculum calls for teacher training, new district oles*. Accessed from https://thejournal.com/articles/2015/12/04/research-move-to-digital-curriculum-calls-for-teacher-training-new-district-roles.aspx.

Schaffhauser, D. (2020). Updated: Free resources for schools during COVID-19 outbreak. *The Journal, 13*. https://thejournal.com/articles/2020/03/13/free-resources-edtech-companies-step-up-during-coronavirus-outbreak.aspx.

Zuboff, S. (1988). *In the age of the smart machine: The future of work and power*. Basic Books, Inc.

Contents

Part I
Experiences with Digital Changes

Introduction

Deborah Cockerham

The most dangerous experiment we can conduct with our children is to keep schooling the same at a time when every other aspect of our society is dramatically changing.

– Chris Dede,

written statement to the Presidential Council of Advisors on Science and Technology panel (1997)

During the 1920 presidential campaign, Warren G. Harding's campaign boasted the slogan "Return to Normalcy." World War I and the Spanish flu pandemic were coming to an end, and the turbulence and chaos caused by these events still gripped the country in fear. The future president argued that people should forget the impact of these events and focus on resuming school, business, and daily life practices as they were before the war and the Spanish flu pandemic. Nothing needed to change, he argued, other than the perspective with which people viewed the world. According to Harding, returning to the pre-pandemic "normal" life would bring "serenity" and make life more robust. Yet Harding's hope for a return to normalcy was short-lived. Regardless of his claims, a "normal" pre-pandemic life was not realistic. Innovation was needed to build a stronger post-pandemic world (Deverell, 2020).

One hundred years later, the world changed again. As the COVID-19 pandemic closed stores and shuttered school buildings, the routines and social encounters of everyday life gave way to unpredictability and isolation. Yet, in contrast to the Harding era, this time society had an answer: digital tools that would provide the ability to participate in business, school, and socialization even while isolated.

D. Cockerham (✉)
University of North Texas, Fort Worth, TX, USA
e-mail: deborah.cockerham@unt.edu

© The Author(s), under exclusive license to Springer Nature Switzerland AG 2023
D. Cockerham et al. (eds.), *Reimagining Education: Studies and Stories for Effective Learning in an Evolving Digital Environment*, Educational Communications and Technology: Issues and Innovations, https://doi.org/10.1007/978-3-031-25102-3_1

However, as many soon discovered, tools alone were not enough. Participating in life online required reliable Internet service, but only 55% of households worldwide were connected to the Internet (ITU/UNESCO, 2019). The connectivity deficit of 45% left approximately 3.7 billion individuals, often located in marginalized communities, unable to access online resources and activities or to develop adequate digital skills. Even individuals who had Internet access often lacked the necessary skills, technical support, or accessible training for implementing technology (Molino, Cortiso, & Ghisleri, 2020).

The pandemic not only exposed inequitable educational opportunities such as these but also revealed incongruencies between learning resources and needs (International Commission on the Futures of Education, 2020). Schools that could afford appropriate tools and training tended to serve wealthier communities, and schools that served economically underprivileged students had for years focused more on tools and training to support basic word processing than on resources to support higher-order thinking skills (Becker, 2000). In addition, technology products purchased by schools did not always match technology needs or provide educator training. The move to online education required educators to adapt or replace teaching approaches that were effective in the physical classroom as they quickly moved to a virtual format. For many, this process involved learning digital tools and developing strategies that would better meet the emerging student needs.

The transformation of educational practices to better meet student needs has long been a goal of educational researchers. Dewey (1938) called for education based on experiences that were relevant to students. Education, according to Dewey, takes student needs into account as active learning is melded with concrete experience and reflection. Freire (1970) called for the teacher-student relationship to move beyond a "banking" approach, in which the teacher narrates ("deposits") the information and students receive and repeat the teacher's instruction. He suggests that an educational approach in which all parties are simultaneously teachers and students can build critical thinking and creative skills and may also more effectively address student and societal needs.

In more recent years, Kozma (1991) argued that technology has the potential to change education and learning, noting that the medium can support problem-solving growth as the user and the machine interact in a continually progressing cycle. Kozma also observed that, with appropriate design and implementation, technology can provide affordances not possible in face-to-face settings. Underwood (2009) likewise notes that, when digital technologies are implemented, the user learns and processes differently than when technology is not involved. A consideration of the impact of technology on learning and education can help in understanding implementations that may support more effective learning.

Technology in the Twenty-First Century

As the pace of technology development increased around the turn of the century, society experienced major changes in almost every area of life. Music and entertainment became portable, and online news outpaced printed newspapers. Global positioning systems directed travel, medical facilities transferred records to data-bases, and businesses increased accounting accuracy through computer-based spreadsheets. In addition, email and social media began to transform communication practices, and a wealth of resources was available at the touch of a button. Mobile technology, when combined with wireless connectivity, sparked increasingly personalized experiences and anywhere, anytime access to online information and connections. Experts recommended technology tools that could support education and even suggested that half of all middle and high school education would move online by 2019 (Christensen, Horn, & Johnson, 2011, cited in Reich, 2020).

Yet, even as technology has become infused into much of daily life, education has not kept pace. Traditional teaching practices still predominate in many educational settings, and many instructional approaches continue to focus on recall as a primary manifestation of learning. However, the ease of accessing the overabundance of available online information has lessened the need for pure memory work. In today's education, the ability to sift quickly through large quantities of information, determine most salient aspects, and use the information in problem solving are increasingly relevant. Twenty-first century skills, including critical thinking and creativity, can leverage technology as a tool for enriching learning.

Furthermore, twenty-first century schools face different challenges than those faced by twentieth century schools. While public schools in the 1950s and 1960s aimed to build national citizenship and support individual development, today's world must address serious issues related to the future of humanity and our planet (UNESCO, 2022). In order to address these challenges, individuals must communicate across cultures, collaborate for the common good, and consider innovative solutions. As education is reinvented to prepare students for the future, schools must ensure that students are developing the communication, collaboration, critical thinking, and creative skills needed to address current and future societal challenges.

New Perspectives on Online Education

During the shutdowns of the COVID-19 pandemic, educators, students, and parents viewed formal education through their computer screens. This vantage point provided the educational community with unique opportunities to reflect upon educational priorities, approaches, and needs. Before memories of recent online educational experiences fade, we must evaluate instructional approaches, student responses, and learning outcomes in light of educational priorities and goals. Insights into these experiences may promote the development of innovative approaches and educational practices that better prepare students for a future in which technology is likely to play an even larger role than today.

Reimagining Education: Stories and Studies for Effective Learning Practices in an Evolving Digital Society aims to encourage readers to rethink education and consider opportunities provided by new technologies for effective teaching and learning. How can educational communities of practice be reimagined to support a growth mindset for learning? Educational approaches that worked well, challenges that were difficult to overcome, and potential benefits of effective technology integration will encourage readers to reimagine education and implement practices that can strengthen the future of K-12 education. The chapters explore innovative visions for twenty-first century learning through a sequence of topics: educational experiences with digital changes, research studies highlighting innovative strategies and technologies, and reflections on reimagining education in an evolving digital environment.

Part I: Experiences with Digital Changes

This section provides a practical foundation for the book as it documents educational experiences of teachers and other academic personnel during the pandemic-related shift from classroom to online or hybrid learning. Readers can relive the emotional ups and downs experienced by a high school teacher returning to the physical classroom during the pandemic (Strawn, chapter "A Year in Tandem: A Teacher's Reflections of Doubt and Hope Amid COVID-19 School Year 2020–2021") and the challenges of a lab-based microbiology instructor in moving to a fully remote instructional environment (Bradshaw-Ward, chapter "Transition to Virtual Instruction: A Microbiology Instructor's Challenges"). Norton (chapter "Entering Education During the COVID-19 Pandemic") explores the difficulties of a new teacher in adjusting to the virtual teaching environment while building relationships with students and peers and learning campus and district expectations.

Although not as visible as teachers and faculty, other professionals supported the continuity of educational instruction through their leadership in various roles during the pandemic. Mukuni et al. (chapter "Instructional Designers' Perspectives on Faculty Experiences with Digital Changes") highlight the role of instructional designers in securing faculty acceptance of online learning and note the importance of a collaborative approach for ensuring quality online instructional experiences. In addition, Jordan et al. (chapter "Behind the Scenes Action Makes Shift to Online Possible") describe the importance of complete administrative teams, including administrators and staff, working behind the scenes to proactively address the numerous challenges and details of educational sustainability. Support from technology coordinators and connections with teaching colleagues encouraged elementary and secondary teachers in Belgium to "jump and swim" as they worked to learn remote instructional skills amid the challenging emergency move to remote learning (Torbeyns et al., chapter "Jump and Swim!? Lived Experiences of Flemish Elementary and Secondary School Teachers in COVID-19 Emergency Teaching Times").

A critical factor in sustaining education during the pandemic was communication between students, faculty, and other educational leadership (Li et al., chapter "Adapting to Digital Changes in Health Education: A Case Study"). Together, educational teams "integrated technology, worked through sickness, adapted to an ever-changing environment, maintained student relationships, learned new ways of instruction…and supported…students when the world was in crisis" (Strawn, 2023). The lived experiences highlighted in Part I bridge the reality of practice during the pandemic with the state-of-the-art research and innovations described in Parts II and III.

Part II: Research Studies Highlighting Innovative Strategies and Technologies

The second section consists of empirical studies of evidence-based learning technology and effective educational strategies and technologies. Investigations into the online experiences and perspectives of teachers in various educational areas provide insights into the teachers' creativity, concern for students, and resilience as they faced unexpected challenges. To support understanding of teacher adaptations as they moved from location-based classrooms to remote learning, the research of Kaiser et al. (chapter "Barriers to Technology Adoption Among K-12 Teachers During the COVID-19 Crisis") uncovers challenges to teaching online, discusses the importance of teacher self-efficacy, and suggests barriers that might have interfered with teacher use of technology tools.

Through interviews with higher education faculty and students, Audon et al. (chapter "The Lockdown in Retrospect: An International, Mixed Methods Perspective on Student and Faculty Experiences with COVID-19 Remote Learning") concluded that, overall, faculty understood and worked to remedy student issues during the pandemic-related shutdowns. Communication, a flexible approach to teaching content, and supporting student needs appeared to be keys to successful online instruction.

In secondary education, teachers struggled to find strategies and tools that would enhance online learning. Norton and Hernandez (chapter "Secondary Education Remote Learning Experiences and Challenges") provide a narrative review of secondary education tools that showed promise both during the pandemic and for the future. In contrast, teachers and parents of kindergarteners faced challenges related to the young children's developmental needs. Kindergarten students were often expected to attend synchronous online class sessions in order to "learn how school works" and develop social skills (Ndolo and Cockerham, chapter "Online Experiences of Kindergarten Teachers and Parents During the Pandemic: Hope for the Future"). Although teachers and parents alike indicated concerns that these two goals were not being met in online environments, they did see growth in the students' independent learning and technical skills.

In another elementary school study (Eustler, chapter "Influence of Pandemic-Induced Technology Use on Literacy Instruction"), analysis of K-5 teacher feedback suggests that teaching in the twenty-first century, by definition, requires the integration of technology. After contrasting technology skills with technology-based *teaching* skills, the author presents a clear case for teacher preparation and training that focuses on developing technology-related teaching skills rather than on learning-specific tools.

However, teachers and students also realized the potential of enriching learning through technology tools. Second-language learners enjoyed opportunities to interact with classmates from a distance and increased their sense of presence when participating in class sessions through virtual reality headsets (Thrasher, chapter "Meeting in the Metaverse: Language Learners' Insights into the Affordances of Virtual Reality"). Other teachers learned the value of using mobile devices to provide social and academic support as students used these devices for class assignments (Mulvey & Novak, chapter "COVID Teaching Experiences as Disrupting Events to Promote a Paradigm Shift in K-12 Mobile Technology Integration"). These authors suggest that, with technology, teachers are "increasingly ready to be the change."

Some educational areas presented complex challenges when moving to remote learning. For example, school counselors struggled with the idea of providing counseling services online while upholding their commitments to the ethics of the American School Counseling Association. Counselors determined which technologies were best suited for their online needs and created new tools to support their practice while adhering to ethical standards (Howard, chapter "Professional School Counselor Technology Use for Communication During COVID-19"). Students who were blind or visually impaired (BVI) also experienced unique challenges in online learning. In a case study of a blind student, Kaplan-Rakowski and Heap (chapter "Emerging Technologies for Blind and Visually Impaired Learners: A Case Study") reveal the student's challenges, perspectives, and successful strategies in navigating the online environment. The chapter concludes with suggested technologies for supporting BVI students.

Part II concludes with results of the Texas Technology Needs Assessment (Strawn et al., chapter "Texas K-12 Teachers Technology Needs Assessment"). This chapter describes a unique research study in which twelve K-12 teachers who were enrolled in a doctoral program examined the technology challenges and needs of 73 K-12 teachers in Texas schools. Training, tools, and strategies are suggested for future online K-12 education. The research in Part II leads directly into the future visions suggested in Part III.

Part III: Reflections on Reimagining Education in an Evolving Digital Environment

The final section focuses on lessons learned, innovative trends, and skills needed to address current and future societal challenges. Forward-facing educational visions incorporate inclusive, engaging learning environments that meet the needs of all learners. Edyburn (chapter "Reimagining the Future of Special Education

Technology") uses trend analysis to suggest future directions for special education technology. Inclusive technologies such as screen magnification and word prediction can benefit individuals both with and without special needs. Along these same lines, Bollinger et al. (chapter "Universal Design for Learning Access: Faculty-Centered Community Design") examined a faculty-centered Community of Practice in which all members worked to implement Universal Design for Learning. Reflections from participants suggest that inclusive, accepting learning spaces engage students in both place-based and online learning spaces.

Additionally, Knox (chapter "Game-Based Learning Design Optimized for Cognitive Load") suggests that the interaction, challenges, and clear, progressive goals of a game-based learning approach may engage and motivate students to learn. As students engage in realistic problem solving through games, they think both critically and creatively while refining strategies for navigating future challenges.

Other topics to consider include privacy literacy and "instructional disobedience." Rivera and Grotewold (chapter "Privacy Literacy and Library Instruction") suggest that, as technology is increasingly integrated into education, privacy literacy should be a priority for all students. To function as digital citizens, students must be aware of and prepared to address privacy challenges. Educators must also consider reasons that students engage in "instructional disobedience," or learning behavior that does not match classroom expectations (Goeman et al., chapter "Instructional Disobedience in Flipped Higher Education Classrooms: An Exploration"). The authors consider why higher education students in flipped classrooms may engage in instructional disobedience and suggest responses to such behavior.

Part III closes by emphasizing the need for instructional strategies that empower students to navigate an uncertain future. Cockerham (chapter "Reimagining Higher Education Pedagogy: Building an Active Understanding of the Research Process") considers the need for students to develop and practice foundational skills such as critical thinking, creativity, collaboration, and communication. The chapter examines higher education instructional pedagogies and their impacts upon students' abilities to address current and future challenges. While memories of challenges and inequities uncovered during the COVID-19 pandemic are still strong, action must be taken to fortify school policies and opportunities. Now is the time to evaluate current practices and develop instructional strategies that develop student agency and twenty-first century skills.

Reimagining Education

The COVID-19 pandemic has impacted all sectors of the educational system, revealing inequities, needs, and misalignments that must be addressed. At the same time, it has illuminated new possibilities and potential directions for building stronger educational opportunities. Learning is, by nature, transformative (Mezirow,

1997). As educational practices are re-envisioned for the future, a return to normalcy is not the answer. Insights from the pandemic have the potential to completely reshape education. A reimagining of education must consider student needs, provide skills and strategies to solve unimagined global issues, and empower the younger generation to make effective choices as the leaders of tomorrow.

References

Becker, H. J. (2000). Who's wired and who's not: Children's access to and use of computer technology. *The Future of Children*, 44–75.

Christensen, C. M., Horn, M. B., & Johnson, C. W. (2011). *Disrupting class: How disruptive innovation will change the way the world learns* (Vol. 1). McGraw-Hill.

Deverell, W. (2020). *Warren Harding tried to return America to 'normalcy' after WWI and the 1918 pandemic. It failed.* In https://www.smithsonianmag.com/history/warren-harding-back-to-normalcy-after-1918-pandemic-180974911/#:~:text=The%20lesson%20from%20 Harding%E2%80%99s%20time%20is%20that%20%E2%80%9Cgoing,%E2%80%9Cequip oise%2C%E2%80%9D%20which%20is%20hardly%20a%20conventional%20political%20 promise

Dewey, J. (1938). *Experience and education*. Prentice-Hall.

Freire, P. (1970). *Pedagogy of the oppressed* (MB Ramos, Trans.). Continuum Press.

International Commission on the Futures of Education. (2020). *Education in a post-COVID world: Nine ideas for public action*. UNESCO.

ITU/UNESCO Broadband Commission for Sustainable Development. (2019). *The state of broadband 2019: Broadband as a foundation for sustainable development*. Accessed from https://www.itu.int/dms_pub/itu-s/opb/pol/S-POL-BROADBAND.20-2019-PDF-E.pdf

Kozma, R. B. (1991). Learning with media. *Review of Educational Research, 61*(2), 179–211.

Mezirow, J. (1997). Transformative learning: Theory to practice. *New Directions for Adult and Continuing Education, 1997*(74), 5–12.

Molino, M., Cortese, C. G., & Ghislieri, C. (2020). The promotion of technology acceptance and work engagement in industry 4.0: From personal resources to information and training. *International Journal of Environmental Research and Public Health, 17*(7), 2438.

Reich, J. (2020). *Failure to disrupt: Why technology alone can't transform education*. Harvard University Press.

Strawn, S. (2023). A year in tandem: A teacher's reflections of doubt and hope amid COVID-19 school year 2020–2021. In D. Cockerham, R. Kaplan-Rakowski, W. Foshay, & M. Spector (Eds.), *Reimagining Education: Studies and Stories for Effective Learning Practices in an Evolving Digital Society* (Chapter 2). Springer.

Underwood, J. D. (2009). *The impact of digital technology: A review of the evidence of the impact of digital technologies on formal education*. British Educational Communications and Technology Agency.

UNESCO. (2022). *Reimagining our futures together: A new social contract for education*. United Nations.

A Year in Tandem: A Teacher's Reflections of Doubt and Hope Amid COVID-19 School Year 2020–2021

Shelby L. Strawn

Introduction

This story is a lived experience from my time teaching during the 2020–2021 school year. Recalling my internal dialogue, I attempted to capture the essence of last year's occurrences in summary. I describe my changing feelings and thoughts taking place last year toward being face-to-face with students, evolving administrative expectations, and the impact of COVID-19.

Shock

It was July of 2020 when I learned my school district opted to begin the school year as regularly scheduled that August. We were charged with the responsibility of teaching both face-to-face and virtual learners simultaneously. Fear of the unknown perpetually plagued my mind until summer's end with feelings of anger, stress, anxiety, and an overall loss of hope. I worried that my disgust with a global pandemic, my severe disillusionment with the public education system, and how the previous school year ended in such turmoil, would severely affect me and bleed over to my students. Influxes of panicked thoughts frequented my days as I considered preparing conceivably impossible lesson plans for three different secondary science courses:

S. L. Strawn (✉)
University of North Texas, Denton, TX, USA
e-mail: shelbystrawn@my.unt.edu

© The Author(s), under exclusive license to Springer Nature Switzerland AG 2023
D. Cockerham et al. (eds.), *Reimagining Education: Studies
and Stories for Effective Learning in an Evolving Digital Environment*,
Educational Communications and Technology: Issues and Innovations,
https://doi.org/10.1007/978-3-031-25102-3_2

How am I going to conduct lab activities? My classroom is too small, and I can't distance them. Will they wear their masks and follow safety guidelines, or will this lead to yet another discipline issue? How will I teach virtual students and face-to-face students at the same time? How will I modify lessons for virtual learners? Will they still learn science if I can't do hands-on activities with them? What if I or my family gets horribly sick? Do I have to use my sick days each time I am required to quarantine? What if students do not have the resources they need to learn from home? How am I going to get through this?

How?

Silence

A pleasant surprise the first day back was that my students were genuinely excited to be there in person. I could see their smiles even behind their masks as they returned to their familiar classrooms and friends. District policy stated that all individuals must wear masks and sanitize regularly, but there was no possibility of socially distancing with full class sizes. Even so, the worries I had before beginning the school year dissipated. I decided that because the students were willing, this crazy year may not be that bad. Teachers were expected to simultaneously teach virtual learners via Google Meets and in-person students because there were initially fewer virtual learners enrolled. We were provided with a noise cancelling microphone so we could speak and listen to the virtual learners' questions, two computer monitors, and a projector screen. The district also provided document cameras for all teachers. I admit to a smooth transition in these technology devices because I regularly used dual monitors and embedded Google Classroom activities into daily instruction. I remember several teachers expressed challenges with Google Meets, coordinating screen views, and communicating to virtual learners in a bustling in-person classroom. My biggest challenge with teaching remote and face-to-face learners was engaging everyone at the same time. The dual assignment ultimately resulted in a significant loss of instructional time per class period. I began to see the detriment of not splitting up in-person and virtual classes within the first few days of school. Teaching 14–18-year-old students in advanced and college-level biology courses brought about opposition, as rigorous subject matter resulted in remote learners struggling to understand concepts that were better understood by in-person learners. Virtual learner needs were inadvertently but continually shelved during class in favor of in-person student needs. Providing equitable and accommodating assignments for virtual learners proved futile. I know that learning transfer must have occurred at least for some fully online students due to end-of-year assessment performance, but a rich educational experience was not had.

Silence was the most significant issue from both virtual and in-person learners throughout the year. Face-to-face learners often exhibited an unengaged or unenthusiastic attitude during lessons or activities, as if they were simply going through the motions of school. Those characteristics may have been related to me having to talk to the virtual learners simultaneously. By contrast, there was a daily struggle to interact with my virtual learners, from turning on cameras to being responsive when I asked if they were there or if they heard and understood my instructions. Still, we moved forward with lessons and assessments. Social factors that I did not previously consider worked against their academic honesty and participation. Some students were truthful, stating they had just woken up and logged in and did not want their camera on. Others exhibited a much more secretive home life. Some preferred to stay home without their cameras on because school had never been a happy place. Some did not want to show their home to their peers or me. Several, though marked 'present,' did not participate the duration of the school year.

Where are they?

Stress

As anticipated, the infection spread throughout the high school campus after the first couple of weeks. Students began trading quarantine time like baseball cards, resulting in staggered attendance throughout the year. As teaching ensued, the mental and physical stress was unavoidable as I continuously followed safety protocols, taught two classes at once, and exhausted my throat from hours-long voice projection through my mask. My mind and body did not appreciate the juggling act, as I was so depleted at the end of the day compared to years past. Not a day went by that I did not need a nap after school to make it through the evening. I kept moving forward, but quite frequently found gaps in learning due to the previous year's March shutdown. Tutoring the most basic concepts became a daily occurrence.

In addition to my regular duties of lesson planning, teaching, grading, intervening, documenting, communicating, and setting up laboratory activities, other district-mandated changes exacerbated my waning positivity. Our district exhibited an evolution in curriculum on top of teaching during the pandemic. The expectations placed upon teachers were nearly impossible to meet. Teachers were required to dramatically alter their instructional to accommodate a more streamlined, vertical approach, also known as a 'professional learning community.' The lack of effective professional development regarding the 'new way' of instructional design, data analysis, and documentation due to summertime shutdown proved to be the final straw for some teachers. Expectations placed on us were modified on a weekly and sometimes daily basis. An 'it's time to go back to normal,' neglectful aura was ever-present from those in charge. Instructional resources and personnel were stretched thin. Teachers the same. I did the minimum that was required of new curriculum mandates for my own mental health. I resented being required to change an already effective teaching methodology in such a tumultuous time – a time when no one was sure about anything. Had I aligned with the 'shape up or ship out' mentality and bore the stress of penciling in every new way of measuring learning and performance on four different documents, I probably would have quit at the end of the first semester.

How do they expect us to do it all?

Sickness

The entire science department quarantined at the same time in mid-October as we all tested positive for COVID-19. Most teachers were symptomatic, including myself. At that time, countless individuals were testing positive for the disease daily, but I could not help feeling personally attacked by the infectious microbe. It was as if the virus had manifested the most abusive and cruel human-like characteristics that left me feeling physically, mentally, and emotionally inadequate. I woke each morning with a small vehicle resting on my chest, my vision blurred, and my brain a maze. My symptoms of coughing, feverishness, exhaustion, severe muscle soreness, and obviously no taste or smell compounded with figuring out how our two school-age children without everyone falling behind. None of these symptoms compared to the disillusionment and resentment I felt. The idea that I could make someone sick with an unknown outcome deafened me. The possibility of my own children and my students losing class time was an impossible thought. I immediately posted on Google Classroom that I would be out for two weeks. For fear of falling behind, I felt that I still needed to be available to explain content because I had projects and tests planned that could not be moved. So, after getting my own children sorted with remote learning (a kindergartner trying to learn and follow along on a synchronous meeting was difficult to witness), I logged in almost daily to teach lessons, explain assignments, and review for tests. I learned that because of the lack of substitutes, teachers were filling in for absent teachers during their conference periods. This act of selflessness made an unforgettable impression.

Why aren't teachers allowed to be sick?

Still

Still, teachers persevered, rallying until the end, but it is never truly the end. I did everything I could to meet the academic needs of my students, which was the best medicine for making it through the year. I practiced positivity and patience toward my students, which resulted in lasting camaraderie because we were all in this situation together. Though there was no resolution this year, there were moments of success bred from the refusal to give up, as teachers across the world experienced. The applauding moment was that my students holistically performed well on their final assessments, showing that they can also persevere and make light of a difficult situation.

Though I would never want to relive the experience, last year was an opportunity. There should be drastic changes in the way teachers are supported if we are to progress toward better education. My worst days were when I felt I was not being heard. We were told that there was support available if we needed, but I felt alone most of the time. There was no incentive when teachers were made to endure the process of full curriculum redesign. There was no acknowledgement when teachers spent their own money on classroom materials and technology resources or earned additional credits and certifications. As far as technology is concerned, resources should have been allotted to purchase new laptops rather than purchasing blanket classroom technology devices for all teachers (I did not use my document camera once the whole year). Rather, we became 1:1 in March of 2020 via reuse of years-old laptops, removing the existing laptops from teacher's classrooms. Because the students knew the laptops were dated, there was a severe lack of care in the way the laptops were treated. In understanding the experience of teachers last year, meaningful administrative support, individualized and specific professional development, and digital pedagogy training are an absolute necessity. Every teacher is unique in their craft, and thus so are their classroom requirements. Teachers deserve the professional responsibility of assessing their classroom material and technology needs and have the freedom to communicate those needs to administration. Solutions of classroom technology optimization and streamlined curriculum design are possible if teachers are treated as equals to administrative staff with a voice in classroom decision-making. If anything, this year has shed light on the dire need for teachers to be upheld as high-quality, respected, professional people. Not everyone could have pushed boundaries the way my colleagues, and every teacher around the globe, did last school year. Pushed beyond our comfort zones, we accomplished what we thought was impossible and supported our students when the world was in crisis. Teachers integrated technology, worked through sickness, adapted to an ever-changing environment, maintained student relationships, learned new ways of instruction, and managed to survive.

Statistic

Despite the arguably successful and proud year I had, I decided to end my teaching career after five years and move into another profession for my own well-being. I have read that the fifth year of teaching is a deciding factor on whether you stay or go.
    I am a statistic.
    Can they hear us now?

Instructional Designers' Perspectives on Faculty Experiences with Digital Changes

Kizito Mukuni, Douglas Asante, and Maha Alfaleh

Introduction

We discuss our perspectives on faculty experiences with digital changes as instructional designers (IDs) employed at two different universities in the United States between the early Spring of 2020 and the Summer of 2021 when school administrations decided to move from face-to-face to fully online, and the interventionary measures employed by two institutions. Our reflections cover IDs and faculty challenges in technology adaptation, continuity plans, and pedagogical strategies during the period. Our findings and concluding recommendations are meant to be of resource to the field of instructional design (ID) and higher education.

The transition to online learning during the pandemic warranted the need for sound instructional design services. Instructional design is the "reflective process of translating principles of learning and instruction into plans for instructional materials, activities, information resources, and evaluation" (Smith & Ragan, 2004, p. 4). IDs assist faculty with course design and redesign, assist faculty to identify appropriate digital tools and technology for use in their courses, and recommend pedagogical approaches to meet their goals in online, hybrid, or face-to-face learning environments.

K. Mukuni (✉)
Fayetteville State University, Fayetteville, USA
e-mail: kizito1@vt.edu

D. Asante · M. Alfaleh
Virginia Polytechnic Institute and State University, Blacksburg, VA, USA
e-mail: douglasa@vt.edu; mahaa89@vt.edu

© The Author(s), under exclusive license to Springer Nature Switzerland AG 2023
D. Cockerham et al. (eds.), *Reimagining Education: Studies and Stories for Effective Learning in an Evolving Digital Environment*, Educational Communications and Technology: Issues and Innovations, https://doi.org/10.1007/978-3-031-25102-3_3

Background

At both institutions, there is a dedicated department within which a team of IDs functions. However, one of the institutions has an instructional technology department and curriculum department that collaborate to support faculty. Faculty members are free to make use of the services provided by the departments either on a contract (usually to develop a new course or convert an existing face-to-face course to an online or hybrid course) or on a walk-in basis (usually to consult on a particular instructional problem). Pre-pandemic, both institutions followed appropriate guidelines for moving courses online. This included providing instructional design services and course reviews, based on institutional policies and rubrics.

These departments encouraged faculty to rethink how they had taught courses pre-pandemic and provided up-to-date devices, access to online resources, and professional development, among other resources. Pre-pandemic, both institutions provided traditional and online courses, but mainly conventional face-to-face courses. During the pandemic, the instructional modality was emergency remote teaching (ERT), not to be confused with online learning (Hodges et al., 2020). Online course design typically requires time and systematic procedures to design (Branch, 2009). ERT requires an immediate, temporal shift to remote teaching. These approaches and necessities compromised certain significant areas of conventional online course design, including accessibility and assessment, among others (Hodges et al., 2020). In this chapter, digital changes refer to the change in faculty use and orientation of communication and collaborative technologies for teaching and learning online.

Challenges Faced During the Transition

As IDs, one of the challenges we faced was securing faculty buy-in. We did encounter faculty who were resistant to change and were unwilling to consider our recommendations for improving their courses using educational tools. For example, one faculty member retorted, "Why should I do all that you're telling me when it is my course?"

Technological tools facilitate the transmission of instructions, communication, and collaborative experiences for teaching and learning. According to Yordming (2017), "In the digital age, information and communication technology (ICT) plays a key role in creating and exchanging knowledge and information around the globe" (p. 45). Given the prevailing conditions then, technology integration was prominent in instructional design. It was quite overwhelming for faculty to adhere to best practices for online course design, especially adapting to digital technology integration into instructions. Learning new digital applications like Equatio, Read&Write, and digital labs regardless of their essence at the time for most STEM courses, created a significant level of anxiety among faculty.

Technology anxiety is often attributed as being the reason behind the reluctance of faculty to design and teach online courses (Johnson et al., 2012). One of the causes of the anxiety is the fear of the time it would take to learn and use the technology (Butler & Sellbom, 2002). According to Makoe (2012), being accustomed to former teaching methods and lack of technical skills and knowledge prove to be barriers to faculty's integration of technology.

Among the many other fears and concerns faculty raised, the most common was not knowing how to use technology (e.g., the grade book, collaborative tools, video editing software, etc.) for instructional purposes. One faculty asked, "How can I use discussions in a graduate seminar under the Hyflex model?" Faculty were also concerned with facing problems connecting to live class sessions, system login problems, and not being accustomed to the system. Some feared that the technology would fail to work, hence disrupting the class. Others complained that they had to learn how to use new tools besides providing training and technical support to their students in some cases. A few were struggling with old devices.

In one of the online Zoom consultations during the transition, a faculty member requested tutorials on using Zoom for teaching, as they had never used it before. The faculty member wanted to know how students could collaborate with each other in Zoom classroom sessions and increase student–student interactions. The faculty revealed that they had previously taught the course using teacher-centered methods with no student interactions. Other faculty who had not taught online before were introduced to best practices for online course design, as some were under the impression that moving a course online simply meant posting PowerPoints on the LMS and grading the assessments. We provided them with strategies for appropriately using technology to enhance learning and ways to create meaningful learning experiences using models like the Community of Inquiry (COI) framework (Fiock, 2020).

Though we introduced various educational tools to faculty, we advised them to adapt only user-friendly tools they were familiar with. The tools recommended were LMS tools (discussion boards, Wikis, Journals, etc.), and collaboration tools (Teams, Zoom, Collaborate Ultra, etc.). We encouraged faculty to make their content interactive by using video tools like VoiceThreads, YuJa, and Kaltura. Even though training workshops and consultation services on various academic tools were provided at both institutions pre-pandemic, some faculty only became aware of them during the transition.

Mitigating the Challenges

At both institutions, though in different capacities, an approach similar to a three-way intervention was engaged by the ID teams to meet the needs of faculty while they transitioned to the new modes of teaching. The three-way approach involved just-in-time professional development – workshop training to reorient and assist faculty to build new and repurposing existing courses for online teaching and learning; a continuity site – stocked with quick-learning resources for faculty, and an ID consultation request; and templates – course shells and online-based course design and teaching aids for faculty. One of the differences between the two institutions in this approach was that one was solely online whereas the other was hybrid in its operations.

Workshops

At one of the institutions, the just-in-time professional development involved creating and teaching workshops centered around teaching online. For example, a condensed workshop session on best practices for transitioning online and integrating learning tools into the course, and a Hyflex session were offered to faculty and graduate-teaching assistants.

Resources and Services

At one of the institutions, quick learning resources for faculty and graduate students were produced and distributed. These resources included tips for using proctor services and exam security tools. Faculty had the opportunity to have one-on-one consultations with instructional designers to request more information and guidance on best practices and tools for teaching online. There was an increase in consultation requests during this period. At one of the institutions, faculty were enrolled in a best practices course for teaching online, which provided various pertinent resources for faculty.

Templates

Instructors were provided course shells with templates on how to structure their lessons. This included where to add objectives, to-do lists, activities, assignments, and assessments. This was intended to guide faculty on what should be included in the lessons.

Discussion

Our experiences working with faculty exposed us to anxieties that haunted faculty about learning, using, and integrating technology tools into their instructions. We identified that the three-pronged approach we used was significant in preparing faculty to intrinsically learn to use and select tools they were comfortable to teach with during such challenging times. The technology tools for LMS use were imperative not only for blended and Hyflex instructional modalities but for the ERT as a whole.

Conclusion and Recommendations

Transitioning to alternative instructional design and delivery has been an age-long challenge for higher education and became more profound during the COVID-19 pandemic. Lessons drawn from such periods indicate the use of templates, deepened consultations, and remodeling modalities for teaching and learning. Preparing faculty for a digital change during crises would require consistent training on technology use and integration, pertinent pedagogical strategies, and advanced template design for multiple modalities. Hyflex design allows for the integration of multiple modalities to reach a wider range of learners (Abdelmalak & Parra, 2016). We recommend that institutions commit to template design that facilitates a Hyflex design to accommodate a wider range of learners.

It is important to support the knowledge, skills, and positive attitudes of faculty to reduce the challenges of online teaching (Borup & Evmenova, 2019). The educational system needs qualified faculty able to develop fast and change the context of information that combines theory and practice based on the need and situation (Guven et al., 2012). Our prediction is that the skills gained by IDs and faculty during the transition will be useful in improving teaching and learning in general and not just in emergency transitions.

Acknowledgment We would like to thank Dr. Joseph Mukuni for his input and support.

References

Abdelmalak, M. M. M., & Parra, J. L. (2016). Expanding learning opportunities for graduate students with HyFlex course design. *International Journal of Online Pedagogy and Course Design, 6*(4), 19–37. https://EconPapers.repec.org/RePEc:igg:jopcd0:v:6:y:2016:i:4:p:19-37

Borup, J., & Evmenova, A. S. (2019). The effectiveness of professional development in overcoming obstacles to effective online instruction in a college of education. *Online Learning, 23*(2), 1–20. https://doi.org/10.24059/olj.v23i2.1468

Branch, R. M. (2009). *Instructional design: The ADDIE approach* (Vol. 722). Springer.

Butler, D. L., & Sellbom, M. (2002). Barriers to adopting technology. *Educause Quarterly, 2*(1), 22–28. https://www.learntechlib.org/p/92849/

Fiock, H. (2020). Designing a community of inquiry in online courses. *The International Review of Research in Open and Distributed Learning, 21*(1), 135–153. https://doi.org/10.19173/irrodl.v20i5.3985

Guven, M., Kurum, D., & Saglam, M. (2012). Evaluation of the distance education pre-service teachers' opinions about teaching practice course (Case of Izmir City). *Turkish Online Journal of Distance Education, 13*(1), 112–127. https://dergipark.org.tr/en/pub/tojde/issue/16899/176124

Hodges, C., Moore, S., Lockee, B., Trust, T., & Bond, A. (2020, March 27). The difference between emergency remote teaching and online learning. *Educause Review, 3*. https://er.educause.edu/articles/2020/3/the-difference-between-emergency-remote-teaching-and-online-learning

Johnson, T., Wisniewski, M. A., Kuhlemeyer, G., Isaacs, G., & Krzykowski, J. (2012). Technology adoption in higher education: Overcoming anxiety through faculty bootcamp. *Journal of Asynchronous Learning Networks, 16*(2), 63–72. https://eds.s.ebscohost.com/eds/pdfviewer/pdfviewer?vid=0&sid=21a6f35b-82a5-4a5f-85e9-0992bf7015e2%40redis

Makoe, M. (2012). Teaching digital natives: Identifying competencies for mobile learning facilitators in distance education. *South African Journal of Higher Education, 26*(1), 91–104. https://www.learntechlib.org/p/69027/

Smith, P. L., & Ragan, T. J. (2004). *Instructional design*. Wiley.

Yordming, R. (2017). Teachers' perspective towards digital teaching tools in Thai EFL classrooms. *International Journal of Languages, Literature and Linguistics, 3*(2), 45–48. https://doi.org/10.18178/ijlll.2017.3.2.108

Jump and Swim!? Lived Experiences of Flemish Elementary and Secondary School Teachers in COVID-19 Emergency Teaching Times

Joke Torbeyns, Katie Goeman, Annelies Raes, and Fien Depaepe

Introduction

The COVID-19 crisis undoubtedly challenged education worldwide. School environments were transformed into virtual realities. Teachers—at all levels of education—were forced to shift to emergency remote teaching and to adapt their practices at an exceptionally high pace (e.g., Bozkurt & Sharma, 2020; Dhawan, 2020). We aimed to identify (a) the major challenges that Flemish elementary and secondary school teachers were confronted with during the first COVID-19 lockdown period (i.e., the months of March–October 2020, in Flanders, Belgium) (research question 1), and (b) the resources they could rely on to address these challenges (research question 2). We individually interviewed 17 elementary and 19 secondary school teachers using a semi-structured questionnaire. The questionnaire was developed on the basis of the e-capacity model, an empirically tested conceptual framework concerning school and teacher-level conditions to foster effective Information and Communication Technology (ICT) integration for instructional purposes (Vanderlinde & van Braak, 2010).

Teachers' responses revealed major challenges related to the available ICT infrastructure, the school's ICT vision and policy and the development of their own digital competencies—challenges that mainly echo the findings of studies

J. Torbeyns (✉) · K. Goeman · F. Depaepe
Katholieke Universiteit Leuven, Leuven, Belgium
e-mail: joke.torbeyns@kuleuven.be; katie.goeman@kuleuven.be; fien.depaepe@kuleuven.be

A. Raes
Katholieke Universiteit Leuven, Leuven, Belgium

Centre Interuniversitaire de Recherche en Education de Lille, Lille, France
e-mail: annelies.raes@kuleuven.be

© The Author(s), under exclusive license to Springer Nature Switzerland AG 2023
D. Cockerham et al. (eds.), *Reimagining Education: Studies and Stories for Effective Learning in an Evolving Digital Environment*, Educational Communications and Technology: Issues and Innovations, https://doi.org/10.1007/978-3-031-25102-3_4

conducted before the COVID-19 crisis (e.g., Goeman et al., 2015; Sailer et al., 2021). Secondary school teachers pointed to the summative evaluation of students' competencies as an additional, and new, challenge during the COVID-19 crisis. The ICT coordinator was mentioned as primary resource to address all challenges. Teachers also referred to their colleagues as important additional resource to overcome their individual difficulties. We exemplify the major challenges and resources as reported by the teachers in the following sections.

How to Reach All Pupils

The first major challenge, shared by primary and secondary school teachers, relates to both the technical and practical facilities needed to effectively reach all pupils. Neither all teachers nor all pupils were equipped with the required infrastructure to organize online distance education. Some teachers had to use their own private laptops to meet with their pupils and provide online instruction, as there were no laptops available at their schools. Likewise, not all pupils were equipped with a laptop or desktop at home. These pupils relied on their cell phones, if available, to meet with their teachers and follow classes.

Confronted with these difficulties, teachers actively—and successfully—looked for solutions. They bought their own private laptops to organize their online distance education and launched, with the help of their school's directors, calls to hand in secondhand laptops for pupils who did not possess a laptop at home.

Unfortunately, the supply of needed infrastructure to the pupils was not sufficient to effectively reach them. Teachers were not able to reach all pupils, even those that were equipped with the required technical tools, due to student behavior that challenged the effective implementation of online instruction. Not willing or not being able to participate in online classes, being reluctant to turn on the camera during online classes, and remaining silent even when invited to contribute to the online discussions were most frequently mentioned as additional barriers. But, again, teachers actively created solutions to deal with the barriers by visiting the pupils' houses and actively inviting these pupils to participate in the online classes. Or, if the latter turned out to be impossible, the teacher offered these pupils the possibility to come to the school to follow classes.

So Many Webinars … But Luckily There's the ICT Coordinator and the Colleagues!

In contrast to the limited number of professional development initiatives related to ICT prior to COVID-19, teachers were offered an extremely high number of webinars and online courses during this first lockdown and were challenged to get a clear overview of all initiatives. Teachers reported being overwhelmed with initiatives from various organizations and with e-mails announcing potentially relevant courses and webinars. It required much time to find out whether the courses and webinars were relevant for them individually, and the advice of their ICT coordinator at school was highly welcomed at this point. The ICT coordinator was not only of great help to select the most relevant webinars and courses but was also continuously on standby to respond to individual problems related to the implementation of online distance education, to explain specific technological challenges, and to create self-made tutorials for the teachers at his/her school.

The teachers further referred to their colleagues—from not only within but also outside their own schools—and especially the spontaneously created online groups as building blocks to address their problems and uncertainties. Being confronted with highly similar challenges and difficulties, they tried to help each other by dividing the questions that needed to be answered to address these challenges and difficulties and sharing the results of their individual search processes.

We Need a Clear Vision and Policy at School

Teachers did their very best to deal with all challenges they were confronted with, but missed a clear vision and policy at school level about how to deal with the challenges related to the organization of online distance education. For some teachers, the absence of a clear vision and policy at school level was not new (i.e., no school vision or policy related to ICT before COVID-19). For other teachers, the school's vision and policy was not adapted to the new situation and required quick and clear changes in view of online distance education. The absence of a clear vision and policy at school level resulted in highly various and inconsistent tool use and teaching practices among teachers within a school, making the delivery of digital education to and for pupils even more complex.

How About Summative Evaluation?

A major challenge for secondary school teachers that was not mentioned by the primary school teachers was the summative evaluation of their pupils. This summative evaluation was not only difficult to implement in terms of content (how to effectively evaluate all core competencies?) and practical organization (how can we know whether the pupils did not cheat or help each other?), but also seriously questioned by parents (can all core competencies reliably and validly be evaluated via online tools, is it correct what the teachers are doing?). Some teachers, having had positive experiences with this type of summative evaluation, expressed their interest in further professional development related to the design and implementation of digital evaluation and related teacher competencies.

Learned ... and Continue to Swim!

Teachers had to jump and swim—and they did! With the help of the ICT coordinator and their colleagues, they learned how to swim and reach the other side. The interviews also echoed a willingness to continue to swim—but not without the necessary infrastructure for teachers and pupils, a sustainable and future-oriented vision and policy at school, and focused professional development initiatives. So, as already called for in 2015 (Goeman et al., 2015): time for action, again!

References

Bozkurt, A., & Sharma, R. C. (2020). Emergency remote teaching in a time of global crisis due to CoronaVirus pandemic. *Asian Journal of Distance Education, 15*(1), i–vi.

Dhawan, S. (2020). Online learning: A panacea in the time of COVID-19 crisis. *Journal of Educational Technology Systems, 49*(1), 5–22. https://doi.org/10.1177/0047239520934018

Goeman, K., Elen, J., Pynoo, B., & van Braak, J. (2015). Time for action! ICT integration in formal education: Key findings from region-wide follow-up monitor. *TechTrends, 59*(4), 40–50. https://doi.org/10.1007/s11528-015-0890-6

Sailer, M., Murböck, J., & Fischer, F. (2021). Digital learning in schools: What does it take beyond digital technology? *Teaching and Teacher Education, 103*, 103346. https://doi.org/10.1016/j.tate.2021.103346

Vanderlinde, R., & van Braak, J. (2010). The e-capacity of primary schools: Development of a conceptual model and scale construction from a school improvement perspective. *Computers & Education, 55*(2), 541–553. https://doi.org/10.1016/j.compedu.2010.02.016

Transition to Virtual Instruction: A Microbiology Instructor's Challenges

Danita Bradshaw-Ward

The Transition

The sudden transition from a traditional (face-to-face) learning environment to a virtual learning environment during the COVID-19 pandemic created a frenzy to adopt and incorporate imaginative digital tools. This hurried change in modality often failed to explore student ease of use and accessibility as well as the appropriate selection and integration of digital tools in addressing the learning objectives. The integration of digital tools to quickly transform an in-person course into a virtual learning environment is challenging and requires the proper vetting to ensure a seamless and suitable implementation. This is a challenge I had to undertake in a short few weeks. For me, the challenges were even greater with the addition of the unique obstacles community colleges face, especially institutions with predominantly minority and low socioeconomic populations.

Traditionally, microbiology is delivered in a face-to-face format to ensure students acquire a "consistent core set of skills needed (and expected) to work safely and effectively in laboratory settings" (Noel et al., 2020, p. 603). Health programs and seasoned faculty often frown upon the idea of offering microbiology in any alternative modality. While the transition to a virtual environment created an opportunity for change in instructors' beliefs and attitudes, technology adaptation methods, and online learning practices, many instructors were not equipped or enthused about the transition. This period of exclusively teaching microbiology in an online environment challenged me to adapt to the once-identified limitations of virtual learning and to explore and incorporate digital tools to "ensure that microbiology

D. Bradshaw-Ward (✉)
University of North Texas, Denton, TX, USA
e-mail: danitabradshaw-ward@unt.edu

© The Author(s), under exclusive license to Springer Nature Switzerland AG 2023
D. Cockerham et al. (eds.), *Reimagining Education: Studies and Stories for Effective Learning in an Evolving Digital Environment*, Educational Communications and Technology: Issues and Innovations, https://doi.org/10.1007/978-3-031-25102-3_5

27

students remain engaged and able to acquire essential skills" (Noel et al., 2020, p. 604). Additionally, I had to be innovative in helping microbiology students "develop practical skills which are otherwise unattainable through lectures and readings" (Brockman et al., 2020, p. 4).

Challenges of Institution Closure and Digital Tool Use

Upon the lifting of mandated educational institution closures and social distancing, my institution and many educational institutions converted microbiology courses back to an in-person delivery format. Other educational institutions continue to offer online or hybrid microbiology courses due to convenience, flexibility (Adams et al., 2015), and higher enrollment. I agree with those institutions that appreciate the flexibility and convenience of an online format microbiology course. However, I have come to realize, and studies show, that proper analysis is necessary before integrating digital tools to achieve learning objectives in virtual laboratory courses (Adil et al., 2021; Radhamani et al., 2021).

The integration of poorly researched digital tools and laboratory kits in my microbiology courses from the Spring of 2020 to the Spring of 2021 was a challenge, but also an opportunity for growth, innovation, and insight into the appropriate selection and implementation of digital tools to enhance students' experience regardless of the modality. Like instructors around the world, I received a two-week timeline to convert my existing in-person microbiology and three anatomy and physiology courses into a virtual learning environment for the remaining eight weeks of the semester. Two weeks is far from enough time to convert one class to an online format, and I had four classes. Receipt of the email mandating course conversions and campus shutdown caused an immediate wave of emotions, ranging from panic, doubt, fear, sense of being overwhelmed to renewed focus, insight, inquisitiveness, and determination. There was no time to dwell on uncertainty. Instead, I needed to quickly prepare virtual learning environments that proceeded with the established learning objectives for the semester. The task was daunting, yet necessary.

The Conversion to Online

The conversion of microbiology to an online course within a two-week time frame was a challenge due to the limited inventory of free supplemental lab resources available. Fortunately, the lab topics in the final weeks of the course consisted of protozoa, fungi, and helminth, which include microscopic slides, organism models, and specimens, all a part of my personal repository. Therefore, creating virtual lab exercises, activities, quizzes, and exams was manageable. The greatest challenge materialized in the Fall 2020 semester, when the full microbiology course creation began.

Microbiology is a unique course that requires distinctive and specific requirements in a virtual learning environment due to the expectation of "'hands-on' practical active learning techniques" (Joshi, 2021, p. 2). Microbiology students are expected to properly handle live bacterium and possess basic hands-on laboratory skills. As a solution to address the expectations and requirements of hands-on laboratory experiences, a decision was made by the district-wide biology curriculum committee to use general microbiology lab kits. The quick adoption of no-expense, at-home laboratory kits eliminated the opportunity to customize the microbiology lab kits to accommodate the current established curriculum and to aid in my teaching style. The lab kits provided additional exercises outside of the adopted curriculum while missing important concepts, which created the need for course modification. However, a positive attribution of the microbiology lab kits is that they simulated a modified laboratory experience for students by creating an engaging at-home learning environment with specifically designed exercises using live bacterial cultures.

Initially, lab kits seemed like the most logical and appropriate solution to recreate an in-person, hands-on experience for my microbiology students. However, first semester evaluation of student performance, engagement, and completion of exercises indicated unforeseen challenges that would persist for the duration of laboratory kit use during online microbiology course offerings during the COVID-19 pandemic. Students' lack of focus on the laboratory portion of the course was evident in the poor participation and performance.

How Can I Improve?

A common experience seen each semester of virtual microbiology instruction was the lack of participation and completion of at-home lab exercises by students. As in every course, there are students that remain engaged and focused on completing assignments and performing well in the course. However, there was a group of students that displayed random commitment and failed to complete required assignments, and thus performed poorly in the course. The latter group was larger than in previous semesters before the pandemic, and over 50% of lab exercises were incomplete or not completed.

For me as an instructor, this was discouraging. The lack of instructor academic freedom in regard to the adoption of the general lab kits generated a personal sense of helplessness during this unprecedented instructional transition. Further, the failure to adequately meet the learning objectives and address the required "hands-on" lab skills was disconcerting. Components of biology laboratories are vital to student learning and laboratory skill development and proficiency. Virtual laboratories should meet the core learning outcomes and be equipped with the necessary tools to create a "realistic, immersive lab environment" (Dustman et al., 2021, p. 1).

Therefore, attentiveness to student preparation for sequential courses and/or professional programs is a necessary goal for instructors, especially those in the unique educational settings of community colleges. My inability, due to lack of selective resources and training, to prepare my students for the next step in their educational career was frustrating.

The longitudinal impact of at-home laboratory kits during the pandemic on student success is a warranted area of exploration. In alternate circumstances of unlimited time and restrictions, educational tools vetted and selected for virtual laboratories might look quite different in my courses. My personal post-COVID-19 research aimed at investigating the impact of virtual laboratory implementation during the pandemic; it was found that adoption of digital tools should be based on virtual learning behaviors (Zhang et al., 2021). Again, my personal limitations in virtual laboratory implementation generated an unintentional mishap in creating an appropriate engaging environment for my students. The lack of engagement in this virtual learning environment nudged me to research and expand my perspective on student engagement. Through literature research, I discovered recommendations to increase student engagement. Instructor–student engagement was identified as important in a virtual learning environment and implementation of student self-reflective activities and student and instructor training in navigation in an online environment that utilizes digital tools "reduces attrition and improves grades in an online biology course" (Davis & Pinedo, 2021, p. 2). This information prompted me to incorporate synchronous concept review sessions and additional asynchronous lectures that homed in on traditionally harder-to-grasp topics.

In conjunction with at-home laboratory kits, recorded videos explaining processes and concepts as they relate to everyday interaction with microbes were incorporated in an attempt to create an engaging virtual learning environment. The recorded videos provided students with visual explanations of how to complete the laboratory exercises and provided a sense of connection between myself and the students. While this does not simulate the in-person experience, it brought engagement and relatability to the virtual experience. In subsequent semesters, the level of participation and completion increased. This direction came about after scouring literature for ideas for ways to create an engaging virtual learning environment that met learning objectives and that could be implemented quickly with no expense.

Students' Challenges Impact on Innovative Implementation

The unique challenges of my students of low socioeconomic status with limited access to Wi-Fi or devices and minority populations consisting of language barriers made adoption of digital tools and virtual activities challenging. Requiring my students to obtain the latest version of a software through purchase or an update to their current device could create an additional burden during this unprecedented time. I received emails from students expressing their journey to access Wi-Fi by driving to campus to sit in the parking lot to complete assignments. Libraries were closed during the initial transition to online, which created a tremendous stress on students' accessibility to Wi-Fi and devices. Therefore, consideration of accessibility and software requirements reduced available digital tools and technology.

In the search for solutions, other virtual activities found in the literature included semester-long virtual case studies and/or research projects that encouraged students to interact with their environments (Adil et al., 2021; Joshi, 2021). Gamification for virtual microbiology laboratories was also suggested as a low-cost, engaging alternative to in-person laboratory experiences (Dustman et al., 2021; Sánchez-Angulo, 2021). Unfortunately, my inexperience in gamification design eliminated its execution in my microbiology virtual laboratories. In addition, time constraints and unrealized demands of virtual instruction hampered training of new educational tools, such as gamification. In hindsight, the time of the pandemic was entirely focused on providing the best microbiology course possible with readily available, low or no cost, familiar tools. As we move towards normalcy, my focus has now evolved into enhancing microbiology courses with the use of digital tools.

Microbiology Instruction

Although my institution discontinued microbiology in an online format, thus eliminating the use of at-home laboratory kits, acquisition of digital tools to enhance the students' learning experience is tempting. The learning environment, virtual or in-person, is in constant need of modification and the search for alternative approaches using digital tools should be intentional among instructors (Joshi, 2021). Research suggests that digital tool utilization for virtual laboratories can be effective in many aspects, but areas that are lacking and should be addressed are student engagement and collaboration (Dustman et al., 2021), which was evident in my virtual microbiology courses during the pandemic. While addition of self-made videos and the incorporation of at-home lab kits appeared promising, student participation and collaboration was average. In hindsight, the implementation of a group virtual project, such as a virtual research project that engages to "virtually travel to a destination and conduct research about the microorganisms in that environment" (Adil et al., 2021, p. 1) would bring an engaging, relatable element to the course.

The implementation of digital tools and instructors' previously learned pedagogical approaches during the pandemic has changed the fabric of education and e-learning forever (Abu Mallouh et al., 2021). This shift is evident in the increase in online, hybrid, and blended course offerings at my institution. While the sudden thrust into virtual instruction and learning was not ideal, the abrupt nudge and "voluntold" circumstances generated a drive for me to be innovative, ambitious, and intentional in implementing new educational digital tools in, once seen as limited, microbiology courses. Although I have resumed in-person instruction of microbiology, many digital tools and virtual activities are permanently implemented into my courses. I continue to provide (1) access to self-recorded mini-lecture videos explaining harder-to-grasp topics; (2) explanation videos for laboratory techniques used during in-person laboratories; and (3) opportunities for self-reflection to promote student engagement. Post-pandemic, my institution considers online microbiology course offerings as unorthodox, contrary to the results of research studies. Recent research exploring digital tool use during the pandemic provided evidence that the incorporation of virtual simulations (Davis & Pinedo, 2021), 3D imagery programs (Owolabi & Bekele, 2021), virtual group projects (Adil et al., 2021), and gamification (Dustman et al., 2021) are acceptable options in delivering an engaging virtual microbiology learning environment that meets the learning objectives. All in all, I am pondering the possibility of offering online microbiology in the future that incorporates appropriate and vetted virtual activities, along with digital tools that meet the learning outcomes and foster student engagement.

References

Abu Mallouh, R. A., Asadi, S., Nilashi, M., Minaei-Bidgoli, B., Nayer, F. K., Samad, S., Mohd, S., & Ibrahim, O. (2021). The impact of coronavirus pandemic (COVID-19) on education: The role of virtual and remote laboratories in education. *Technology in Society, 67*, 101728. https://doi.org/10.1016/j.techsoc.2021.101728

Adams, A. E., Randall, S., & Traustadottir, T. (2015). A tale of two sections: An experiment to compare the effectiveness of a hybrid versus a traditional lecture format in introductory microbiology. *CBE Life Sciences Education, 14*(1), 1–8. https://doi.org/10.1187/cbe.14-08-0118

Adil, A., Sami, S., & Morales, T. P. (2021). Remote online project: Traveling in a virtual world, researching microbes. *Journal of Microbiology & Biology Education, 22*(1). https://doi.org/10.1128/jmbe.v22i1.2367

Brockman, R. M., Taylor, J. M., Segars, L. W., Selke, V., & Taylor, T. A. H. (2020). Student perceptions of online and in-person microbiology laboratory experiences in undergraduate medical education. *Medical Education Online, 25*(1), 1710324, 1–12. https://doi.org/10.1080/10872981.2019.1710324

Davis, C. P., & Pinedo, T. (2021). The challenges of teaching anatomy and physiology laboratory online in the time of COVID-19. *Journal of Microbiology & Biology Education, 22*(1). https://doi.org/10.1128/jmbe.v22i1.2605

Dustman, W. A., King-Keller, S., & Marquez, R. J. (2021). Development of gamified, interactive, low-cost, flexible virtual microbiology labs that promote higher-order thinking during pandemic instruction. *Journal of Microbiology & Biology Education, 22*(1). https://doi.org/10.1128/jmbe.v22i1.2439

Joshi, L. T. (2021). Using alternative teaching and learning approaches to deliver clinical microbiology during the COVID-19 pandemic. *FEMS Microbiology Letters, 368*(16). https://doi.org/10.1093/femsle/fnab103

Noel, T. C., Rubin, J. E., Acebo Guerrero, Y., Davis, M. A., Dietz, H., Libertucci, J., & Sukdeo, N. (2020). Keeping the microbiology lab alive: Essential microbiology lab skill development in the wake of COVID-19. *Canadian Journal of Microbiology, 66*(10), 603–604. https://doi.org/10.1139/cjm-2020-0373

Owolabi, J., & Bekele, A. (2021). Implementation of innovative educational Technologies in Teaching of anatomy and basic medical sciences during the COVID-19 pandemic in a developing country: The COVID-19 silver lining? *Advances in Medical Education and Practice, 12*, 619–625. https://doi.org/10.2147/AMEP.S295239

Radhamani, R., Kumar, D., Nizar, N., Achuthan, K., Nair, B., & Diwakar, S. (2021). What virtual laboratory usage tells us about laboratory skill education pre- and post-COVID-19: Focus on usage, behavior, intention and adoption. *Education and Information Technologies, 26*(6), 7477–7495. https://doi.org/10.1007/s10639-021-10583-3

Sánchez-Angulo, M. (2021). Teaching microbiology in times of plague. *International Microbiology, 24*(4), 665–670. https://doi.org/10.1007/s10123-021-00179-9

Zhang, X., Al-Mekhled, D., & Choate, J. (2021). Are virtual physiology laboratories effective for student learning? A systematic review. *Advances in Physiology Education, 45*(3), 467–480. https://doi.org/10.1152/advan.00016.2021

Entering Education During the COVID-19 Pandemic

Samantha Marie Norton

Entering Education During the COVID-19 Pandemic

Computers, black boxes, silence – my first year of teaching was one I will never forget. I started teaching middle school science in August 2019 in the Dallas-Fort Worth Metropolitan Area of Texas. The district was innovative and used technology daily; every student from 6th grade to 12th grade had a personal Chromebook provided to them by the district. Elementary students had devices on campus for their daily use.

There were so many things to learn about instruction, but overwhelmingly, professional development was centered around the technology. I was provided a crash course on the learning management system, Moodle. Within my professional learning community, I learned about Google Suite and how lessons were shared from the campus level to the district level. Having grown up with technology, I saw the opportunity to teach my students how to use their devices beyond entertainment purposes.

My passion for embedding technology in education began during my undergraduate career. Transitioning from required notes to personal choices was mind-blowing for me. Ever since I could remember, I needed a composition book for each class, and most classes had notebook checks throughout a grading period. My professors allowed me the freedom of choice when it came to notetaking and the submission of assignments. I was familiar with submitting notes online, but I discovered that I preferred taking my notes on the computer as opposed to handwritten material; I typed much faster and could reread the work because it wasn't written in

S. M. Norton (✉)
University of North Texas, Denton, TX, USA
e-mail: samanthanorton@my.unt.edu

lackadaisical writing. The foundation of my learning began to revolve around my computer and the accessibility of information it provides. It was this experience that drove my passion to relay the same opportunity to my students.

March 2020

When I became a teacher, I aimed to supply the flexibility I saw in college, but in a controlled environment, to meet the needs of my students' adolescent limitations. I developed online notebooks using Google Slides for my students, with expectations that introduced the new style of notetaking, but had safety nets for students to transition to handwritten notes if they were not connecting with the material. Most of my students switched to the digital platform, and I saw the biggest change in my students with special needs. If a student's progress began to slip on assignments, I started with their note-taking skill and offered lessons on proper digital notetaking or suggested transitioning to handwritten notes.

I never realized how thankful I would be for embedding technology in my classrooms until spring break of 2020. I said goodbye to my students, not realizing I would never see them again face to face. When the news came that we would not be returning to campus, I began adjusting my lessons by shifting them a week, anticipating a return to in-person learning after a brief break. It was towards the end of that first week that we were notified we would be switching to "distance learning," with little guidance about the logistics. At the time, all I knew was I needed to create digital lessons for my students that taught the essentials for each of my courses. While my students had their devices at home, a lot of them neglected to charge their devices and some students lacked Internet at home. Additionally, not all students had possession of technology.

While the district had the administrative team working toward solving these logistical issues, the professional learning communities met to create lessons for the weeks ahead. I was part of two communities at the time, 7th-grade science and the 8th-grade elective course within the Career and Technology Education (CTE) department. Having a background in technology, I was tasked with developing the new curriculum that would be used for the CTE course across the district for all 8th-graders enrolled in the class. The administration determined that because of the pandemic, only an hour per week should be expected from each course. The time, while relatively brief, was widely attributed to various unique situations many of our families found themselves in – some had parents out of work, younger siblings they had to take care of, limited Internet connectivity, and exposure to illness. At this time, we still had no synchronous meeting times. Each week, I had to sacrifice information and promote the most fundamental knowledge. I also had to find a way to provide interactive instruction in the hopes that my students would still engage with the material. I ended up creating Google Slide lessons for lessons about each part of the brain. By completing the templates I provided, my students were able to make connections from their personal lives to the different parts of the brain as a means to promote memorization. While there was so much supplemental information I wanted to share with them, my students only acquired the basics in this asynchronous environment.

We ended the year with a quick, two-minute "have a good summer" video. I hosted office hours, which no student attended. My heart was heavy knowing that spring break was the last time I would see many of my students. The next year, I was moving up to instruct the biomedical academy and forensic science courses at the high school level. All I could think about at this time was, "please let us be back to normal." I didn't know how to define normal after the experiences we just went through.

2020–2021 School Year

Leading up to fall 2020, the district decided to ensure the safety of staff and students. We would begin the year 100 percent remote for the first 3 weeks, then parents had the choice to have their students remain online or return in person. The first 3 weeks, while at the time seemed impossible to do, were some of the easiest compared to what was to come. We had A-days and B-days where students went to half of their schedule but were double-blocked. This allowed for 45-minute synchronous instruction via Zoom, followed by 45-minute asynchronous instruction, where students completed assignments related to the course. Many of my assignments were already embedded within the learning management system, so the adjustment wasn't challenging. The hardest part was getting students to tune in and participate. I began using Pear Deck to present all material to my students. In live-time, I was able to see who was actively in class and who wasn't participating. This became a precursor to student success and a talking point when parents became concerned.

Since I knew some of the learning obstacles my students could be faced with while at home, I attempted to create asynchronous alternatives. Within Moodle, I had attendance check-ins via the quiz feature with short answer questions. Typically, the questions related to something presented that day or to an upcoming asynchronous lesson. For students who were unable to attend the Zoom meetings, I also had YouTube videos of a lecture for them to watch on their own time. It felt like instead of preparing for three courses, I had six to plan: my students who would be in Zoom for my three courses, and then the students who missed the meetings. During the first 3 weeks, I was still able to find time to complete these preps because I had the 45-minute asynchronous time allotted for each class period each day with the double-blocked schedule.

After the first 3 weeks, I was excited to meet my students face-to-face! I was incredibly nervous about their safety, but I also knew most of them needed to be in person for social and emotional development. While I attempted to have students discuss in class, only two or three each class period were willing to discuss, and most breakout rooms were silent. I knew in person I should expect students to be talkative and just enjoy the presence of each other, but I was not prepared for the stress and anxiety that came with teaching my in-person students, while also managing remote students.

With students returning in person, all schedules were switched back to an 8-class period day and there were no more double-blocked classes. This meant the time I had originally spent creating new digital content for my remote students was taken away and the only time I had was my conference period. Additionally, only some courses were allowed to continue requiring Zoom meetings of their remote students. While this seemed odd at the time, I quickly realized the district was thinking about our students and putting them first. Most remote students remained remote due to health or risk of exposure from their parents' jobs. That also meant all their siblings were staying home with them. To meet the needs of all students, flexibility was key. Two of my courses, biomedical science for 11th-graders and biomedical science for 12th-graders, met the requirement for Zoom meetings. This required managing both in-person class and virtual Zoom meetings at the same time. I found attendance and discussions between the two were the most stressful parts of class, as I didn't want to waste the valuable time I had to complete these tasks. I found that requiring my in-person learners to log into the meeting aided in discussions because they could go into breakout rooms with the virtual learners, and I could hear discussions by simply walking around the room.

My forensic science course, on the other hand, was much simpler. Most asynchronous courses were provided with an online program that students followed. I just had to report their grades and whether they logged into the program each day or not. The main difficulty I had with the forensic science course was when students were sick or out due to exposure to COVID-19. The online course didn't align with the time in which I was presenting content for in-person learners. It also required enrollment and funding for each student within the program. That meant if a student was in-person and then had to go remote for a 2-week quarantine, the instructors had to create content for them to engage with. I didn't want to sacrifice the hands-on experiences for my in-person learners, but that also meant I had to find substitutes for my remote students. For most experiences, I either created videos or interactive lessons using Google Slides and Genial.ly. Google Slides was the quickest way to adapt lessons for virtual environments. However, when I had the time, Genial.ly provided more interactive lessons for my students. This website allowed me to take any picture and expand upon it with interactive buttons and animations. With minimal coding skills, I knew I couldn't program a lab simulation, but with this tool, I could create a simple virtual lab that came close to a simulation. The only challenge with this tool was dedicating creation time.

Conclusions

Looking back, I am thankful for the unique experiences I had during college which led me to create a digital environment in my classroom from day one. While many of my coworkers were challenged by technology issues, I was able to dedicate time to adjusting my content. I also learned how to present professional development. I spent the summer of 2020 hosting Zoom meetings with educators across Texas to teach about digital tools. I taught many professionals Google Classroom, Pear Deck, and the basics of Zoom.

My technology integration has been affirmed through these experiences of teaching during COVID-19. While online classes have been around for years, now the door has been opened for public school systems to provide remote opportunities. When I imagine my future classroom, I reflect on how the global workforce has changed and students need to be competitive with machines just as much as other applicants. I refer to emerging technologies and professional development to provide familiarity with technologies that are used outside of the educational setting. COVID-19 forced education and companies to be remote. Due to these changes, there are still many employers relying on remote settings, stressing the critical importance of student familiarity and skill with technology.

Acknowledgments I would like to offer my special thanks to Dr. Dave Edyburn for his constructive suggestions during the development of this paper. His professional guidance and willingness to give his time have been much appreciated.

I would also like to extend my thanks to Christine Santarelli-Harris and Emma Norton for their valuable critiques throughout the editing of my story.

Adapting to Digital Changes in Health Education: A Case Study

Yun Li, Rania Cannaday, Laura Patricia Luna Arviz, Hilario Hinojosa, and Sherry S. Lin

Background

In March 2020, Texas A&M University (TAMU) administrators decided to transition all courses from on-campus to emergency remote teaching (ERT) due to the COVID-19 pandemic. ERT is a temporary teaching method that provides reliable access to students during a crisis (Bozkurt & Sharma, 2020; Ferri et al., 2020). The primary goal is to quickly set up instruction and support rather than re-creating a new learning system (Affouneh et al., 2020; Bond et al., 2021). Still, the sudden shift brought challenges to our instructors, such as the technical skills needed to set up online courses (Abel, 2020; Dubey & Pandey, 2020) and the knowledge required to modify the strategies for online teaching (Ferri et al., 2020). In this chapter, we provide two case studies from TAMU, describing the different transition processes for a course delivered in a lecture-based format and a course taught in a flipped classroom format.

Case Study 1: The School of Public Health (SPH)

Data Management and Assessment is a 2-credit course to introduce students to the basics of biostatistics and familiarize students with using Excel and Epi-info software for managing, analyzing, and assessing population health data.

Y. Li (✉) · R. Cannaday · L. P. L. Arviz · H. Hinojosa · S. S. Lin
School of Medicine, Texas A&M University, College Station, TX, USA
e-mail: liyun215@tamu.edu; cannaday@tamu.edu; pluna@tamu.edu;
Hilarioh1000@tamu.edu; sslin@tamu.edu

© The Author(s), under exclusive license to Springer Nature Switzerland AG 2023
D. Cockerham et al. (eds.), *Reimagining Education: Studies
and Stories for Effective Learning in an Evolving Digital Environment*,
Educational Communications and Technology: Issues and Innovations,
https://doi.org/10.1007/978-3-031-25102-3_7

Prior to the pandemic, this course adopted a traditional lecture-based format in which the instructor delivered lectures with occasional in-person group discussions and paper-based assignments. To cope with the emergency, the instructor used Zoom to deliver synchronous online lectures. Meanwhile, students had access to other learning materials to expand their knowledge after the classes, such as lecture recordings, assigned LinkedIn videos, and e-textbooks. The additional resources helped address students' questions that they could not ask due to Internet issues. For the group projects, the instructor used the Zoom breakout rooms to facilitate online group collaboration. Students first joined the main room in Zoom, and the instructor briefly introduced the project. Subsequently, students were assigned to the corresponding breakout rooms for group discussions. Upon completing the group discussion, students returned to the main Zoom room to present their work. Before the pandemic, the instructor printed the exams from ExamSoft, a computer-based testing software, and used scantron to grade students' test responses. During the pandemic, the instructor moved all the assessments online and used Canvas for quizzes and Examplify for exams. Taking the test online provided an efficient testing environment and shortened the time it took to deliver test results. Besides occasional and minor technical issues, the overall positive experience of using Canvas quizzes and Examplify assessments led to the instructor's decision to continue using the assessment tools after the post-ERT era.

Case Study 2: School of Medicine (COM)

The Clinicopathologic Correlations (CPCs) are an integral component of the medical curriculum in the pre-clerkship years in the School of Medicine. The CPCs provide the foundation for understanding the pathophysiology of diseases and the basis of how patients present clinically.

Before the pandemic, the CPCs were delivered using the flipped classroom format. Students received a CPC paper handout of several patient clinical cases and reading materials such as assigned textbook chapters, articles, and a digital library of microscopic images. The CPC live session was divided into three parts, including a short PowerPoint presentation delivered by the instructor, a group study session where students reviewed all the cases and consolidated the information learned, and a closed-book individual quiz. Students attended the CPC in-class sessions on their assigned regional campuses with their campus instructor. The instructors on each campus rotated throughout the groups to answer any further questions when students were studying in groups.

During the pandemic, Zoom was used to deliver synchronous online CPC sessions with about 170 students simultaneously participating in an online environment. Unlike the CPC live sessions, online CPC connected the different campuses using Zoom, and one pathology instructor was designated to deliver the presentation. Students could ask questions directly during the presentation that simulated the CPC live sessions. Students also utilized the Zoom chat to send their questions to the host, and the host presented the questions to the instructor. The breakout rooms were used to host students in groups of 4–5 students in individual rooms. When students were studying in their groups, the coordinator circulated the instructors to the breakout rooms so that they could check on students and provide further clarifications or answer questions. Since the students were designated in groups per their campus, the instructor initially assigned to that campus would circulate among their respective student groups. Meanwhile, students could use the "Ask for help" function in Zoom if they had questions. All students were brought back to the main room for the closed-book quiz.

Discussion

While a lecture-based and a blended course are different in the transition process, we have observed some commonalities that affect the ERT. First, suitable pedagogical strategies and practices depend on exposure and access to resources such as online learning infrastructure for institutions, instructors, and learners. In our case, several support systems aid instructors and students in dealing with the challenges they may face during the transition. At the university level, the Office for Academic Innovation created two websites named Keep Teaching for Instructors and Keep Learning for Students, where tutorials for tools such as Canvas and Zoom were hosted for instructors and learners to use on demand. At the school level, instructional designers and technologists at the School of Public Health (SPH) and the College of Medicine (COM) actively collaborated with the instructors via various communication tools such as Slack, Zoom, and emails when they needed support to develop digital content and consulting for tools to facilitate online interactions and assessment.

Second, communicating with students and peer faculty upfront about new learning routines is essential. Remote learning is fundamentally different from an in-person learning experience. The uncertainty and stress caused by a sudden change to a new learning environment can be anxiety-provoking for students and the faculty. Explicitly teaching new routines and processes to students can help them better adapt to digital changes. For example, our instructors created a step-by-step student guide and faculty guide for virtual Zoom CPC sessions. By giving students clear directions, they understood what they needed to do and what they were expected in virtual CPC sessions.

Third, Internet connectivity is critical to the online learning infrastructure system. Instructors and students cannot engage in meaningful online learning if Internet connectivity becomes an issue. Research has discovered that one of the major concerns among students since the COVID-19 outbreak is to have a reliable Internet connection, particularly when required to use a webcam and microphone (Castelli & Sarvary, 2021). We have also observed Internet connectivity issues in our cases. Though the problem was noted, there was no clear solution other than having students ask for hotspots near the university or go to different locations with possibly better Internet services. In addition, some students had to connect to audio through a phone call with cameras off to avoid Internet disconnections. To minimize disruptions in students' learning, our instructors pre-recorded lectures that allowed students to review the content they might have missed during their connectivity issues at their own pace.

Last, constant connection to video conferencing tools decreases the level of online interaction. While Zoom has been extremely helpful, overusing this virtual platform to deliver synchronous courses can result in Zoom fatigue that reduces activity level (Wiederhold, 2020). In our second case, the instructors also noted that there was often little to no interaction between students during the small group sessions via Zoom, where the students were placed in the breakout rooms for group study. Moreover, the instructors would walk around the room in the live CPC session to observe what students were doing, where they were lost, and when they needed clarification. This instructor–student interaction was difficult to accomplish in the virtual room, especially when students had their cameras off.

On a positive note, the sudden shift to remote teaching provided opportunities for instructors to re-evaluate their teaching modalities, consult with instructional designers and technologists for best practices and expectations, and test ideas about educational strategies and digital tools for effective online teaching. Due to this pandemic, instructors had to adapt their instructional practices to remote teaching environments. In the first case, the instructor mainly used Examplify to store test questions rather than a computer-based assessment tool before the pandemic. When students took exams in Examplify during the pandemic, the instructor recognized how this assessment tool could improve grading efficiency with a detailed learning analytics report for each exam. In the second case, having one instructor deliver the presentation to all students utilizing Zoom to connect remote campuses was implemented with great success. The preliminary data showed no significant drop in quiz grades with this new teaching practice compared to prior years. Moreover, the instructors believed that being able to deliver one standardized presentation would be desirable to eliminate the perception of variation among campuses and have decided to continue this practice after the post-ERT era.

Conclusion

Overall, adopting online teaching in an emergent situation requires an evaluation of remote readiness from all stakeholders' perspectives at the early stage of online transition. In this chapter, we have shared our insights from the institutions' and instructors' perspectives. The institutions can investigate available resources to better support instructors and students during online transition. The instructors can examine what pedagogical adjustments are needed for online teaching and identify strategies to engage students in online learning.

A significant change in instructors that emerged from this ERT experience is their awareness of using technology for pedagogical purposes. Such awareness is recognized as teachers' understanding of the interactions between pedagogy and technology to deliver effective teaching with technology (Li et al., 2021). The awareness of the purposeful implementation of technology is the first step toward effective technology integration. Next is to prepare instructors with knowledge of how to use technology appropriately and effectively in their teaching. Hence prompt training for instructors on all aspects of technology integration is necessary. Koehler and Mishra (2009) have proposed a technological Pedagogical Content Knowledge (TPACK) model that elucidates three components of teachers' knowledge (i.e., content, pedagogy, and technology) and interactions among them. As digital technology is continuously playing a critical role in the post-ERT era, we propose professional development training on models like TPACK to help instructors better integrate technology into different learning environments for effective teaching and learning.

References

Abel, A., Jr. (2020). The phenomenon of learning at a distance through emergency remote teaching amidst the pandemic crisis. *Asian Journal of Distance Education, 15*(1), 127–143.

Affouneh, S., Salha, S., & Khlaif, Z. N. (2020). Designing quality e-learning environments for emergency remote teaching in coronavirus crisis. *Interdisciplinary Journal of Virtual Learning in Medical Sciences, 11*(2), 135–137.

Bond, M., Bedenlier, S., Marín, V. I., & Händel, M. (2021). Emergency remote teaching in higher education: Mapping the first global online semester. *International Journal of Educational Technology in Higher Education, 18*(1), 1–24.

Bozkurt, A., & Sharma, R. C. (2020). Emergency remote teaching in a time of global crisis due to CoronaVirus pandemic. *Asian Journal of Distance Education, 15*(1), i–vi.

Castelli, F. R., & Sarvary, M. A. (2021). Why students do not turn on their video cameras during online classes and an equitable and inclusive plan to encourage them to do so. *Ecology and Evolution, 11*(8), 3565–3576.

Dubey, P., & Pandey, D. (2020). Distance learning in higher education during pandemic: Challenges and opportunities. *International Journal of Indian Psychology, 8*(2), 43–46.

Ferri, F., Grifoni, P., & Guzzo, T. (2020). Online learning and emergency remote teaching: Opportunities and challenges in emergency situations. *Societies, 10*(4), 86.

Koehler, M., & Mishra, P. (2009). What is technological pedagogical content knowledge (TPACK)? *Contemporary Issues in Technology and Teacher Education, 9*(1), 60–70.

Li, Y., Sutedjo, A., Ramos, S. J., Garcimartin, H. R., & Thomas, A. (2021). A naturalistic inquiry into digital game-based learning in stem classes from the instructors' perspective. In *Game-based learning across the disciplines* (pp. 229–244). Springer.

Wiederhold, B. K. (2020). Connecting through technology during the coronavirus disease 2019 pandemic: Avoiding "Zoom Fatigue". *Cyberpsychology, Behavior and Social Networking, 23*(7), 437–438.

Part II
Research Studies Highlighting Innovative Strategies and Technologies

Behind the Scenes Action Makes Shift to Online Possible

Beth E. Jordan, Davina M. DeVries, Debbie L. Fratus, Brenda L. Holt, and Amy H. Schwartz

Introduction

Transitioning a curriculum to remote instruction involves more than partnering with an online-meeting software vendor. The sudden move to online instruction can be very challenging for predominantly classroom-based programs with many workshops and lab requirements. This chapter describes the processes undertaken by the Office of Academic Affairs (OAA) at a college of pharmacy to address the array of challenges during the pandemic. The OAA staff includes the Associate Dean for Academic Affairs (ADAA), Administrative Specialist (AS), Academic Services Administrator (ASA), Learning and Development Manager (LDM), and an Instructional Designer (ID). Few colleges of pharmacy in the United States have staff with advanced degrees in education, but having two (i.e., LDM and ID) proved especially useful with a rapid transition to remote learning. Similarly, having staff with business degrees and logistics backgrounds (i.e., AS and ASA) facilitated efforts regarding operational changes for the curriculum and other offices within the College.

Our office supports a Doctor of Pharmacy (PharmD) program, which includes four years of didactic and experiential coursework. Typically, 85 to 100 students transition through the program as a cohort each year. Several courses utilize hybrid delivery, and one is fully online. In March 2020, the pandemic necessitated transition to fully online instruction with 48-hour notice. The OAA team reacted with all hands-on.

B. E. Jordan (✉) · D. M. DeVries · D. L. Fratus · B. L. Holt · A. H. Schwartz
University of South Florida Taneja College of Pharmacy, Tampa, FL, USA
e-mail: bjordan@ut.edu; dmdevrie@usf.edu; dfratus@usf.edu; bholt@usf.edu;
aschwartz@uttyler.edu

© The Author(s), under exclusive license to Springer Nature Switzerland AG 2023   49
D. Cockerham et al. (eds.), *Reimagining Education: Studies
and Stories for Effective Learning in an Evolving Digital Environment*,
Educational Communications and Technology: Issues and Innovations,
https://doi.org/10.1007/978-3-031-25102-3_8

News of faculty experiences and innovative teaching strategies began appearing in publications and presentations across the country. While these stories are vital to reimagining education, the logistics supporting the stories are similarly important. The support academic staff provides is often overshadowed by faculty successes. The OAA team was fortunate, as leadership recognized our efforts through a college award of gratitude. Faculty also honored several of us with annual staff awards when similar administrative teams may not be shown such gratitude. The hope is by sharing this story, other colleges and schools will recognize the impact of OAA staff on a program, not just during urgent times.

Process

As the pandemic crossed the globe, universities realized they would have to enact swift changes. Our university immediately convened a COVID taskforce, which consisted of faculty, health professionals, and university leadership. College leadership tasked the OAA with developing and executing plans to ensure students received quality remote education without delaying progression. Based on state and national COVID information, university administration directed all programs to transition to remote instruction; students, faculty, and staff were not to return to campus after spring break. Whereas most of the university was leaving on spring break, affording a week to transition, the college of pharmacy, using an alternate calendar, had already resumed classes. Thus, the directive provided on a Friday necessitated a transition before classes resumed on Monday. The college had to work quickly to transition, which affected multiple departments. What follows is the OAA journey.

The university held its first academic continuity meeting on a Monday and, by Friday, the OAA team posted links to educational technology and related materials and provided training for the faculty. The OAA staff interfaced with the professional academy and accreditation liaisons to appreciate acceptable remote training options to sustain quality clinical experiences and meet accreditation requirements (Accreditation Council for Pharmacy Education, 2015), while concurrently addressing university policies, state regulations, and healthcare practice site requirements, which were changing in real time as new information arose.

Additional issues beyond academics facing faculty and staff were related to the transition from campus to home, which impacted access to equipment and other resources. Within a week of the university edict, the OAA team developed and administered a survey to faculty and staff assessing access to necessary equipment and resources. Within 48 h, 85% of those surveyed responded, identifying the following challenges: 55% either did not know Internet speeds or had less than 100 mbps; 42% did not have Microsoft operating systems; and 22% described other barriers they perceived would prevent them from maintaining normal responsibilities. Additionally, although faculty shared comfort level with software pertinent to online instruction as a barrier, the majority (59%) were comfortable with the software. Responses were shared with college administration and assistance was provided to those experiencing technology challenges or requiring alternative work solutions.

The OAA team shared resources created to assist during the transition via the OAA Canvas LMS portal. Additional resources were developed to address anticipated faculty and staff needs and those expressed in the survey. For example, the Learning and Development Manager (LDM) created a matrix to compare features for the different online meeting platforms. One-on-one faculty support was provided upon request. The Department Chairs developed an Excel spreadsheet to collect faculty plans for addressing course student learning outcomes remotely and corresponding needs for assistance, including Advanced Pharmacy Practice Experience (APPE). The OAA staff enhanced the spreadsheet to ensure accurate collection of information and guide support processes.

As the semester ended, neither the university nor the college could host face-to-face graduation or graduation-affiliated activities. The college Office of Student Affairs (OSA) oversees the annual graduation celebration and awards event during the week prior to commencement. Administration asked the OSA staff to host the event virtually in real time. However, the OSA staff did not have the necessary technical skills, thus, OAA's LDM assisted. Whereas the OSA developed the script and faculty supported ceremony activities, the LDM oversaw three technical synchronous rehearsals, and managed technical backend, camera views, and real-time direction of the event using Microsoft Teams Events. The event was successful with only limited streaming or technical issues, garnered over 400 real-time viewers, and included appearances by the university President, health science center senior Vice President, and the college Dean.

Upon successful completion of the semester and graduation, energies shifted to future semesters. Introductory Pharmacy Practice Experiences (IPPE), which comprise 33% of the curriculum, occur during the summer; as do fourth-year APPE rotations, which encompass 90% of the curriculum in the final year. To mitigate COVID transmission, healthcare institutions restricted student and faculty access to facilities, which impacted experiential training. Institution policies and procedures were fluid, requiring constant monitoring and adjustments. Concurrently, accrediting bodies and universities remained diligent monitoring requirements to ensure curricular quality and integrity. The college needed a plan that would remain compliant with all requirements, maintain high-quality instruction, and flexible to support future adjustments.

The pharmacy academy and accreditation body held meetings with pharmacy program administrators to discuss options for maintaining quality experiential education when physical presence at a practice site was not possible. When considering student summer IPPE needs, it became clear that curricular adjustments were necessary. The OAA team proposed shifting forthcoming fall didactic courses to the summer, affording time in the fall for IPPE. The hope was that the pandemic would ease, and students and faculty would be permitted to return to practice sites. Selected courses were those that did not require knowledge from experiential rotations and could be held remotely. The OAA worked with the Office of Experiential Education, OSA, and Department Chairs to develop the proposal. The LDM and ID worked with faculty to modify the impacted fall courses for remote instruction (using available educational technology) and adjusted for the shorter ten-week summer semester.

The OAA worked with several colleges and university departments to adjust other instructional logistics to meet all requirements. The OSA focused on registration and general communications with students. A student agreement to address the uncertainty of experiential rotations during the pandemic, with the possibility of instructional interruptions was developed with guidance from the University Office of General Counsel. The university Office of Graduate Studies provided guidance aligned with the Southern Association of Colleges and Schools Commission on Colleges' communications (2021) and the Board of Governors. After determining the best path and draft schedule, the Office of Financial Aid was consulted to ensure compliance. The college Dean performed the final review and approval. The entire process was completed in two weeks and implemented for summer courses beginning in May.

In June, the university announced limited classroom capacities for fall, which resulted in no classrooms being able to hold a cohort of 85–100 students. With fall semester starting the first week of August, the OAA staff provided guidance and instructional support to faculty regarding options for administering courses that required face-to-face instruction.

The third-year students completed the remaining fall didactic courses in a condensed manner to allow time for concurrent IPPE. Didactic courses were scheduled three days per week, leaving four consecutive days for experiential rotations. Guidance was provided to faculty to adapt course delivery. As hoped, practice sites began allowing students into their facilities early fall. The scheduling adjustments successfully allowed all students to complete the program requirements without impacting progression.

Social distancing requirements remained unchanged for Spring 2021, and OAA staff classroom scheduling efforts continued to support educational needs. More classes resumed on-campus instruction utilizing a hybrid approach. Some in-person courses continued with multiple smaller sessions. Faculty support and training for educational technology continued. Some changes that occurred because of COVID led to improvements in usage of educational technology.

The University returned to full, on-campus instruction in fall 2021. Some recommended COVID protocols continued; however, most instruction returned to pre-COVID conditions. With the development of COVID variants, many courses maintained some aspects of remote instruction. Moving forward, the OAA team remains ready to assist.

Discussion/Implications

Even for programs designed to be taught face-to-face, with enhanced live engagement and interaction, there are opportunities for effective blended learning. To do so, faculty need easy access to resources to support them when teaching online.

Effective utilization of instructional design theory can lead to course redesign that leverages the benefits of technology yet continues to support students academically, physically, and emotionally. The OAA espoused the use of educational technologies before the pandemic. Although the pandemic accelerated utilization, continued guidance is required to ensure maintenance of elements that support and enhance learning and retention.

Similarly, ensuring maintaining alignment with policies, procedures, and regulations is essential to ensure continued program success during unexpected crises. Ensuring continued collaboration and communication between offices is vital.

Conclusion

When faced with a great challenge, the success of academic programs is not solely reliant on the faculty. Rather, the resilience, diligence and invaluable insight provided by administrative and support personnel must be recognized and supported. Academic programs need to consider the value of these individuals when creating position descriptions and developing compensation packages.

Acknowledgments We gratefully recognize that our efforts would not have been as successful were it not for the administration, faculty, and staff in our college who valued our input. The Associate Dean for Academic Affairs leads our team with respect and confidence in our abilities. The other offices mentioned in our story provided perspective and information from their areas that helped inform the work. A special thanks to the Director of Student Services for her editorial remarks.

References

Accreditation Council for Pharmacy Education. (2015). *Accreditation standards and key elements for the professional program in pharmacy leading to the Doctor of Pharmacy degree*. Retrieved from https://www.acpe-accredit.org/pdf/Standards2016FINAL2022.pdf

Southern Association of Colleges and Schools Commission on Colleges. (2021). *Coronavirus and the Commission*. Retrieved from https://sacscoc.org/coronavirus-and-the-commission/

The Lockdown in Retrospect: An International, Mixed Methods Perspective on Student and Faculty Experiences with COVID-19 Remote Learning

Audon Archibald, Tania Heap, Heather Lucke, Dominique Verpoorten, Lin Lin-Lipsmeyer, Neil Guppy, and Silvia Bartolic

Background

COVID-19 Impact on the Classroom

The COVID-19 pandemic has impacted higher education worldwide, affecting more than 1.3 billion students from all education levels across 142 countries (Karalis & Raikou, 2020). Prior to the pandemic, online education had become a mainstream phenomenon across the globe (Kumar et al., 2017). As of Fall 2014, approximately 1 in 4 students in higher education in the United States took at least one online course, and 1 in 7 students (or approximately 2.8 million) took their courses exclusively online (Allen et al., 2016). In spring 2020, the emergence and rapid spread of COVID-19 prompted universities across the globe to transition from in-person teaching to remote online teaching (Trust & Whalen, 2020), greatly increasing the already existing need to understand the nuances of online course delivery.

A. Archibald (✉) · T. Heap · H. Lucke
University of North Texas, Denton, TX, USA
e-mail: audon.archibald@unt.edu; tania.heap@unt.edu; heather.lucke@unt.edu

D. Verpoorten
Université de Liège, Liège, Belgium
e-mail: dverpoorten@uliege.be

L. Lin-Lipsmeyer
Southern Methodist University, Dallas, TX, USA
e-mail: LLipsmeyer@smu.edu

N. Guppy · S. Bartolic
University of British Columbia, Vancouver, BC, Canada
e-mail: neil.guppy@ubc.ca; bartolic@mail.ubc.ca

© The Author(s), under exclusive license to Springer Nature Switzerland AG 2023
D. Cockerham et al. (eds.), *Reimagining Education: Studies and Stories for Effective Learning in an Evolving Digital Environment*,
Educational Communications and Technology: Issues and Innovations,
https://doi.org/10.1007/978-3-031-25102-3_9

While many universities offered online or hybrid courses prior to the COVID-19 pandemic, this emergency shift to almost exclusive online instruction was the best solution universities had for continuing instruction amid the COVID-19 crisis (Donham et al., 2022). This rapid transition left many instructors with little time and resources to alter their face-to-face courses to suit this new modality without reducing their pedagogical rigor. The stress of the transition was lessened for some instructors with prior online teaching experience or courses readily translated to an online format. However, many instructors felt considerably less prepared and were forced to rely on department or university-provided support, the likes of which were often of dubious quality (Pagoto et al., 2021). Although emergency remote instruction during the pandemic is different from other online courses due to the swift improvisation required to move classes online (Donham et al., 2022), this transition also brought with it a myriad of options for how to adapt traditional learning activities into a digital space. For example, synchronous lectures delivered in real time via videoconferencing platforms (e.g., Zoom or Microsoft Teams) allow for more traditional lecture activities and student engagement patterns. In contrast, asynchronous lectures, often delivered as prerecorded videos with self-directed student activities, allow more flexibility for students to work at their own pace (Hickling et al., 2021). Some instructors even combined these methods by recording live lectures and then posting them to the learning management system for maximum flexibility, a method that proved effective among STEM students (Pagoto et al., 2021).

Beyond content delivery, other factors also impacted higher education during the pandemic. Research on courses that switched from face-to-face to remote delivery during the pandemic has indicated a general detriment to student attitudes and engagement with remote courses (Armstrong et al., 2022). In one study, 51% of surveyed students reported being "very satisfied" with their courses before the emergency transition, but that percentage dropped to only 19% after the transition (Means & Neisler, 2021). One specific barrier that negatively impacted both instructors and students was attempting to navigate home environments that were often noisy, busy, crowded, and not conducive to learning (Bartolic et al., 2022a, b; Donham et al., 2022).

Like their instructors, students were also forced to rapidly adjust to the emergency transition, sometimes with poor communication from their instructors and universities (Pagoto et al., 2021). In facing the transition, up to 80% of students reported having difficulty staying motivated, with an additional 1 in 6 students professing consistent issues with access to reliable technology that hampered their ability to learn. Furthermore, 46% of surveyed students reported physical or mental health concerns that interfered with their course participation (Means & Neisler, 2021). Caregiving responsibilities, occupational demands, and demographic differences, such as race, socioeconomic status, and location also created additional challenges for students (Pokhrel & Chhetri, 2021). Quantitative findings from a separate study also indicate that Hispanic, first generation, and sexual or gender minority students experienced the greatest challenges regarding distance learning relative to the other student populations (Fruehwirth et al., 2021). One focus group additionally found that 11% of students reported feeling uncared for by instructors who were inflexible to students who had accessibility or accommodation concerns, those in different countries or time zones, or those that did not have sufficient course infrastructure present in the chosen learning management system (LMS) (Pagoto et al., 2021).

Despite these barriers, the flexibility of online learning, due to the lack of rigid course schedules, is a boon for students who have extensive commitments outside school, such as work or caring for family. Further, using software such as Zoom can improve the accessibility of education. For example, Zoom offers the option to produce automated closed captions, and lecture recordings allow students to move back and forth through the lecture to repeat content as needed (Donham et al., 2022). For students whose attendance may be impacted by health issues, lecture recordings also allow them to access any content they may miss. For instructors, the ability to create course content asynchronously on their own time may offer similar flexibility (Hickling et al., 2021).

Given the extensive impact of the pandemic on higher education, research on online teaching and learning has rapidly proliferated. Although many universities have reopened their doors, online instruction and assessment are continuing to be offered in greater amounts alongside face-to-face education (Tartavulea et al., 2020). Therefore, in the wake of the emergency transition to remote instruction, instructors can use their experiences and emerging research to improve their teaching practices and be better prepared to transition online again in the event of a future crisis (Trust & Whalen, 2020).

However, despite the strides we have made in understanding how we might improve our pedagogies based on our experiences during the pandemic, there is still much we can learn from student and faculty experiences during the pandemic. Specifically, understandings of individual student differences, and if those differences were perceived and acted upon by faculty, remain as key research areas still worth exploring. This is particularly true from an international perspective, as the nature of learning is not bound to Americentric expectations. As a result, the present study seeks to derive meaning from the synthesis of over 4000 student and 500 faculty perspectives worldwide on their experiences during the transition by means of a multi-institutional consortium of academics, each collecting data from their own students and faculty.

Existing consortium work has revealed considerable lessons of note for institutions of higher education. Perhaps most noteworthily is that many of the original fears held by students and educators around the world at the onset of the COVID-19 pandemic, while not completely assuaged, did not come to the cataclysmic conclusions many anticipated (Bartolic et al., 2022a). While it may have been a reality for pockets of instructors and students, data suggests that a majority of faculty did not, as many feared, abandon all pretenses of teaching during the pandemic in favor of pre-recorded lectures or standalone PowerPoints without additional support. Additionally, students, while many underwent (and continue to experience) considerable duress due to COVID-19, many found the support they needed to continue their education. Mass dropouts, swaths of students abandoning their degree programs, and like fears largely did not come to pass. That said, while reviews of study data suggest these more dire fears about how the pandemic would change higher education did not come to fruition, there is still much to learn from exploring what additional factors may have influenced student experiences during the transition.

An International Perspective on COVID-19 Responses

Nine higher education institutions from seven countries (Australia, Belgium, Canada, the Netherlands, the Philippines, the UK, and the United States) formed the bulk of this unnamed academic consortium. Each participating university collected data from their students, faculty, and, if possible, course support staff and department administrators. During data collection, each partner university made use of a base, self-completed, online survey that partners could add, but not subtract, questions from. One survey existed for students and another for faculty. Additionally, each university collected one-on-one interview data using a base set of open-ended qualitative questions from faculty. Of this consortium, two universities, one based in the United States and one in Belgium, provided additional qualitative analysis of study data. All quantitative data collection was organized and coordinated by a Canada-based university.

Process: Quantitative Analysis

To assess a general summation of student takeaways from the emergency remote transition, students were asked to pick a specific course that underwent a full or partial transition as the subject of their experience. This was coupled with more generalized attitudes about how students fared during the transition, as well as contextual, student-specific factors such as demographic information. Alongside other findings previously presented by the consortium, student responses to the emergency transition overall were cataloged in a series of 23 Likert scale questions (from 1 to 7 on an Agree–Disagree axis) that captured their personal, rather than mechanical, perspectives about how the transition was handled by themselves and their instructors, alongside their general perspectives on their learning values. For ease of interpretation, these 23 items were then evaluated using an exploratory factor analysis to group items with overlapping variance in the students' experiences.

After two iterations, making use of varimax rotation to clarify factor loadings, four items were deleted from the factor solution based on either significant factor cross-loadings or not loading onto any factor in the solution using a coefficient cut-off of 0.40. This final factor solution suggested the existence of four overall factors for these student perspectives and learning values: negative beliefs about transition outcomes (e.g., after the transition, the quality of my work declined, 7 items), confidence in the instructor to handle the transition (e.g., I was confident as my instructor transitioned to online learning, 4 items), willingness to engage with difficult course material (e.g., In general, I prefer more challenging courses, 4 items), and preference for avoiding academic risk (e.g., I would rather drop a difficult course than earn a low grade, 4 items).

Findings: Student Individual Differences and Transition Perspectives

As anticipated, high confidence in the instructor's ability to handle the transition was strongly, inversely correlated with negative outcomes post-transition for students ($r = -0.54$, $p < 0.001$, $n = 3179$). Interestingly, students who professed a preference for less challenge appeared to experience more negative outcomes with the transition than students who did not show this preference ($r = 0.10$, $p < 0.001$, $n = 2799$), but this pattern was not inversely identified for students who expressed an explicit preference for more challenging courses ($r = 0.03$, $p = 0.07$, $n = 2824$).

Across demographic lines, overall negative experiences from the transition were not significantly different in terms of gender (note: no non-binary participants included), nor between students who had or had not ever taken a course online before. However, there was a positive correlation between negative experiences post-transition alongside student age ($r = 0.15$, $p < 0.001$, $n = 3201$) and student academic level ($r = 0.05$, $p = 0.003$, $n = 3220$), which was mirrored for both demographic points in the anticipated, inverse direction for how confident students were in their instructors ($r = -0.10$, $p < 0.001$, $n = 3420$; $r = -0.07$, $p < 0.001$, $n = 3446$, respectively). Accordingly, data suggests that general patterns of student experience during the transition to remote instruction was one of greater perceived difficulty and more distrust in "the system" for students who were older and had progressed further in their academic tracks.

These negative experiences with the transition also had considerable overlap with students' home environments. Both more negative experiences with the transition as well as a lack of confidence in instructors post transition were significantly correlated with students having slower Internet access, their home environments being too noisy or crowded, a lack of study space, and their work schedule being unaccommodating to their academic needs. However, while this might be expected, comparisons of these results to student beliefs about their academic abilities provide some additional context to these responses. Students who were academic challenge-averse *also* indicated (at the $p < 0.05$ level) that they had more problems with slow Internet, too much noise, a lack of space, and difficulty with their work schedule. This was not mirrored for students who displayed explicit confidence to challenge themselves academically. Students who scored highly in a desire for academic challenge only indicated greater difficulties with slow Internet and a lack of study space, with no effect detected for how they reported on disruptiveness of their home environments, as well as for how likely their work schedule was to interfere with their studies.

While these results by no means diminish the very real effects of home environment and life stability of students during the emergency remote transition, they do underlie the possible role of existing student academic outlook in how they processed their remote learning. That is, while a student's desire for more challenging vs. less challenging classes is unlikely to have a strong direct effect on their home environment, the same lack of desire for challenge may still incur more sensitivity to disruptions affecting their studies. This is not to say that students less confident in their abilities were unfairly oversensitive. Rather, the present pattern suggests that the effects of the pandemic were felt most harshly among those who may have already been struggling both at home and in their academic convictions, with resiliency to these effects present for students who maintained their desire for challenge during the pandemic.

Findings: Personal vs. Community Resilience (Single University)

To understand more about other possible factors that created protective effects for students facing the transition, a single university based in the United States also had students complete two additional scales, the short-form Connor–Davidson Resiliency scale [CDRISC10, (Connor & Davidson, 2003)], as well as a university-focused, modified version of the short-form Conjoint Community Resiliency Assessment Measure [CCRAM10, (Leykin et al., 2013)], focusing on individual, and community, resiliency, respectively. As one might expect, personal ($r = -0.21$, $p < 0.001$, $n = 310$) and community ($r = -0.30$, $p < 0.001$, $n = 0.307$) resilience were both inversely correlated to the perception of negative transition outcomes for students. As predicted by the aforementioned results about home environment, students who showcased a higher drive for challenging courses also reported higher levels of personal ($r = 0.32$, $p < 0.001$, $n = 313$) and community ($r = 0.12$, $p = 0.04$, $n = 309$) resiliency.

The students who indicated that they avoided academic challenge showed a correlation with lower personal resiliency ($r = -0.29$, $p < 0.001$, $p = 312$, $n = 312$) but, surprisingly, no relationship with levels of community resiliency ($r = -0.04$, $p = 0.45$, $n = 309$). Ultimately, these results perhaps suggest that a key experience during the remote transition for students was one of what one might be called privilege. Students who were already driven academically were spared (at least according to their beliefs) much of the harshest pandemic realities, while students who may have been struggling to push themselves reported greater difficulty at home, more severe negative outcomes due to the transition, and a dearth of support from their communities.

Process: Qualitative Analysis

To aid in contextualizing student responses, two universities, one in the United States and one in Belgium, also provided qualitative assessments of faculty perspectives on the transition. From the open-ended faculty interviews, three questions were selected as the subject of qualitative analysis as both a concession to time and for their poignant, surface-valid use for understanding faculty experiences. Additionally, this question gave faculty a chance to offer both their perspectives looking back on the choices they made during the pandemic and how their perspectives had changed since. These questions were, "How was teaching during the emergency remote transition informed your opinions about the future?" "How do you think your students fared with this transition?" and "What could have been done differently or better?"

In a structured approach to qualitatively code what the perceived underlying patterns of how faculty members responded were, the US-based university created a coding tree that described prevailing trends in how faculty answered the questions of interest based on recommendations by Braun and Clarke (2006) within NVivo, with final codes iterated until they reached an acceptable Cohen's Kappa of greater than 0.80. Sharing this coding tree with the university based in Belgium (note: quotes from Belgium faculty translated from French), the independent conclusions drawn by each organization were then compared against one another (see Appendix A for complete breakdown of which elements of the coding tree were detected/not detected across faculty at both universities).

Findings: Faculty Perspectives Within the United States and Belgium

Analysts at both universities identified noteworthy overlaps (and lack of overlap) in how their respective faculty responded to our three target questions (see Table 1). Faculty at both universities indicated that the accessibility of course materials, as well as their awareness of contextual student hardships (e.g., housing or food insecurity) was of importance to their takeaways from the pandemic. Echoing a sentiment espoused by dozens of faculty, one US faculty chose not to focus their response on how they believed students fared during their transition on academic outcomes, but on the context-based hardships students were experiencing.

"For the students it was an extremely stressful time. Their lives were changing, their schedules had changed, the environment in which they were trying to learn had changed. So, some people were letting go. Some people were in a bad housing situation. Some were not sure where their next meal was coming from. And some were working 50 hours a week and trying to figure out how to learn at the same time…"

Some faculty, however, also conceded that the pandemic's switch to virtual lectures, while inhibiting some benefits of face-to-face learning, "… was a really

Table 1 Qualitative coding theme comparison between the US and Belgian universities

Accessibility Concerns About Course (Parent Code)	*Concerns about Course Materials*[a]
Concerns about Course Assessment	Awareness of Student Mental Health Issues
Awareness of Student Contextual Hardships[a]	Compliance with the Office of Accommodations
Awareness of Student Physical Health Issues	
Adaptation Styles to the Remote Transition (Parent Code)	
Reported Difficulties Using Technology	Positive Experiences Using Technology
Awareness of Student Preparedness	*Awareness of Student Lack of Preparedness*[a]
Evidence of Lack of Preparedness of Faculty	*Evidence of Preparedness of Faculty*[a]
Overcoming Transition Anxiety[a]	
Concerns about Assessment During the Transition (Parent Code)	
Concerns about Academic Dishonesty	Concerns about Fairness of Assessment
Concerns about Privacy of Assessment	
Evidence of Ineffective vs. Effective Pedagogy in Remote Model (Parent Code)	
Difficulties Communicating with Students	Ease of Communicating with Students
Learning Environment Disruption (Students)	*Learning Environment Disruption (Technology)*[a]
Difficulties Communicating in General[a]	Flexibility of Remote Work
Faculty Confidence in Handling of Transition	Lack of Confidence in Handling of Transition
Negative Beliefs about Remote Work[a]	Positive Beliefs about Remote Work
Successful Faculty Support from University[a]	*Unsuccessful Faculty Support from University*[a]
Changing Levels of Course Engagement (Parent Code)	
Decreased Engagement in Remote Model[a]	*Increased Engagement in Remote Model*[a]
Lack of Focus/Concentration in Faculty	*Lack of Focus/Concentration in Students*[a]

Note: [a]Faculty response in line with code detected at both the US and Belgian Universities; parent codes are displayed in bold font.

important disability accommodation issue that made my class accessible to everyone... everyone gets to be more physically comfortable too. You know, chairs are not comfortable at all..." – *US-based faculty.*

Additionally, some faculty from both universities espoused they believed themselves adequately prepared for the emergency remote transition while simultaneously observing students may have lacked the opportunity to appropriately prepare. One Belgium-based faculty professed, in response to what they thought about how students fared: "The first week was complicated for them. Some of them expressed anxiety in relation to the recordings to be produced and regarding the examination, the technical problems to be solved...The course contents remained the same and it made them anxious in terms of workload."

For some faculty, this awareness that students were having to overcome a lot of anxiety drove a need to be prepared and available to handle the uncertainty students were facing. At both universities, some faculty went so far as to invest in their home-teaching station in advance of courses being formally transitioned during March 2020, or commit to additional office hours that they might otherwise have not.

A great deal of faculty attitudes toward the remote transition found across both universities was particularly intense surrounding issues within classroom communication in the remote model. Many faculty felt that, while initial university responses may have been appropriate, how exactly courses changed during the transition to distance learning may have not been clear enough: "At the beginning, we had a fairly clear view of what the distance version of the course should look like, but we did not convey our view very clearly to students. Communication on course organization should have been more precise." – *Belgium-based faculty, in response to question on what could have been done better.*

The software universities made use of to facilitate distance learning was an oft-cited reason for the breakdown of communication between students and faculty as well. Many faculty professed that they were forced to choose between a more stable, audio-only lecture vs. a more choppy but more engaging audio and video (i.e., cameras on) setup for their courses. One US-based faculty member lamented, in response to the question on what could have been done better, while they understood that choppy Internet was a valid concern (particularly for low-income students), letting students turn their camera off always led to "... teaching and all you have are these black windows. You don't know what they're doing, and it feels strange that you don't know what they're doing. I guess I take it personally, like [even those who aren't low income] are not interested in being there."

This sentiment surrounding how the remote model may be negatively affecting the teaching experience did not stop there. One other Belgium-based faculty recalled, in reference to what could have been done better, how, for them, the remote transition was a major problem due to the situational pressures and inequitable nature of eLearning technology for many students.

> This was a major problem: not having the opportunity to check understanding and conditions of learning. I just had insights through e-mails of students with very small homes, doors slamming, trains passing, noises of motorcycles in the street, slow bandwidth... It just means that inequalities were reinforced by lockdown and that we did not collectively

provide enough support. How many students did we lose? I feel bad thinking thereabout…
Technologies are not neutral. If one wants more eLearning without taking account of this,
eLearning will be a socio-economical nightmare and disaster. – *Belgium-based faculty*

Yet, despite some of these harsher condemnations from faculty, the reality of
whether the transition to remote education was more of a boon or bane for learning
continues to be controversial on an international scale. Claims that they saw
increases *and* decreases in engagement from students were numerous from faculty
at both universities, sometimes even from the same faculty. From the faculty perspective, playing into the lack of neutrality (and perhaps the nature of student preferences for a challenge vs. less challenging academics) of pandemic effects, faculty
noted that about a third of students appeared to struggle above and beyond their
peers, leading to a drop in attendance, lack of engagement in synchronous lectures,
and, in some cases, dropping out of courses altogether. Other students, conversely,
found features of distance education, such as the "chat" feature during lectures, the
ability to screenshare relevant links to the whole class under their own power, or
even just being in their own space while they were learning to be much more conducive to staying on task.

Discussion

The findings from the quantitative analysis appear to suggest a possible impact of
existing (i.e., prior to the pandemic) student academic outlook in how students perceived their household environment. Students with lower confidence in their academic prospects may have been sensitive to disruptions in their household, impacting
their learning more compared to those with more confidence. Also, the transition to
remote instruction appeared to be more difficult for students who were older than
traditional college learners and were more progressed in their academic studies
(e.g., advanced undergraduate or graduate courses). This might be because students
in this demographic category tend to juggle multiple commitments, such as employment and a family and, as a result, have fewer dedicated opportunities for learning
and tend to study in noisier households.

The trends overall suggest that the effects of the pandemic were felt most harshly
among those who may have been previously struggling both at home and in their
academic convictions, with individual resiliency to these effects mildly present for
students who maintained their desire for challenge during the pandemic.

The rationale for employing a mixed method empirical study was to use the
qualitative data to dig deeper into the trends identified in the quantitative data sets.
In this chapter, we qualitatively focused on the faculty attitudes and beliefs as they
were handling the remote transition. More specifically, at the university in the
United States, we attempted to better understand if the shift to the remote model was
ultimately successful or not for them, how faculty perceived student success in the

remote model compared to the in-person model and how aware were faculty of students' hardships or complaints.

One of the most common sentiments in the faculty dataset was their awareness of student hardships and were largely supportive in nature. However, faculty seemed more likely to hedge for a theoretical hardship happening behind the scenes rather than having a specific student or concern in mind. A component of a theoretical theme here is how faculty support of students in this time manifested. Manifestations were largely in how faculty conceded the need for flexible due dates to their students, with less emphasis on lowering their academic standards.

As we have seen in the analysis, a faculty desire to be fair to their students was also prevalent. Faculty wanted students to have a fair shot at both an education and good grades, but did not want this to come as a consequence of them lowering their pedagogical standards. Faculty had to expand their definitions of student academic success, beyond a letter grade, in light of the pass or fail system adopted by many of the universities present in our international consortium, to incorporate more real-life oriented successes, such as in students maintaining their mental well-being or teachers imparting on students how to learn in an environment shifted to online mid-semester. Faculty awareness of students' mental health and isolation being a risk factor in their learning experience reflect the findings across the nation and globally, indicating that prolonged social isolation during the pandemic can lead to mental health issues that contribute to cognitive decline (Morgan, 2022). Evidence from the last 2 years of studying this phenomenon indicates that the rapid shift to remote learning disrupted students' social and cognitive functions (Guppy et al., 2022a) as well as emotional well-being (Ferdig et al., 2021).

We did find that students suffering from harsher lockdowns in their homes, perhaps due to the crowding of their space or other difficulties, did appear to have lower confidence in their ability to learn. However, faculty appeared to be aware of these issues, and made remedying them a key feature of their approach to remote learning (Guppy et al., 2022a). Students, even with less-than-ideal housing conditions (e.g., noisy and shared environments, lack of a dedicated study space), rated their confidence in learning higher when they felt their instructor provided strong navigational support for online learning (Guppy et al., 2022b). One caveat is that the nine institutions in our research tilted toward medium and large institutions, most with a strong pre-pandemic presence in online learning and a pre-existing learning technology infrastructure. Regardless, one "success" we can take away from the pandemic is that faculty, and students, appear to have a greater understanding of remote learning technology and how to make use of it in education. Faculty were aware of support for technology amongst their peer groups and amongst the university, such as teaching and learning centers, and seemed to know where to turn to if they needed support (Bartolic et al., 2022a).

Gathered primarily from responses from Belgium faculty, it is apparent that faculty were aware of a variety of different patterns of response to the pandemic in students. One of these most prominent response sets to this end is that a minority of faculty (3 out of 51) did identify that certain students appeared to not undergo almost any academic-related negative outcomes to the pandemic, and appeared to showcase only academic success in their courses. While only a few faculty high-lighted this as part of their experience, it is nonetheless a salient pattern worth mentioning.

Another recurring theme that emerged at both the American and the Belgian institutions is communication (or lack thereof) being a cornerstone of faculty experience. In some cases, students themselves, rather than other faculty, were very difficult to reach in the wake of the emergency remote transition. Furthermore, as so many faculty were unwilling to require students to find and keep on webcams to attend synchronous lectures, most students, far more than can be reasonably explained by the number of students who lack access to technology, elected to keep their cameras off. This "teaching to black boxes" made it especially difficult for faculty to keep tabs on whether students were struggling or not during lectures. This left the responsibility of communicating difficulty up to the students, who were not hugely likely to communicate to faculty unprompted. However, faculty who were proactive in seeking communication and student interaction were much more likely to have a smooth understanding of student hardships.

Lastly, faculty at both universities appeared to prioritize a balance of flexibility with time spent on good pedagogy and supporting students' pandemic living. Faculty were aware of their own increased personal flexibility, but also student hardships and the need to be flexible with them, as well as being aware that they need to reconcile it with efforts required to create a good, pedagogically sound remote course (beyond Zoom lectures). For example, faculty often found themselves spending time researching resources for students' well-being, such as counseling services and food banks, rather than the delivery of the course content.

Limitations and Conclusions

Our consortium attempted to glean a global perspective on the COVID-19 pandemic and its impact on higher education teaching, learning, and pedagogy across the continents. Our multinational research employed a mixed methods design, with a combination of quantitative data from a large student population and qualitative data from faculty members to answer consortium research questions. Our study is not without limitations and challenges. Only the US university collected data about individual and community resiliency, so caution is advised before generalizing the findings to other institutions in and outside of the country.

Our data is also aging, having been collected in the early months of the pandemic. To investigate the long-term impact of a global disruptive event, leading to rapid shift to remote instruction, a follow up may be necessary. Since our study was conducted, COVID-19 vaccinations have been approved and administered globally, and most higher education institutions and workplaces experienced a gradual return to an in-person or hybrid model (Singh et al., 2021; Yang et al., 2021). A follow-up study examining the possible long-term impact could help identify any new or deeper gaps among students and vulnerable populations, and whether the digital divide and digital disconnect gap identified early on (Guppy et al., 2022a) is closing or deepening. For example, some countries still lag with vaccination rates and appropriate healthcare response to the pandemic, which might impact or mirror the digital divide and the higher education support infrastructure. This could in turn affect students, faculty, and administrators' current (1.5 years later) perception of the future of online and remote learning and where they perceive higher education is heading in the long term. While a hybrid model is gaining popularity, some institutions, particularly those focused historically on serving traditional college learners, are seeking to return at least partly to pre-pandemic practices. For example, MIT is re-embracing standardized testing for their admissions protocol, despite inconclusive scientific evidence of their validity (Bello, 2022). Are we facing a return to pre-pandemic "normality" or a balance of the old and new reshaping normal? Further research might help shed light on these emerging questions.

References

Allen, I. E., Seaman, J., Poulin, R., & Straut, T. T. (2016). *Online report card: Tracking online education in the United States*. Babson Survey Research Group. Babson College, 231 Forest Street, Babson Park, MA 02457. Retrieved from: https://files-eric-ed-gov.libproxy.library.unt.edu/fulltext/ED572777.pdf

Armstrong, K. E., Goodboy, A. K., & Shin, M. (2022). Pandemic pedagogy and emergency remote instruction: Transitioning scheduled in-person courses to online diminishes effective teaching and student learning outcomes. *Southern Communication Journal, 87*, 1–14.

Bartolic, S. K., Boud, D., Agapito, J., Verpoorten, D., Williams, S., Lutze-Mann, L., Matzat, U., Moreno, M. M., Polly, P., Tai, J., Marsh, H., Lin, L., Burgess, J. L., Habtu, S., Rodrigo, M. M., Roth, M., Heap, T., & Guppy, N. (2022a). A multi-institutional assessment of changes in higher education teaching and learning in the face of COVID-19. *Educational Review, 74*(3), 1–17.

Bartolic, S., Matzat, U., Tai, J., Burgess, J. L., Boud, D., Craig, H., Archibald, A., De Jaeger, A., Kaplan-Rakowski, R., Lutze-Mann, L., Polly, P., Roth, M., Heap, T., Agapito, J., & Guppy, N. (2022b). Student vulnerabilities and confidence in learning in the context of the COVID-19 pandemic. *Studies in Higher Education, 47*(12), 2460–2472.

Bello, A. (2022, April 19). *MIT is bringing back the SAT. Your college shouldn't*. The Chronicle of Higher Education. Retrieved from: https://www.chronicle.com/article/mit-is-bringing-back-the-sat-your-college-shouldnt

Braun, V., & Clarke, V. (2006). Using thematic analysis in psychology. *Qualitative Research in Psychology, 3*, 77–101.

Connor, K. M., & Davidson, J. R. (2003). Development of a new resilience scale: The Connor-Davidson resilience scale (CD-RISC). *Depression and Anxiety, 18*(2), 76–82.

Donham, C., Barron, H. A., Alkhouri, J. S., Changaran Kumarath, M., Alejandro, W., Menke, E., & Kranzfelder, P. (2022). I will teach you here or there, I will try to teach you anywhere: Perceived supports and barriers for emergency remote teaching during the COVID-19 pandemic. *International Journal of STEM Education, 9*(1), 1–25.

Ferdig, R. E., Baumgartner, E., Mouza, C., Kaplan-Rakowski, R., & Hartshorne, R. (2021). Editorial: Rapid publishing in a time of COVID-19: How a pandemic might change our academic writing practices. *Contemporary Issues in Technology and Teacher Education, 21*(1), 1–18.

Fruehwirth, J. C., Biswas, S., & Perreira, K. M. (2021). The Covid-19 pandemic and mental health of first-year college students: Examining the effect of Covid-19 stressors using longitudinal data. *PLoS One, 16*(3), e0247999.

Guppy, N., Boud, D., Heap, T., Verpoorten, D., Matzat, U., Tai, J., Lutze-Mann, L., Roth, M., Polly, P., Burgess, J. L., Agapito, J., & Bartolic, S. (2022a). Teaching and learning under COVID-19 public health edicts: The role of household lockdowns and prior technology usage. *Higher Education, 84*, 1–18.

Guppy, N., Matzat, U., Agapito, J., Archibald, A., De Jaeger, A., Heap, T., Moreno, M. M., Rodrigo, M. M., & Bartolic, S. (2022b). Student confidence in learning during the COVID-19 pandemic: what helped and what hindered?. *Higher Education Research & Development*, 1-15. https://doi.org/10.1080/07294360.2022.2119372

Hickling, S., Bhatti, A., Arena, G., Kite, J., Denny, J., Spencer, N. L., & Bowles, D. C. (2021). Adapting to teaching during a pandemic: Pedagogical adjustments for the next semester of teaching during COVID-19 and future online learning. *Pedagogy in Health Promotion, 7*(2), 95–102.

Karalis, T., & Raikou, N. (2020). Teaching at the times of COVID-19: Inferences and implications for higher education pedagogy. *International Journal of Academic Research in Business and Social Sciences, 10*(5), 479–493.

Kumar, A., Kumar, P., Palvia, S. C. J., & Verma, S. (2017). Online education worldwide: Current status and emerging trends. *Journal of Information Technology Case and Application Research, 19*(1), 3–9.

Leykin, D., Lahad, M., Cohen, O., Goldberg, A., & Aharonson-Daniel, L. (2013). Conjoint community resiliency assessment measure-28/10 items (CCRAM28 and CCRAM10): A self-report tool for assessing community resilience. *American Journal of Community Psychology, 52*, 313–323.

Means, B., & Neisler, J. (2021). Teaching and learning in the time of COVID: The student perspective. *Online Learning, 25*(1), 8–27. https://doi.org/10.24059/olj.v25i1.2496

Morgan, H. (2022). Alleviating the challenges with remote learning during a pandemic. *Education Sciences, 12*(2), 109. https://doi.org/10.3390/educsci12020109

Pagoto, S., Lewis, K. A., Groshon, L., Palmer, L., Waring, M. E., Workman, D., et al. (2021). STEM undergraduates' perspectives of instructor and university responses to the COVID-19 pandemic in Spring 2020. *PLoS One, 16*(8), e0256213.

Pokhrel, S., & Chhetri, R. (2021). A literature review on impact of COVID-19 pandemic on teaching and learning. *Higher Education for the Future, 8*(1), 133–141.

Singh, J., Steele, K., & Singh, L. (2021). Combining the best of online and face-to-face learning: Hybrid and blended learning approach for COVID-19, post vaccine, & post-pandemic world. *Journal of Educational Technology Systems, 50*(2), 140–171.

Tartavulea, C. V., Albu, C. N., Albu, N., Dieaconescu, R. I., & Petre, S. (2020). Online teaching practices and the effectiveness of the educational process in the wake of the COVID-19 pandemic. *Amfiteatru Economic, 22*(55), 920–936.

Trust, T., & Whalen, J. (2020). Should teachers be trained in emergency remote teaching? Lessons learned from the COVID-19 pandemic. *Journal of Technology and Teacher Education, 28*(2), 189–199. Retrieved from https://www.learntechlib.org/primary/p/215995/paper_215995.pdf

Yang, E., Kim, Y., & Hong, S. (2021). Does working from home work? Experience of working from home and the value of hybrid workplace post-COVID-19. *Journal of Corporate Real Estate*. Retrieved from: https://doi-org.libproxy.library.unt.edu/10.1108/JCRE-04-2021-0015

Influence of Pandemic-Induced Technology Use on Literacy Instruction

Lauren Eutsler

Background/Rationale

The COVID-19 pandemic mandated teachers use educational technology in unprecedented ways that impacted their instructional design and implementation. In response to the pandemic, schools intermittently closed their physical doors, and teachers and students were expected to learn from the confines of their homes, subject to remote learning via live instruction delivered over a device (e.g., computer, tablet, mobile phone). This period of "emergency remote teaching" (Hodges et al., 2020) was intended to be temporary in an attempt to social distance and combat the virus. However, this change was all but temporary and has forced teachers to be flexible in how they manage their classrooms, whether instruction is remote, in-person, or hybrid. A profound change is the use of technology to deliver instruction through asynchronous and synchronous videos, utilizing screen sharing tools and document cameras. This can be compared to pre-pandemic, when some teachers might have perceived technology as an addition to their curriculum (Mitchell et al., 2016), which can be caused by perceptions regarding the usability of a given technology (Xie et al., 2019).

Following a year of teaching with remote learning, with data collected in summer 2021, this chapter reports on the lived experiences of 21 teachers from 14 states within the United States, with the intention to reveal ways to improve technology use within literacy instruction. Experienced teachers reflect on teaching before and during the pandemic, to relay their successes, challenges and concerns, and predictions about teaching in post-pandemic contexts.

L. Eutsler (✉)
University of North Texas, Denton, TX, USA
e-mail: lauren.eutsler@unt.edu

Previous literature focuses on teachers' technology integration in literacy, teaching successes, and teaching challenges and concerns. These experiences call for the need to prepare new teachers and provide professional support in response to the changed academic landscape.

Technology Integration in Literacy

Pre-pandemic, technology integration in classrooms was influenced by teacher-level factors such as teacher beliefs and confidence (Fehti & Lawther, 2010; Henriksen et al., 2019). Integration factors hinged on motivation and perceived utility-value (Backfish et al., 2021), anxiety (Henderson & Corry, 2021), and engaging hands-on with technology (Jones & Dexter, 2018). These successes, challenges, and concerns demonstrate promise and lessons learned when integrating technology within the field of literacy. Literacy, for the context of this chapter and study, is defined broadly to span reading, writing, speaking, and listening—across all subject areas.

Research that highlights technology use in literacy demonstrates promise to support literacy instruction. Successful use constitutes the ability to use technology to improve learning or increase student engagement. A systematic review of mobile technology to improve early literacy found that technology positively impacted learning in more than 85% of the 61 studies investigated (Eutsler et al., 2020). In one example, first graders who used the Letterworks app on the iPad improved their literacy skills (D'Agostino et al., 2016). With regard to engagement, another study with 37 young children found that of the 65% who chose to read a digital book with an adult instead of a print book, half of children who read digitally requested to read more books (Eutsler & Trotter, 2020). A desire to read more digital books implies that today's children enjoy reading digitally.

Success is not achieved without encountering challenges and concerns. These span teacher-level decisions to device adoption considerations. With regard to teaching, a primary concern is how to prepare teachers pedagogically to integrate technology into literacy instructional planning (Eutsler, 2021a; DeCoito & Richardson, 2018). Some additional challenges include students' inequitable access to technology (Lynch, 2020; Semingson et al., 2020), teacher resistance to use a new technology tool (D'Agostino et al., 2016), and technical factors, such that digital reading requires an awareness of video and audio quality (Semingson et al., 2020).

Preparing New Teachers and Providing Professional Support

Concerns, challenges, and successes when integrating technology in literacy are important to acknowledge, because transferring these experiences is necessary to prepare preservice teachers to teach with technology. It is essential that programs recognize teacher perceptions and provide support for engaging with technologies relative to their future classrooms (Xie et al., 2021). Since the pandemic, teachers no longer have a choice to use technology. Instead, technology has become the key connector to communicate with students, parents, and other teachers. Developing professional knowledge of teachers is shaped by the experiences of higher education faculty and their ability to support future teachers to integrate technology. Professional development programs aimed at identifying, selecting, and integrating twenty-first century tools have been shown to improve teacher educators' (Archambault et al., 2010) and classroom teachers' (Liao et al., 2017) technology integration skills. A review of literature regarding teacher educators' ability to foster preservice teachers' technology-rich experiences found that teacher educator competences remain limited (Uerz et al., 2018). These limits hinge upon teacher educators' lack of experience using technology, specifically, to recognize and adopt innovative technology to teach course content.

New teachers entering the classroom require hands-on technology experiences because they did not use educational technology to the extent that it is expected of teachers today. Few beginning teachers foster opportunities for student-centered technology-rich experiences (Tondeur et al., 2016). Teachers assert reduced uses of technology due to a lack of time to explore and practice with technology, inadequate access to devices, limited knowledge, and little ongoing support (Hutchison, 2012). Experiences with technology remain limited, but need to be embedded within teacher preparation programs. One example, preservice teachers were tasked with using the iPad to locate and integrate apps and create content for lessons using a gradual release of responsibility approach with a focus on pedagogy, where they designed more innovative and comprehensive literacy instruction (Eutsler, 2021a). Another technology-rich hands-on experience involved preservice teachers learning basic block coding skills to design digital books viewable in virtual reality, conducted through a synchronous workshop held during emergency remote instruction (Eutsler, 2021b).

Preservice teachers report that teaching online requires greater effort than in-person planning (Rosenberg-Kima & Mike, 2020). The pandemic forced teachers to pivot pedagogically and become online educators without formal training (Short et al., 2021). During the early stages of the pandemic, teachers fumbled to use new technology (An et al., 2021). By investigating teacher experiences integrating technology into the curriculum during the pandemic, this knowledge can be shared to benefit other teachers who have endured similar situations (Fox, 2020). More research is needed that examines how the pandemic has influenced teacher technology use beyond the initial months following the lockdown in March, 2020 (An et al., 2021). To further investigate these teacher experiences, this study investigates teacher experiences using technology in literacy instruction 1 year following the pandemic. Findings from this study provide opportunities to improve teachers' pedagogical strategies, and the field of education can benefit from innovative uses of technology to scaffold literacy instruction.

Process

Guided by a qualitative case-study design (Merriam, 1998), a survey with open-ended response questions was distributed in summer 2021, where teachers reflected on their experiences using technology during the pandemic within literacy instruction. To temper bias and broaden recruitment, three schools from each state (and Washington D.C.) were randomly selected from the National Center for Education Statistics (https://nces.ed.gov/ccd/schoolsearch/). This list was generated by curating a list of the K-5 teachers at each of the 153 schools, for a total sample of 1730 teachers. Participants were invited via email three times in June 2021. Concurrent recruitment occurred on 53 private Facebook groups (e.g., English Teachers & Linguists, Teachers for the USA, Teachers of Reading). The entire survey contained three different sets of questions, to include a focus on integrating technology into literacy: before the pandemic ($n = 6$), during the pandemic ($n = 8$), and predictions beyond the pandemic ($n = 4$). Each question was open-ended, and included probing questions, to mimic an interview context. Since the dataset is abundant, four questions addressed in this book chapter include:

- Thinking beyond the pandemic, what do you predict about how the pandemic may impact your use of technology when planning literacy instruction? Reflect on: What worked? What challenges have you faced? What lessons have you learned? (750 character min)
- Beyond the pandemic, what is your greatest concern about using technology to support students' literacy development? (250 character min)
- Beyond the pandemic, what are you hopeful for about using technology to support students' literacy development? (250 character min)
- In what ways might the pandemic impact how new teachers need to be trained to plan literacy instruction? (750 character min)

To participate, teachers needed at least 2 years of teaching experience (required to compare pandemic teaching experiences with prior teaching), to reside in the United States, and teach grades K-5. Teachers reported on their demographic characteristics and school context.

Twenty-one teachers, all female, from 14 states teaching grades K-5 in suburban ($n = 9$; 42.86%), urban ($n = 6$; 28.57%), and rural ($n = 6$; 28.57%) classrooms, fully responded to the survey. The survey was open-ended and requested teaching vignettes and examples through character minimums, for an average response time of 2 hours and 36 minutes. Races included European American/White ($n = 16$; 76.19%), African American/Black ($n = 2$; 9.52%), Latin American ($n = 2$; 9.52%), and Mixed ($n = 1$; 4.76%). Teacher ages ranged from 35 to 44 ($n = 9$; 42.86%), 25 to 34 ($n = 6$; 28.57%), 45 to 54 ($n = 5$; 23.81%), and 18 to 24 ($n = 1$; 4.76%). Most schools were public ($n = 16$; 76.19%), some charter ($n = 4$; 19.05%), and one private (4.76%). During the 2020–2021 school year, each teacher's mode of instruction was hybrid ($n = 10$; 47.62%), in-person ($n = 6$; 28.57%), or online/remote ($n = 5$; 23.81%).

Data analysis included descriptive statistics (frequencies, percentages, means) of teacher demographics, educational technology devices, and technology usage. Open-ended responses were analyzed inductively to develop a data-driven understanding (Merriam, 1998). The analysis is descriptive and non-experimental to encapsulate "an intensive, holistic description and analysis of a single entity, phenomenon, or social unit" (p. 16). The single unit of focus is elementary teachers in the United States. More specific to this analysis, meaning was derived from the dataset, whereby "making sense out of data involves consolidating, reducing, and interpreting what people have said and what the researcher has seen and read – it is the process of making meaning" (Merriam, 1998, p. 178).

Findings

Reflective of case study design, findings are reported within the pretense that reality is constructed by an individual's experience, with the purpose that "research is, after all, producing knowledge about the world – in our case, the world of educational practice" (Merriam, 1998, p. 3). Empirical data suggests how the pandemic influenced teacher technology use and subsequent student use, to reveal teaching successes, teaching concerns. These experiences lead to recommendations to improve technology integration in literacy instruction.

Pandemic-Induced Changes to Technology Use

When examining how the pandemic impacted teacher uses of technology when planning literacy instruction, teachers reported an increase in access to technology and educational technology programs (i.e., apps, software). Descriptive analyses of technology devices before and during the pandemic capture the substantial increase in technology use. Every teacher said their students had individual device access the year following the pandemic. This differs from before the pandemic, where 66.67% ($n = 14$) of their students had 1:1 device access. Teachers also reported increased access to devices, with many using a Chromebook ($n = 16$; 76.19%), Laptop ($n = 15$; 71.43%), and Document Camera ($n = 14$; 66.67%). After more than a year of teaching during the pandemic, all teachers in this study self-identified as technologically savvy.

With student and teacher access to technology devices, all teachers reported using technology daily as part of their instruction, an increase from two-thirds of teachers prior to the pandemic. When asked about subject use, all teachers integrated technology into English Language Arts, followed by Science and Social Studies ($n = 20$; 95.24%), Math ($n = 17$; 80.95%), with the least integration in Music ($n = 14$; 66.67%) and Art ($n = 12$; 57.14%). When asked to clarify how technology is integrated into literacy, the majority of teachers reported using literacy apps and software (n = 15; 71.43%), such as Seesaw, NearPod, Reading Eggs, Waterford, Achieve 3000, Reading Horizons, Discovery Phonics, Epic, and Kindle. More than one-third of teachers (n = 8; 38.10%) described using technology to assess students' literacy skills. Teachers questioned the reliability of these online measures of achievement because

> their [students'] ability to use technology really affects their achievement. If they are unable to use tech, they receive low scores. I have a lot of supports set in the google forms (like audio of me reading the questions and images).

Though some teachers desired more hands-on and off-screen activities (n = 5; 23.81%), they expressed the need to help students use technology more effectively, such as integrating online reading and facilitate typing practice to create guided technology lessons for students, citing the importance that "young students need more learning about technology before implementing it further." This knowledge is important to foster in students because, "we will have more online reading and typing integrated into the younger classrooms." A strategy to introduce students to new educational technology included, "I learned to have students master a tool before teaching them another one."

Teaching Successes

Successes emphasized by teachers include students' ability to learn and document their knowledge using technology, while teachers claimed increased efficiency for some aspects of their job. Teachers praised their students for quickly becoming highly proficient technology users, to virtually read, write, and discuss text together, where "students enjoyed being content creators, and not just content consumers." Technology enabled students to connect socially and one fourth-grade teacher said she "would continue to use the technology tools to allow students to communicate with one another, especially given the fact that many students preferred this mode of communication over in-person speaking." Students' technological independence was noted by one first-grade teacher:

> Technology will be utilized much more in the younger elementary grades than pre pandemic. These young learners are capable of far more than they had been doing previously. Part of that was due to access to devices as one to one tech wasn't seen as necessary for K-4 students. Access to technology devices and quality apps, software, and websites opens the door to endless possibilities. That is overwhelming and wonderful at the same time.

Teachers also acknowledged benefits when using technology to support their planning and instruction. For instance, data analytics within digital programs helped increase accountability because teachers tracked time spent and student achievement, where technology tools served as a tool to monitor student progress. For example, "Having students turn in things electronically helps me keep them accountable. I can easily see who did the work and not have a large stack of papers to look through." To help with planning instruction, one teacher reflected that she "learned the power of audio on technology both for myself in giving directions to students and for students in recording their thoughts and idea." Another teacher capitalized on digital audio features. To illustrate, "Because I made PowerPoints of read aloud books, I was able to make them into videos for students to watch on their own. I will continue to do this."

Technology provided access to more learning material, which allowed for flexible remote planning, helped organize instructional planning, and improved communication with parents. By locating existing material, "I learned that I do not need to do everything, since others have already done a lot of it. I just need to find the resources and tweak them to meet my specific students' needs." Reflecting on improved efficiencies, a teacher reflected, "Honestly, some things are easier. This proved to be true with online assessments! They grade themselves!!!" Similarly, another teacher found that, "Digital resources have also proved to be a huge time saver and it saves paper and ink as well."

Technology enabled teachers to provide students with unlimited reading material, especially to support individualized student learning. Technology gives students "access to newer information and [to] be able to find current events more readily." Also, educational technology is capable of supporting individualized instruction, such as "interventions to students," "provide an unlimited amount of reading material," and "help pin point [sic] deficits to help better teach to the student's specific needs and close the gaps created before during or after the pandemic." One teacher explained that she would "continue to use websites like Pathblazer and reading a-z for independent activities as they are easy to give focused skills and reading levels."

Teaching Concerns

Concerns primarily focused on device access, at-home support, and deleterious impacts of using the technology. Access to technology was initially a concern, especially in the earliest months of the pandemic. In the beginning, one teacher reflected on how "some students did not have Internet or devices at home. When Internet was offered to those families at no cost, some families still refused to take up the offer." This same teacher added that for students with no device, consequently, "the ONLY instruction these students got was a work packet of sheets to send home and a weekly phone call (which was rarely answered). How do you teach students who you don't see or have access to?" Even students with access to devices required parent or sibling support to learn new programs and oversee online learning. But for many students, their caregivers were busy working and could only provide minimal support. Some could help, but outside of typical school hours, which stretched teachers' work hours thin since, "many parents wanted students to do work when they were home at night or on weekends and I felt like I was on call 24-7." One teacher shared another challenge, that her "students relied on parents to complete assignments and parents were not taught the same methods we now use to teach literacy." At-home distractions created an additional hurdle for teachers because, "students could 'tune you out' if they wanted to. I didn't know if they were really listening or focused on the lesson since they were in their homes. Families in the background often hampered learning for some."

Teachers were expected to operate as technical support, therefore a challenge was "getting students to use the technology appropriately. I teach first grade so the learning curve was very high." Every teacher expressed concerns regarding excessive screen time, citing that it could negatively impact students' eyesight, social-emotional development, and interest in reading. A teacher suggested that "schools need to supply students with blue light blocking glasses." One teacher feared that accessibility features (i.e., screen reader) could lead to laziness in students' independent reading skills. If students spend too much time on technology, it is possible that "students will lose interest in real world activities and be glued to the screens." Teachers expressed a desire to carefully avoid screen time, even though technology was expected by the school. As an illustration:

> My district will require students to have 30 minutes per week of a digital math program and 30 to 90 minutes per week of a digital literacy program. I don't think I will use much additional technology if I can do a hands-on activity instead.

Another teacher noted that avoiding an overuse of technology should be forefront, observing that "everyone seems to worry about student [sic] spending so much time on screens after school, but I'm concerned that we're doing the exact same thing in school with technology being the basis for literacy and math instruction." If students use too many digital devices, teachers "fear that so much time on computers will cause a setback in students handwriting development." Instead, teachers recommended a balance of on and off-screen time:

> I know that we must prepare today's students for the world they live in but students need to know how to engage with each other, self monitor and advocate for their learning within the social context of school. I don't want them to hide behind a screen but nurture the development as must [much] as possible within the context of the classroom.

Teachers expressed concern about future misuses of technology. To illustrate, "technology will be used as a one size fits all babysitter to replace quality in person instruction." Similarly, "I worry that parents and teachers will think Technolgy [sic] can replace what we do in the classroom." An admission by one teacher was that, "sometimes when we use it, it becomes a crutch. Some teachers use technology to promote learning, whereas others use it for the entire lesson and never interact with their students." Another concern centered on choosing quality technology programs to benefit student learning. To demonstrate:

> I fear that many teachers/administrators will purchase poor quality programs because they are popular, cheap or free rather than researching and finding truly beneficial, quality programs that will help students grow their literacy skills. Teachers may assign students to work in a literacy program but never check on their progress.

Teachers emphasized careful technology selection. To illustrate, "I worry that publishers will create programs that claim to remediate when they really do not. Nothing will replace robust individualized instruction." Another teacher suggested, "Teachers need to advocate for quality, research backed products and methods for their students. Stop buying into the latest and greatest method or TPT fad because it's cute and fun or seems like it would work." Teachers clearly ruminated on their school's technology software selection decisions.

Teacher Preparation and Professional Development

Teachers acknowledged that today's classrooms do not reflect past classrooms. Understandably, today's classrooms do not mirror teachers' own school experiences, nor their prior years of teaching and teacher preparedness. As one experienced teacher relayed, "The pandemic has taught this 30 year veteran to embrace change and to take chances." As a result of pandemic teaching experiences, "new teachers are going to need lots of supports for the post-pandemic years of teaching."

Despite planning to teach in-person in the months following this study's data collection in June 2021, teachers remarked about future uses of technology. For instance:

> I will continue to use the Google programs such as Google slides, Google docs, and Google forms. I enjoyed being able to conference in real time with the students as they were writing. I will continue this in the upcoming year. We are getting a new LMS platform called Schoology for the upcoming year. I will utilize this platform when sharing online text and having the students respond to reading digitally. I also will continue to record mini lessons using Screencastify and share them on our LMS page.

Teaching remotely required that teachers use new technologies, such as "a document camera and share my screen on zoom to model instruction." Thinking about teacher preparation, "new teachers need to be taught tech programs to be prepared." For instance, "new teacher courses need to be implementing new technologies all the time." Teachers said that changes are necessary to adapt teacher preparation programs, to equip teachers how to teach, albeit online or in-person, and they called for an emphasis on learning how to teach online. To illustrate how a teacher preparation program might adapt, one teacher suggested:

> Online teaching should probably be included in the required education courses. When students are doing their student teaching, they should spend a portion of that time as a virtual teacher and providing virtual assignments to students. Assignments should follow the universal design for learning and be accessible for face-to-face students as well as those who are virtual learners.

Teachers relayed the importance of continually learning new tools, where "every semester those new teachers need to learn new apps and new websites they can use in the classroom." A more specific reflection of tools and skills required of teachers was described:

> Teachers will need to know how to use google classrooms, progress online, virtual reading and highlighting. They will also need to learn how to use smart boards, share screens, and projectors. They will use it to create work plans, communicate with parents, and coworkers. New teachers will have to learn how to create spreadsheets and share documents with others. They should also learn how to use sign- up genius or another form of sign up. Also make sure they have connections to multiple media sites that allow them to show quick videos and even musical songs to students.

Teachers contended that digital literacy instruction should be responsive to students' needs. This could be accomplished by creating targeted video clips for individual practice, and using adaptable digital tools like Pathblazer, Reading A-Z, and Lalilo. This requires support from IT support specialists to develop online teaching skills, specifically, (a) using learning management systems (i.e., Google Classroom, Schoology) and utilizing learning analytics, (b) virtual reading, highlighting, recording, and screen-sharing, and (c) creating online content and sharing documents (i.e., Google forms, Kindle cloud).

Teachers called for professional development that focuses on adapting to students' needs, such as the "need to be trained [on] how to assess skill gaps created by the pandemic." Teaching during the pandemic required that, "we learned how to do everything with technology this year, and for some lessons it worked better but for some lessons it was a limitation. Determining which are which, will be a challenge." Relatedly, "some students (myself included) can get overwhelmed with the options of technology and become paralyzed before getting started." Consequently, one teacher cautioned:

> I think my greatest concern is the push to continue to introduce new technology to students without teachers always having training. More technology is not the answer. Students, parents and teachers get overwhelmed when they have too many resources. Simple is best. Technology is helpful. Technology is good. But too much of it, can be a bad thing.

Instead of focusing on one approach, "Students need a variety of methods to learn, not just one way. Children have different modalities of learning, so we as teachers should use different ways to teach. To me, kids will learn better this way." Moreover, "With all the technology we have, we don't need to teach students facts and rote information. We need to teach them to question, respond, and interact with information."

Teachers suggested helping students navigate new educational technologies. This may include partnering with parents to better support at-home uses of educational technology. To accomplish this partnership, teachers require strategies to support parents, such that, "New teachers need to be trained on how to train parents to use different tools for literacy, too. Parent support is important, especially when kids are learning online." A suggestion, teachers "should also be trained in any apps that help behavior management and communication with families. I found communication with families so important this year and wish it were streamlined in one mode of communication (email, BehaviorFlip, google voice etc)."

Discussion/Implications

Though the pandemic required all teachers to use technology, K-12 online learning was gaining momentum before the pandemic (Martin et al., 2021). Schools requested students use educational technology in the home, typically to obtain learning benchmarks, as noted in a study of 120 parents, where 119 reported adopting mobile technology to support their child reading in the home (Eutsler & Antonenko, 2018). Given the pandemic-induced requirements to use technology to deliver instruction and support student learning, the purpose of this study was to investigate how teachers reflected on their pandemic teaching experiences after more than a year, and to examine teacher perceptions of technology use beyond the pandemic. Although the study is based on a limited sample, 21 teachers from 14 states in the United States relayed how the pandemic influenced their technology use. They described these experiences with vignettes, reflecting on their teaching successes and teaching concerns, to provide recommendations to prepare new teachers and support experienced teachers. Though these reflections were thorough, it is important to acknowledge that these experiences are limited by the small sample and unique experiences of each teacher in this study.

With regard to *pandemic-induced changes to technology use*, findings from this study reveal how teacher mindset and levels of support influences perceptions of teaching experiences. This study identified that all students had individual access to technology a little more than a year into the pandemic, an initial barrier during the early stages of the pandemic (An et al., 2021; Lynch, 2020; Semingson et al., 2020). Teachers also utilized multiple devices and learned the importance of mastering one technology tool before introducing another. Digital tools enabled teachers to more efficiently and effectively communicate with their students, support individualized learning, and assess student learning.

This study provides evidence that teachers no longer have a choice to integrate educational technology. Teachers used technology daily, and so did their students. In fact, teachers reported using technology in nearly all subjects. Following more than a year of ubiquitous technology use, all teachers in this study self-identified as technologically savvy. These findings suggest teacher-level factors such as confidence and teacher beliefs (Fehti & Lawther, 2010; Henriksen et al., 2019) increased after a year of teaching during the pandemic.

Teaching remote and online was a new experience that allowed teachers to explore new technology implementation strategies. These experiences were met with successes and concerns. In terms of *teaching successes*, because teachers found themselves using technology more, they discovered new ways to improve their efficiency processes as a teacher. Despite an early finding within the pandemic that teaching online required increased effort over teaching in-person (Rosenberg-Kima & Mike, 2020), teachers in this study found that using technology during the pandemic increased grading efficiency and ability to monitor individual students' progress, while, improving ease to design recorded lessons for students. Teachers also noted high-quality literacy programs helped differentiate student learning. *Teaching concerns* attuned to access and use of devices. Early in the pandemic, device access barred teachers from physically (albeit remotely) accessing students. Challenges with parental support were caused by remote work in the home, and teachers were expected to deliver instruction to elementary students who were abruptly expected to use technology as a learning tool, an unfamiliar experience for many. Teachers noted their professional expertise, because parents are not professionally trained to teach literacy; as a result, teachers felt students did not receive adequate literacy instruction. The technology itself also raised concerns, especially adverse reactions of excessive screen time. Teachers advocated for a balance of screen and off-screen time, utilizing hands-on learning techniques. When implementing technology, teachers contended the programs need to be supported by research, purposefully integrated, and teacher monitored.

Changes in how teachers perceive and use technology requires change in *teacher preparation and professional development*. Because new technological skills are required to teach in today's classroom, teachers stated that teacher preparation programs are responsible for equipping teachers with technology training. Though prior research focused on the importance of providing teachers with hands-on technology opportunities (e.g., Jones & Dexter, 2018), teachers in this study emphasized the skill set required of newly trained teachers to focus on pedagogy, such as how to use technology devices and manage education software. Teachers suggested providing virtual teaching opportunities to mimic the new strategies required to teach online. Teacher preparation programs might consider investing in virtual teaching programs such as simSchool (Christensen et al., 2011).

A need to shift how teachers are prepared to teach in digital classrooms also highlights the importance of providing teacher professional development. When asked, "What does it take beyond digital technology?" it was discovered that teachers need basic digital skills and technology-related teaching skills rather than digital technology resources (Sailer et al., 2021). Teachers in this study support this assertion and added that training and support should emphasize systematic processes and procedures, where digital pedagogy is focused on learning. Selecting and integrating technology tools into lesson planning is time-intensive and requires experiences to increase user confidence (Henriksen et al., 2019). All teachers in this study relayed the need for a change in how new teachers are prepared to teach with technology reflective of their pandemic teaching experiences. Professional development requires more than identifying, selecting, and integrating tools, efforts once considered effective (Liao et al., 2017). Schools can better support teachers with their technology integration efforts by hiring more educational technology specialists. A more immediate strategy might involve peer teacher mentors as advocates to support teachers with their technology integration efforts. As digital innovations continue to evolve, teachers require ongoing support that is adaptive, flexible, and responsive to the needs of their students.

Implications

This study's findings demonstrate the importance of studying new teacher experiences to inform future teaching practices. The findings reported in this chapter provide implications to indicate a shift in how teachers and students increasingly use technology within literacy instruction. For app developers and digital designers, increased digital uses require the development of high-quality, research-supported software and apps to meet individualized teaching and learning demands (e.g., adaptive; student-friendly virtual collaboration spaces). Innovations in technology integration efforts enable researchers to develop new theories and explain digital literacy teaching and learning that extend beyond sociocultural theory (Vygotsky, 1978) and technology adoption frameworks (e.g., TPACK, Koehler & Mishra, 2009). Teacher experiences using technology should continue to be investigated to inform how teachers across all subjects and grade-levels are prepared to teach in post-pandemic, or endemic contexts. This study provides evidence for the need to engage in continuous and ongoing reform in how teachers are prepared and supported. These experiences also call for teacher professional development and the need for additional specializations in educational technology within teacher preparation programs and graduate degrees. Teachers and teacher educators alike can benefit from the in-depth reflections of teachers in this study by using technology more effectively to save time when planning instruction and monitoring student progress. Future research should continue to investigate teacher and student experiences, to identify more effective strategies when integrating technology into the classrooms of tomorrow.

Conclusions

After more than a year of teaching during the pandemic, teachers in this study demonstrate that teaching and learning with technology is no longer a separate entity. Since the pandemic, teachers are required to use technology to deliver instruction, communicate with students and peers, and monitor student learning. This requires a shift in how teachers are prepared to teach with technology during their teacher preparation programs. Teacher experiences indicate the importance of considering limitations such as access to and knowledge of how to manage technology devices and educational software. Teachers require support to design differentiated digital instruction that is intentional, efficient, and meaningful. To teach in today's classrooms as suggested by a teacher in this study, "You must broaden your definition of learning and think creatively to be sure that the next curveball is not the one that knocks you out!"

Acknowledgments Without the support of Maria Svennson, University of North Texas PhD student, this project would not have been possible. Maria worked enthusiastically as my research assistant, where she helped in monumental ways to recruit participants and support with analyzing the large dataset. Thank you, Maria.

References

An, Y., Kaplan-Rakowski, R., Yang, J., Conan, J., Kinard, W., & Daughrity, L. (2021). Examining K-12 teachers' feelings, experiences, and perspectives regarding online teaching during the early stage of the COVID-19 pandemic. *Educational Technology Research and Development, 69*(2), 2589–2613. https://doi.org/10.1007/s11423-021-10008-5

Archambault, L., Wetzel, K., Foulger, T. S., & Kim Williams, M. (2010). Professional development 2.0: Transforming teacher education pedagogy with 21st century tools. *Journal of Digital Learning in Teacher Education, 27*(1), 4–11. https://doi.org/10.1080/21532974.2010.10784651

Backfish, I., Lachner, A., Sturmer, K., & Scheiter, K. (2021). Variability of teachers' technology integration in the classroom: A matter of utility! *Computers & Education, 166*. https://doi.org/10.1016/j.compedu.2021.104159

Christensen, R., Knezek, G., Tyler-Wood, T., & Gibson, D. (2011). SimSchool: An online dynamic simulator for enhancing teacher preparation. *International Journal of Learning Technology, 6*(2), 201–220. https://doi.org/10.1504/IJLT.2011.042649

D'Agostino, J. V., Rodgers, E., Harmey, S., & Brownfield, K. (2016). Introducing an iPad app into literacy instruction for struggling readers: Teacher perceptions and student outcomes. *Journal of Early Childhood Literacy, 16*(4), 522–548. https://doi.org/10.1177/1468798415616853

DeCoito, I., & Richardson, T. (2018). Teachers and technology: Present practice and future directions. *Contemporary Issues in Technology and Teacher Education, 18*(2), 362–378. https://www.learntechlib.org/p/180395/

Eutsler, L. (2021a). TPACK's pedagogy and the gradual release of responsibility model coalesce: Integrating technology into literacy teacher preparation. *Journal of Research on Technology in Education, 54*, 327. https://doi.org/10.1080/15391523.2020.1858463

Eutsler, L. (2021b). Making space for visual literacy in teacher preparation: Preservice teachers coding to design digital books. *Tech Trends. Online First, 65*, 833. https://doi.org/10.1007/s11528-021-00629-1

Eutsler, L., & Antonenko, P. (2018). Predictors of portable technology adoption intentions to support elementary children reading. *Education and Information Technologies, 23*, 1971–1994. https://doi.org/10.1007/s10639-018-9700-z

Eutsler, L., & Trotter, J. (2020). Print or iPad? Young children's text type shared reading preference and behaviors in comparison to parent predictions and at-home practices. *Literacy, Research, and Instruction, 59*(4), 324–345. https://doi.org/10.1080/19388071.2020.1777229

Eutsler, L., Mitchell, C., Stamm, B., & Kogut, A. (2020). The influence of mobile technologies on preschool and elementary children's literacy gains: A systematic review spanning 2007–2019. *Educational Technology Research and Development, 68*, 1739–1768. https://doi.org/10.1007/s11423-020-09786-1

Fehti, A. I., & Lawther, D. L. (2010). Laptops in the K-12 classrooms: Exploring factors impacting instructional use. *Computers & Education, 55*, 937–944. https://doi.org/10.1016/j.compedu.2010.04.004

Fox, K. (2020). Bidirectional benefits from school to home literacy practices in the early childhood virtual classroom. In R. E. Ferdig, E. Baumgartner, R. Hartshorne, R. Kaplan-Rakowski, & C. Mouza (Eds.), *Teaching, technology, and teacher education during the COVID-19 pan-*

demic: Stories from the field (pp. 133–140). Association for the Advancement of Computing in Education (AACE). https://www.learntechlib.org/p/216903/

Henderson, J., & Corry, M. (2021). Teacher anxiety and technology change: A review of the literature. *Technology, Pedagogy, and Education.* https://doi.org/10.1080/1475939X.2021.1931426

Henriksen, D., Mehta, R., & Rosenberg, J. M. (2019). Supporting a creatively focused technology fluent mindset among educators: A five-year inquiry into teachers' confidence with technology. *Journal of Technology and Teacher Education, 27*(1), 63–95. https://www.learntechlib.org/p/184724/

Hodges, C. B., Moore, S., Lockee, B. B., Trust, T., & Bond, M. A. (2020). *The difference between emergency remote teaching and online learning.* EduCAUSE Review. https://er.educause.edu/articles/2020/3/the-difference-between-emergency-remote-teaching-and-online-learning

Hutchison, A. (2012). Literacy teachers' perceptions of professional development that increases integration of technology into literacy instruction. *Technology, Pedagogy and Education, 21*(1), 37–56. https://doi.org/10.1080/1475939X.2012.659894

Jones, M., & Dexter, S. (2018). Teacher perspectives on technology integration professional development: Formal, informal, and independent learning activities. *Journal of Educational Multimedia and Hypermedia, 27*(1), 83–102. https://www.learntechlib.org/p/178511/

Koehler, M., & Mishra, P. (2009). What is technological pedagogical content knowledge (TPACK)? *Contemporary Issues in Technology and Teacher Education, 9*(1), 60–70. https://www.learntechlib.org/p/29544/

Liao, Y. C., Ottenbreit-Leftwich, A., Karlin, M., Glazewski, K., & Brush, T. (2017). Supporting change in teacher practice: Examining shifts of teachers' professional development preferences and needs for technology integration. *Contemporary Issues in Technology and Teacher Education, 17*(4), 522–548. https://www.learntechlib.org/p/178710/

Lynch, M. (2020). E-learning during a global pandemic. *Asian Journal of Distance Education, 15*(1), 189–195. https://eric.ed.gov/?id=EJ1290016

Martin, F., et al. (2021). A systematic review of research on K-12 online teaching and learning: Comparison of research from two decades 2000–2019. *Journal of Research on Technology in Education, 1* 20. Online first. https://doi.org/10.1080/15391523.2021.1940396

Merriam, S. B. (1998). *Qualitative research and case study applications in education.* Jossey-Bass Publishers.

Mitchell, G. W., Wohleb, E. C., & Skinner, L. B. (2016). Perceptions of public educators regarding accessibility to technology and the importance of integrating technology across the curriculum. *The Journal of Research in Business Education, 57*(2), 14–25.

Rosenberg-Kima, R. B., & Mike, K. (2020). Teaching online teaching: Using the task-centered instructional design strategy for online computer science teachers' preparation. In R. E. Ferdig, E. Baumgartner, R. Hartshorne, R. Kaplan-Rakowski, & C. Mouza (Eds.), *Teaching, technology, and teacher education during the COVID-19 pandemic: Stories from the field* (pp. 119–124). Association for the Advancement of Computing in Education (AACE). https://www.learntechlib.org/p/216903/

Sailer, M., Murböck, J., & Fischer, F. (2021). Digital learning in schools: What does it take beyond digital technology? *Teaching and Teacher Education, 103,* 103346, 1–13. https://doi.org/10.1016/j.tate.2021.103346

Semingson, P., Owens, D., & Kerns, W. (2020). "Connected" literacies: Virtual storybook reading and digital writing during the COVID-19 pandemic. In R. E. Ferdig, E. Baumgartner, R. Hartshorne, R. Kaplan-Rakowski, & C. Mouza (Eds.), *Teaching, technology, and teacher education during the COVID-19 pandemic: Stories from the field* (pp. 85–90). Association for the Advancement of Computing in Education (AACE). https://www.learntechlib.org/p/216903/

Short, C., Graham, C. R., & Sabey, E. (2021). K-12 blended teaching skills and abilities: An analysis of blended teaching artifacts. *Journal of Online Learning Research, 7*(1), 5–33. https://www.learntechlib.org/primary/p/217689/

Tondeur, J., Pareja Roblin, N., van Braak, J., Voogt, J., & Prestridge, S. (2016). Preparing beginning teachers for technology integration in education: Ready for take-off? *Technology, Pedagogy and Education, 26*(2), 157–177. https://doi.org/10.1080/1475939X.2016.1193556

Uerz, D., Volman, M., & Kral, M. (2018). Teacher educators' competences in fostering student teachers' proficiency in teaching and learning with technology: An overview of relevant research literature. *Teaching and Teacher Education, 70*, 12–23. https://doi.org/10.1016/j.tate.2017.11.005

Vygotsky, L. S. (1978). *Mind in society: The development of higher psychological processes.* Harvard University Press.

Xie, K., Vongkulluksn, V. W., Justice, L. M., & Logan, J. A. (2019). Technology acceptance in context: Preschool teachers' integration of a technology-based early language and literacy curriculum. *Journal of Early Childhood Teacher Education, 40*(3), 275–295. https://doi.org/10.1080/10901027.2019.1572678

Xie, K., Nelson, M. J., Cheng, S. L., & Jiang, Z. (2021). Examining changes in teachers' perceptions of external and internal barriers in their integration of educational digital resources in K-12 classrooms. *Journal of Research on Technology in Education*, 1–26. https://doi.org/10.1080/15391523.2021.1951404

Barriers to Technology Adoption Among K-12 Teachers During the COVID-19 Crisis

Sara Kaiser, Shelby L. Strawn, and Deborah Cockerham

Introduction

When times of crisis such as the COVID-19 pandemic require K-12 schools to move to remote instruction, classrooms depend heavily on technology. During these times, teachers' technology proficiency is critically important to academic continuity (Day, 2015).

A teacher's technology proficiency in the classroom is based upon their perceived technology self-efficacy. The level of self-efficacy appears to affect all aspects of the instructional experience, from teaching methodology and student engagement to student acceptance and performance (Gomez Rey et al., 2018). In the Teacher's Confidence Report, 65% of the teachers surveyed were very or extremely confident in their ability to use educational technology, and almost all teachers surveyed (95%) saw the benefits of using educational technology. Houghton Mifflin Harcourt (2018) similarly reported teachers' confidence levels in technology implementation, with 58% reporting extreme or high confidence. However, many teachers were slow to implement potentially beneficial technologies in the classroom.

This study explored teachers' perceived technology self-efficacy and the barriers that impeded their classroom technology implementation during the 2020 COVID-19 crisis. Results revealed factors that commonly influenced adoption of new technologies during the rapid move to online learning amidst pandemic-related school closures. Understanding these factors can support preparation for effective educational technology implementation in the future.

S. Kaiser (✉) · S. L. Strawn · D. Cockerham
University of North Texas, Denton, TX, USA
e-mail: sarakaiser@my.unt.edu; shelbystrawn@my.unt.edu; deborah.cockerham@unt.edu

© The Author(s), under exclusive license to Springer Nature Switzerland AG 2023
D. Cockerham et al. (eds.), *Reimagining Education: Studies and Stories for Effective Learning in an Evolving Digital Environment*,
Educational Communications and Technology: Issues and Innovations,
https://doi.org/10.1007/978-3-031-25102-3_11

Background/Rationale

Theoretical Framework

Albert Bandura's Social Learning Theory and Acceptance of Change (Bandura, 1982) provided the theoretical framework for this study. Bandura posited that self-efficacy, or the level to which individuals believe they can regulate and master specific aspects of their lives, impacts performance. In the classroom, self-efficacy can impact teacher behaviors. For example, one study found that teachers with increased levels of self-efficacy were more likely to implement new strategies in the classroom (Ross, 1994).

According to Bandura (2012), a person's self-efficacy influences their willingness to accept change. Even knowledge and skills are insufficient to produce acceptance or motivation without self-efficacy, since decisions and attitudes are often influenced by perceived capabilities (Bandura, 2012). Self-efficacy has been applied to technology acceptance and can directly impact teacher attitudes toward and acceptance of technology (Holden & Rada, 2011).

Self-efficacy in a specific discipline is based primarily on three factors: personal achievements in the specified area, observation of others' accomplishments, and social prompting (Bandura, 1982, p. 126). Personal experience and achievements are developed through practice and mastery of a given skill, vicarious experience from observing others, social cues that individuals receive from others, and general social/emotional mental states. In education, mastery in skillsets for a given experience may be based on the instructor's interpretation and evaluation of results. Self-belief is then revised and created according to those interpretations. Personal achievements may take the form of micro-steps, as a person experiences success on a single performance of a skill, subskill, or task. Realizing that they can complete the task, the individual's confidence begins to grow. The initial success provides motivation to continue developing the skill, and self-efficacy continues to increase with each sequential practicing of the skill. For example, when a beginning piano student plays his first song, he realizes that he can make music. The desire to play more songs can motivate the student to continue to practice, leading to more success and personal achievements that strengthen self-efficacy.

In like manner, a teacher's judgements of personal competence with digital technology may also be created by vicarious experiences and social feedback as fellow teachers, administrators, and students evaluate their personal performance (Bandura, 1997). In addition, an individual's self-efficacy may be related to emotional and psychological states, so that a negative experience with digital educational technologies may diminish self-efficacy toward educational technologies. Accomplishments of others can also underscore self-efficacy by serving as visual demonstrations of the tasks or skills to be accomplished. Social prompts can take the form of positive feedback through verbal and/or nonverbal cues. Words of encouragement, imitations of behavior, a thumbs-up, or even a smile can build confidence in one's ability to perform the skill (Bandura, 1997).

While self-efficacy is driven by individual and personal perceptions based on social modeling and feedback, factors that increase perceived technology abilities (and therefore the likelihood of technology implementation) are not yet known. This study sought to explore the relationship between self-efficacy and rapid implementation of technology during a crisis such as the COVID-19 global pandemic. We first explored the topic by investigating existing empirical studies focused on teacher perceptions and technology use. The main questions asked were: to what extent did teachers' perceptions of self-efficacy influence their adoption of technology during the COVID-19 pandemic? What barriers commonly impeded teachers' technology implementation?

Teacher Perceptions

Existing evidence of relationships between self-efficacy and use of technology, as well as stress experienced by teachers during sudden change (Poitras et al., 2017; Ramadan, 2017), provides a foundation for investigating the influence of abrupt changes such as pandemic-related shutdowns upon a teacher's self-efficacy with technological skills. The COVID-19 crisis presents a unique opportunity to evaluate the simultaneous impact of these phenomena.

Teacher implementation of classroom technologies offers insight into their readiness to adopt modern digital technologies. Tondeur et al. (2012) suggest that planning lessons with technology presents challenges because educators do not all possess the same level of technology skills as the students they teach. The acceptance and effective implementation of technology influences the ability to reach students (Schrum & Levin, 2016). Classroom use of educational technology allows students to engage in learning in meaningful and student-centered ways (Prensky, 2008). Li et al. (2019) explored the predictors that independently contribute to teacher use of technology by surveying high school teachers. Their results showed that teachers' technology self-efficacy was a significant predictor of their technology usage, impacted by teachers' pedagogical and technological readiness. Additionally, attitudes toward technology appeared to have a significant and positive effect on perceived self-efficacy and feelings associated with the implementation of educational technologies (Celik & Yesilyurt, 2012). Confident teachers with a high degree of computer self-efficacy are more likely to have a positive attitude about technology-supported education (Ritter, 2015).

In addition to a person's perceived technological skills influencing their implementation of educational technology (Poitras et al., 2017), a higher level of self-efficacy may produce stronger effort toward developing new skills (Shen et al., 2013). Potential barriers between the instructor and technology may diminish the instructor's technology use in an educational setting (Heinonen et al., 2019). Lack of time, inadequate organizational support, and limited collegial support may hinder the learning of new technology (Heinonen et al., 2019).

Technology Use and Implementation

Teacher technology adoption propensity correlates with willingness to participate in the change process (Aldunate & Nussbaum, 2013). Early adopters of technology tend to dedicate ample time and resources to developing learning materials that incorporate educational technologies, regardless of the complexity of the implementation process. Conversely, late adopters spend significantly less time creating content with technology components and consistently exit the adoption process at earlier stages (Aldunate & Nussbaum, 2013).

Moreover, organizational factors (e.g., the level of autonomy associated with implementation), technological factors (e.g., purpose and complexity), and individual factors (e.g., age, intellectual capabilities, and past experiences) influence technology acceptance and implementation in the classroom. Such moderating factors influence technology acceptance and should be considered when evaluating technology acceptance. The potential impact of perceived usefulness (defined as the degree to which a person believes that using a technological tool will enhance their performance), ease of use, purpose, technological complexity, gender, and experience on adoption practices may have profound effects on technology acceptance, with the strongest factors seen as experience and age (Sun & Zhang, 2006).

Although most existing research focuses on adoption of technology in typical, non-crisis circumstances, examples of technology implementation in crisis provide insights into technology adoption and barriers during the current widespread crisis. One such example investigated the use of Facebook at a Syrian university during the Syrian political crisis, which prevented many students from commuting safely (Ramadan, 2017). In the study, many students who were displaced due to the Syrian crisis conflict had difficulty commuting to the university. Prior to the crisis, school had been conducted in person, but social networks became pedagogical tools once live instruction was less feasible. Student and teacher use of Facebook appeared to play a supportive role in collaboration, and authors concluded that Facebook helped create collaborative learning models by facilitating connections between communities (Ramadan, 2017).

As part of the response to Hurricane Katrina in 2015, universities in New Orleans rapidly developed mobile learning models for online coursework and implemented the use of mobile devices (Day, 2015). Based on average test scores from local assessments given by the university professors, no negative impact to learning occurred during the transition to virtual learning. The University of New Orleans' infrastructure and response time supported continuity and underscored the need for planning, response time, and academic continuity. In educational institutions, these critical functions can mitigate the impact of future unplanned school closures. In like manner, technology implementation was sudden during the COVID-19 crisis.

Pilot Study

In late spring of 2020, we interviewed four teachers in a pilot focus group. Although the pilot was for a study surrounding teacher technology adoption, it occurred during the beginning stages of remote instruction. The objective of the focus group was to identify the degree to which a relationship may exist between a teacher's perceived proficiency in technology and the use of classroom technology. Other factors were analyzed as well, including perceptions and readiness to adopt technology. There was significant discussion about rapid transfer to all-online learning due to COVID-19 school closures, which became a major focus in our present study. The findings prompted further research into teacher self-efficacy and the adoption of technology during the 2020 COVID-19 school closures.

Methods

Purpose of the Present Study

In the present study, we sought to understand the experiences and barriers teachers encountered while adapting to an all-online learning environment during the 2020 COVID-19 crisis. Understanding technology use in the classroom, barriers that impede technology implementation, and perceived self-efficacy may broaden understanding of the factors that influence adoption of new technologies during times of crisis and provide insights into technology adoption during typical conditions. We sought to answer two research questions: To what extent did teachers' perceptions of self-efficacy influence their adoption of technology during the COVID-19 pandemic? What barriers commonly impeded teachers' technology implementation?

Participants and Sampling Methods

The research proposal was approved by the university's Institutional Review Board. Twenty teachers participated in semi-structured interviews (see Tables 1, 2 and 3 for participant demographics). All participants were active full-time secondary school (grades 6–12) teachers who were not serving in administrative roles. Participants represented rural, urban, and suburban schools in both public and private districts with varying socioeconomic levels. See Appendix A for the demographic questionnaire.

Table 1 Participant demographics

Participant	1	2	3	4	5
State	MN	CT	CT	TX	CT
Years of teaching	21	31	6.5	16	9
Type of school	Private	Public	Public	Public	Public
Age	49	54	28	55	31
Subject taught	Biology	Life Consumer Science	Spanish	Science	French
Grade levels taught	9th–12th	5th–8th	7th–8th	9th–12th	7th–8th
Highest education level	Masters	Masters	Bachelors	Masters	Masters
Region	Suburban	Rural	Suburban	Urban	Rural
Perceived socioeconomic status of school	Upper middle class	Middle/upper	Unsure	Low SES	Middle Class
1–10 scale technology self-efficacy prior to COVID-19	7	7	8	6.5	7
1–10 scale technology self-efficacy post COVID-19	8	8.5	8	8.5	7
Participant	6	7	8	9	10
State	PA	CT	TX	CT	CT
Years of teaching	28	14		12	21
Type of school	Public	Public	Public	Public	Public
Age	53	34	41	34	47
Subject taught	World cultures	General ED	English, language arts, reading	Social studies	Spanish
Grade levels taught	9th–12th	1st	5th	9th–12th	9th–12th
Highest education level	Masters	Masters	Masters	Masters	Masters
Region	Rural	Urban	Suburban	Rural	Suburban
Perceived socioeconomic status of school	Middle class	Low	Low	Middle class	Upper middle class
1–10 scale technology self-efficacy prior to COVID-19	5	10	8	8	8
1–10 scale technology self-efficacy post COVID-19	5	10	8	8	9
Participant	11	12	13	14	15
State	TX	TX	TX	NJ	CT
Years of teaching	3	5	4	16	10
Type of school	Public	Private	Public	Public	Public
Age	32	40	26	37	36

(continued)

Table 1 (continued)

Subject taught	Algebra 2	Math & Science	Math	Spanish	ELA
Grade levels taught	9th–12th	7th–8th	7th	9th–12th	11th–12th
Highest education level	Bachelors	Masters	Masters	Masters	Masters
Region	Suburban	Suburban	Suburban	Suburban	Urban
Perceived socioeconomic status of school	Middle where is debatable	Middle to upper middle class	Low	Upper	Middle to lower
1–10 scale technology self-efficacy prior to COVID-19	8	7 or 8	9–10	8	7
1–10 scale technology self-efficacy post COVID-19	8–9 same	7 or 8	9–10 same	8–9 same	7 same
Participant	**16**	**17**	**18**	**19**	**20**
State	MA	TX	CT	TX	MD
Years of teaching	6	2	3	11	19
Type of school	Private	Public	Public	Public	Private
Age	40	24	31	36	42
Subject taught	Science	Art	Art	Science	ALL subjects
Grade levels taught	9th–12th	5th–8th	6th–8th	6th	5th
Highest education level	Doctorate	Bachelors	Bachelors	Masters	Masters
Region	Urban	Rural	Urban	Urban	Suburban
Perceived socioeconomic status of school	Upper	Low	Low	Low	Middle-Upper
1–10 scale technology self-efficacy prior to COVID-19	7–8	8	7	9–10	9
1–10 scale technology self-efficacy post COVID-19	7–8	8	8	10	9

Participant Demographic Frequencies

Materials

Materials included computer web cam with Internet access. DocuSign allowed participants to add their signatures on the participant consent forms, and Zoom video conferencing platform was used to conduct, record, and transcribe each interview. The researchers cleaned and verified Zoom interview transcripts prior to analyzing results. No participant compensation was provided. Participants answered open-ended questions in one-to-one virtual semi-structured interviews to evaluate perceived self-efficacy of technology and the barriers that impacted adoption during the COVID-19 crisis.

Table 2 Participants by state

State	Number and percentage
Texas	7 (35%)
Connecticut	8 (40%)
Pennsylvania	1 (4%)
New Jersey	1 (4%)
Maryland	1 (4%)
Minnesota	1 (4%)
Massachusetts	1 (4%)

Table 3 Participant years of teaching experience

Years of teaching experience	Number and percentage
1–5	5 (25%)
6–10	5 (25%)
11–15	3 (15%)
16–20	3 (15%)
21–25	2 (10%)
26–30	1 (5%)
Over 30	1 (5%)

Procedure

A recruitment flyer inviting K-12 public and private school teachers was posted publicly on the researchers' Facebook pages. Teachers who emailed to indicate interest in participating were emailed the approved consent form via DocuSign e-signature platform to review and sign. Each participant then took part in a one-to-one 30–45-minute Zoom interview with one of the study authors. After introductions, participants were asked to answer eight demographic questions, including their name, discipline, years of experience, description of school system, and age group taught. Two interview questions required participants to rate their confidence and comfort using personal and educational technology both before and during COVID-19 on a 10-point Likert scale. Participants were then asked nine open-ended questions. They were asked about the types of technology used for education during the COVID-19 crisis, and about challenges they encountered when using technology during the crisis. They were also asked to reflect on their ability to adapt to new technology, their perceived technology proficiency before and during COVID-19 school closures and their opinions on the effectiveness of distance education for their students. The interview questionnaire is included in Appendix A.

Analysis of Data

Two researchers conducted first cycle coding, and commonly worded responses were noted (Saldana, 2016). During second-cycle coding, researchers independently conducted pattern coding to determine meaning from the themes and patterns (Saldaña, 2012, pp. 236–239). Words and phrases that best illustrate the themes were included in the study findings.

For example, in response to the question, "How does your environment contribute to your use of technology amid COVID-19 school closure?" respondents often replied with answers regarding their immediate home environment and conditions that affected or did not affect teaching in their home environment. Thus, the barrier "Environment" became a collective code for responses related to the influence of the environment upon teaching.

Results

The researchers identified four primary themes: Self-Confidence, Technology Proficiency, Socioeconomic Status (Environment), and Effectiveness of Online Learning. The counts of responses in each category were then entered into SPSS Statistics Software for further analysis of trends in qualitative responses.

Self-Confidence

To answer the primary research question, "To what extent did teachers' perceptions of self-efficacy influence their adoption of technology during the COVID-19 pandemic?" participants were asked to rate themselves from 1 to 10, with 1 being the least confident and 10 being the most confident in their skills with technology use before and after COVID-19 school closures. Most teachers (90%) rated their confidence level as high or very high ($M = 7.6$) before the COVID-19 school closures. After the shutdowns, five of these participants rated their confidence 1 to 1.5 points higher ($M = 8.3$), and two teachers showed no change. Two other teachers rated their confidence as an "average" score of 5 ($M = 5$) prior to the pandemic and did not change their rating post-school closure.

Socioeconomic Status (Environment)

To answer the secondary research question, "What barriers commonly impeded teachers' technology implementation?" a one-way analysis of variance (ANOVA), first developed by Ronald Fisher in 1925 as an extension of t- and z-test method, compared the effects of socioeconomic status on perceived self-efficacy. Results revealed a statistically significant relationship between the teachers' perceptions of the socioeconomic status of the school district and perceived efficacy of online learning ($F = (5, 14)$, $F = 4.139$, $p = 0.016$). A post-hoc analysis showed highest perceptions of efficacy with higher socioeconomic status. Additionally, resources were cited as a barrier encountered during the COVID-19 crisis ($M = 2.45$, $SD = 2.012$). Participants most often discussed barriers related to lack of resources ("It's [online learning] academically not the best thing … parents just don't have the ability to provide the devices and the internet that they need") and safety concerns for the students ("Since my kids are low socioeconomic kids, a lot of them see school as a safe place to go"). These barriers could have contributed to a lack of student involvement and accountability, as one middle school teacher in Connecticut noted: [if students] "…were passing before the quarantine hit…they would pass the entire year whether they did their online learning through quarantine or not. It was unfair to hold students accountable when they didn't have the resources."

Technology Proficiency

A one-way ANOVA was run for a potential mean change in self-reported proficiency and yielded 0.375 ($SE = 0.626$). The data did not, however, demonstrate normal distribution as assessed by Shapiro-Wilk's test ($p = 0.000$).

Social/Emotional

Again, to answer the secondary research question, the second most cited barrier was social/emotional challenges ($M = 2.30$, $SD = 1.302$). Participants discussed the impact of social challenges encountered by the students, impacting the process of virtual teaching. They mentioned feeling like they were therapists, since students were "home, and …parents are stressed out." In addition, social engagement was seen as lacking. Teachers felt that the "in-person dynamic of conversations and deep questioning and probing…" can't be recreated "asynchronously by technology." As one participant noted, "The main objective in high school is trying to teach them [students] how to be good people, and when there is not the regular interaction and building of those relationships…student achievement drops."

Table 4 Primary tools participants used

Purpose	Digital technology tool
Learning management	Google classroom
	Canvas & Microsoft Applications
	Powerschool learning
Communication	Email
Recording software	YouTube
	Google meets
	Screencastify
	Zoom
Formative assessment	Quizizz
	Edpuzzle
	Quizlet
Collaboration	Flipgrid
	Google docs
	Google slides
	Google hangout
Additional support	YouTube
	Ted-ED
	Khan academy

Technology

Teachers reported using a variety of programs during in-class learning both before and during COVID-19 school closures (see Table 4). All participants except for two reported a decrease in the quantity of technology tools used in online learning during COVID-19 school closures. However, the types of technology used during closures were new adoptions because of the changed instructional method. Other participants reported using the same digital platforms before and during the closures, but were required to add others, including web cam, and recording software, to live stream lessons.

Moreover, there were commonalities both in the programs used by participants and in the reported experiences. Some teachers reported having to shift from one learning management system to a new one. In one such case, the participant reported using PowerSchool Learning, but because PowerSchool Learning continually had technical difficulties, the administration made a sudden switch to Google Classroom during the closure. This type of change was often required by administrators. As one participant mentioned, "I felt like every week there was some new wrench thrown in the plan. So, any plans we started with we started here, and the path was not linear at all, it just curved every which way. Every week there was a new email and here's a new site and here's a new way, so it was constantly just reforming what you thought you were going to do and then changing it all over again. Trashing it and starting all over again. Readjusting and changing as the weeks went on."

Teachers also reported receiving multiple administrative emails throughout the quarantine that changed the expectations of online learning and updated existing plans for technology use. Teachers used a variety of websites for formative assessment, including Quizizz, Edpuzzle, and Quizlet. Collaboration applications included Flipgrid, Google Docs, Google Slides, and Google Hangout. Video websites such as YouTube and Ted-ED were used by the participants for additional learning support.

Common learning management systems were Google Apps for Education and Canvas. Most participants (95%) had access to Google Classroom at some point during school closures, and the remaining participants (5%) had access to Canvas and Microsoft Office Applications. The participants attained varying levels of expertise on these platforms prior to school closures. Participants also reported having to quickly familiarize themselves with video and recording software such as YouTube, Zoom, Google Meets, and Screencastify. Many teachers experienced a substantial learning curve for the new tools and technology. However, teachers felt that confidence in classroom technology increased because they were "forced to try a couple of those things…" that they "hadn't used for classroom purposes."

Additional Barriers

In addition to technology adaptability, resource availability, and socioeconomic disadvantages, other barriers may have contributed to the teacher's overall thoughts on effectiveness of online learning during COVID-19 school closures. Teachers noted needing to adapt to their personal home environments because their family members were home also. Multiple participants reported having to quickly change modems and increase their Internet bandwidth plans. Likewise, they needed to prioritize their time because their children were also at home participating in online learning. Many teachers reported that they were also parents and had to divide their online time between instructing their students and homeschooling their own children.

Additional barriers such as resource availability for students, technology availability, and socioeconomic disadvantages are consistent with the theme of tumultuousness that contributes to the disarray in daily instruction: "Well, it was very chaotic working from home because I have three young children. I would say the environment was chaotic at best, so we had to just kind of get through. We weren't doing weekly lessons; we met our classes daily as if we were in person."

Student engagement was another challenge for the participants. Teachers reported that many students could not log in for synchronous meetings or would not participate in the lessons. Teachers also reported that assignment submissions and student communication drastically diminished during COVID-19 school closures. As one teacher commented, "In class they wouldn't stop talking. Online they were silent."

Effectiveness of Online Learning

When asked whether distance learning is effective for their students, 80% of teachers agreed that distance education was largely ineffective, noting "…when you're in a classroom and you see a kid struggling, you can see them walking down the hallway and pull them aside and have a chat. Those little things you can do to keep an eye on your students you can't do online. Distance education is ineffective because remote instruction lacks an integral part of building teacher-student relationships. The students simply cannot receive the same level of instruction at home that they would at school."

Only one middle school teacher stated that distance learning was very effective because of the support received from their school district and administration. The participant also indicated that distance education would not be effective without substantial support from the school district, "For my students for 5th grade and up [through 8th grade], I think as long as it's laid out and planned out well, I think it's very effective. What we did with what we had was great."

Discussion and Implications

The primary findings in this study were that a relationship appears to exist between success with online learning during COVID-19 and barriers such as student resources, home environment, administrative support, and district infrastructure. The presence of these barriers reduced perceived confidence with online learning. Those with strong institutional support often experienced high self-efficacy. While responses indicated the presence of stress, perceived self-efficacy and existing confidence with educational technology appeared to support a certain adaptive flexibility when shifting to online learning. Poitras et al. (2017) stated that a person's perceived technological skills influencing their implementation of educational technology and a higher level of self-efficacy may produce stronger effort toward developing new skills. Barriers between the instructor and technology device may diminish the instructor's technology use in an educational setting (Heinonen et al., 2019). Additionally, lack of time, inadequate organizational support, and limited collegial support may hinder the learning of new technology (Heinonen et al., 2019). Bandura addressed that personal experience is developed through practice and mastery of a given skill, vicarious experience from observing others, social cues that individuals receive from others, and general social/emotional mental states. In education, mastery for a given experience may be based on the instructor's interpretation and evaluation of results. Self-belief is then revised and created according to those interpretations (Bandura, 1982, p. 126). The primary findings of this study support preceding literature of teacher self-efficacy and barriers that impeded technological self-efficacy through the context of COVID-19 pandemic as a crisis event.

Other findings were that teachers reported using fewer forms of technology during the 2020 COVID-19 school closure than before the crisis. Many teachers reported that if remote instruction were planned more thoroughly, they would have had more classroom success, thus easily scalable educational interventions for students transitioning to online learning are needed. Furthermore, school districts must have programs prepared in case the need to rapidly implement streamlined online learning occurs again in the future.

Participant comments revealed how teachers frequently adapted to varying scenarios of remote instruction during the 2020 COVID-19 crisis. While responses indicated the presence of stress, perceived self-efficacy and existing confidence with educational technology appeared to support adaptive flexibility when shifting to online learning. This was illustrated by comments such as, "[Remote learning] did give me the opportunity to try new things such as photography in the classroom that I wasn't able to do. If I had the opportunity to use technology in my classroom on a regular basis, I definitely would."

Most participants interviewed in this study noted that, upon school closures, they received different instructions from their local administration based on state regulations, which caused varying degrees of comfort and adaptability to remote instruction. Many teachers reported that, if remote instruction were planned more thoroughly, they would have had more classroom success.

Some participants stated that distance education could be effective under certain conditions, such as with specific students who may benefit from online instruction. As one participant summed up, "I think it depends so much on the individual student. Overall, I think missing out on the interaction that we have in the classroom is more detrimental than any of the bonuses. Before the closure, it sounded like a dream to sleep in and stay home, but I think as the weeks went on, they missed being at school."

A relationship appears to exist between success with online learning during COVID-19 and barriers such as student resources, home environment, administrative support, and district infrastructure. The presence of these barriers appeared to reduce perceived confidence with online learning. Those with strong institutional support often experienced high self-efficacy ("My immediate boss was very supportive. It all went pretty seamlessly really"), and those with lower self-efficacy were less willing to try new tools ("I think [my confidence levels] caused me to try to avoid new things.")

Overall, teachers reported using fewer forms of technology during the 2020 COVID-19 school closure than before the crisis. This may have been to reduce technological complications, promote student engagement, prevent miscommunication, minimize stress, or follow administrative mandate. As stated in one participant's response: "The students when we first said we were going to work from home they thought it was amazing and within two weeks the reality kicked in. That meant no spring sports, possibly no soccer in the fall, and we definitely started to lose them the last two weeks. The engagement wasn't there. And the more extrovert kids, the kids that need company, were the ones that suffered the most. So that was tough."

Teachers' perceptions of the effectiveness of learning online were related to barriers and support received during the school closures. The rapid transition and lack of choice for using technology also impacted teachers' sense of self-efficacy. Various participants reported that if online learning were planned effectively or "laid out differently," online learning would be more effective than it was during the school closures. As one teacher summed up: "[Educational technology] is a nice tool, but it is just that, a tool. When you sign up for higher level classes beyond high school you can choose whether to sit in class or to do it online, whereas these kids weren't given a choice."

These findings suggest the need to prepare for future crisis events that might lead to widespread virtual learning. It is evident that school districts should have programs in place to be able to rapidly implement streamlined online learning if necessary. The study also indicates the need to provide easily scalable educational interventions for students transitioning to online learning. As one teacher commented, "In some instances, basic family survival kicked in and…pushed school to the back burner."

The current research strongly informs how educational stakeholders must make decisions now to positively influence the future of American education. To mitigate chaotic or stressful educational transitions during future crisis events, teachers' technology uses and needs must be understood and schools must be prepared to adjust quickly. As teacher responses suggest, inconsistency due to sudden change and unknown subsequent events negatively impacts the greatest influencers of future generations: teachers.

Limitations

The qualitative nature of the study required a small sample size, and not all states were represented. As a result, findings may not be generalizable to a larger teaching population.

Recruitment was conducted on Facebook, which may have impacted the technology acceptance level of participants. All participants were already using social media and technology, so it is possible that the sample comprises primarily of early adopters of technology. Participants who responded may have already been comfortable with technology, thus potentially biasing the results. A follow-up study using a variety of recruitment techniques could yield more robust results.

While this study contemplated the types and number of technologies used during the COVID-19 crisis, it did not evaluate the presence of novel instructional interventions. It is possible that the interventions employed were intended to be direct replacements for classroom modalities, as opposed to new content and delivery. If instructors employ the same strategies virtually as in physical settings, their perceptions of confidence toward commonly used educational technologies may be impacted.

Future Directions

Participant responses were aligned with accounts of previous pandemics and other crises that led to school closures. When a school closure occurred in 1937 because of a polio outbreak (Strauss, 2020), a similar disparity of technology and ability to effectively communicate a lesson was reported to exist across the country (Navarro et al., 2016). The already existing disparity in educational resources increases in times of crisis, presenting significant risks for widening the academic attainment gap related to socioeconomic status. A better understanding of technological inequalities among specific socioeconomic groups may highlight the need for policy changes, administrative communication, and future development of computerized instructional models.

Lastly, literature supports the idea that stress negatively affects teachers and students, and that stress and anxiety may manifest as depression following crisis events (Seyle et al., 2013). Teachers in this study reported that inconsistency and lack of student resources both increased the chaos for in their home environments and stressed them when planning and carrying out lessons. This may negatively affect teachers in the long term, just as the COVID-19 pandemic delayed schools reopening. Thus, a longitudinal study that gathers long-term effects of school closure events is warranted.

Appendix A

Questionnaires

Demographic questions:

1. State
2. Years of experience teaching
3. Public/private
4. Age (if comfortable)
5. Discipline/grade level taught
6. Age group taught
7. Highest level of education
8. Rural/urban/suburban school district
9. Socioeconomic status of the school district

Interview questions:

1. What would you rate yourself, on a scale of 1–10 with 1 being the least and 10 being the most confident in your use of personal (non-educational) technology devices prior to the COVID-19 school closure?

2. What would you rate yourself, on a scale of 1–10 with 1 being the least and 10 being the most confident in your use of personal (non-educational) technology devices now?
3. Were you comfortable with classroom technology use prior to COVID-19 school closure? Explain.
4. Are you comfortable with classroom technology use post COVID-19 school closure? Explain.
5. What are the types of technology used in the classroom pre COVID-19?
6. What types of technology were used during COVID-19?
7. How does your environment contribute to your use of technology amid COVID-19 school closure?
8. What barriers have you noticed in your experience regarding technology during the COVID-19 crisis?
9. How would you have described your confidence level with technology pre, during, and post COVID-19?
10. How have your perceived tech abilities from the previous question influenced your utilization of it during the COVID-19 crisis?
11. How effective is distance education for your students, in your opinion? Why?

References

Aldunate, R., & Nussbaum, M. (2013). Teacher adoption of technology. *Computers in Human Behavior, 29*(3), 519–524. https://doi.org/10.1016/j.chb.2012.10.017

Bandura, A. (1982). Self-efficacy mechanism in human agency. *American Psychologist, 37*(2), 122–147. https://doi.org/10.1037/0003-066X.37.2.122

Bandura, A. (1997). *Self-efficacy: The exercise of control.* W H Freeman/Times Books/Henry Holt & Co.

Bandura, A. (2012). On the functional properties of perceived self-efficacy revisited. *Journal of Management, 38*(1), 9–44. https://doi.org/10.1177/0149206311410606

Celik, V., & Yesilyurt, E. (2012). Attitudes to technology, perceived computer self-efficacy predictors of computer supported education. *Computers & Education, 60*, 148–158.

Day, T. (2015). Academic continuity: Staying true to teaching values and objectives in the face of course interruptions. *Teaching and Learning Inquiry, 3*(1), 75–89. https://doi.org/10.20343/teachlearninqu.3.1.75

Gomez-Rey, P., Barbera, E., & Fernandez-Navarro, F. (2018). Students' perceptions about online teaching effectiveness: A bottom-up approach for identifying online instructors' roles. *Australasian Journal of Educational Technology, 34*(1), 116–130. https://doi.org/10.14742/ajet.3437

Heinonen, K., Jaaskela, P., Hakkinen, P., Isomaki, H., & Hamalainen, R. (2019). University teachers as developers of technology-enhanced teaching: Do beliefs matter? *Journal of Research on Technology in Education, 51*(2), 135–151.

Holden, H., & Rada, R. (2011). Understanding the influence of perceived usability and technology self-efficacy on teachers' technology acceptance. *Journal of Research on Technology in Education, 43*(4), 343–367. https://doi.org/10.1080/15391523.2011.10782576

Houghton Mifflin Harcourt. (2018). *4th annual Educator Confidence Report.* https://
    prod-hmhco-vmg-craftcmsprivate.s3.amazonaws.com/documents/WF696716_
    ECR_2018_NTL_ResearchReport.pdf?X-Amz-Content-Sha256=UNSIGNED-
    PAYLOAD&X-Amz-Algorithm=AWS4-HMAC-SHA256&X-Amz-Credential
    =AKIAJMFIFLXXFP4CBPDA%2F20230225%2Fus-east-1%2Fs3%2Faws4_
    request&X-Amz-Date=20230225T124122Z&X-Amz-SignedHeaders=host&X-
    Amz-Expires=3600&X-Amz-Signature=97af19bb5e37ae65ba09352e9148c8808
    02e7590ff1079aa65a7192a5cd5df0d
Li, Y., Garza, V., Keicher, A., & Popov, V. (2019). Predicting high school teacher use of technol-
    ogy: Pedagogical beliefs, technological beliefs and attitudes, and teacher training. *Technology,
    Knowledge and Learning, 24*(3), 501–518. https://doi.org/10.1007/s10758-018-9355-2
Navarro, J. A., Kohl, K. S., Cetron, M. S., & Markel, H. (2016). A tale of many cities: A contem-
    porary historical study of the implementation of school closures during the 2009 pA(H1N1)
    influenza pandemic. *Journal of Health Politics, Policy and Law, 41*(3), 393–421. https://doi.
    org/10.1215/03616878-3523958
Poitras, E. G., Doleck, T., Huang, L., Li, S., & Lajoie, S. P. (2017). Advancing teacher technol-
    ogy education using open-ended learning environments as research and training platforms.
    Australasian Journal of Educational Technology, 33(3). https://doi.org/10.14742/ajet.3498
Prensky, M. (2008). Turning on the lights. *Educational Leadership, 65*(6), 40–45.
Ramadan, R. (2017). Unravelling Facebook: A pedagogical tool during the Syrian crisis. *Open
    Learning, 32*(3), 196–213. https://doi.org/10.1080/02680513.2017.1345303
Ritter, R. (2015). *The relationship of K-12 teachers' technology self-proficiency among curriculum
    areas and grade level: A pilot study.*
Ross, J. A. (1994). Beliefs that make a difference: The origin and impacts of teacher efficacy. In:
    Annual meeting of the Canadian Association for Curriculum Studies, (Vol. 44).
Saldaña, J. (2012). *The coding manual for qualitative researchers.* SAGE.
Saldana, J. (2016). *The coding manual for qualitative researchers.* SAGE.
Schrum, L., & Levin, B. B. (2016). Educational technologies and twenty-first century leadership
    for learning. *International Journal of Leadership in Education, 19*(1), 17–39. https://doi.org/1
    0.1080/13603124.2015.1096078
Seyle, C., Widyatmoko, S., & Silver, R. (2013). Coping with natural disasters in Yogyakarta,
    Indonesia: A study of elementary school teachers. *School Psychology International, 34,*
    387–404.
Shen, D., Cho, M.-H., Tsai, C.-L., & Marra, R. (2013). Unpacking online learning experiences:
    Online learning self-efficacy and learning satisfaction. *Internet and Higher Education, 19,*
    10–17. https://doi.org/10.1016/j.iheduc.2013.04.001
Strauss, V. (2020). In Chicago, schools closed during a 1937 polio epidemic and kids learned from
    home – over the radio. *The Washington Post.*
Sun, H., & Zhang, P. (2006). The role of moderating factors in user technology acceptance.
    International Journal of Human-Computer Studies, 64(2), 53–78. https://doi.org/10.1016/j.
    ijhcs.2005.04.013
Tondeur, J., Van Braak, J., Sang, G., Voogt, J., Fisser, P., & Ottenbreit-Leftwich, A. (2012). Preparing
    pre-service teachers to integrate technology in education: A synthesis of qualitative evidence.
    Computers & Education, 59(1), 134–144. https://doi.org/10.1016/j.compedu.2011.10.009

Online Experiences of Kindergarten Teachers and Parents During the Pandemic: Hope for the Future

Sharon Ndolo and Deborah Cockerham

Introduction

Face-to-face classrooms in the United States were disrupted in Spring 2020 by the spread of COVID-19, requiring in-person learners of all ages to suddenly shift to online learning environments. This chapter describes the experiences of teachers and parents as they led online education with kindergarten students. Twelve teachers and nine parents shared their online educational approaches, concerns, and perceived student benefits. Findings from the study provide insights into experiences with young learners during online schooling that School stakeholders can utilize the findings during decision-making as they implement policies that ensure educational continuity in future crises.

Background/Rationale

Developmental trajectories suggest that appropriate kindergarten learning instruction includes opportunities for both social learning and physical action, which appear to be highly intertwined with perception and cognition in young learners (Taylor & Boyer, 2020; Vygotsky, 1967). However, during the COVID-19 pandemic, the sudden move to online learning created barriers in teachers' abilities to support these needs (Cockerham et al., 2021; Safrizal et al., 2021). In addition, kindergarten students' limitations in navigating online schooling required learning

S. Ndolo · D. Cockerham (✉)
University of North Texas, Denton, TX, USA
e-mail: sharonndolo@my.unt.edu; deborah.cockerham@unt.edu

© The Author(s), under exclusive license to Springer Nature Switzerland AG 2023
D. Cockerham et al. (eds.), *Reimagining Education: Studies
and Stories for Effective Learning in an Evolving Digital Environment*,
Educational Communications and Technology: Issues and Innovations,
https://doi.org/10.1007/978-3-031-25102-3_12

103

support, frequently involving parents in the learning experience (Hung Lau & Lee, 2020; Safrizal et al., 2021). The students' limitation in navigating online schooling required extra parental supports, some of which led to assessment challenges as teachers expressed concerns with parents helping their students during assessments (Aliyyah et al., 2020; Safrizal et al., 2021). The virtual learning environment created challenges that not only had a direct impact on students' academic outcomes (Basilaia & Kvavadze, 2020; Cockerham et al., 2021; Stoijkovic, 2020) but also increased teacher and parental stress as the challenges and time demands of online instruction negatively impacted students (Hung Lau & Lee, 2020; Safrizal et al., 2021). The increased stress and burnout is evidenced in a qualitative study that sought to predict student learning outcomes during the pandemic using reading losses that occur in the summer (Bao et al., 2020). An assessment of 18,170 kindergarten students from the Early Childhood Longitudinal Study, Kindergarten Class of 2010–2011 predicted that reading ability would decrease by 66% during school closures and warned of continued decrease if children remain out of school for prolonged periods (Bao et al., 2020). The authors suggested that activities as simple as parental and teacher involvement in reading books to kindergarteners every day could mitigate up to 31% of pandemic literacy loss. However, other researchers (Dong et al., 2020; Tomasik et al., 2021) noted that student learning outcomes may depend on the input of parents.

Academic evaluations were expected to report minimal learning gains due to the abrupt shift of instruction to digital platforms (Tomasik et al., 2021). However, some researchers suggest that COVID-19 involuntarily supported improvements in the learning process and cognitive development by encouraging students to learn independently (Basilaia & Kvavadze, 2020; Weiss et al., 2006; Wright & Bartholomew, 2020). Additionally, online learning materials and strategies that were used during this period continued to support learning because of their availability to educators after the pandemic (Basilaia & Kvavadze, 2020).

Prior scholars have highlighted teacher and parental concerns with student engagement during instruction. For example, a case study that sought to identify instructor difficulties during the pandemic with 67 primary school teachers in Indonesia found that the instructors experienced difficulties maintaining enthusiasm among young learners during instruction (Aliyyah et al., 2020). Authors connected the lack of engagement with distractions from the students' home environments and interruptions from other students, such as discussions of unrelated topics.

Lack of social interaction in online environments for the young learners was a major concern for both teachers and parents, many of whom believed that face-to-face social learning had been replaced with digital interactions (Cockerham et al., 2021; Dong et al., 2020). The lack of social interaction in online learning environments is evidenced in a qualitative study that sought to identify the changed nature of kindergarten learning with 13 kindergarten teachers from Texas and West Virginia. The study found that teachers were concerned with the increased focus on academics and assessments since "they [kindergarten students] need to have more time to socialize, time to figure out how to solve their problems, learning how to take turns, they learn through playing" (Brown et al., 2020, p. 8).

Given the challenges and concerns expressed by teachers and parents, it is imperative to investigate their firsthand lived experiences in the digital learning spaces with young learners. This study aims to explore teacher and parent experiences with kindergarten students' online learning and to share their stories in order to create awareness of their stories and provide hope for the future. Findings provide critical documentation and a resource for school stakeholders to use during future crises.

Methods

This qualitative study investigates the experiences of teachers and parents who taught or assisted with teaching kindergarteners online during the pandemic. Primary questions included:

- What challenges did kindergarten teachers face during online schooling?
- What challenges did kindergarten parents face during online schooling?
- How was student engagement in digital lessons maintained?
- How have teacher and parent understandings of the primary goals of kindergarten impacted their perspectives of online learning?
- What did participants see as benefits of online learning?

Participants

This study was approved and conducted in accordance with the ethical standards of the university's Institutional Review Board. Purposeful/judgmental sampling was used due to its ability to select proficient participants who provided rich data (Etikan et al., 2016). Participants were recruited through a snowball technique, in which participants recommended other potential participants (Patton, 2002). Participants represented both public and private schools in Texas, New York, and California. A total of twelve teachers (12 F, ages 24–65; M_{age} = 39) and nine parents (9 F, ages 36–46; M_{age} = 42) participated in the study.

Materials

Interview questions (see Appendix A) were derived from common themes found in the literature. To comply with COVID-19 protocols, interviews were conducted via Zoom videoconferencing tool, which provided audio transcriptions of interviews.

Procedures

Participants were recruited via email. All participants provided written informed consent prior to their inclusion in this study. Demographic data was gathered online through a Qualtrics survey. Each participant took part in a 30–60 min one-to-one semi-structured interview.

Data analysis consisted of first cycle coding, in which two researchers and one research assistant independently read and explored the data for initial highlights and themes. Patterns and important features were noted through analytic memos and in vivo analyses (Saldana, 2012, pp. 43–64; 105–110). During second-cycle coding, pattern coding (Saldana, 2012, pp. 236–239) was conducted independently by the researchers to ascertain meaning from previous analyses. Words and phrases that best illustrate the themes were included in the study findings.

Results

The main goal of the study was to investigate the experiences of teachers and parents who taught or assisted with teaching during the pandemic. Results are reported by topic below.

Research Question 1: What Challenges Did Kindergarten Teachers Face During Online Schooling?

Primary challenges reported by teachers involved technical problems, assessment challenges, difficulty maintaining student engagement, and increased social isolation among learners. Most teachers reported technological challenges such as zoom glitches, difficulties with video recording features, zoom login concerns, and zoom security. One teacher noted that her main concern was "poor connectivity on the student's side. If the signal is not good, I cannot do anything, and it is very frustrating." Challenges such as this created a feeling of helplessness since the ability to strengthen Internet connectivity was beyond the teacher's control.

Teachers generally needed increased time to plan strategies and activities that would keep students engaged, but student distraction and lack of motivation remained concerns during online learning. For many, the most difficult issue was the need to simultaneously teach "students at home doing virtual while I'm here with other students that are in person." This limited teachers' abilities to attend to either online or face-to-face students, resulting in teacher frustration. The need to simultaneously teach was also interrupted by pandemic-related attendance inconsistencies.

Some teachers reported that they required more time for planning and conducting instruction during the pandemic. However, district and school guidelines also added to teacher frustration when planning. As one teacher noted, "We cannot divert from what we have planned so we feel very confined."

In addition, increased levels of parental involvement in the children's learning resulted in teacher concerns with online learning assessment. Some teachers felt that the students were receiving too much assistance from parents ("I can't really monitor or gauge because I don't know if the parent is actually doing the work or the child") and others felt that "the challenge with the kindergarten...is that [online] I can't assess you." See Table 1 for themes, defining characteristics, and examples related to teacher challenges.

Research Question 2: What Challenges Did Kindergarten parents Face During Online Schooling?

Technological issues also challenged parents. One parent reported that, because of device charging issues, she was "popped out of class in the middle of the session." Another parent commented that she missed an entire class session due to Zoom log in issues: "Sometimes you will not even be able to login so that means you've missed a class for that day."

Other parents were concerned about the mental well-being of their children. During online schooling, one child "...became very, very anxious and that led to a lot of behavior issues..." and another child did well during the school day, "...but then, as soon as it was over, she just had a total meltdown, just like a complete full-on tantrum afterwards..." Another parent commented that her child actually "hated" the online schooling experience.

Parents often expressed concerns with the inability to adequately perform their own work or school responsibilities while supporting their children's learning. As one parent noted, "I'm thinking...do I have to do this and work at the same time?" Another had figured out a compromise with her son's school schedule and her own graduate studies: "Sometimes when I have my classes, like in the afternoon, I finish up with him [child] and then leave him halfway, so I can attend my classes as well. It [online learning] interrupted my schedule a little bit." Parents who were stay-at-home mothers noted fewer scheduling conflicts ("I am fortunate to be a stay-at-home mother, so it [online learning] works well"). See Table 2 for themes, defining characteristics, and examples related to parent challenges.

Research Question 3: How Was Student Engagement in Digital Lessons Maintained?

Teachers and parents employed a variety of strategies to keep students engaged during instruction. While one teacher involved students with "thumbs up, thumbs down, or touch your nose, touch your head," others incorporated "active songs...some

Table 1 Teacher challenges during online instruction

Category	Theme	Defining characteristics	Illuminative examples
Teacher challenges	Technology challenges	Zoom glitches, web camera issues, Zoom login, Internet connections, Zoom security issues	"It [zoom] has been finicky, it wouldn't uncheck the one I did not want to share" "If you pause because of screen issues, they start to look around and then they are completely off, and you have lost them, so now you are struggling and have to bring them back to focus on the same time" "My camera not working, because it really is a disadvantage to not have the students see me" "Poor connectivity on the student's side. If the signal is not good, I cannot do anything, and it is very frustrating" "If [the Internet] goes down or something [is] wrong with this Google, my software program [for] my online kids can't get logged in [and] can't get their work" "A lot of security breaches with Zoom" "I would be doing hand over hand, with a physical handwriting but I cannot, this must be in person"
	Student distractions	Distractions at home, confusion, strategies for engagement, unrelated topics during instruction	"I have to be creative, because it's easy to be distracted at home. We hear the TV going on back there" "In the middle of the lesson, you have the child that raises their hand and says something that has nothing to do with what you're doing, and that's typical but it's [it's] difficult with the virtual kids. It takes so much. It's not just like 'yes,' you know, ask a question. No, it's usually running to my computer because they can't hear me"
	Time and scheduling	Lesson planning	"A lot of time devoted to planning lessons" "Limited with activities to do, we cannot divert from what we have planned so we feel very confined" "…it's like double planning" "Assessments take too much time to plan"

| Inconsistency | Inconsistent student attendance, inconsistent administration expectations, unrelated topics during instruction | "I never know exactly how many are going to be on when I turn on my meeting, sometimes I see the kids I'm doing oh you're absent today, you know because they haven't walked in the room yet and I thoughts they were going to be tardy but, no—they are online"
"We do have kids that are you know like this coming week we have another virtual kiddo [coming] because of exposure to COVID"
"Five students virtual, 14 students face-to-face. Numbers change frequently from 5–9 students"
"…a lot of switching goes on…" |
| Assessment Challenges | Assessments | "Parent may write instead of having the child do the work by themselves"
"They really can't write; their parents have been writing for them"
"There's some students you'd rather not be correcting while you have parents' listening ears"
"If there needs to be a correction, it is awkward with parents. I don't like correcting their child when they are there"
"The challenge with the kindergarten…is that I can't assess you [online]"<br>"I can't really monitor or gauge [progress] because I don't know if the parent is actually doing the work or the child"
"[I need] to see that and hear it at the same time, to solidify that 'hey they they know what they're doing'. So that's a problem right there that we're not able to see or know about, you know…" |

Table 2 Parental challenges during online instruction

Category	Theme	Defining characteristics	Illuminative examples
Parental challenges	Technology challenges	Laptops/Chromebooks, Zoom login, Internet	"Sometimes when you forget to charge your Chromebook, and you are popped out of class in the middle of the session" "I remember the day particularly…we didn't have like [internet] connection, like there was a problem in the school side" "Sometimes you will not even be able to login so that means you've missed a class for that day" "…Like you know your Internet goes down because we have many devices using the same internet" "The ones that we've experienced are the ones that everybody's experienced—when, you know, the district had a Zoom gateway failure"
	Children's attitude and mental health in the home environment	Anxious, patience, toys, TV	"…but then, as soon as it was over, she just had a total meltdown, just like a complete full-on tantrum afterwards. I think it was just like—it was just too much" "He hates it [online schooling]" "It was hard for her to be here at the table, knowing that all the toys and the things that she wanted to be playing with were there…" "If you were at the building, you can't just leave, you can't just go get a snack, you stay in your spot until the teacher says you can go" "He's totally unfocused, like very unfocused. I have to, we have to do some learning"
	Schedules	Conflicting school schedules with work	"The really difficult thing was that I didn't even start my workday, most of the time until one o'clock" "I'm thinking…do I have to do this and work at the same time?" "Sometimes when I have my classes, like in the afternoon… I finish up with him and then leave him halfway, so I can attend my classes as well. It interrupted my schedule a little bit" "I am fortunate to be a stay-at-home mother, so it works well" "I mean fortunately or unfortunately I wasn't working but there's no way I could have been working"

dancing or maybe act out a story..." Other strategies included physical movements, breaks, calling on students, and treats. Teachers felt the need "...to be creative, because it's easy [for the child] to be distracted at home. We hear the TV going on back there."

Likewise, parents used a variety of strategies to keep their children engaged during instruction. While some would "...offer reminders like 'remember, you need to look at the teacher, you need to do what the teacher is saying'," others allowed the child to use the iPad only for school-related tasks so that engaging in schoolwork had a special feel. Other strategies included stickers, reminders, and treats. See Table 3 for themes, defining characteristics, and examples related to teacher and parent experiences with student engagement.

Research Question 4: How Have Teacher and Parent Understandings of the Primary Goals of Kindergarten Impacted Their Perspectives of Online Learning?

The majority of parents and teachers agreed that a primary goal of kindergarten is to build social skills and "learn how school works," but online, social opportunities were limited. Teachers expressed frustrations with the challenges of conducting hands-on activities with their online students and felt that "the challenges...for kindergarten online are the socialization--working with others and things like that or even learning by playing. That's very difficult to accomplish over Zoom." Teachers who had some students returning for face-to-face instruction were concerned about student inability to share supplies: For example, one teacher shared that "One little girl dropped her box of crayons on the floor and another sweet little girl jumped down to the floor and started to you know REACH, to help pick them up with her, and I was going, 'No, no, no...sorry...I know you're trying to be a helper. I know you're wanting to be kind, but during COVID, we don't, we don't touch each other's things. (Pause)...It just hurt my heart to have to tell a little girl who is being so sweet and helpful that we don't help our friends in kindergarten."

Similarly, parents expressed concerns with the lack of social interactions in online learning environments during the pandemic. Two parents commented that they would prefer to have their children go back to in-person learning even during COVID to avoid having the students miss out on social interaction. One parent noted, "She is lagging behind on social skills and that's one of the reasons why I will change my mind and have her go back to school so that she doesn't fall behind so much." See Table 4 for themes, defining characteristics, and examples related to teacher and parents view on social interactions.

Table 3 Teacher and parent experiences with student engagement in online learning environments

Category	Theme	Defining characteristics	Illuminative examples
Student engagement	Teacher strategies for online engagement	Brain breaks, physical movements, singing	"Hey guys, let's stop for a minute, let's wiggle, let's stretch. Then we'll start back up" "I do a lot of thumbs up, thumbs down, or touch your nose, touch your head, and things like that. That is the best way I realized to keep them focused and let me do some formative assessment while they're working" "I use equity sticks so that everybody has a name in there, so that I'm not just calling on the kids that are in person. I have the kids online as well, and so everybody gets an equal opportunity to answer questions, or you know stuff like that" "We do active songs for each lesson, or we might have some dancing or maybe act out a story that we really like" "I have incorporated videos like little cute animations" "I give them a break to keep them engaged. In-person we move a lot from table to floor to outside—So I constantly do something that is different" "I do silly things, like have them were a hat on Fridays" "I give him an hour off so they're offline from 10:10 to 11:30, [so] they are totally off the computer" "We do a lot of brain breaks, more so than I have had in the past…"
	Parent strategies for online engagement	Prompts and reminders, stickers, encouraging child to respect teacher	"His attention span sometimes is low, so you have to keep an eye on him. We had to tell him: you know, the teacher can see you…" "He gets so distracted, so I had to keep telling him remember you're in class, you know" "…offering prompts, offer reminders like remember, you need to look at the teacher, you need to do what the teacher is saying…" "It was sort of like a kind of like a special treat to get to use the iPad to do her homework" "Sitting next to the child, stickers" "He's totally unfocused, like very unfocused. I must, we have to do some learning"

Category	Theme	Defining characteristics	Illuminative examples
Goals of kindergarten	Teacher perceptions	Socializing, hands on activities, sharing, solving disputes	"Parents are making a sacrifice of not having their kids interact with other kids because of the virus"
			"The challenges I see for kindergarten online is the socialization working with others and things like that or even learning by playing and that's very difficult to accomplish over zoom"
			"In the online environment, they're missing the interactive process"
			"They do not know how to solve a dispute because they do not have their peers to be upset with"
			"It has been really frustrating for me because I am an educator that loves to interact with my students and love being able to help them with things like tying shoes"
			"It has taken a lot longer on the computer for them to warm up to me just because they've never met me there's no usual you know kindergarten greeting and then hugs that usually happens so they're a little bit quieter noticed"
			"They're missing sharing the interaction with a partner, how to problem solve with a partner. – I think that's gonna be like a shock to them when they do come back in person. – kids like the project to do the hands on and hands on activities"
			"Kindergartener's love hugs and they don't get that online"
			"They miss out on things, the excitement in the hall, the Friday before vacation"
			"Trying to teach social skills to kids that can't touch each other or be close together or learn how to share things. – I mean they're missing that social piece, that is so, so valuable in the younger years"
			"Distancing and not sharing supplies [are issues]"
			"Kids can't share supplies and do their usual kind of activities…"
			"…the virtual kiddos meet up together for lunch through Zoom because the parents wanted that, so they eat together and they, you know, have their recess together, and then after that, they join back with us through the afternoon"
	Parent perceptions	Socializing, hands-on activities, sharing	"Kindergarten is a year of focusing on social emotional skills and setting expectations about how to be at school, what it's like to be at school"
			"We can't get social interaction in the same way remotely, but I don't think that they are missing out that much"
			"She is lagging on social skills and that's one of the reasons why I will change my mind and have her go back to school so that she doesn't fall behind so much"
			"I think that is a challenge …it's just something I can't do much about, so I hope that next year, you know, hopefully they go back"

Research Question 5: What Did Teachers and Parents See as Benefits of Online Learning?

Online learning benefits for the students included growth in independent learning skills and increased technological competence. Even though "most classes don't teach computers, and how to use them, the kids at home are seeing it more often because they're watching their parents' login.," and Students were becoming "technologically savvy at a very early stage and that might stem into careers and engineering, computer science and coding." Several teachers struggled to identify any benefits, and one teacher saw "…no benefits on their [students'] part…" unless it was "maybe that they don't have to get up as early" and could get more sleep. See Table 5 for themes, defining characteristics, and examples related to teachers' and parents' perceptions on the benefits of online instruction.

Table 5 Teachers and parents' perceptions on the benefits of online instruction for young children

Category	Theme	Defining characteristics	Illuminative examples
Benefits		Technology skills, personalized learning, independent learning, bedtime/waketime	"General computer knowledge" "Most classes don't teach computers, and how to use them, the kids at home are seeing it more often because they're watching their parent's login" "They are definitely learning how to be amazing technological geniuses" "Technologically savvy at a very early stage and that might stem into careers and engineering, computer science and coding" "Students feel connected to me because it seems like its one on one since they are alone on the screen. Because they are desperate to talk to somebody" "They're functioning in some ways, like a college course you know preparing them to take responsibility for their own education" "Most of my students now kindergarten can work the interface of Google meets without an adult can get on their assignments without an adult" "They are using zoom independently when they are five" "I don't see any that I can honestly see true benefits. No benefits on their part, maybe that they don't have to get up as early"

Discussion

The purpose of this qualitative study was to investigate the experiences of teachers and parents who taught or assisted with teaching kindergarten during the pandemic. Primary findings related to each question are described below.

Social Skills in Kindergarten

The majority of teachers and parents agreed that the development of social skills is a primary focus of kindergarten, and all teachers and parents were concerned with kindergarteners missing opportunities to socially interact with each other. Teachers noted that students "...do not know how to solve a dispute because they do not have their peers to be upset with" and that students missed "sharing the interaction with a partner, how to problem-solve with a partner..." Teachers reiterated the value of social skills for their young learners and expressed difficulty with teaching social skills virtually. These findings concur with Dong et al. (2020), who found that parents and teachers were concerned with increased student isolation in online learning environments, and with Brown et al. (2020), who stated that kindergarten learning should be centered in social skills development that enables young learners to function in the community. If a solid social foundation is not established early in life, individuals may experience a lifetime of social challenges. As one teacher expressed, "Trying to teach social skills to kids that can't touch each other or be close together or learn how to share things – I mean, they're missing that social piece that is so, so valuable in the younger years."

Student Engagement in Learning

Findings suggest that both teachers and parents experienced issues with student engagement during instruction. Challenges with maintaining student engagement prompted teachers and parents to be prepared with a variety of strategies to support student focus. Teachers and parents commented that it is difficult to maintain young students' attention in online learning environments due to both home and online learning distractions, and most participants shared stories illustrating the challenges. For example, "in the middle of the lesson, you have the child that raises their hand and says something that has nothing to do with what you're doing, and that's typical, but it's difficult [to address the disruption] with the virtual kids." Since there were "some students you'd rather not be correcting while you have parents' listening ears," teachers were not always able to confront the distractions. In addition, they had no control over home distractions such as a television or other media competing for the child's attention at home while he attended online class. This finding is in line with Aliyyah et al. (2020), who found that distractions during online learning were often either interruptions from students who discussed unrelated topics or distractions from the home environment. The addition of home distractions to the online classroom multiplied the number of challenges teachers would typically encounter in a face-to-face classroom, adding to teacher stress.

Technological Issues

Difficulties logging in to online classes, unexpected disconnections from class, and lack of sufficient Internet connectivity compounded the challenges of online learning for both parents and teachers. Teachers were particularly concerned with students who had insufficient Internet access, since, as one teacher stated, "if the signal is not good, I cannot do anything [to help], and it is very frustrating." Because online education depends upon sufficient technological support, the ability of the teacher to intervene and support student progress was limited by issues with technology. This is in line with the findings of Basilaia and Kvavadze (2020), who noted that technological challenges can have a negative impact on the learning process.

Teacher concerns with students' deficits in reading and writing skills were generally associated with the online environment: "I would be doing [my] hand over [the child's] hand, [guiding him] with physical handwriting, but I cannot [in the online environment]. This has to be in person." Similar concerns were highlighted by Stoijkovic (2020), who noted the negative effects of online instruction upon student reading and writing skills. The ability to stay connected with students during the pandemic-related shutdowns would not exist without technology, but the frustrations when current technology doesn't work can impede student growth and lead to faster teacher burnout.

Increased Levels of Parental Involvement in Kindergarten Instruction

Parental help was required to help students navigate the online environment. At the beginning of the year, many of the kindergarteners were unable to log onto their devices or open the needed technology tools. Since most were non-readers or were just beginning to read, they could not decipher directions without help. In addition, kindergarten is the entry point for many years of schooling, and children needed to learn "expectations about how to be at school, what it's like to be at school." For most kindergarten students, step-by-step assistance was required in order to participate in online schooling.

Although parental presence in online classes was a benefit for students, having parents in class created challenges for parents and teachers. Parents suddenly needed to give up a portion of their own day to keep their children in school. Finding enough time to complete their own tasks and responsibilities while assisting a kindergartener online was difficult for all parental participants. For those who worked outside the home or had children of multiple ages, scheduling became an additional hurdle. In addition, many parents who had protected their children from screen usage were now encouraging their children to use screens in order to attend school. Each of these factors created stress for parents, but the combination of all factors intensified the stress load. As Hung Lau and Lee (2020) noted, the increased stress negatively impacted students.

For teachers, parental presence in the classroom increased the pressure they felt, especially when parents critiqued their instructional techniques or management style. In addition, when they needed to correct a child, it was "awkward with parents. I don't like correcting their child when they are there." Teachers commented that parental involvement also interfered with assessment, since they couldn't determine "if the parent is actually doing the work or the child." The inability to assess students compounded teachers' lesson planning, since the amount of progress students make on a skill or concept influences future instructional plans. Challenges such as these increased stress and burnout among teachers.

Benefits for Online Learning During the Pandemic

Pandemic-related disruptions led to new learning approaches that required students to learn via digital devices, increasing time and practice with using technology. It was not surprising that all teachers and parents mentioned student improvements in technology usage and independent learning skills. This is consistent with Wright and Bartholomew (2020), who stated that COVID-19 involuntarily caused improvements in the learning process that were favorable for independent learning. Further, it coincides with Basilaia and Kvavadze (2020) and Weiss et al. (2006), who linked improved cognitive developments for kindergarten students with independent learning during the pandemic.

Conclusions

With the possibilities of future crises, kindergarteners face a chance of disrupted face-to-face learning routines. Hence it is important to provide an understanding of online kindergarten schooling experiences during pandemics such as the COVID-19 pandemic that can establish a critical foundation for online educational continuity during future crises. Additionally, kindergarten is an important transitional year in which instruction focuses on developing social skills and learning "how school works." Based on insights from the current study, preparation for future online schooling will require an emphasis on social interactions and technology resources.

Strategies and tools that support social interaction during online instruction must be maximized. To re-imagine education, it is crucial that research focuses on developing new and improved resources for supporting social skill development in young children. Acquiring a strong base of social understanding and skills is essential as these students build life skills that enable them to positively contribute to society.

Further, advancements in technology provide the opportunities for continuity of learning anywhere at any time during crisis. Hence, resources must be refined to ensure that the frustrations experienced with log-in glitches or sudden disconnections from class that disrupted learning and decreased motivation are minimized. Online tools and apps must be strengthened to provide dependable, consistent, and equitable technology to avoid having situations where individuals lack sufficient Internet access, which leads to extra challenges and limited learning opportunities.

However, even amidst the challenges of online kindergarten learning, teachers and parents found reasons to be optimistic: schooling was able to continue during the shutdowns, friends could be reached online, and student growth was observed in technology skills and independent learning. One teacher's comment that "technology has been the biggest change, and I am learning day by day" showed the hope with which most participants viewed online learning. The positive mindset shared by teachers and parents who experienced so many instructional challenges during the COVID-19 pandemic brings renewed educational hope for the future.

Limitations and Future Directions

The primary limitation in this study was the small participant pool. Technical challenges and the lack of student engagement during instruction illuminate the need for future researchers to examine the effectiveness of the new learning materials and strategies that kindergarten teachers utilized during the pandemic. Future research could focus specifically on kindergarten teachers and parents from low-income families to gain deeper understanding of their learning experience during the pandemic.

Appendix A

Teacher Interview Questions

1. Have you experienced changes in your teaching since the pandemic? If so, describe.
2. Approximately what percentage of your time is spent teaching students virtually? What percentage is face-to-face? How many students of your students are online and how many are face-to-face?

3. What challenges do you see for kindergarten students who are learning online? What benefits do you see for kindergarten students who are learning online?
4. Describe how you kept students engaged during instruction time.
5. What kind of support and/or feedback have you received from parents? Do you think the parents provided the support needed for smooth learning? Explain.
6. Take me through a typical school day.
7. What do you think the students are learning in an online learning environment? What are they missing?
8. How has your school supported you? Has technology training been provided? If so, explain.
9. Did you have any technology challenges during instruction? If yes, explain.
10. Please share a story or example from your online educational experiences.
11. Is there anything else you'd like to share?

Parent Interview Questions

1. How much total time per day is your child expected to attend synchronous online class sessions?
2. How much total time per day do you support your child with remote learning? How does your schedule work with your child's schedule?
3. What, in your opinion, has your child learned/is your child learning in a remote learning environment? Do you think he/she is gaining adequate skills?
4. Describe any strategies that you used to keep your child engaged during instruction time. (If none were needed, how did the teacher keep students engaged?)
5. What is your child's attitude toward remote instruction? Has this changed during the time he/she has attended online classes? How motivated is your child to learn?
6. Describe how you feel/have felt when assisting your child to write new letters or numbers or to read.
7. What do you see as the primary goal(s)/purpose(s) of kindergarten? Do you feel that your child is moving toward this goal? Explain.
8. Which of these best describes the educational resources your school provides for you with remote learning?
   Not enough
   Just right
   Too much
   Explain. How do you feel about the amount of support your school provides?
9. What is your biggest challenge in relation to your child's remote learning?
10. Describe any technology issues you've encountered during class sessions.
11. Is there anything else that I did not ask that you would like to share?

References

Aliyyah, R. R., Rachmadtullah, R., Samsudin, A., Syaodih, E., Nurtanto, M., & Tambunan, A. (2020). The perceptions of primary school teachers of online learning during the COVID-19 pandemic period: A case study in Indonesia. *Journal of Ethnic and Cultural Studies, 7*(2), 90–109. https://doi.org/10.29333/ejecs/388

Bao, X., Qu, H., Zhang, R., & Hogan, T. P. (2020). Modeling reading ability gain in kindergarten children during COVID-19 school closures. *International Journal of Environmental Research and Public Health, 17*(17), 6371. https://doi.org/10.3390/ijerph17176371

Basilaia, G., & Kvavadze, D. (2020). Transition to online education in schools during a SARS-CoV-2 coronavirus (COVID-19) pandemic in Georgia. *Pedagogical Research, 5*(4), 10.29333/pr/7937.

Brown, C. P., Ku, D. H., & Barry, D. P. (2020). "Kindergarten isn't fun anymore. Isn't that so sad?": Examining how kindergarten teachers in the US made sense of the changed kindergarten. *Teaching and Teacher Education, 90*, 103029. https://doi.org/10.1016/j.tate.2020.103029

Cockerham, D., Lin, L., Ndolo, S., & Schwartz, M. (2021). Voices of the students: Adolescent well-being and social interactions during the emergent shift to online learning environments. *Education and Information Technologies, 26*(6), 7523–7541. https://doi.org/10.1007/s10639-021-10601-4

Dong, C., Cao, S., & Li, H. (2020). Young children's online learning during COVID-19 pandemic: Chinese parents' beliefs and attitudes. *Elsevier Enhanced Reader*. (n.d.). https://doi.org/10.1016/j.childyouth.2020.105440

Etikan, I. Musa, S., Alkassim, R. (2016). Comparison of convenience sampling and purposive sampling. *American Journal of Theoretical and Applied Statistics, 5*(1),1–4, https://doi.org/10.11648/j.ajtas.20160501.11

Hung Lau, E., & Lee, K. (2020). Parents' views on young children's distance learning and screen time during COVID-19 class suspension in Hong Kong. *Early Education and Development*. https://doi.org/10.1080/10409289.2020.1843925

Patton, M. Q. (2002). *Qualitative research & evaluation methods*. Sage.

Safrizal, S., Yulia, R., & Suryana, D. (2021). Difficulties of implementing online learning in kindergarten during the Covid-19 pandemic outbreak: Teacher's perspective review. *Journal Pendeikan dan Pengajaran, 54*(3), 406.

Saldaña, J. (2012). *The coding manual for qualitative researchers*. Sage.

Stoijkovic, C. (2020). The impact of the Covid-19 pandemic on the educational work of kindergarten teachers. *International Journal of Cognitive Research in Science, Engineering and Education, 8*(3),123–133. https://doi.org/10.23947/2334-8496-2020-8-3-123-133. *Proceeding International Webinar Series- Educational Revolution in Post Covid Era*. ISBN:978-602-5445-13-2.

Taylor, M. E., & Boyer, W. (2020). Play-based learning: Evidence-based research to improve children's learning experiences in the kindergarten classroom. *Early Childhood Education Journal, 48*(2), 127–133.

Tomasik, M. J., Helbling, L. A., & Moser, U. (2021). Educational gains of in-person vs. distance learning in primary and secondary schools: A natural experiment during the COVID-19 pandemic school closures in Switzerland. *International Journal of Psychology, 56*(4), 566–576. https://doi.org/10.1002/ijop.12728

Vygotsky, L. S. (1967). Play and its role in the mental development of a child. *Soviet Psychology, 5*, 6–18.

Weiss, I., Kramarski, B., & Talis, S. (2006). Effects of multimedia environments on kindergarten children's mathematical achievements and style of learning. *Educational Media International, 43*(1), 3. https://doi.org/10.1080/09523980500490513

Wright, G. A., & Bartholomew, S. R. (2020). Hands-on approaches to education: During a pandemic. *Technology & Engineering Teacher, 80*(4), 18–23.

Secondary Education Remote Learning Experiences and Challenges

Samantha Marie Norton and Ruthi Hernandez

Secondary Education Remote Learning Experiences and Challenges

COVID-19 required educators to revamp their teaching methods in an attempt to meet the diverse learning needs of students, with little advance notice. Dadhe and Kuthe (2021) found that COVID-19 contributed to students' daily technology use, but motivation and engagement played more important roles in digital learning outcomes. Gopal et al. (2021) evaluated student satisfaction and performance during online classes and found a positive impact on performance when satisfaction was high. To understand student preferences for digital environments, Noskova et al. (2021) found that students prefer multimedia and video lectures over simple text materials. These findings suggest that motivation and satisfaction with virtual learning environments influenced student performance during the pandemic. However, these studies were conducted using college-level participants. While transitions to remote and distance learning were difficult for many universities, online college programs have been in place for years using Learning Management Systems that made the remote adjustment easier.

March 2020 led to the closing of school buildings across the world and a pivot to virtual, remote instruction (Prescott, 2021). While colleges and universities had online programs in place, secondary education experienced challenges with the pivot to virtual learning. Many systems found solutions in remote and hybrid learning, but increased the divide between students who had access to digital materials and those who did not. Educators assumed many roles and were forced to develop

S. M. Norton (✉) · R. Hernandez
University of North Texas, Denton, TX, USA
e-mail: samanthanorton@my.unt.edu

© The Author(s), under exclusive license to Springer Nature Switzerland AG 2023
D. Cockerham et al. (eds.), *Reimagining Education: Studies
and Stories for Effective Learning in an Evolving Digital Environment*,
Educational Communications and Technology: Issues and Innovations,
https://doi.org/10.1007/978-3-031-25102-3_13

121

curricula that involved the use of technology to find solutions to provide students with learning materials. Changes to secondary instruction required remote education, and digital learning became one of the new priorities and buzzwords. In a study on senior high school students, most students demonstrated a general understanding of "digital learning and innovation," but their level of understanding was merely at the surface level (Yang & Ding, 2021, p. 5). The researchers concluded that educators need to develop students' overall understanding and choose their digital tools to meet the students where they are and slowly develop digital literacy before diving into complex systems. This will become a key topic in the literature discussed and provide a foundation for future steps in secondary education.

The emerging literature describes the challenges and adaptations of education for undergraduate and graduate students (Dadhe & Kuthe, 2021; Gopal et al., 2021; Yang & Ding, 2021). However, research concerning the impact of the pandemic on secondary education, more specifically, grades 9–12 is harder to find. While many pre-built, ready-to-use lessons and digital platforms are readily available for primary grades, there exists a dearth of ready-to-go lessons and gamified experiences for students in high school. This study provides a review of sources focusing on the adaptations seen for secondary education during the COVID-19 pandemic, specifically, the challenges and tools used during this time.

Method

This review of the literature used a narrative review to provide context about the challenges of educating during the COVID-19 pandemic and the tools that aided in overcoming these obstacles. According to Greenhalgh et al. (2018), a narrative review is written with the purpose of interpretation to deepen understanding (p. 2). The inclusion criteria limited articles to those that were (1) published between the years 2020 and 2022, (2) written about secondary education, grades 9–12, and (3) available in full-text format.

Five databases were searched (Academic Search Complete, ERIC, SAGE, JSTOR, and Google Scholar). Key terms for the searches include: "secondary education," "digital learning," "digital education platforms," and "digital tools." Inclusion criteria included secondary education and COVID-19. Documents not available in English were excluded. Documents were gathered in PDF form and stored in a Google Drive Folder for analysis by the researchers.

Literature Review

Through the database search, emerging themes centered around virtual challenges and tools for remote learning. Within the remote environment, student engagement and motivation decreased and many reported increased stress and concern for mental health. Tools that emerged to combat isolation and increase motivation included synchronous video platforms, asynchronous video platforms, and unique interactive experiences.

Virtual Challenges

Studies of education during COVID-19 start by discussing the challenges found with adapting to new systems (Holquist et al., 2020; Lin et al., 2022; Megawati et al., 2021). In their research, Holquist et al. (2020) sought to determine the effects of virtual and distance learning during COVID-19 on student engagement. Overall, they found the pandemic hurt the motivation and performance of participants; many students cited stress and mental health issues, lack of resources to access and complete lessons, and communication with teachers as their leading concerns. Students had to continue with their education while they sought to understand the pandemic, life in quarantine, and a new normal. The transition to virtual learning took place abruptly, and neither students nor teachers were ready. This was noted as a barrier to engagement by the researchers.

Research studies also highlighted the exacerbation of issues related to equity in the school system (Holquist et al., 2020; Prescott, 2021). Students, who previously did not have adequate access to technology at home or a steady, reliable Internet connection, continued to struggle – more so than their peers. The difficulties with accessing and completing lessons and turning in work caused engagement to suffer. Both studies found that these difficulties seemed to undergird students' growing frustration and highlighted the weaknesses of an education system that needed significant reform before the pandemic. As one student described the situation: "It [the biggest problem with digital tools] is that [the] Internet isn't up all the time, so then [it is] impossible to use the iPad" (Almén et al., 2020, p. 299).

Additionally, secondary students reported challenges with unstable Internet connections, lack of access to adequate technology, and challenges regarding mental health (Cevik et al., 2021; Holquist et al., 2020; Morgan et al., 2021; Megawati et al., 2021; Prescott, 2021). Learners found it difficult to complete assignments, and some even addressed concerns regarding academic integrity. One student elaborated that when they could simply look up the answers online without any negative consequences, they did not care as much about their learning (Holquist et al., 2020). When describing additional challenges, students stated they struggled to engage and/or remain engaged in virtual learning environments. They experienced "decreased interactions with teachers and peers, a lack of resources, and increased busywork" (p. 8).

When comparing learning conditions in pre- and post-pandemic situations, Holquist et al. (2020) found a correlation between teachers' and students' perceptions of engagement. Those teachers who students reported as engaging in the physical classroom continued to be seen as engaging in the virtual classroom. The converse was also true; if a teacher was not considered engaging before the pandemic, they were not perceived as engaging during virtual learning either. Students noted that the teachers who showed care and concern for them and their well-being helped foster engagement in learning during the pandemic. The more teachers engaged with students, the more likely students would be motivated.

Though distance learning brought many challenges, teachers and students identified new strategies and practices that translated well into virtual learning environments. In pre-pandemic, traditional learning settings, the authors listed the following as supportive engagement practices: "a collaborative classroom setting, relating content to the real world, and fostering relationships with teachers and peers" (Holquist et al., 2020, p. 7). While they later assert that these elements can also exist in a virtual learning context, it was challenging to instantaneously determine what this would look like and how it would be done. Students, teachers, administrators, parents, and the larger community could not foresee how different education would soon look in the spring semester of 2020. Teachers had to shift to a whole new paradigm of lesson planning, creation, delivery, and assessment – all while maintaining and continuing to build relationships with their students.

Synchronous Video Platforms

Due to COVID-19, many schools went completely virtual or implemented a hybrid system of instruction. Several studies found that Zoom and Google Meet were the most common tools used by 9–12 educators during the pandemic (McPherson et al., 2021; Megawati et al., 2021; Morgan et al., 2021; Ramadhan et al., 2022; Zuidema & Zuidema, 2021). Ramadhan et al. (2022) discussed the implementation of blended formats in a way that did not overwhelm the educator or the student. The learning environment suggested and observed during the pandemic, combined software like Blackboard Collaborate, Zoom, Google Meet, or related software and the use of a learning management system to deliver content. Educators needed to be accessible, primarily through email for asynchronous times. The implementation of blended learning, following this framework, was a solution that was best suited for many; however, it was noted that there was no single best solution.

Benefits of the synchronous video platforms include communication and relationship-building from afar that provided real-time assistance and social–emotional needs (Morgan et al., 2021). However, these systems require a lot of Internet capability and are seen to create "zoom fatigue," in which users were exhausted from sitting in front of their device for extended periods (Megawati et al., 2021; Morgan et al., 2021). Morgan et al. (2021) found that opening informal check-ins on Monday and check-out on Friday, with additional office hours once a week, allowed for a community sense and interpersonal skills to be developed. Additionally, the synchronous video meetings allowed for instructor-guided lab experiments to take place.

Another use of the Zoom environment involved 11th graders using Zoom Annotation to facilitate discussion with drawing or text features for learners to express their thoughts to the group without speaking over each other (Megawati et al., 2021; Zuidema & Zuidema, 2021). One of the features students and educators alike enjoyed was the use of the camera (Hamlin et al., 2021; Zuidema & Zuidema, 2021). In a study about art during the pandemic, these live video-streaming services allowed for "Long Distance Portraits" to be created, where students connect through the use of portraits of each other over Zoom (Zuidema & Zuidema, 2021). These connections built a sense of belonging and community.

McPherson et al. (2021) described virtual field trips as a strategy to deliver high-quality, meaningful lessons, whether learning in person or virtually. They acknowledged that increased time in distance learning was connected to levels of student engagement – that is, the longer students are learning from home, the more likely engagement would wane. Virtual field trips helped to address this concern and were well received by the students in the study. The virtual field trips were conducted through Zoom, YouTube Live, and Slido.

These virtual field trips were designed to be cross-curricular and make real-world connections with students' current science units (McPherson et al., 2021). The teachers and researchers partnered with companies who would provide a guided tour via Zoom and interact with students by answering real-time questions and posing points for reflection. To increase student engagement, the tour "[emphasized] relationships between industry, society, and the environment" (p. 46). Teachers and students reported positive experiences with the virtual field trips, stating that they were "rewarding and stimulating" (p. 51).

Asynchronous Video Platforms

While there are benefits to synchronous meetings, the biggest drawback is the Internet connectivity to support these systems (Cevik et al., 2021; Holquist et al., 2020; Morgan et al., 2021; Megawati et al., 2021; Prescott, 2021). To overcome this barrier, asynchronous video platforms provided a solution (Huang et al., 2022; Lin et al., 2022; Megawati et al., 2021). These asynchronous tools can be used in a variety of ways such as flipped classrooms, khan-style videos, and social media platforms for quick instruction.

Educational videos are not a new technology introduced due to the pandemic. On the contrary, they were widespread in flipped, blended, and online courses, and many schools used asynchronous videos as the primary tool for content delivery (Huang et al., 2022). One valuable design feature of video lectures is that they allow students to comprehend course material through the use of playback features. In their study they used pre- and post-test data to validate the video lecture curriculum with 83 secondary students. Overall, student empathy and self-efficacy showed an increase, but also a decrease in student interest.

Lin et al. (2022) conducted a study with 38 upper-secondary students. These learners were divided into two groups: Khan-style video and online practice; attention (measured by an electroencephalogram) of those in the video lecture group was higher than in the online practice group; no relationship between students' attention and academic achievement. The khan-style video was a lecture with a handwritten tutorial with no lecturer face/gestures, just a walk-through of problems with a digital pen and tablet with audio voice explanations. The online practice consisted of the instructor posting problems for students with only a yellow icon to provide hints to aid in solving the problems; students answer on real paper and submit online. Both environments allowed for student achievement enhancement. The study found that attention was higher for virtual learning, but also found that there was no correlation between attention and understanding as both groups performed the same on academic achievement.

An interesting tool used for asynchronous learning was the social media platform TikTok (Megawati et al., 2021). Using only a smartphone with an Internet connection, students watched teacher-created videos to learn the content and respond through comments. The platform was used as an asynchronous YouTube video. Students were able to take the meaning of recounting text and write about a personal experience in the correct structure. The social media application allowed for student connectivity without the requirement of high Internet speed and connectivity during a set time.

Interactive Experiences

There existed a learning curve for educators regarding awareness of interactive digital tools and how to use them. Almén et al. (2020) noted that students lacked engagement in learning when teachers relied solely on PowerPoint presentations, YouTube videos, and other digital tools that were less interactive. To combat disinterest in content, educators attempted to find tools that provided interactive experiences for the learners (Davey et al., 2020; McPherson et al., 2021; Megawati et al., 2021). Tools that are identified as interactive experiences in these articles include Nearpod, Slido, Canva, iSpring Suite 9, Google Jamboard, and Google Slides. Student learning was found to increase content knowledge, student engagement, and collaboration (Davey et al., 2020; McPherson et al., 2021; Megawati et al., 2021).

In their NASA eClips study, Davey et al. (2020) observed substantial gains in science literacy for students who used Nearpod for their lesson platform. Developers describe this platform as one that provides "real-time insights into student understanding through interactive lessons, interactive videos, gamification, and activities" (Renaissance Learning, n.d.). The authors of the NASA eClips study explained that "classroom teachers are tasked with developing 21st-century skills in their students and often turn to the Internet to find educational materials such as videos, activities, and visualizations to incorporate into their lessons" (p. 385). NASA designed their eClips lessons to integrate videos into an interactive platform according to the 5E Model – engage, explore, explain, elaborate, and evaluate (Davey et al., 2020).

While their study noted significantly increased gains with the use of Nearpod, interactive PDFs (or iPDFs) brought positive outcomes to the learning experience as well. These interactive portable document files included "embedded links to media, resources, and lesson elements" (p. 388). However, one of the major benefits of Nearpod is that the teacher has more control over the pace of the lesson as students are not able to advance or lag in the slides on their devices. This helps keep students on task and on the topic to maximize understanding and engagement. This was demonstrated in the study results that showed significantly higher post-test scores for this group than for those who used iPDFs. Specifically, the students who used Nearpod "scored significantly higher on four of the five test items" (p. 392).

The teachers who used Nearpod for their lesson delivery platform felt that it supported student learning very well in terms of each area of the 5E model and rated it higher than teachers who used iPDFs. The authors noted, "The method of delivery seems to play a potentially important role in student learning. Nearpod students showed significantly greater gains in content knowledge over their iPDF peers, and Nearpod teachers, when comparing teacher research group ratings, also reported finder greater value, ease of use, and more impact delivering the Spotlite lessons" (p. 396).

Classroom management remains a key component in both virtual field trips and in-person field trips. Slido is a web-based learning platform that provides for interactivity between the presenter and attendees (or teachers and students) while meeting online. It includes live polls, Q&A, quizzes, and word clouds (Slido, n.d.). In their article, McPherson et al. (2021) noted that moderators "staffed" the Slido platform and censored language and usernames deemed unprofessional or outside behavior expectations to mitigate inappropriate behavior or comments. Another step teachers utilized required students to log into the Slido platform with their student accounts. This helped to directly identify participating students.

For these virtual and digitally interactive field trips, teachers scaffolded question prompts in Slido with content presented from the prior lesson(s). The company tour guide could then elaborate upon student responses, and this helped to increase student engagement. After the virtual field trip, teachers assigned group projects to assess learning goals. Students used breakout rooms via Zoom and other digital platforms like Google Jamboard and Slides to discuss and build their projects. To keep the momentum going and drive student participation, the teachers would come in and out of the different breakout rooms to see how things were progressing for each group. Students shared their finished projects with the class via virtual gallery walks (McPherson et al., 2021).

Another interactive presentation was found on the Canva website that provided students the opportunity to apply e-materials creatively (Megawati et al., 2021). Teachers and students were able to design e-materials ranging from interactive presentations to infographics. Students could also use student videos to present their work in a video format. Through the use of iSpring Suite 9, the materials were also able to be created using narrative text (Megawati et al., 2021). Within this platform, students could receive instant feedback for incorrect answers and get immediate progress checks on interactive questions embedded in presentations.

When exploring interactive learning experiences and the use of social media sites, Dennen et al. (2020) noted in their research that the integration of social media into lessons and learning activities can bring benefits and concerns. The authors reiterated the notion that social media use and engagement typically happen around the early teenage years when many students receive their first smartphones. While social media can be a powerful force for learning, the authors cautioned, "…social media is a holistic force in the lives of teenagers and young adults…social media can be addictive and lead to negative behaviors, which can carry over into the classroom" (p. 1636).

Discussion

Changes in instruction were inevitable when COVID-19 caused rapid school closures for public safety in March 2020. These changes led to the publication of adaptations that occurred for education in a variety of fields, from elementary to professional schooling. A gap in the literature was identified for secondary education, grades 9–12. This study worked to analyze literature that met this gap, using papers published between the years 2020 and 2022 that focused on the challenges and tools used during the pandemic for secondary education.

The challenges identified were like those experienced by all grade levels, including student engagement, technology fatigue, and unstable Internet connections. Most notable was the observed disparity of access across social classes (Cevik et al., 2021; Holquist et al., 2020; Morgan et al., 2021; Megawati et al., 2021; Prescott, 2021). The repercussions of this learning loss gap are predicted to continue for years to come (UNICEF, 2022). Future studies will need to focus on adjusting the status quo and creating digital equity and culturally responsive education systems (Prescott, 2021).

Through the literature review, tools such as synchronous video platforms, asynchronous video platforms, and interactive experiences were identified as solutions to the loss of student engagement. Through the use of Zoom, Google Meet, and similar platforms, social needs were met by students through the use of live-video streaming, breakout rooms, and Zoom Annotation. These synchronous tools should not be forgotten as schooling practices return to normal. These platforms can be used for students who are absent for extended periods of time. By meeting with these students, the transition back to the classroom becomes easier as they will not have missed content.

The biggest downside to synchronous video streaming was the drain on Internet connectivity that it caused. To combat this, many educators turned to asynchronous settings through the use of educational videos. While these tools are not new, they were found to be a positive online practice that increased student achievement. Asynchronous videos may be a more practical alternative for excessive absences and aid students in their return to the classroom. These videos can provide additional supports for students who may have been present for a lecture but forgot how to complete the homework.

Ultimately, the most engagement was seen through the use of interactive experiences such as Nearpod, Slido, Canva, iSpring Suite 9, Google Jamboard, and Google Slides. These interactive experiences could be completed synchronously or asynchronously, making them adaptable to the educational needs of the content and student alike. A good trait about these opportunities was the real-time feedback students were able to receive that guided them during their learning experience. These real-time opportunities for feedback are powerful for students and should continue to be used. Feedback is imperative for the learning process and these tools can make it easier on the teacher to provide these experiences.

A McREL Research report argues that the need for future research should be directed toward studying the qualities of interpersonal interactions rather than the sites where learning takes place (Holquist et al., 2020, p. iii). In addition, they suggest that future research should be conducted that incorporates student feedback to better understand their perspectives and integrate it into a more holistic construct of engagement. It is hoped that through this, educators will be able to build upon and modify existing pedagogical practices to better meet student needs, especially in a post-pandemic learning environment.

Teacher professional development should focus on building upon these pedagogical practices and enhancing learning. The technologies discussed in this paper were not only advantageous for remote learning but can be tools to improve learning for in-person education as well. For example, these strategies and tools might be used for students who are absent due to doctor appointments, illness, extracurricular activities, etc. and miss out on experiences held in class. Many of these tools can be used to aid in bridging the gap expected due to absences. Inservice and pre-service teachers should be provided with tools to accommodate absences such as these.

These technologies that were used during crises can provide insight into the future of education. Because student engagement and achievement were achieved during the crisis, many of these tools can continue to be developed and used. Questions about a transition to remote learning linger in the minds of educators and learners alike. These technologies were shown to create relationships when the world was shut down, but there were many flaws. For one, the social divide between the less fortunate was never addressed, and a gap now resides in its place. There were also many reports of lack of Internet connectivity, which led to difficulty accessing the virtual experiences discussed. Future studies should reflect on the continued use of these technologies upon a return to in-person learning. Additionally, the gap in education caused by COVID-19 can be explored. These studies will provide further insight into how education will be reimagined to overcome the pause in learning due to the pandemic.

Acknowledgments We would like to extend our deepest gratitude to Dr. Dave Edyburn for his professional guidance and constructive suggestions during the development of this paper. His flexibility and willingness to provide his time and wisdom are much appreciated.

References

Almén, L., Bagga-Gupta, S., & Bjursell, C. (2020). Access to and accounts of using digital tools in Swedish secondary grades. An exploratory study. *Journal of Information Technology Education: Research, 19*, 287–314. https://doi.org/10.28945/4550

Cevik, M., Baris, N., Sirin, M., Ortak Kilinc, O., Kaplan, Y., Atabey Ozdemir, B., Yalcin, H., Seref, G., Topal, S., & Delice, T. (2021). The effect of digital activities on the technology awareness and computational thinking skills of gifted students (eTwinning project example). *International Journal of Modern Education Studies, 5*, 205–244.

Dadhe, P. P., & Kuthe, G. D. (2021). Assessment of availability and use of technology by students for online education during COVID -19 pandemic in rural India: A case study. *Library Philosophy and Practice* (e-journal), 6005. https://digitalcommons.unl.edu/libphilprac/6005

Davey, B. T., Bowers, S., & Spears, S. (2020). NASA eclipse TM Interactive Lessons: A three-year study of the impact of NASA educational products on student science literacy. *Journal of Computers in Mathematics and Science Teaching, 39*(4), 383–398.

Dennen, V. P., Choi, H., & Word, K. (2020). Social media, teenagers, and the school context: A scoping review of research in education and related fields. *Educational Technology Research and Development, 68*(4), 1635–1658. https://doi.org/10.1007/s11423-020-09796-z

Gopal, R., Singh, V., & Aggarwal, A. (2021). Impact of online classes on the satisfaction and performance of students during the pandemic period of COVID 19. *Education & Information Technologies, 26*, 6923–6947. https://doi-org.libproxy.library.unt.edu/10.1007/s10639-021-10523-1

Greenhalgh, T., Thorne, S., & Malterud, K. (2018). Time to challenge the spurious hierarchy of systematic over narrative reviews? *European Journal of Clinical Investigation, 48*(6), e12931. https://doi.org/10.1111/eci.12931

Hamlin, J., Gibbons, C., & Lambrou, A. (2021). Portraits across the distance: Connecting and collaborating through film and photography in a pandemic. *Art Education, 74*(6), 48–54. https://doi.org/10.1080/00043125.2021.1954478

Holquist, S. E., Cetz, J., O'Neil, S. D., Smiley, D., Taylor, L. M., & Crowder, M. K. (2020). *The "silent epidemic" finds its voice: Demystifying how students view engagement in their learning.* McREL International.

Huang, B., Jong, M. S. Y., & Chiai, C. S. (2022). The design and implementation of a video-facilitated transdisciplinary STEM curriculum in the context of COVID-19 pandemic. *Journal of Educational Technology & Society, 25*(1), 108–123.

Lin, C. H., Wu, W. H., & Lee, T. N. (2022). Using an online learning platform to show students' achievements and attention in the video lecture and online practice learning environments. *Journal of Educational Technology & Society, 25*(1), 155–165.

McPherson, H., Frank, G., Pearce, R., & Hoffman, E. (2021). Virtual field trips: Pivoting cross-curricular experiential learning to an online platform. *Science Teacher, 88*(6), 45–51.

Megawati, F., Mukminatein, N., Permana, A. I., Dewi, L. A., & Fitriati, F. (2021). Emergency remote teaching and learning: Technology-based instructional plan across grade levels. *Teaching English with Technology, 21*(2), 112–126. http://www.tewtjournal.org

Morgan, B., Gaitan, E., Polletta, V., Cheung, C., Aslan, L., Wolff, L., Cheung, V., Sassanfar, M., & Wallace, L. J. (2021). Adapting a hands-on youth development STEM program in the age of COVID-19:the LEAH Knox Scholars program. The Journal of STEM Outreach, 4(3). 10.15695/jstem/v4i3.08.

Nearpod. (n.d.). Retrieved February 2022, from https://nearpod.com/

Noskova, T., Pavlova, T., & Yakovleva, O. (2021). A study of students' preferences in the information resources of the digital learning environment. *Journal on Efficiency and Responsibility in Education and Science, 14*(1), 53–65. https://doi.org/10.7160/eriesj.2021.140105

Prescott, S. (2021). *Bridging digital equity and culturally responsive education in PreK-12.* Retrieved from: http://newamerica.org/education-policy/reports/bridging-digital-equity-and-culturally-responsive-education-in-prek12/

Ramadhan, A., Pradono Suryodiningrat, S., & Hendric Spits Warnars, H. L. (2022). IT blueprint for an effective online learning system with a blended approach for upper secondary education system during COVID-19 pandemic. *TEM Journal, 11*(1), 446–453. https://doi.org/10.18421/tem111-57

Slido. (n.d.). Retrieved February 2022, from https://sli.do

UNICEF. (2022, January 23). *COVID:19 scale of education loss 'nearly insurmountable', warns UNICEF.* Media Factsheet. https://www.unicef.org/press-releases/covid19-scale-education-loss-nearly-insurmountable-warns-unicef

Yang, X., & Ding, Y. (2021). Research on the current situation and teaching strategies of "digital learning and innovation" literacy of senior high school students. *EDP Sciences.* https://doi.org/10.1051/shsconf/202112301026

Zuidema, D. R., & Zuidema, R. H. (2021). From passive observers to active participants: Using interactive remote demonstrations to increase student involvement in online chemistry instruction. *Journal of Chemical Education, 98*(3), 843–849. https://doi.org/10.1021/acs.jchemed.0c01081

Professional School Counselor Technology Use for Communication During COVID-19

Erin L. Howard

School Counselor Technology During COVID-19

The four components of the American School Counseling Association (ASCA, 2016) national model support the standards in programming, ethics, academics, career readiness, and social/personal development for all K-12 students. ASCA recommends that professional school counselors have a caseload of the student to counselor ratio of no more than 1:250 and that the ASCA Deliver component should be prioritized. Specifically, 80% of the comprehensive counseling program should consist of the Deliver component providing direct and indirect services to students, such as guidance lessons, individual and student group meetings, and consultation with faculty and other mental health professionals. The other 20% of the comprehensive counseling program should be split between the ASCA Define, Manage, and Assess components: Additionally, time should be spent on collaboration and leadership to create systemic change and provide leadership in the school and within the community. The professional school counselors' primary focus should be on supporting mental health and social–emotional learning (SEL) to remove barriers to learning in the school environment. However, what all of the domains have in common is communication. The professional school counselor must communicate with students and their families to effectively address the Direct component of the ASCA model. They must communicate with stakeholder, faculty, and staff to effectively execute the ASCA Define, Manage, and Assess components. Therefore, this study focuses on the immediate need of professional school counselors to communicate during school closings and remote education using technology available. This

E. L. Howard (✉)
University of North Texas, Denton, TX, USA
e-mail: ErinHoward2@my.unt.edu

© The Author(s), under exclusive license to Springer Nature Switzerland AG 2023   133
D. Cockerham et al. (eds.), *Reimagining Education: Studies*
and Stories for Effective Learning in an Evolving Digital Environment,
Educational Communications and Technology: Issues and Innovations,
https://doi.org/10.1007/978-3-031-25102-3_14

prompts the question: How was this technology used, and what was the satisfaction and comfort level of the professional school counselors using it to provide school counseling services across the ASCA national model components?

Role Change During COVID-19

Abdillah et al. (2020) observed that during the pandemic, remote learning became necessary to keep students engaged in education, while attempting to decrease the spread of the deadly virus. The COVID-19 pandemic has made technology use a necessity to provide school counseling services to students. The study examined the level of technology acceptance by school counselors in Indonesia during the COVID-19 pandemic. The results suggest that the participants did not have high anxiety about general computer use. They also had positive perceptions of technology usefulness and perceived ease of use, specifically during the COVID-19 pandemic. The results reported that when school counselor's computer use anxiety rose, then the perceived usefulness and perceived ease of use regarding technology went down. Currently, the professional school counselors in this study were using Google Classroom, Zoom, and other media, to provide a myriad of counseling services such as programming and classroom guidance. This has been achieved through a high level of collaboration with other professionals and self-efficacy. In conclusion, the study observed that responsive services such as individual and group counseling have still not been provided using technology at the time of this study. The author discusses that to reach this high level of comfort with technology use in school counseling, in responsive services, it is possible that there will need to be continued intense collaboration, training, and continued self-efficacy.

Professional school counselors are taking the lead during this time of crisis with their unique educational backgrounds and experiences. Pincus et al. (2020) looked at the unique background, education, training, and role of the professional school counselor as the school mental health leader during the COVID-19 crisis. The authors reported that these counselors were required to have a master's level degree in counseling, including an internship and a professional school counseling certification along with past teaching experience. The Counseling graduate degree includes learning to provide group, individual, and crisis counseling along with specific counseling techniques and theory, making them experts in mental health. This level of knowledge in mental wellness and required experience teaching led to counselors assuming a role of leadership, especially when the top priority of the campus was on mental wellness. Professional school counselors meet short-term mental health needs and serve as community liaisons who refer students, families, faculty, and staff to community resources acting as mental health triage. In addition, professional school counselors have been trained to be leaders in the school community collecting data and advocating for systemic change in response to all students, faculty, staff, and stakeholders in the Assessment component of the ASCA national model. By the nature of their role, professional school counselors are generally in communication daily with students, faculty, and staff so they build effective relationships and feel the pulse of the school community.

Technology for Monitoring Students

The Manage Domain of the ASCA (2016) National Model organizes the school's professional school counseling comprehensive program. This includes prioritizing the components of the program based on action plans, advisory councils, data, calendars, and annual agreements. A study completed before COVID-19 included 507 professional school counselors across all the regions of the United States, with a focus on suburban schools, examined the use of technology in the Manage component of the ASCA national model (Mason et al., 2019). The results found that most professional school counselors did use technology in the Manage component, but not the other ASCA components of Direct, Define, and Assess.

Most professional school counselors either had created or maintained a website specifically for their counseling program. Most communicated with students through that website, texting through Remind, or a newsletter using an electronic format such as a S'more website (https://www.smore.com). Some even regularly used social media, such as Facebook and Twitter were tools to communicate with staff, colleagues, and stakeholders, but did not often use social media to communicate with students. The professional school counselors in this study used electronic files to manage data, track activity, and organize school events daily with organization being the top reason to use technology. However, they did not use technology in counseling, or the Direct component of the ASCA domain. The number of participants that reported never using technology in these components was higher than expected in this study (Mason et al., 2019). This was to change suddenly with the challenges of the onset of COVID-19.

COVID-19 Technology Complications

The COVID-19 pandemic and subsequent shutdowns made some school communities starkly aware that they were not equipped to support student mental health needs during a time of crisis. When Renjan and Fung (2020) examined the impact of the pandemic on schools in Singapore, they found that the onset of the COVID-19 stay-at-home orders and the longer-term continuation of remote school and isolation were causing mental distress to a large number of students. Singapore was already equipped with regional mental health centers to address the needs of its youth called Response, Early Intervention, and Assessment in Community Mental Health (REACH). During the pandemic, REACH was overwhelmed by the influx of people needing assistance and was unable to meet its current clients' needs and began to use telehealth and video conferencing as appropriate or cancel sessions with clients completely. As the isolation and trauma of the COVID-19 pandemic took their toll, referrals rose to a three-month wait for REACH, social welfare, and health services. To decrease wait time, REACH considered possible viable solutions for the future such as synchronous mental health care, telephone helplines, live web chat, online applications, online self-help software, and artificial intelligence robots.

Technology for Monitoring Students

The Manage Domain of the ASCA (2016) National Model organizes the school's professional school counseling comprehensive program. This includes prioritizing the components of the program based on action plans, advisory councils, data, calendars, and annual agreements. A study completed before COVID-19 included professional school counselors across all the regions of the United States, with a focus on suburban schools, examined the use of technology in the Manage component of the ASCA national model (Mason et al., 2019). The results found that most professional school counselors did use technology in the Manage component, but not the other ASCA components of Direct, Define, and Assess.

Most professional school counselors either had created or maintained a website specifically for their counseling program. Most communicated with students through that website, texting through Remind, or a newsletter using an electronic format such as a S'more website. Some even regularly used social media, such as Facebook and Twitter were tools to communicate with staff, colleagues, and stakeholders, but did not often use social media to communicate with students. The professional school counselors in this study used electronic files to manage data, track activity, and organize school events daily with organization being the top reason to use technology. However, they did not use technology in counseling, or the Direct component of the ASCA domain. The number of participants that reported never using technology in these components was higher than expected in this study (Mason et al., 2019). This was to change suddenly with the challenges of the onset of COVID-19.

Intervention Programs and Technology

In a study by Steele (2014), professional school counselors reported using technology to support professional development and program management in the Define component of the ASCA national model. In this study, the professional school counselors often used online software to carry out intervention programming and to record data for evidence of student growth and learning, while also tracking at-risk indicators. Using student information systems that allow counselors remote or online access created a means to collect and aggregate student data remotely. Knowledge of this technology was helpful for the professional school counselors in this study to learn how their students' progress would be measured and the expected outcome. As a result, they were able to provide direct and indirect responsive services developing gap interventions and programming to meet the student's needs.

When designing how best to organize the Deliver component of the ASCA national model of the comprehensive counseling program, the professional school counselors in this study considered what form of communication was preferred by the students in their schools (Glasheen et al., 2015).

Traditionally, most secondary school students met with their school counselor face-to-face to speak about the topics that they chose most important. Still, some students did not reach out to their professional school counselors, even when they needed guidance or interventions. Many students in this study communicated with others through online formats and social media on a regular basis. The results indicated that 84% of males and 80% of females would contact a professional school counselor if one was available to them online. Further, 94.5% of students with moderate to severe concerns about depression and 96% of students with moderate or severe stress reported they would utilize online school counseling sessions. The study revealed about half of the students would prefer to discuss topics such as sexuality, and more personal issues, online rather than in person. The fact that the majority of students reported that they would utilize online school counseling, and even prefer it, supports its inclusion in the comprehensive school counseling program.

The professional school counselors in the study by Goodrich (2020) reported using technology to design pathways for communication, coordinate community providers, and effectively strengthen support systems for students in the Deliver and Manage components of the ASCA national model. In this study, technology was used to provide a platform for continuing education and staff or community meetings, events, and interventions. This was especially important in rural areas that covered large geographical areas to make attendance possibly virtually, when not possible physically. The professional school counselors used online forums, chats, and blogs as a part of the counseling program to open communication with students and provide a space for the positive feedback. In addition, the professional school counselors were able to give assessments, share schedules, and track academic progress using technology with students and their families, making their comprehensive counseling program more effective.

Social Emotional Learning (SEL) and Technology

SEL is a focus of the Deliver component of the ASCA national model. According to Slovák and Fitzpatrick (2015), SEL has become a focus at all levels of education. This study identified the main five core competencies of SEL: self-awareness, self-management, social awareness, relationship skills, and responsible decision-making skills. These skills are paired with the ongoing goal to improve the skills of communication, self-control strategies, identifying and understanding feelings, and dealing with conflict. The results suggested that technology could be used to support these SEL learning targets through extending learning support and scaffolding.

For example, support could be extended by using a personal device, such as Fitbit, to provide stress detection based on physiological data. The device would alert the person anytime the body showed physical signs of stress to serve as a cue to begin mindfulness coping skills such as breathing or walking. Additionally, a Fitbit could give a vibration as a cue for awareness of a social skill need and be followed with a prompt of what to do next, such as stop-think-proceed. Another supporting technology would allow on-the-go reflection for social interactions by creating and watching videos to analyze the social interaction and evaluate the experience. The results indicated that there is much more research to be done to find out about the possibilities of teaching SEL-using technology as it is a relatively new field.

Digital Game-Based Learning in SEL

SEL is integral to the Deliver component of the ASCA national model. Craig et al. (2015) investigated Social Skills Training (SST) or SEL delivery using adaptive digital gaming. The game *Zoo U* was created as an adaptive interactive online game for elementary-age children to learn SEL strategies at school and at home. The adaptive game provides opportunities to solve real-life age-appropriate social problems in a virtual world with more than one attempt allowed to choose the correct use of social skills.

The participants in the experimental group reported a higher level of progress in the areas of social initiation, impulse control, emotion regulation, internalizing behaviors, externalizing behaviors, and assertiveness than those in the control group. There were no significant differences found when comparing the test group and control group in the areas of communication, cooperation, or empathy. The results show that adaptive gaming may be a reasonable option for teaching SEL to elementary-age children and may be effective. This format would remove the barriers of location and access to trained professional school counselors to provide SEL to students who otherwise would not have access (Craig et al., 2015).

Digitizing Career Guidance

The Assess component of the ASCA national model examines data to improve the comprehensive school counseling program. Upon auditing their program, professional school counselors at a rural high school in Washington state found their dropout rate to be higher than the state average (Gruman et al., 2013). This study also found that those graduating and going to college from this school had a higher rate of requiring a remedial course in college. Their counseling program was not spending the ASCA recommended 80% of the time on the Deliver component and, with the time constraints, there was almost no time spent on the social/personal needs of the students. Given this data, the professional school counselors looked to technology to meet their needs to design, coordinate, and deliver a comprehensive counseling program more closely following the ASCA national model. They chose Navigation 101 adaptive software to become the cornerstone of academic and career planning for the school's comprehensive counseling program.

Navigation 101 included lessons in academic goal setting, career exploration, post-secondary readiness, and financial planning. These lessons were followed up by small group advisory lessons that the teachers could create in Navigation 101 to monitor and follow their advisory group through high school (Gruman et al., 2013). In addition to advisory groups, Navigation 101 also supported student portfolios, offered a platform for student-led parent conferences, provided student-driven analytics, and collected data to create reports of student activity and a list of at-risk students. Parents had the option to be notified if their child was falling behind in academics or was presenting concerning behavior at school. Students surveyed reported they felt supported in their graduation projects and parent involvement increased during the use of Navigation 101.

One rural school in Washington decided to overlay their current software with a computerized identification system. This system monitored the mental wellness of students and supported case management. Through the use of this interactive and responsive technology, counselors and teachers could instantly identify students' at-risk status (Gruman et al., 2013). The program granted access to parents so they could also monitor their child's at-risk status, including credits for graduation and standardized testing results and progress. Having this information readily available to counselors and parents facilitated a smooth transition to making connections with community resources and effective community referrals to benefit students and their families.

Process

The purpose of this research study was to examine the technology use of professional school counselors during COVID-19. Technology use had to change with COVID-19 and school closures to stop the spread of the virus. Professional school counselors had to resolve confidentiality and ethical issues of the ASCA national model component in order to serve the needs of students and families across the components using technology.

Participants and Procedures

Insituttional Review Board (IRB) approval was obtained from the Denton Independent School District (DISD) and the University of North Texas. The IRB-approved recruitment email was sent to a convenience sample of known certified professional school counselors in the district/region. Each eligible counselor that showed interest in taking the survey was given an informed consent form along with the survey link. The link was accessed without collecting any identifying information and submitted directly to the research team. A total of 55 certified professional school counselors and interns all over age 18, all at a master's level degree or taking an intern level course that completed graduate programs, and all serving various levels in K-12 schools participated in the study. Data was collected and analyzed to assess trends in technology use during COVID-19.

Materials

The Survey for Professional School Counselors was created by the author with four demographic questions, two open-ended questions and two sections of Likert scale questions. The goal of the survey was to determine the attitudes and perspectives of professional school counselor toward technology use during COVID-19. Section one gathers information of how satisfied the participants were with aspects of technology use as a professional school counselor. Section two asks about the comfort level of the participants with same tasks as section one. The survey was created by the author using Google Forms as the platform for the survey as it is accessible and commonly used by professional school counselors.

Findings

The purpose of the study was to analyze professional school counselors'use of technology, specifically video conferencing platforms to communicate with students, families, community members, stakeholders, and other educators, along with required confidential communication, during COVID-19 closures and pandemic stay-at-home mandates.

The participants represented a variety of age ranges: 20–25 (4%), 25–35 (16.4%), 35–45 (36.4%), 45–55 (38.2%), and 56+ (4%). Almost all professional school counselors in this study had completed a master's degree as their highest level of education, and 98.6% were female. The professional school counselors were fairly evenly divided across grade levels: elementary (30.9%), middle (38.2%), high school (27.3%), and EC-12 (3.3%). Almost all counselors, 98.2%, had consistent Internet service at their homes.

Years as a school counselor varied much more than the age ranges, providing a diverse sample of professionals as shown in Fig. 1.

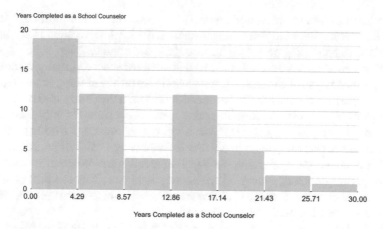

Fig. 1 Years completed as a school counselor

Most professional school counselors in this study, 58.2%, used Zoom, and 14.5% used Microsoft Teams, while 23.6% reported using other than listed, and a minuscule 3.6% used WebEx when video conferencing with colleagues. Over 75% of the participants were completely comfortable or somewhat comfortable with their video conferencing experience with colleagues. Similarly, about 70% of the participants were completely or somewhat satisfied with their video conferencing experience with colleagues. Only about 1% were very uncomfortable or very unsatisfied.

Most, (56.4%) of the professional school counselors reported being somewhat or completely unsatisfied with using video conferencing to work with students to solve peer conflict and advising. Only 1.8% were completely satisfied, and 14.5% were even somewhat satisfied. In turn, 45.5% of the participants reported being completely or somewhat uncomfortable with peer conflict and advising over video conferencing. A very small amount, 1.6%, were completely comfortable, and 20% somewhat comfortable.

The satisfaction and comfort level with the use of technology drops when direct responsive services are addressed. The majority (41.8%) of participants reported being completely unsatisfied and 40% were completely uncomfortable with meeting with students for personal issues, such as sexuality, self-harm, and anxiety, through video conferencing. The participants in this study did have a rate of 38.25% somewhat satisfied and 29.1% somewhat comfortable, but zero participants rated video conferencing on these confidential topics as either completely satisfactory or completely comfortable.

Parent nights provide pertinent information to parents such as upcoming events, course selection to choose classes to take the next year, open house, and orientation. The professional school counselors had varied responses with an even split at 25.5%, for somewhat satisfied, neutral, and somewhat unsatisfied, and 27.3% for somewhat comfortable and neutral, with 21.8% somewhat uncomfortable. A smaller number, 12.7%, was completely unsatisfied, and 18.2% were completely uncomfortable with presenting parent nights through video conferencing.

Connected Learners denoted students that attended school virtually without ever coming to the physical campus. All instruction was provided through video conferencing, including counseling guidance and services. In this study, about 48% of the participants were most comfortable and somewhat comfortable with their experience teaching counseling lessons through video conferencing. Working with connected learners was rated completely uncomfortable by 14.5% of participants with 21.5% somewhat uncomfortable. Satisfaction levels mirrored comfort levels with 36% of participants rating working with connected learners as completely satisfied or somewhat satisfied. Finally, 14.5% were completely unsatisfied, and 21.8% were somewhat unsatisfied with the experience.

The final survey question was open-ended: "What do you see as the biggest challenge in technology use for professional school counselors during the COVID-19 Pandemic?" Constructivists, according to Guardo (2019), view the human experience of learning as that people experience the world and reflect upon those experiences, build their own representations, and incorporate new information into their pre-existing knowledge to create schemas. Participants reflected on their experiences of technology use during COVID-19 as a professional school counselor.

The analysis procedures for this study involve narrative inquiry analysis in order to encourage participants to construct their own stories and narrative from their own personal experiences with technology during the pandemic. Responses were somewhat varied, but the frequency of phrases and their interpretation clarifies the perspective of professional school counselors and technology use during the COVID-19 pandemic. The responses were coded and categorized by the author, as shown in Table 1.

The results of the open-ended question reflected a feeling of unrest and dissatisfaction with the current technology climate during the COVID-19 pandemic.

Table 1 Coded catalog of open-ended questions

Category	Number of references	Description	Example
Video conference, zoom, telehealth	17	Usage was up substantially than before the pandemic	"I use video conferecing100% more than I did pre COVID"
Communication, speak with, talk to	10	Frustration was shared with using the technology.	"Technology-based communication limits the information you receive in meeting with individuals"
Confidential	8	"Confidentiality, the fear of being recorded." counseling mandated confidentiality that counselors struggled with meeting using technology	"Confidentiality, the fear of being recorded"

The participants shared that technology is no longer optional and now a mandate with challenges that have come with this rapid change. Video conferencing was the most common challenge for professional school counselors, followed by communication and confidentiality concerns. The participants expressed a specific fear of confidential guiding session being recorded due to a lack of control over the technology being used. For example, one participant reported the biggest challenge for them to be "Limits of confidentiality due to not knowing who can hear the conversation during consultations." The results in general reflect a feeling of a lack of training and confidence creating dissatisfaction and frustration with the current technology climate as another participant shared, "Technology is viewed more as a necessity, as opposed to an option. With that, Professional School Counselors have to navigate providing virtual services and set up new boundaries surrounding technology. They are now more accessible with technology, but that also poses its challenges."

Discussion/Implications

The COVID-19 pandemic has caused a myriad of changes in the use of technology within education, including within the field of professional school counseling. Technology use is no longer a choice among professional school counselors, but is now a necessity to be able to successfully provide school counseling services to students across the ASCA (2016) national model components. Professional school counselors have adapted to the needs and challenges set before them the first full year of educating children and adolescents during the COVID-19 pandemic using online technology. This study sought to understand how this technology was used, and what was the satisfaction and comfort level of the professional school counselors using it to provide school counseling services across the ASCA national model components?

In this study, the certified professional school counselors mostly used the Zoom video conferencing platform to communicate with students, parents, and colleagues. The participants were generally uncomfortable and dissatisfied with teaching lessons to connect with learners through video conferencing. However, there was an even larger percentage that reported low levels of comfort and satisfaction with presenting virtual parent nights and responsive services such as sexuality and self-harm. These results may be a symptom of the differing levels of self-efficacy, the inability to assure confidentiality, and a lack of training and time to spend learning new technology for professionals with a range of experience and expertise (Steele et al., 2014). In addition, the negative feelings reported may be due to inadequate professional training, a preference to face to face learning over online, general stress caused by a low level of support during this abrupt transition from completely in person to completely remote.

Conclusion

In the past, technology use across all ASCA national model components was a challenge due to training and accessibility. Professional school counselors questioned confidentiality and how to uphold the strict ethics of the profession using technology (Steele & Nukols, 2020). In this study, the professional school counselors reported still having a lack of training, preparation, and time to learn about technology. However, due to COVID-19, the professional school counselors reported additional responsibilities to an already exhausting role to be very difficult, especially finding time to fit in training for new technology. This could be due to schools relying heavily on professional school counselors to take the lead with mental wellness and leadership in schools during COVID-19. The unique training and background made professional school counselors the much-needed leader in this time of crisis (Pincus et al., 2020). The Deliver domain that provides direct and indirect services requires the highest level of confidentiality, leaving it with the lowest level of confidence by the participants in using technology to provide. However, the use of technology to track progress, at-risk factors, and career interests have been found successful (Gruman et al., 2013). It is possible that the use of technology in the future may reduce gaps in accessibility to professional school counseling comprehensive programs.

Limitations and Future Research

This study was conducted completely online. Future research should consider interviews with participants to gain additional information about the motivation for certain behaviors and decisions. Also, the study sample size is small and includes one geographical area. Increasing the sample size and including more diverse geographical participants would allow for more confidence in generalizing the results to populations beyond the locale sample. Future studies should examine the type of technology that could meet the unique ethical needs of school counselors, specifically to meet the needs of students across the ASCA national model. Future studies must also be considered specifically regarding improvement in attitudes and perceptions of the Deliver component using technology that calls for confidentiality. This information could possibly contribute to the decisions of school professionals about what technology to use and develop in the future. Security with computers, systems, and software can leave counselors and students both vulnerable to hackers and breaches possibly making its use unethical. In conclusion, the field of school counseling in education can be reimagined with seamless technology and a positive outlook on digitization, using the knowledge and experiences gained during COVID-19.

Appendix A: Survey Instrument

Table 1: Survey for professional school counselors
Part 1: Demographics
Highest level of education completed:

① Bachelors	③ Doctoral
② Masters	

Age range:

① 20–25	④ 46–55
② 26–35	⑤ 55+
③ 36–45	

Gender: ①Male ②Female ③Decline to Answer
What level do you serve:

① Early Childhood	④ High School
② Elementary	⑤ All level EC-12
③ Middle School	

Do you have access to consistent Internet at home? ① No ② Yes
Which form of video conferencing do you use most often with colleagues?

① TEAMS	④ Other
② Zoom	
③ Webex	

Which form of video conferencing do you use most often with students?

① TEAMS	④ Other
② Zoom	
③ Webex	

Which form of video conferencing are you most comfortable using in your work setting?

① TEAMS	④ Other
② Zoom	
③ Webex	

Part 2

Looking at satisfaction level: Ranging from 1–5, with 5 being completely satisfied and 1 being completely unsatisfied

D = Completely Dissatisfied, SD = Somewhat Dissatisfied, N = Neutral, SS = Somewhat Satisfied, CS = Completely Satisfied

		D	SD	N	SS	CS
1.	How satisfied are you with communication with colleagues through video conferencing?	①	②	③	④	⑤
2.	How satisfied are you with meeting with students for advising/guidance/peer conflict issues through video conferencing?	①	②	③	④	⑤
3.	How satisfied are you with meeting with parents for Parent Nights through video conferencing?	①	②	③	④	⑤
4.	How satisfied are you with meeting with students for personal issues (such as sexuality, self-harm, anxiety) through video conferencing?)	①	②	③	④	⑤
5.	How satisfied are you with meeting with connected learners at class time through video conferencing?	①	②	③	④	⑤

Part 3

Looking at comfort level: Ranging from 1–5, with 5 being completely comfortable and 1 being completely uncomfortable

CU = Completely Uncomfortable, SC = Somewhat Uncomfortable, N = Neutral, SC = Somewhat Comfortable, CC = Completely Comfortable

		CU	SU	N	SC	CC
1.	How comfortable are you with meeting with connected learners to teach lessons at class time through video conferencing?	①	②	③	④	⑤
2.	How comfortable are you with meeting with students for advising/guidance/peer conflict issues through video conferencing?	①	②	③	④	⑤
3.	How comfortable are you with communication with colleagues through video conferencing??	①	②	③	④	⑤
4.	How comfortable are you with meeting with students for personal issues (such as sexuality, self-harm, anxiety) through video conferencing	①	②	③	④	⑤
5.	How comfortable are you with meeting with parents for Parent Nights through video conferencing?	①	②	③	④	⑤

(Open Ended)

What do you see as the biggest change in technology use for Professional School Counselors during the COVID-19 Pandemic?

Years completed as a school counselor.

References

Abdillah, H., Setyosari, P., Lasan, B., & Muslihati, M. (2020). The acceptance of school counselor in the use of ICT during school from home in the Covid-19 era. *Journal for the Education of Gifted Young Scientists, 8*(4), 1569–1582. https://doi.org/10.17478/jegys.804939

American School Counselor Association. (2016). *ASCA ethical standards for school counselors.* https://www.schoolcounselor.org/asca/media/asca/Ethics/EthicalStandards2016.pdf

Craig, A. B., Brown, E. R., Upright, J., & Derosier, M. E. (2015). Enhancing children's social-emotional functioning through virtual game-based delivery of social skills training. *Journal of Child and Family Studies, 25*(3), 959–968. https://doi.org/10.1007/s10826-015-0274-8

Glasheen, K., Shochet, I., & Campbell, M. (2015). Online counselling in secondary schools: Would students seek help by this medium? *British Journal of Guidance & Counselling, 44*(1), 108–122. https://doi.org/10.1080/03069885.2015.1017805

Goodrich, K. M., Kingsley, K. V., & Sands, H. C. (2020). Digitally responsive school counseling across the ASCA national model. *International Journal for the Advancement of Counselling, 42*(2), 147–158. https://doi.org/10.1007/s10447-020-09396-9

Gruman, D. H., Marston, T., & Koon, H. (2013). Bringing mental health needs into focus through school counseling program transformation. *Professional School Counseling, 16*(5), 333–341. https://doi.org/10.1177/2156759X1201600506

Guardo, A. (2019). Constructivism, intersubjectivity, provability, and triviality. *International Journal of Philosophical Studies, 27*(4), 515–527. https://doi.org/10.1080/0967255 9.2019.1632369

Mason, E. C. M., Griffith, C., & Belser, C. T. (2019). School counselors' use of technology for program management. *Professional School Counseling, 22*(1), 1–10. https://doi.org/10.117 7/2156759X19870794

Pincus, R., Hannor-Walker, T., Wright, L., & Justice, J. (2020). COVID-19's effect on students: How school counselors rise to the rescue. *NASSP Bulletin, 104*(4), 241–256. https://doi.org/10.1177/0192636520975866

Renjan, V., & Fung, D. S. S. (2020). Debate: COVID-19 to the under 19 – A Singapore school mental health response. *Child and Adolescent Mental Health, 25*(4), 260–262. https://doi-org.libproxy.library.unt.edu/10.1111/camh.12426

Slovák, P., & Fitzpatrick, G. (2015). Teaching and developing social and emotional skills with technology. *Association of Computing Machinery Transactions on Computer-Human Interaction, 22*(4), 1–34. https://doi.org/10.1145/2744195

Steele, T., & Nukols, G. (2020). Technology trends in school counseling. *Journal of School Counseling, 18*(10), 1–30.

Steele, T. M., Jacokes, D. E., & Stone, C. B. (2014). An examination of the role of online technology in school counseling. *Professional School Counseling, 18*(1), 125–135. https://doi.org/1 0.1177/2156759X0001800118

COVID Teaching Experiences as Disrupting Events to Promote a Paradigm Shift in K-12 Mobile Technology Integration

Bridget K. Mulvey and Elena Novak

Background/Rationale

Globally, the coronavirus (COVID-19) pandemic forced schools to rapidly transition to remote learning, starting a new era in the educational world where technology integration is a necessity. This transition forced teachers to rethink the role of mobile devices in classrooms and beyond, as a mobile device is oftentimes the only device that marginalized students have at home (Dede, 2020). Mobile learning refers to "learning across multiple contexts, through social and content interactions, using personal electronic devices" (Crompton, 2013, p. 4.). It involves the use of portable handheld devices, such as smart phones and tablets, that can be easily turned on and off with a button. Mobile learning emphasizes learning on the move with learners being mobile (Scanlon et al., 2005). An important characteristic of mobile learning is that it reflects a learner-centered approach that enables an acquisition of new knowledge, experiences, and skills through mobile technologies (Sharples et al., 2009). Although the field of mobile learning is rapidly developing, offering numerous mobile applications and learning opportunities, effective K–12 educational integration of mobile devices has been lagging (Christensen & Knezek, 2018) as teachers are reluctant to use mobile devices.

Teacher reluctance to use mobile devices in schools is attributed to disruptive use of mobile devices in a classroom, lack of administrative and technological support to implement and monitor mobile learning, and lack of appropriate mobile devices and curriculum to support their use for learning. Inequitable resources and conditions in students' homes increased educational inequalities as classes largely shifted

B. K. Mulvey (✉) · E. Novak
Kent State University, Kent, OH, USA
e-mail: bmulvey@kent.edu

to remote delivery, with a mobile device to be likely the only device that marginalized students, who live in rural areas or come from a low socioeconomic background, have at home (Dede, 2020).

Despite these barriers to mobile learning, the pandemic provided most teachers with experience facilitating remote learning and learning with mobile devices. These experiences may have impacted teachers' perceptions of mobile learning and its potential educational benefits. Teachers' perceptions of teaching and technologies are directly correlated with instructional approaches they use in their classroom and student achievement (Nikolopoulou et al., 2021; Taylor & Booth, 2015). A majority of research on mobile technology integration examined student learning or mobile learning systems' design (Chee et al., 2017; Wu et al., 2012). Considerably less research examined mobile technology from pedagogical perspectives (Chen & Tsai, 2021). Thus, there is a need to explore K-12 teachers' pandemic experiences and how they impacted their perspectives of mobile learning during the pandemic.

Disruption Framework

As rapid technological development is situated in a complex system of modern society, that development is unpredictable with impacts that can span levels of the system (Kilkki et al., 2018). A significant body of research has focused on disruptive *technologies* that necessitate behavior changes to access the related innovation (Albors-Garrigos & Hervas-Oliver, 2014; Bessant et al., 2010). Yet we focus on a disruptive *event* or *process,* the COVID-19 global pandemic, "in which an agent must redesign its strategy to survive a change in the environment" (Kilkki et al., 2018, p. 275); a disruption can result in unequal costs and benefits, yet the potential for innovation – a term with more positive connotations – remains. In their view, when boundaries blur, new emergent conditions may lead to the need for substantial adaptations. We adapted the 'disruption framework' of Kilkki et al. (2018) intended for the firm/industry level of the system to apply to the formal educational system in the United States of America, with a focus on teachers' perspectives on technology use for mobile learning in the context of the COVID-19 pandemic.

For the present study, the potential disruptive event is the COVID-19 pandemic that forced teachers to redesign their teaching strategy to survive the change in their educational environment. Prior to the COVID-19 pandemic, many teachers tended to be wary of mobile devices in the classroom, as they commonly were considered a distraction from learning (e.g., Christensen & Knezek, 2018; Thomas et al., 2014). The pandemic has the potential to lead to innovation in teaching and communication methods, also known as disruptive innovation (Christensen, 2013). We investigate this potential by investigating teachers' perceptions of mobile learning early in 2020, when much K–12 learning was done remotely.

Purpose and Research Questions

To consider how teachers rethought the role of mobile learning during the pandemic, this exploratory mixed methods study investigated 16 teachers' perspectives about mobile learning and how COVID-19 influenced those perspectives. In this context, the COVID-19 pandemic is viewed as a disruptive event that forced teachers to redesign their teaching strategy to survive the change in their educational environment (Kilkki et al., 2018). Such a disruptive event can lead to innovation in teaching and communication methods, also known as disruptive innovation (Christensen, 2013).

The present investigation focused on the following research questions:

1. What were K–12 teachers' perspectives of mobile learning during the early months of the shift to remote or hybrid instruction due to the COVID-19 pandemic?
2. How did the teachers' experiences during the COVID-19 pandemic influence their perspectives of mobile learning?

Process

This exploratory mixed methods study examined K–12 teachers' perspectives of mobile learning in a COVID world, offering insights into their experiences with digital changes.

Participants and Setting

Teachers ($N = 16$; age $M = 33.81$; 4 males) enrolled in an online graduate introductory course in educational technology entitled, *Trends in Educational Technology*, and participated in the study. The course was taught at a large Midwestern university in the United States during the early months of the shift to remote or hybrid instruction in 2020. Each teacher taught in a different school. On average, they reported 6.31 years of teaching experience. Four teachers taught at the elementary level, five were middle school teachers, and seven were high school teachers. The teachers taught a variety of subjects, including English/language arts, mathematics, social studies, foreign languages, career-based intervention, and library.

Based on participant self-report, the participants represent a specific group of teachers who consider themselves sufficiently proficient with using technology ($M = 3.75$, $SD = 0.68$ on a 1–5 scale: 1 = Terrible; 5 = Excellent). Using the Stages of Technology Adoption instrument (Christensen, 1997), teachers rated their technology adoption stage as 1 = Awareness; 2 = Learning the process; 3 = Understanding and application of the process; 4 = Familiarity and confidence; 5 = Adaptation to other contexts; and 6 = Creative application to new contexts. It is a single item survey that was developed based on Rogers' (1983) Diffusion of Innovation theory. Teachers reported themselves as being either in Stage 5 (Adaption to other contexts) or Stage 6 (Creative application to new contexts) related to technology adoption (see Table 1). This suggests a high technology integration ability within the participants ($M = 5.50$, SD = 0.52 on a 1–6 scale).

The *Trends in Educational Technology* course included an introduction to the field of educational technology, followed by weekly modules that explored different trends in the field. One module focused on mobile learning, which introduced the concept of mobile learning through guided readings and websites with examples of schools and communities utilizing mobile devices for teaching and learning. After completing the readings, students discussed their ideas about mobile learning on a discussion board.

Data Collection

Quantitative data included participant responses to a questionnaire, Mobile learning readiness (Christensen & Knezek, 2018), completed after the course module on mobile learning. The survey measures the extent to which classroom teachers perceive mobile learning as an effective teaching and learning tool. The survey includes 28 five-point Likert-type items representing four subscales: possibilities, practices

Table 1 Frequencies of stage of technology adoption

Stages	Frequency	%
1. *Awareness:* I am aware that technology exists but have not used it – perhaps I am even avoiding it. I am anxious about the prospect of using computers	0	0.0
2. *Learning the process:* I am currently trying to learn the basics. I am sometimes frustrated using computers. I lack confidence when using computers.	0	0.0
3. *Understanding and application of the process:* I am beginning to understand the process of using technology and can think of specific tasks in which it might be useful.	0	0.0
4. *Familiarity and confidence:* I am gaining a sense of confidence in using the computer for specific tasks. I am starting to feel comfortable using the computer.	0	0.0
5. *Adaptation to other contexts:* I think about the computer as a tool to help me and am no longer concerned about it as technology. I can use it in many applications and as an instructional aid.	7	43.8
6. *Creative application to new contexts:* I can apply what I know about technology in the classroom. I am able to use it as an instructional tool and integrate it into the curriculum.	7	43.8
Missing	2	12.5
Total	16	100.0

for improving classroom instruction, mobile device preferences, and environmental/contextual factors. Participants rated each item on a scale of 1 = Strongly Disagree to 5 = Strongly Agree. The scale had good internal consistency and reliability (Cronbach $\alpha = 0.762$).

Qualitative data included course activities and assignments such as participants' discussion board responses to the following reading prompts:

1. Describe three major ideas and/or practices associated with mobile learning.
2. How would you describe the differences between electronic learning (e-learning) and mobile learning (m-learning)?
3. Describe the differences between a technology-oriented approach and learner-centered approach in mobile learning. Which approach is more beneficial for learning in your point of view?
4. Consider how our new COVID world might have challenged educators' and parents' ideas about mobile learning. How has your opinion about mobile learning changed in light of your and your students' socially distanced life?

Data Analysis

Participants' responses to surveys were analyzed using descriptive statistics to learn about teachers' perspectives of mobile learning. The quantitative analysis was followed up by a qualitative analysis of analytic induction (Bogden & Biklen, 2003) of course artifacts to further investigate their perspectives of mobile learning, helping to explain the quantitative results. Inductive analysis of qualitative data was used to learn about how their experiences during the COVID-19 pandemic influenced their perspectives of mobile learning.

Findings

Perspectives of Mobile Learning

Participant responses to the mobile learning readiness survey (see Table 2) indicated that, on average, possibilities associated with mobile learning were rated considerably high ($M = 4.40$). For instance, participants considered mobile devices to bring new opportunities for learning ($M = 4.27$ on a 1–5 scale); enhance learning ($M = 4.73$) in more flexible ways ($M = 4.47$); improve twenty-first century skills ($M = 4.53$); and connect learners to people, content, and resources ($M = 4.47$). In addition, teachers rated their agreement with mobile technology as being able to improve classroom instruction moderately high ($M = 3.64$). The m-learning environmental and contextual factors, such as technical infrastructure, wireless network, administrative support, and curriculum, were rated moderately high as well

Table 2 Mobile learning readiness (*n* = 15)

Possibilities	Mean	SD
Mobile devices can play an important role in K-12 education	4.27	0.594
Mobile learning will bring new opportunities for learning	4.27	0.704
Mobile technology should be used to connect learners to people, content, and resources	4.47	0.516
Mobile learning will increase flexibility of learning.	4.47	1.06
Mobile learning can be used to improve traditional literacy programs.	4.07	0.917
Mobile technology can be used to improve twenty-first century skills	4.53	0.743
Technology can be used to level the playing field for special needs students	4.40	0.737
Mobile devices can enhance learning if there is adequate support for teachers	4.73	0.594
Subtotal	4.40	0.468
Practices for improving classroom instruction		
Mobile devices would introduce a significant distraction in my classroom	3.40	0.828
The use of mobile technology in school makes students more motivated to learn	3.13	0.990
The use of mobile technology in school increases student participation in classroom/remote discussions	3.53	0.834
The use of mobile technology in school increases student engagement	3.67	0.617
The use of mobile technology in school allows students to own their learning	3.60	0.828
The use of mobile devices in school allows students to work together more often	3.87	0.834
The use of mobile technology in school allows students to develop creativity	3.60	0.828
Mobile learning will improve communication between students and teachers	3.93	0.799
Mobile learning devices improve communication between students	4.33	0.724
Having a mobile device would improve student organization	3.33	0.900
Subtotal	3.64	0.352
Mobile devices preferences		
Using a mobile device will help me be better organized in my daily activities	3.27	0.961
Using a mobile device will allow me to be better organized in my teaching	3.27	0.884
I prefer to read a book on a mobile device rather than a traditional book	1.53	0.915
I prefer to use an electronic textbook rather than a traditional textbook	1.93	1.44
I prefer to use a mobile device rather than a computer for learning	1.93	1.10
Subtotal	2.39	0.652
Environmental/contextual factors		
Students are more knowledgeable than I am when it comes to using mobile technologies	3.53	0.834
My school is doing a good job of using technology to enhance learning	3.67	1.18
My campus technical infrastructure and wireless network can accommodate students bringing their own technology	3.20	1.27
My curriculum is conducive to students having their own technology	3.20	1.15
My administration is supportive of students having their own device	3.67	1.18
Subtotal	3.45	0.498
Total	3.60	0.333

Note: Possible score range: 1–5; 1 – strongly disagree, 5 – strongly agree

(M = 3.45). Nevertheless, participants were more concerned about the availability of curriculum that is conducive to mobile learning (M = 3.20) and school technical infrastructure for using mobile devices (M = 3.20). Finally, teachers' preferences for using mobile technology to organize and support their daily activities and teaching were rated the lowest (M = 2.37). These areas can be seen as barriers to successful mobile learning integration in the classroom.

Inductive analysis of course artifacts resulted in the development of two overlapping themes about mobile learning to explain the quantitative results, informed by participants' experiences during the pandemic: (1) mobile learning supports differentiation and flexibility and (2) mobile learning increases connection between people. Both themes are presented below.

Mobile Learning Supports Differentiation and Flexibility

Related to differentiation and flexibility, participants acknowledged the perspective of many older students who appreciated being more in control of their own learning and its pace. For example, P2 reflected: "Distance learners… many of them actually like [mobile learning] because they can work at their own pace and aren't expected to be in the same place (both literally and figuratively) as everyone else. … This is what they were really craving all along." Indeed, many secondary school students told teacher participants that they were more successful when they could take more or less time with certain topics. Others noted flexibility of the timing of learning: "Having all of these tools accessible 24/7 also allows for asynchronous learning anytime" (P6). Participants also identified flexibility in the location of learning: "I not only had students at home, learning from me on their couches or beds, but I had students get into Zoom on their phones while riding in the car. They took their phones outside to show me things at their house when we were talking about the weather" (P2). When some schools transitioned back to in-person, some teachers continued to use mobile devices for learning, using them for observations and other data collection on school grounds related to science investigations.

Participants also noted ways that mobile devices promoted different, "fresh" ways for students to engage differently and in different learning environments. For example, P7 commented, "With mobile devices, students can learn, share and connect with peers in a variety of different learning environments. In my opinion, mobile learning makes virtual learning feel fresh, relevant, and engaging."

For others, mobile technology helped teachers challenge students more, helping each student to grow in their own ways. This included how remote and mobile learning promoted more student questions and other forms of academic risk taking. P1 noted, "Students were asking questions and making speculations about how to use the other operators with fractions. This is something students could be shy about when we were in person." She continued, "That experience really opened my eyes to my students and the way they learn, especially when I am not around." She decided that, when back in person, she would help students "to explore the content not only when they need help, but also when they have a spark of interest. I want them to feel safe sharing their ideas and new ways to solve problems. I want to include more [mobile]-learning in my classroom." In these ways, participants' experiences with mobile learning helped them recognize its benefits for developing a safe, welcoming space for student growth.

Mobile Learning Increases Connection Between People

Participants also highlighted important ways that mobile learning increased connections between themselves and students and between students. P1 noted that students and parents quickly responded with questions to text alerts she sent out. P12 emphasized more in-depth learning via connections:

> At first, I feared that virtual learning would leave my students feeling disconnected from the classroom. However, I ended up understanding that a specific type of virtual learning, called mobile learning, could allow me to connect with and teach my students in new and interesting ways. I could challenge them with assignments that allowed them to simultaneously explore the world around them while staying connected with our class.

P12 highlighted the affordance of mobile technology to support "interesting" ways to connect with students and connect students with the class/each other, while supporting explorations of the world. P15 considered connection with an emphasis on communication:

> I even had separate tutoring times outside of the online lesson for students to ask questions and receive assistance on their assignments. Communication was another important aspect of online learning. Gmail, Google classroom messaging, and Zoom helped me communicate with my students. I feel that students seemed to feel more comfortable asking questions in an online lesson then they did in the actual classroom.

This participant not only differentiated instruction via tutoring sessions but also considered their flipped classroom approach to remote instruction to increase student comfort in asking questions.

Other participants identified mobile devices as a way to promote communication between themselves, students, and parents. Phone video chats with teachers presented another way for students, who stayed home after many students transitioned back to in-person learning, to flexibly connect with teachers for support. Thus, the flexibility supported by mobile devices promoted connections between people in ways that supported student learning.

Influence of COVID-19 Experiences

Inductive analysis of the qualitative data also addressed the influence of participants' experiences during COVID-19 on their perspectives of mobile learning. Participants' personal COVID teaching required many to use mobile devices for teaching and learning for the first time or in new ways. Many participants shared initial fears that mobile learners would further disconnect students from their learning:

> Prior to COVID, I utilized technology as an accessory to my teaching. However, all that changed when our school switched to 100% virtual learning due to the pandemic. Suddenly, technology became the only way to reach my students. ... At first, I feared that virtual learning would leave my students feeling disconnected from the classroom. However, I ended up understanding that a specific type of virtual learning, called mobile learning, could allow me to connect with and teach my students in new and interesting ways. (P7)

With experience, this changed to considering mobile learning "to connect with and teach my students in new and interesting ways. I could challenge them"... "to simultaneously explore the world around them while staying connected with our class" (P7).

In this way, many participants directly connected their perspective of mobile devices, enhancing learning to their experiences during COVID. P6 reflected, "Last year, I required my students to put their phones away in class as to not be 'distracted' by social media and other alerts. Fast-forward a year, and now I am asking my students to sign into my google meet on their phone to have one less tab open on their Chromebook.

Some participants even considered mobile learning to be potentially transformational at the individual to educational system levels. For themselves, participants' personal exposure to mobile learning during pandemic helped them to identify the possibilities. For example, P4 reflected:

> Before COVID, I don't think I really had much of an "opinion" on mobile learning. Sure, I teach in a 1:1 school, and we're also in the middle of [a national park], so we've been encouraged to take kids outside when we can. But I really had no idea of how much mobile learning can be utilized until the pandemic changed everything.

For others, the change was situated at the school and district levels. For example, P8 commented:

> As remote learning has become more common during this pandemic, I've experienced a shift in attitudes toward [electronic] and [mobile]-learning. Prior to the pandemic, many schools/classrooms had a strict no-phones policy as they were viewed as interfering with learning. However, when learning at home, totally different rules apply. One major shift my school has made has been to focus on performance tasks that are not tests/quizzes/multiple choice. With mobile learning and the Internet at their fingertips, kids no longer need to memorize facts and figures that they can easily search. Instead, COVID and mobile learning have pushed teachers to think about what students truly need to be able to do, and to utilize technology to work toward that.

For P10's school, remote learning and mobile learning disrupted school policy, shifting from business-as-usual assessment to performance assessment. The participant considered mobile learning experiences during the pandemic to expand teachers' consideration of the core skills students need, enabling more targeted, focused teaching and learning.

Participants also reflected on the role of "force[d]" use of mobile devices changing content delivery and the perspectives of teachers and parents about the possibilities related to mobile learning. At the school and district levels, P11 noted:

> I think COVID-19 challenged the idea that mobile learning is impossible. I work in a district where teachers initially fought the 1:1 initiative and claimed they would never use our LMS. Well, Covid-19 forced everyone to use devices and changed the way content was

being delivered. What mobile learning taught instructors and parents is that it is possible. Learning can happen online.

COVID mitigated an initial strong teacher push-back against the 1:1 technology initiative in the district, with the pandemic acting as a disruptive event for this district.

Other participants focused more broadly on the educational system being upended by the pandemic. P14 concluded, "Education will forever be shaped by the changes that have happened due to COVID. Mobile learning has been pushed into the spotlight. … I believe mobile learning will be here to stay even once the pandemic has passed." Note that the participant considered the changes initiated by the pandemic to have "forever" shaped education. The participant's perspective emphasized the longevity and great extent of the pandemic's impact.

Discussion/Implications

Findings of the present study include that the teacher participants considered mobile devices to have many affordances, including the potential to bring new opportunities for and enhance learning in flexible ways that can connect learners to people, content, and resources and support differentiated instruction. Most of the teachers also considered the COVID-19 pandemic to have provided themselves and other teachers with extensive experiences facilitating remote, including mobile, learning that they see as a catalyst for longer term change in their instruction, district policy, and beyond. These findings are consistent with prior research that examined K–12 teachers' mobile learning readiness in the United States (Christensen & Knezek, 2018). Research indicates that mobile technologies offer many educational benefits. They are closely associated with student-centered learning (Lai et al., 2019), knowledge-sharing behaviors, and collaboration (Reeves et al., 2017), and transformative learning (Lindsay, 2016; Norris et al., 2011; Norris & Soloway, 2015).

The pandemic disrupted the educational system and provided firsthand experiences implementing remote and mobile learning for most teachers in the United States. Many of the teachers in the present study identified ways in which the pandemic served as a disrupting event for themselves, their school districts, and potentially, for a paradigm shift in education. The teacher participants' general framing of the pandemic as a catalyst for educational change offers hope that, given the appropriate administrative, technological, and curricular support, mobile technologies can transform learning and facilitate a positive pedagogical change in a classroom. Based on this, we believe that the COVID-19 pandemic and associated dramatic changes in teaching and learning may be a "disrupting event" that can be further leveraged to promote innovative mobile learning (Christensen & Knezek, 2018).

This study provided further evidence that teachers need technological and pedagogical support to implement mobile learning in schools, access to curricula conducive to mobile learning, and school technical infrastructure for using mobile devices as these remain serious barriers to mobile learning. One area of mobile learning readiness was rated relatively low by participants in the present study: teacher preferences for using mobile technology to organize and support daily activities and teaching practices ($M = 2.39$ on a 1–5 scale) with quite a large variability in their responses, particularly to questions about using (a) an electronic textbook rather than a traditional textbook ($M = 1.93$, $SD = 1.44$), (b) a mobile device rather than a computer for learning ($M = 1.93$, $SD = 1.10$), and (c) a mobile device to better organize daily activities ($M = 3.27$, $SD = 0.96$). Teachers' low preferences for electronic textbooks are consistent with other studies of reading preferences and behaviors (e.g., Mizrachi et al., 2021; Novak et al., 2018). Although prior research with a large number of US teacher participants ($N = 1430$) reported the Preferences factor among the lowest as well (Christensen & Knezek, 2018), their mean average was considerably higher ($M = 3.09$) than in the present study. Since teachers' attitudes toward technology affect their intention to use technology in a classroom (Nikolopoulou et al., 2021), this area deserves more attention from researchers, educational technology programs, and teacher preparation programs.

A particular aspect of teacher preferences that can be addressed is teachers' preferences for using mobile devices for daily and teaching activities. Oftentimes, educational technology and teacher preparation programs focus on how technology can support student academic performance, overlooking the need to demonstrate how technologies can enhance teachers' everyday experiences. For example, mobile devices can be used for time management and organization, health monitoring, better communication and access to school staff, increased collaboration with colleagues, access the cloud, and reduced operational costs and saved time (replace paper-based assessments, eliminate landline carrier services, scanning and imaging, talk-to-text applications, digital file sharing, etc.). In addition, mobile devices can help self-regulate learning through time tracking and monitoring (Tabuenca et al., 2015).

Given the self-selection of participants in the present study into a graduate-level educational technology course and their considerably high proficiency with technology (stages 5 and 6 technology adopters), it is plausible to assume that their ability to integrate technology in a classroom exceeds many of their colleagues. As such, the teacher participants may have been more likely than most to be open to the benefits of mobile learning. Yet even the high-level technology adopters who were study participants here expressed some reservations to using mobile devices for educational purposes. Because of the significant high proficiency of the participants, the findings may not generalize beyond the local setting. Furthermore, this is a pilot study, and more research is needed.

Teachers who are well-positioned to be educational leaders in K–12 schools, like the participants of the present study, may support other teachers in a continuation of mobile device use for meaningful learning. The COVD-19 teaching experiences of the present study's participants disrupted some teacher participants' emphasis on why mobile learning would not work; their experiences disrupted how they used technology. COVID-19 experiences revealed student needs such as flexibility in the time spent on work and where and how that work is done. Technology, especially mobile devices, helped them to address student needs. Indeed, mobile learning and pandemic experiences have the potential to be transformational.

Conclusions

This study of stage 5 (adaptation to other contexts) and stage 6 (creative application to new contexts) technology adopters provides a window into the world of the possible. K–12 education is poised to more readily accept the need for mobile learning in the post-pandemic world. It is not optional to differentiate instruction or be flexible. It is not optional to help students connect with each other and the content in flexible ways. These are essential, and mobile learning is an important way forward to accomplish these aims. And more teachers acknowledge this now. Teachers, such as the participants of this study who have some training in mobile learning, are increasingly ready to be the change. Yet support from all system levels is needed to realize this potential. Policymakers and school district administrators need to allocate financial resources for this effort. District administrators also need to protect teachers' time for participation in ongoing professional development programs and communities of practice with just-in-time support. Teacher learning experiences should integrate and unpack flexible, differentiated, innovative mobile technologies in teacher preparation programs and professional development programs alike. Peer observations and goal setting within professional learning communities can help teachers support each other, if given time within the workday. With COVID mobile technology teaching experiences acting as a catalyst, we can further disrupt education via innovation; we urge systemic investment in and support of teachers to promote a paradigm shift.

References

Albors-Garrigos, J., & Hervas-Oliver, J. L. (2014). Creative destruction in clusters: From theory to practice, the role of technology gatekeepers, understanding disruptive innovation in industrial districts. In *Proceedings of Portland International Conference on Management of Engineering & Technology (PICMET)* (pp. 710–722).

Bessant, J., von Stamm, B., Moeslein, K. M., & Neyer, A. K. (2010). Backing outsiders: Selection strategies for discontinuous innovation. *R & D Management, 40*, 345–335.

Bogden, R. C., & Biklen, S. K. (2003). *Qualitative research of education: An introduction to theories and methods* (4th ed.). Allyn and Bacon.

Chee, K. N., Yahaya, N., Ibrahim, N. H., & Noor Hassan, M. (2017). Review of mobile learning trends 2010–2015: A meta-analysis. *Educational Technology & Society, 20*(2), 113–126.

Chen, C. H., & Tsai, C. C. (2021). In-service teachers' conceptions of mobile technology-integrated instruction: Tendency towards student-centered learning. *Computers & Education, 170*, 104224.

Christensen, C. M. (2013). Disruptive innovation. In *The encyclopedia of human-computer interaction* (2nd ed.). https://www.interaction-design.org/literature/book/the-encyclopedia-of-human-computer-interaction-2nd-ed/disruptive-innovation. Retrieved January 12, 2021.

Christensen, R. R. (1997). *Effect of technology integration education on the attitudes of teachers and their students.* (Publication No. 9816134) [Doctoral dissertation, University of North Texas]. Proquest Dissertations & Theses Global.

Christensen, R., & Knezek, G. (2018). Reprint of readiness for integrating mobile learning in the classroom: Challenges, preferences and possibilities. *Computers in Human Behavior, 78*, 379–388. https://doi.org/10.1016/j.chb.2017.07.046

Crompton, H. (2013). A historical overview of mobile learning: Toward learner-centered education. In Z. L. Berge & L. Y. Muilenburg (Eds.), *Handbook of mobile learning* (pp. 3–14). Routledge.

Dede, C. (2020). *Remote learning and stone soup*. Retrieved from https://learningpolicyinstitute.org/blog/remote-learning-and-stone-soup

Kilkki, K., Mäntylä, M., Kimmo, K., Hämmäinen, H., & Alisto, H. (2018). A disruption framework. *Technological Forecasting and Social Change, 129*, 275–284. https://www.sciencedirect.com/science/article/pii/S0040162517314622

Lai, A. F., Chen, C. H., & Lee, G. Y. (2019). An augmented reality-based learning approach to enhancing students' science reading performances from the perspective of the cognitive load theory. *British Journal of Educational Technology, 5*, 232–247. https://doi.org/10.1111/bjet.12716

Lindsay, L. (2016). Transformation of teacher practice using mobile technology with one-to-one classes: M-Learning pedagogical approaches. *British Journal of Educational Technology, 47*, 883–892.

Mizrachi, D., Salaz, A. M., Kurbanoglu, S., & Boustany, J. (2021). The Academic Reading Format International Study (ARFIS): Final results of a comparative survey analysis of 21,265 students in 33 countries. *Reference Services Review*. https://doi.org/10.1108/RSR-04-2021-0012

Nikolopoulou, K., Gialamas, V., & Lavidas, K. (2021). Habit, hedonic motivation, performance expectancy and technological pedagogical knowledge affect teachers' intention to use mobile internet. *Computers and Education Open, 2*, 100041. https://doi.org/10.1016/j.caeo.2021.100041

Norris, C., Hossain, A., & Soloway, E. (2011). Using smartphones as essential tools for learning a call to place schools on the right side of the 21st century. *TechTrends, 51*(3), 18–25.

Norris, C., & Soloway, E. (2015). Mobile technology in 2020: Predictions and implications for K-12 education. *Educational Technology, 55*(1), 12–19.

Novak, E., Daday, J., & McDaniel, K. (2018). Using a mathematical model of motivation, volition, and performance to examine students' e-text learning experiences. *Educational Technology Research & Development., 66*(5), 1189–1209. https://doi.org/10.1007/s11423-018-9599-5

Reeves, J. L., Gunter, G. A., & Lacey, C. (2017). Mobile learning in pre-kindergarten: Using student feedback to inform practice. *Educational Technology & Society, 20*(1), 37–44.

Rogers, E. M. (1983). *Diffusion of innovations* (3rd ed.). The Free Press.

Scanlon, E., Jones, A. C., & Waycott, J. (2005). Mobile technologies: Prospects for their use in learning in informal science settings. *Journal of Interactive Media in Education, 2005*(2), Art. 23. https://doi.org/10.5334/2005-25

Sharples, M., Amedillo Sanchez, I., Milrad, M., & Vavoula, G. (2009). Mobile learning: Small devices, big issues. In N. Balacheff, S. Ludvigsen, T. deJong, & S. Barnes (Eds.), *Technology enhanced learning: Principles and products* (pp. 233–249). Springer.

Tabuenca, B., Kalz, M., Drachsler, H., & Specht, M. (2015). Time will tell: The role of mobile learning analytics in self-regulated learning. *Computers & Education, 89*, 53–74.

Taylor, D. L., & Booth, S. (2015). Secondary physical science teachers' conceptions of science teaching in a context of change. *International Journal of Science Education, 37*, 1299–1320.

Thomas, K. M., O'Bannon, B. W., & Britt, V. G. (2014). Standing in the schoolhouse door: Teacher perceptions of mobile phones in the classroom. *Journal of Research on Technology in Education, 46*, 373–395.

Wu, W. H., Wu, Y. C. J., Chen, C. Y., Kao, H. Y., Lin, C. H., & Huang, S. H. (2012). Review of trends from mobile learning studies: A meta-analysis. *Computers & Education, 59*, 817–827.

Emerging Technologies for Blind and Visually Impaired Learners: A Case Study

Regina Kaplan-Rakowski and Tania Heap

Background

Visual content is prevalent on educational platforms, which is not surprising given that out of the five traditional senses, sight is the most valued (Enoch et al., 2019). Established cognitive multimedia learning theories advocate for the instructional implementation of visuals (e.g., Mayer, 2009; Paivio, 1986), claiming that using visuals typically yields more effective learning outcomes (Aisami, 2015). Moreover, most learners indicate preferences of learning with visuals (Kuri & Truzzi, 2002).

Because of the imbalanced focus on visual learning materials, students with visual impairments are often at a disadvantage. Evolving digital environments need to keep pace and offer equivalent learning opportunities to visually impaired individuals. Therefore, the existence of assistive technologies is fundamental to allow for diversity and inclusion. Traditional strategies to overcome barriers are use of colorblind friendly cues, such as texture, written labels, other indicators besides color alone, audio cues, keyboard-only commands, haptic and auditory white cane controller, ability to zoom and focus on one element at a time, and environment descriptions with both audio and text based options (Crutchfield & Haugh, 2018; Siu et al., 2020).

In addition to traditional strategies, innovative technologies are increasingly capable of assisting blind and visually impaired (BVI) individuals with applications using artificial intelligence, speech recognition, text-to-speech software, refreshable braille displays (Fig. 1), smart glasses, robotics, screen readers, and other assistive technologies. These tools can positively impact BVI students' learning because

R. Kaplan-Rakowski (✉) · T. Heap
University of North Texas, Denton, TX, USA
e-mail: Regina.Kaplan-Rakowski@unt.edu; Tania.Heap@unt.edu

© The Author(s), under exclusive license to Springer Nature Switzerland AG 2023
D. Cockerham et al. (eds.), *Reimagining Education: Studies and Stories for Effective Learning in an Evolving Digital Environment*, Educational Communications and Technology: Issues and Innovations, https://doi.org/10.1007/978-3-031-25102-3_16

Fig. 1 Blind person using a braille screen reader. (Photo by Sigmund on Unsplash)

assistive technology is designed to increase, maintain, or improve the functional capabilities of people with disabilities (WHO, n.d.).[1]

However, a large portion of the BVI population lacks sufficient access to assistive technology. This deficit became particularly apparent with the abrupt shift to online learning due to the COVID-19 pandemic outbreak (Ferdig et al., 2020). The switch to remote learning diminished typical struggles of the BVI population, such as navigation and orientation across campus. Instead, other challenges became prevalent and were mostly related to using digital online content. Our chapter describes a case study of a blind student who shared his daily experience with online learning, highlighting both the encountered struggles and the type of assistance received during the pandemic. The discussion on the future use of emerging technologies for the BVI concludes our chapter.

Process

The Blind and Visually Impaired and Online Learning

The global shift to online instruction due the COVID-19 pandemic (Ferdig et al., 2020; Hartshorne et al., 2020) necessitated nearly instantaneous employment of essential techniques (An et al., 2021) to allow learners to continue their education in

---

[1] Throughout this chapter, the authors will use both person-first language, which places the person before their characteristic (e.g., people with disabilities) and identity-first language, which leads with the person's characteristic (e.g., blind user). There are pros and cons to using either approach, but when the opportunity presents, a good practice is to ask each individual which language they prefer.

the digital-only format. This shift not only negatively impacted students' social (Bartolic et al., 2022) and cognitive functions but also disturbed emotional well-being (Kaplan-Rakowski, 2021). Despite some of these unfortunate pandemic consequences, some positive outcomes also occurred (Ferdig et al., 2021). In the context of BVI students, the positive outcome was that the usual challenge of commuting and navigation through campus was eliminated. Instead, students could pursue their learning online, at the comfort of their homes.

Simultaneously, yet new challenges occurred: BVI learners struggled with accessing digital learning content due to some of it being inaccessible. That is, even though some content that was supposed to be accessible per assistive technology products advertisements, as it appeared, not all learning products were accessible. The issue of accessibility or lack thereof is not new. Policies driving compliance with the Americans with Disabilities Act (ADA) and the evolution of technology have contributed to increased opportunities for accessible learning for students with special needs, including the BVI population of learners.

Efforts include the incorporation of Universal Design for Learning (UDL), which improves learning environments aiming to eliminate barriers to any learners (Rose, 2000). UDL is a framework containing principles that guide educators and other educational stakeholders in creating learning experiences that give all students equal opportunity to succeed. Guidelines are centered around providing learners with multiple means of engagement, representation, action, and expression (CAST, 2018).

Even though ADA compliance efforts have been in place, they can be seen as minimum standards to achieve rather than a thorough solution. Designing inclusive online learning content remains to be challenging. One solution to this challenge is employing BVI individuals in the process of designing and testing assistive products (personal communication, 2020). Instructional designers tend to rely on testing products using commercial technology. However, as reported by the BVI community, some of those products are unreliable and inaccurate – consequently, useless.

Some challenges encountered by the BVI community were not as evident before the pandemic. For example, Longhurst (2021) reports on a case of an undergraduate medicine blind student in an anatomy class. Pre-pandemic, the course consisted of a lecture followed by a practical dissection room session. When the shift to remote learning occurred, in-person lectures were replaced with video-based lectures. The practical sessions were substituted with a "virtual online workbook" incorporated in the Canvas Learning Management System (LMS). Students then participated in synchronous interactive questions-answers sessions using a videoconferencing platform.

The sudden challenge was that the traditional (accessible) handbook used for the dissection room sessions was replaced with a multimedia-rich set of webpages. Non-BVI students took advantage of the videos, 3D images, GIF animations, illustrations, and diagrams to learn about dissection, consequently, succeeding in the class. The blind student faced issues. Specifically, the multitude of multimedia was excessive for the braille screen reader. Moreover, the blind student's support worker lacked sufficient expertise in the medical area and, as a result, was unable to effectively assist the blind student with learning. That is, although the support worker was able to read the instructional text to the blind student, describing the technical visual media that were embedded in the instructional materials was challenging. In the end, the blind student could not follow the instructional materials enough to satisfy the requirements of the course.

McBride (2020) reports on another instance of challenges experienced by BVI learners during COVID-19. Taking a broader, survey-based approach, McBride addressed the issues of accessibility and engagement of school-aged BVI individuals. Parents, teachers, as well as orientation and mobility instructors participated in the survey ($N = 312$). The studied aspects included parents' concerns, the ability to access assistive technology, materials, and tools, together with the helpfulness of teachers of BVI students. It became apparent that despite the best intentions and efforts, BVI individuals could not be well supported by parents or guardians due to their lack of time, training, and accessible resources. For example, braille materials or large-print materials are typically stored in public libraries that were closed during the pandemic, which made the assistive materials and tools unavailable.

Examples of some successful strategies of supporting BVI individuals during the pandemic include those documented by Lueders et al. (2020). Using the Individualized Education Program (IEP) process, three interns analyzed the BVI needs and organized distribution of braille materials, iPads, and slant boards to BVI individuals. Some methods of observation included eye gaze tracking of BVI students, who could be individually pinned using videoconferencing tools. The interns prepared focused surveys and other data tracking platforms to facilitate efficient communication, information updates, parental feedback, which could be implemented and addressed immediately, allowing for efficient learning of BVI students.

Study Purpose and Research Questions

The purpose of our study was to conduct an in-depth investigation into the unique challenges experienced by a blind individual who is a full-time assistive technology user enrolled in online courses with emerging technologies as part of their pedagogy. Given the need for BVI individuals to continue their learning efficiently and effectively during the pandemic and beyond, this study aimed to address the following research questions:

1. How did the rapid shift to online learning due to a pandemic affect the learning experience of a blind individual?
2. How can assistive technology and emerging educational technologies help or hinder the learning experience of a blind student?
3. What can educators do to make a positive impact on blind students' learning experiences?

Methods

This is a qualitative analysis of a case study of a blind student who shares his daily challenges with online learning using non-ADA-compliant learning environments. We opted for a case study to allow for a comprehensive analysis of the participant's lived experience (Tellis, 1997). Such an approach draws on several data sources, including interviews, observations, and documents, to form a common understanding based on emerging themes within the case. Case study qualitative research investigates specific idiosyncrasies and offers the development of concepts and theory (Mills et al., 2010). Our participant's input comes from a semi-structured interview, analyzed using a combination of inductive thematic analysis (Braun & Clarke, 2006), saliency analysis (Buetow, 2010), and the content analysis of assignments completed as part of his degree course work. The student's testimony will follow with his positive and negative impressions on using innovative technologies to assist with learning.

Participant

The study participant opted to be referred to with his real name: Jarrod. Jarrod is a young male who lost his sight 4 years prior. He is an undergraduate student of a large, urban university in the south-central part of the United States. The participant was enrolled in a learning technologies course in 2021 as a full-time assistive technology user. This chapter focuses on the findings derived from data based on Jarrod's lived experience as a blind student. Jarrod granted his consent to conduct the study and the Institutional Review Board protocol was completed and approved.

Data Collection

Two sources of data facilitated our analysis: a semi-structured interview and participant's reflection blogs. The semi-structured interview contained questions (see Appendix A) concerning the participant's experience, success, and challenges with online learning and technology use post-pandemic. The participant's reflection blogs were a part of his coursework assignments, which included reading and reflecting on self-selected academic publications on the topic of emerging technologies for BVI. Based on the readings, the participant was to produce six weekly journal reports evaluating and discussing his experience using different emerging technologies, such as AI-driven software, virtual assistants, gaming, and emerging assistive technologies for individuals with disabilities.

Data Analysis

Jarrod's input comes from a semi-structured interview conducted in early spring of 2022, which was audio recorded using Microsoft Teams and was analyzed using inductive thematic and saliency analysis. Data also come from the content analysis of assignments and tasks that Jarrod completed as part of his course work in Spring 2021. Thematic analysis assists researchers in identifying themes or patterns in data by using a coding scheme. It helps to derive the patterns most relevant to the research questions and the most recurrent in the participant sample (Braun & Clarke, 2006). Saliency analysis focuses on the saliency of the themes: some themes may not be as recurrent in the data set but of relevance in answering a research question or over-arching goal (Buetow, 2010). Analysis of both datasets was completed using NVivo. After agreeing on the primary coding patterns and emerging themes, the authors coded the transcripts, allowing for the possibility of additional recurring and salient themes. To ensure inter-rater reliability, the authors reviewed all new recurring and salient themes and any inconsistent themes and dimensions highlighted by NVivo's coding comparison feature, until they reached a Cohen's Kappa for all dimensions of at least 80% (Lavrakas, 2008).

Findings and Disscussion

This section reports on a case study of a BVI learner who shared his perceived barriers and success strategies. Some current barriers discussed in this section include employability, together with societal unawareness and alienation. Success strategies include educators' flexibility (e.g., by allowing BVI to complete assignments using alternative formats).

We are focusing only on several selected dimensions that emerged from the barriers and success strategies discussed in the interview and helped inform the research questions: (1) How did the rapid shift to online learning due to a pandemic affect the learning experience of a blind individual? (2) How can assistive technology and emerging educational technology help or hinder the learning experience of a blind student? (3) What can educators do to make a positive impact on blind students' learning experiences? We are including quotations from the interview and weekly journal logs to illustrate the emerging themes.

Current Barriers: Employability

A recurring perception of a barrier from Jarrod's interview and journal entries appears to be a persistent societal lack of recognition of blind individuals about their ability to complete tasks, live an independent life, and in playing a critical role in breaking accessibility barriers. In turn, that lack of recognition leads to further barriers related to it, namely, employability, unawareness, and mistrust or misconceptions.

Skilled blind people appear to be underutilized and excluded from the possibility of making a positive impact in society, beginning from being offered gainful employment opportunities.

> It seems to me like there are a lot of visually impaired individuals with nothing but time on their hands and I'm sure some of them would be glad to have any kind of job, let alone one having to do with accessibility. I know because I am definitely one of those individuals.

Jarrod is aware of the availability of jobs in his areas of interest and skills, and the impactful contributions that employees with disabilities can make in making the workplace more inclusive, yet his perception is that blind people are not seen as employable despite their skills, even in industries that cater to people with disabilities.

> My counselor asked [the publisher representative] if there was a visually impaired employee (…) who worked there that could help us and he said 'no'. They did not have one person who was familiar with screen readers in their disability department.

The quotation above is Jarrod's description of trying as a student to use a third-party digital publisher platform that was inaccessible and learning that the publisher company had no assistive technology users employed in their disability department to address or even understand his challenges.

Current Barriers: Societal Unawareness and Alienation

Alienation and social isolation are reoccurring in Jarrod's testimony as well. In thinking about current access barriers for blind students engaging with digital and emerging technology, Jarrod's perception is that disabled students and users, in general, are often excluded from conversations around digital accessibility, the initial design, and the development of technologies. Even perhaps more surprisingly, his personal experience indicates that blind users can also be excluded from conversations around the design of products that are specifically targeting blind students, as exemplified here:

> A plan was put into action in order to help visually impaired students navigate the campus of [my university]. I am in an organization (…) called the Blind and Visually Impaired Alliance and our organization was never contacted. After getting in contact with the person in charge of the plan, we found out that they did not consult any visually impaired individuals during any phase of the plan. On top of that, we were sent a PDF of the plan afterwards, and the PDF wasn't even accessible.

Challenges such as orientation and navigation around physical spaces including campuses have been documented for a long time (Brown, 2008). The shift to digital, however, added new challenges on top of the existing ones. The inaccessible PDF file that further hindered campus orientation is an example of the added challenge.

Jarrod's own experience with social isolation documented during his course was possibly further exacerbated during his studies by the forced shift to online learning because of the pandemic (Morgan, 2022).

> I was always, like, afraid of doing everything online. I actually liked being on campus and physically attending classes.

However, AI-driven technology and the use of virtual assistants appear to offer hope in successfully addressing this challenge:

> This disability can also be very isolating [but] … virtual assistants can make it less isolating by being able to relate to others who also use virtual assistants.

The next section further explores the success strategies that enable blind learners to experience high-quality online education, how assistive and emerging technologies can facilitate that experience, and what educators and other stakeholders can do to make a positive impact.

Success Strategies: Flexibility and Other People's Roles

Allowing flexibility by educators, course designers, or product developers appears to be a way to enable blind students to engage in and complete activities at an equivalent standard to visual learners. A strategy could be, for example, to accept completing an activity using a different sensory input (e.g., activities using sound and audio cues instead of only visual cues; Crutchfield & Haugh, 2018). Educators could allow students to complete the same task and achieve the same learning outcome using a different process, sensory input, or tool. That is, educators could be flexible and accept, for example, an audio file instead of a text-based file, which may be more accessible, while producing the same output. Blind users rely on tactile senses and can have increased spatial awareness via auditory or other intact sensory inputs (King, 2014), as also documented by Jarrod:

> When we lose our sight, our brain rewires itself in order to compensate for the loss, allowing us to focus more on the senses that we have left. This is why people with vision think that our senses are on the same level of that of a blind superhero. When, in actuality, it is just our way of compensating for the loss of one of our senses.

His experience does not appear to be just anecdotal evidence. Congenital lack of or later loss of vision appears to result in functional changes in the brain, which can lead to improvement of the intact sensory abilities (Huber et al., 2019; King, 2014). In his weekly journal assignment, Jarrod discussed his review of research by Huber and colleagues, where they found evidence using neuroimaging for systematic changes within the human auditory cortex as a result of blindness. He relates their findings to his own personal experience and social interactions with people who are not blind.

> I get asked all the time if my hearing is like that of the blind superhero Daredevil who has super enhanced senses. Although my other senses are not enhanced to the level of

Daredevil's, they are at a higher level than that of a sighted person. (…) From my under-standing [of Huber et al.'s findings], this means that as a blind individual our brains rewire themselves so that where we would be getting visual information instead, we are getting auditory information.

Flexibility can also take the form of changing other people's roles from a situation where the blind person has to depend on others for orientation and navigation, to one where the other person can be there as needed, or simply be more aware, informed, flexible, and inclusive in their practices. Those practices can range from enabling multiple avenues to achieve the same task, to becoming familiar with basic digital accessibility best practices and UDL principles (Burgstahler, 2020).

Success Strategies: Affordable Emerging Technologies

As mentioned earlier, Jarrod's experience with AI-driven hands-free tools such as virtual assistants and smart glasses (Fig. 2) appears to be positive because the tech-nology enables him to complete day-to-day activities in a more efficient way:

Virtual assistants can streamline situations and their hands-free nature saves so much time.
It can be a hassle to pull out my phone to use the [navigation] app when I already have a cane in my hand. (…) with the phone app I would have to keep the phone out so that the camera could see my surroundings to guide me, but with smart glasses I would just use the camera in the glasses leaving my hands free making the whole process much easier and less stressful.

Affordability of assistive and emerging technology should also be considered as a success factor in increasing access to quality education for BVI students. As Jarrod

Fig. 2 Person wearing smart glasses. (Photo by Quang Tri NGUYEN on Unsplash)

notes when evaluating a text-to-speech app for reading digital documents, his own personal perception is that affordability can help many other blind users who are unable to find gainful employment:

> [the developers] could make the app easier to navigate by adding submenus, so there aren't so many buttons and other things on screen at the same time. They could also lower the price since the majority of visually impaired individuals are unemployed and live off disability.

Looking at the facts, according to the American Community Survey (ACS) data, 44% of BVI people are employed and 10% of BVI people who are in the labor force are unemployed. Just over half of the BVI population (50.9%) does not participate in the labor force (McDonnall & Sui, 2019). Such a large percentage of population removed from the labor market, coupled with the fact that across all ages, people with disabilities are less likely to be employed (U.S. Bureau of Labor Statistics, 2022), might contribute to Jarrod's perception of the affordability barrier. Employability can be perceived by blind users as a barrier, and consequently, the possibility of affording high quality, yet expensive, technology to thrive in online education and everyday life.

Traditional, Web Content Accessibility Guidelines

Thanks to our participant's insights and findings reported in other studies, we stress that guidelines helping the BVI population of learners should be (re-)introduced and reinforced. For example, Longhurst (2021) reminds about the importance of adhering to the Web Content Accessibility Guidelines (Caldwell et al., 2008) that recommend digital teaching materials to be internationally recognized. Some traditional guidelines of how to help BVI learners include:

1. Ensuring that any text or graphics can be enlarged.
2. Providing text alternatives in addition to audio and video transcripts.
3. Color text and background should be sufficiently contrasted in color.
4. When delivering information or learning content, various approaches should be used without solely relying on the use of color.
5. Visuals such as videos or lecture recordings should be supported with accurate captions, not only supporting the BVI students but also ensuring that students with hearing impairments are able to follow the content of the visuals.

Innovative, Emerging Applications and Technologies

Current research is revolving around introducing diversified forms of emerging technologies for BVI users such as tactile radar, Arduino-based device for video games, radio-frequency identification (RFID), assisted gloves or similar wearable technology (Rodríguez et al., 2018; Sooraj et al., 2021). There also has been some research in spatial data gathering using immersive technologies and algorithms to direct the user to take an action. For example, Lee and Cho (2022) report on smart glasses that guide objects in real photos and help users detect the shape of the object through a braille pad. Meanwhile, Zhao et al. (2018) describe white cane haptics to navigate virtual reality environments.

Such technologies often involve an input device (e.g., a camera and a micro-phone), an output device (e.g., a speaker), a sensory device (e.g., vibration modules) as output signals, and usually some form of a headset. Rodríguez et al. (2018) describe the common input, output, and immersion experiences that can be used. Some experiences are audio-based and use auditory icons and earcons to associate information with the sound. However, there are also more sophisticated audio solutions such as spatial or 3D sound, which assign a 3D effect to the sound, allowing it to come from any part of the scene – the concept known as ambisonic sound.

Haptic-based strategies can be used to enhance immersion, for instance, by vibrating when collisions are detected. Video games use a combination of these strategies together with screen readers that turn what is displayed on the monitor into a different, non-standard output such as speech or text on a braille output device (Rodríguez et al., 2018).

Some algorithms currently being studied also focus on being able to read braille and process it to convert into instructions for the user. Example experiments are conducted in high-immersion virtual reality (VR) with the use of a VR headset and a white cane. Users in VR can perceive virtual objects by either seeing, hearing, or touching them. The touching takes place by grasping the objects through haptic feedback devices. Instant, real-time interactions allow for the virtual content to not only be moved around but also scaled. Consequently, that scaling allows the spatial information to be accessible for BVI individuals (Kriemeier & Götzelmann, 2020).

A critical challenge in this area is the involvement of risk – especially if the user is to use the technology in a real world setting that is being converted to VR through computational algorithms. This risk may be physical or health-related, with nausea and dizziness being the most common unpleasant sensation reported by VR headset users (Crossland et al., 2019). Also, the "accessible public facilities such as tactile pavements and tactile signs are installed only in limited areas globally, and visually impaired individuals use assistive devices such as canes or guide dogs, which have limitations" (Lee & Cho, 2022).

While accessible design of emerging technologies is becoming increasingly known and common, there still seems to be a dire need for connecting the three areas – where real or virtual world data input points are analyzed, then processed with deep learning (recognition) algorithms, and then signaling the user in real-time of the necessary actions to be taken. Scalable and affordable immersive technology activities that consider a wide range of users, including assistive technology users and users with visual disabilities, are still far from being mainstream.

Limitations and Future Studies

Like any research, this study has several limitations. First, as with most case studies, this study is difficult to replicate and cannot be easily generalized to a larger population. Future studies should be based on more voices, allowing to infer more robust findings. Second, our study was based in the USA, where learning conditions for BVI users may be more assistive compared to less developed countries. Investigations incorporating a more international view would be more impactful globally. Third, we were limited to only qualitative analysis, while follow-up projects should also provide quantitative data enriching analysis. Fourth, this study was based on self-reported utterances. Future studies should include more data based on performance scores and quantifiable logging metrics.

Conclusions

In this case study, we investigated the experience of a BVI learner who shared his perceived barriers and success strategies. Some current barriers identified include employability, together with societal unawareness and alienation. Success strategies include educators' flexibility (e.g., by allowing BVI to complete assignments using alternative formats). The implementation of traditional and innovative technologies seems promising. Future research should explore the ways emerging technologies can assist BVI learners and other disadvantaged individuals.

Given what we have learned from this case study and the promise of UDL as a framework for reimagining education of next decades, a number of strategies and stakeholders will play a significant role in making learning and emerging educational technologies accessible to everyone. Beyond focusing on BVI learners, following UDL principles can lead to improved access and quality of education to all users, with or without a disability. For example, closed captioning in videos does not solely benefit deaf and hard of hearing users but is also beneficial to students who are second language learners (Alobaid, 2021) or live and study in noisy environments (Kent et al., 2018).

The rapid and large-scale shift to online instruction due to the COVID-19 pandemic highlighted various gaps in education and teacher education, consequently calling for some necessary adjustments that scholars now have a mission to make (Baumgartner et al., 2022; Ferdig et al., 2021; Mouza et al., 2022). Among others, these adjustments include fostering a more accessible and inclusive delivery of instruction to diverse populations of learners (Russ & Hamidi, 2021). Creating technologies and learning experiences that follow universal design principles requires a paradigm shift toward a common goal, "from designing for some to designing for everyone" (Burgstahler & Crawford, 2020, p. 85). It requires buy-in and adequate training and support from multiple stakeholders in education: faculty, IT professionals, instructional designers, media producers, as well as educational policymakers and senior administration. It also requires incorporating accessibility guidelines and feedback from assistive technology users at the course or product design stage, rather than viewing accessibility and universal design as an afterthought.

Appendix

Interview Questions to Jarrod

(i) Online learning

1. What aspects of online learning work well for you?
2. What aspects of online learning do not work well for you?
3. How did the shift to online learning due to the COVID-19 pandemic impacted you?
4. How did the shift to online learning due to the COVID-19 pandemic impacted your community?
5. What support did you receive?
6. What support did you wish you had received?
7. How has the shift to online learning due to COVID-19 informed your opinion about the future of digital accessibility?

(ii) Technology

0. What does not work well for you? How accurate is dictation? Do you feel it is improving?
1. What can be done differently or better?
2. What technologies have you been using that are helpful to you?
3. What innovative technologies are you aware of that you think could be helpful to you?
4. What about screen readers?
5. What about smart speakers?
6. As an assistive technology user and an experienced gamer, what advice do you have for game designers and professors using gaming in their courses?

An additional question:

How much understanding of your situation do you think the sighted people have?

References

Aisami, R. S. (2015). Learning styles and visual literacy for learning and performance. *Procedia-Social and Behavioral Sciences, 176*, 538–545.

Alobaid, A. (2021). ICT multimedia learning affordances: Role and impact on ESL learners' writing accuracy development. *Heliyon, 7*(7), e07517.

An, Y., Kaplan-Rakowski, R., Yang, J., Conan, J., Kinard, W., & Daughrity, L. (2021). Examining K-12 teachers' feelings, experiences, and perspectives regarding online teaching during the early stage of the COVID-19 pandemic. *Educational Technology Research and Development, 69*(2), 2589–2613. https://doi.org/10.1007/s11423-021-10008-5

Bartolic, S., Matzat, U., Tai, J., Burgess, J. L., Boud, D., Craig, H., Archibald, A., De Jaeger, A., Kaplan-Rakowski, R., Lutze-Mann, L., Polly, P., Roth, M., Heap, T., Agapito, J., & Guppy, N. (2022). Student vulnerabilities and confidence in learning in the context of the COVID-19 pandemic. *Studies in Higher Education, 47*, 1–13.

Baumgartner, E., Hartshorne, R., Kaplan-Rakowski, R., Mouza, C., & Ferdig, R. E. (Eds.). (2022). *A Retrospective of teaching, technology, and teacher education during the COVID-19 pandemic*. Association for the Advancement of Computing in Education (AACE).

Braun, V., & Clarke, V. (2006). Using thematic analysis in psychology. *Qualitative Research in Psychology, 3*, 77–101.

Brown, S. E. (2008). Breaking barriers: The pioneering disability students services program at the University of Illinois, 1948–1960. In *The history of discrimination in US education* (pp. 165–192). Palgrave Macmillan.

Buetow, S. (2010). Thematic analysis and its reconceptualization as saliency analysis. *Journal of Health Services Research and Policy, 15*(2), 123–125.

Burgstahler, S. (2020). *Creating inclusive learning opportunities in higher education: A universal design toolkit* (pp. 47–48). Harvard Education Press.

Burgstahler, S., & Crawford, L. (2020). The development of accessibility recommendations for online learning researchers. In S. Burgstahler (Ed.), *Universal design in higher education: Promising practices*. DO-IT, University of Washington. Retrieved from: www.uw.edu/doit/UDHE-promisingpractices/preface.html

Caldwell, B., Cooper, M., Reid, L. G., Vanderheiden, G., Chisholm, W., Slatin, J., & White, J. (2008). Web content accessibility guidelines (WCAG) 2.0. WWW Consortium (W3C), 290, 1–34.

CAST. (2018). *Universal design for learning guidelines version 2.2*. Retrieved from: http://udl-guidelines.cast.org

Crossland, M. D., Starke, S. D., Wolffsohn, J. S., & Webster, A. R. (2019). Benefit of an electronic head-mounted low vision aid. *Ophthalmic & Physiological Optics, 39*(6), 422–431.

Crutchfield, B., & Haugh, J. (2018). Accessibility in the virtual/augmented reality space. *CSUN 2018 Assistive Technology Conference, San Diego, CA, March 22*.

Enoch, J., McDonald, L., Jones, L., Jones, P. R., & Crabb, D. P. (2019). Evaluating whether sight is the most valued sense. *JAMA Ophthalmology, 137*(11), 1317–1320.

Ferdig, R. E., Baumgartner, E., Hartshorne, R., Kaplan-Rakowski, R., & Mouza, C. (2020). *Teaching, technology, and teacher education during the COVID-19 pandemic: Stories from the field*. Association for the Advancement of Computing in Education (AACE). Retrieved from: https://www.learntechlib.org/p/216903/

Ferdig, R. E., Baumgartner, E., Mouza, C., Kaplan-Rakowski, R., & Hartshorne, R. (2021). Editorial: Rapid publishing in a time of COVID-19: How a pandemic might change our academic writing practices. *Contemporary Issues in Technology and Teacher Education, 21*(1).

Hartshorne, R., Baumgartner, E., Kaplan-Rakowski, R., Mouza, C., & Ferdig, R. E. (2020). Special issue editorial: Preservice and inservice professional development during the COVID-19 pandemic. *Journal of Technology and Teacher Education, 28*(2), 137–147. https://www.learntechlib.org/primary/p/216910/

Huber, E., Chang, K., Alvarez, I., Hundle, A., Bridge, H., & Fine, I. (2019). Early blindness shapes cortical representations of auditory frequency within auditory cortex. *Journal of Neuroscience, 39*(26), 5143–5152.

Kaplan-Rakowski, R. (2021). Addressing students' emotional needs during the COVID-19 pandemic: A perspective on text versus video feedback in online environments. *Educational Technology Research and Development, 69*(1), 133–136. https://doi.org/10.1007/s11423-020-09897-9

Kent, M., Ellis, K., Latter, N., & Peaty, G. (2018). The case for captioned lectures in Australian higher education. *TechTrends, 62*(2), 158–165.

King, A. J. (2014). What happens to your hearing if you are born blind? *Brain, 137*(1), 6–8.

Kriemeier, J., & Götzelmann, T. (2020). Two decades of touchable and walkable virtual reality for blind and visually impaired people: A high-level taxonomy. *Multimodal Technologies and Interaction, 4*(4), 79. https://doi.org/10.3390/mti4040079

Kuri, N. P., & Truzzi, O. M. S. (2002). Learning styles of freshmen engineering students. In *Proceedings of the International Conference on Engineering Education (ICEE 2002).*

Lavrakas, P. J. (2008). *Encyclopedia of survey research methods.* Sage Publications.

Lee, D., & Cho, J. (2022). Automatic object detection algorithm-based braille image generation system for the recognition of real-life obstacles for visually impaired people. *Sensors (Basel), 22*(4), 1601, 1–22. Retrieved from:. https://doi.org/10.3390/s22041601

Longhurst, G. J. (2021). Teaching a blind student anatomy during the Covid-19 pandemic. *Anatomical Sciences Education, 14*(5), 586–589.

Lueders, K., Perla, F., Maffit, J., Vasile, E., Jay, N., Kaplan, J., & Hanuschock, W. E., III. (2020). Remote instruction for students who are blind or visually impaired: Experiences of preservice interns. In R. E. Ferdig, E. Baumgartner, R. Hartshorne, R. Kaplan-Rakowski, & C. Mouza (Eds.), *Teaching, technology, and teacher education during the COVID-19 pandemic: Stories from the field.* Association for the Advancement of Computing in Education (AACE).

Mayer, R. E. (2009). *Multimedia learning* (2nd ed.). Cambridge University Press.

McBride, C. R. (2020). *Critical issues in education for students with visual impairments: Access to mathematics and the impact of the Covid-19 pandemic* [Unpublished doctoral dissertation] University of Georgia.

McDonnall, M. C., & Sui, Z. (2019). Employment and unemployment rates of people who are blind or visually impaired: Estimates from multiple sources. *Journal of Visual Impairment & Blindness, 113*(6), 481–492.

Mills, A. J., Durepos, G., & Wiebe, E. (2010). Reflexivity. Encyclopediaof case study research. SAGE Publications, Inc. https://doi.org/10.4135/9781412957397

Morgan, H. (2022). Alleviating the challenges with remote learning during a pandemic. *Education Sciences, 12*(2), 109, 1–12, Retrieved from:. https://doi.org/10.3390/educsci12020109

Mouza, C., Hartshorne, R., Baumgartner, E., & Kaplan-Rakowski, R. (2022). Special issue editorial: A 2025 vision for technology and teacher education. *Journal of Technology and Teacher Education, 30*(2), 107–115.

Paivio, A. (1986). *Mental representations: A dual-coding approach.* Oxford University Press.

Rodríguez, A., Boada, I., & Sbert, M. (2018). An Arduino-based device for visually impaired people to play videogames. *Multimedia Tools and Applications, 77*(15), 19591.

Rose, D. (2000). Universal design for learning. *Journal of Special Education Technology, 15*(3), 45–49.

Russ, S., & Hamidi, F. (2021, April). Online learning accessibility during the COVID-19 pandemic. In *Proceedings of the 18th International Web for All Conference* (pp. 1–7).

Siu, A. F., Sinclair, M., Kovacs, R., Ofek, E., Holz, C., & Cutrell, E. (2020). Virtual reality without vision: A haptic and auditory white cane to navigate complex virtual worlds. In *Proceedings of the 2020 CHI Conference on Human Factors in Computing Systems, Honolulu, HI, April 25–30.*

Sooraj, V. S., Magadum, H. J., & Alluri, L. (2021, December). iTouch–blind assistance smart glove. In *2021 10th International Conference on System Modeling & Advancement in Research Trends (SMART)* (pp. 172–175). IEEE.

Tellis, W. (1997). Introduction to case study. *The Qualitative Report, 3*(2).

U.S. Bureau of Labor Statistics. (2022). *Persons with a disability: Labor force characteristics summary.* Retrieved from: https://bit.ly/2Rt9rgm

WHO. (n.d.). *Assistive technology.* World Health Organization: Health Topics. Retrieved from: https://www.who.int/health-topics/assistive-technology#tab=tab_1

Zhao, Y., Bennett, C. L., Benko, H., Cutrell, E., Holz, C., Morris, M. R., & Sinclair, M. (2018, April). Enabling people with visual impairments to navigate virtual reality with a haptic and auditory cane simulation. In *Proceedings of the 2018 CHI conference on human factors in computing systems* (pp. 1–14).

Meeting in the Metaverse: Language Learners' Insights into the Affordances of Virtual Reality

Tricia Thrasher

Background/Rationale

The COVID-19 pandemic catapulted online instruction forward across all fields of education and highlighted the need to examine how distant learning can be carried out effectively during a time when it was no longer possible to rely on traditional teaching methods. The field of foreign language teaching and learning was particularly impacted by this shift, as a major component of learning a language is being able to practice interpersonal speaking skills face-to-face with others. Although videoconferencing platforms (e.g., *Zoom*) still allowed learners to see each other during the pandemic, the physical distance and disconnectedness between students remained apparent. However, virtual reality (VR) technology, which allows learners to collectively immerse themselves in virtual spaces, could bridge this gap between students who are physically distant and better simulate face-to-face interactions and learning.

Virtual Reality

VR can be divided into two distinct categories: low-immersion VR (e.g., Desktop virtual worlds like Second Life) and high-immersion VR (e.g., head-mounted devices like the Meta Quest 2 headset), with high-immersion VR systems producing a more authentic, fully immersive experience (Kaplan-Rakowski & Gruber, 2019).

T. Thrasher (✉)
Immerse, Inc, Irvine, CA, USA

One major affordance of high-immersion VR is its ability to fully immerse users in a 360° environment that can offer experiential learning (Parmaxi, 2020). This full immersion is critical, as it often leads to a higher sense of telepresence, or the feeling of being inside the virtual environment with others, and ultimately to better learning. Given these affordances and potential, the field of education is expected to experience a 28% growth in VR usage by 2024 (XR Today, 2021), making research that examines how VR can be used for educational purposes imperative (Huang et al., 2021).

VR and Language Learning

In terms of language learning specifically, Computer Assisted Language Learning (CALL) researchers have cited many benefits of VR. These include the ability to provide contextualized, culturally relevant learning by virtually transporting students to different locations (Chien et al., 2019; Huang et al., 2021; Parong et al., 2020) and to create student-centered collaborative interactions (Liaw, 2019; Parmaxi, 2020). Moreover, VR's impact on affective factors has been extensively researched, with studies showing that VR can increase motivation and enjoyment while lowering foreign language anxiety (Gruber & Kaplan-Rakowski, 2020 & 2021; Kaplan-Rakowski & Wojdynski, 2018; Thrasher, 2022; York et al., 2021).

Using VR for language learning has also been found to lead to better learning outcomes. Specifically, it has been shown that VR experiences can help improve vocabulary (Andujar & Buckner, 2019; Chen, 2016; Huang et al., 2021), listening (Chateau et al., 2019), grammar (Chen, 2016; Chien et al., 2019), speaking (Huang et al., 2021; Parmaxi, 2020), and pronunciation skills (Chien et al., 2019; Huang et al., 2021; Thrasher, 2022).

Learners' Perceptions of VR

Given VR's promising potential, it is important to understand whether language learners also perceive VR as beneficial. Researchers have started exploring learners' opinions of this technology, and so far, students have reported enjoying using VR, saying that they find it immersive (Kaplan-Rakowski & Meseberg, 2018; Kaplan-Rakowski & Wojdynski, 2018), interesting (Chatcau et al., 2019; Kaplan-Rakowski & Wojdynski, 2018), fun, and different (York et al., 2021). Moreover, in their study with 30 EFL learners, York et al. (2021) found that students considered communicating in VR to be significantly easier than video calls since they felt physically immersed in the VR environment together. Furthermore, in their 2018 study with 22 EFL learners, Kaplan-Rakowski and Wojdynski (2018) found that VR helped participants focus 100% on the task at hand by minimizing distractions through full immersion.

However, participants have also mentioned the technological challenges that accompany using VR. Specifically, users have noted that VR does not always work well (Huang et al., 2021; Kaplan-Rakowski & Meseberg, 2018; York et al., 2021), which can reduce their sense of presence, motivation, and participation. Participants have also complained about headsets being uncomfortable (Kaplan-Rakowski & Meseberg, 2018; York et al., 2021), poor image quality (York et al., 2021), connection issues (Kaplan-Rakowski & Meseberg, 2018), headaches, tiredness of eyes, and cybersickness (Kaplan-Rakowski & Wojdynski, 2018). Lastly, as VR reduces visual cues (e.g., eye contact) that could be useful when communicating in a second language, it can still be expected that some learners will prefer face-to-face communication where they can see others more easily (York et al., 2021).

This feedback collected thus far from students has been insightful. However, given the rise in popularity of VR and online learning for education after COVID-19, it is imperative that research continues to capture learners' opinions of this technology to ensure that it is being used in a manner that favors students' learning. This study therefore gathered participants' feedback on VR, as well as two other learning environments (*Zoom* and a traditional classroom), with the aim of understanding the benefits and drawbacks of VR for online language learning.

Research Question

This study addressed the following research question: How did learners perceive the VR environment for language learning compared to the traditional face-to-face classroom and *Zoom* in the context of the COVID-19 pandemic?

Method

This qualitative study emerged from a larger mixed-methods project examining how VR benefits foreign language anxiety and, in turn, oral production in French. As part of this project, participants' perceptions of the three learning environments were analyzed in detail through qualitative interview data. Only methods and findings relevant to this data will be presented in the current chapter.

Participants

Thirty-eight intermediate learners of French as a foreign language participated in this study. The participants included ($n = 21$) female students and ($n = 17$) male college students attending a large Midwest university. At the time of data collection, all students were enrolled in a French conversation course that aimed to develop their

Fig. 1 Oculus Go headset

oral proficiency. Data collection was integrated into this course over three semesters: Fall 2020, Spring 2021, and Fall 2021. During their respective semesters, all students were loaned a personal Oculus Go VR headset to use remotely for the duration of the study. Figure 1 shows an image of someone wearing an Oculus Go VR headset.

At the onset of the study, participants completed a language background questionnaire that elicited information about their age, gender, and previous experience using virtual reality. Participants had a mean age of 20.3 years, with 26.32% (10/38) of the participants reporting having some prior experience with VR, but only 7.89% (3/38) having used it specifically for language learning. Participants' background information is presented in Table 1. Pseudonyms are used for all participants.

Training

Before completing any study tasks, participants underwent two 50-minute training sessions where they learned how to use their Oculus Go headset and the VR application used in the study: *vTimeXR*. Specifically, students were taught how to use and care for their headset, how to create their *vTimeXR* account, how to customize their avatar, how to add their classmates, and how to connect with each other and navigate to different destinations in the application. This training was critical, since very few participants had ever used VR, and none had used *vTimeXR*. Participants only completed study activities once they self-reported that they had no further questions pertaining to how to use their headsets or navigate the *vTimeXR* platform. However, participants were allowed to ask questions about their equipment and the platform throughout the semester as they came up.

Table 1 Participant information

Pseudonym	Age	Gender	Previous VR experience
Levi	32	M	None
Selina	26	F	Yes, in previous research study
Scarlett	26	F	None
Rick	25	M	None
Mason	22	M	None
Chris	22	M	None
Mark	21	M	Yes, for gaming
Brody	21	M	Yes, for gaming
Hudson	20	M	Yes, in previous French courses and for gaming
Morgan	20	M	Yes, for gaming
Rohan	20	M	None
Jacob	20	M	None
Iris	20	F	Yes, in previous French courses
Melanie	20	F	None
Lucia	20	F	None
Isabella	20	F	None
Layla	20	F	None
Nick	19	M	Yes, in previous French courses
Justin	19	M	Yes, for gaming
Ethan	19	M	None
Ella	19	F	Yes, for gaming
Jessica	19	F	None
Samantha	19	F	None
Amanda	19	F	None
Talia	19	F	None
Hannah	19	F	None
McKenzie	19	F	None
Katie	19	F	None
Stacey	19	F	None
Violet	19	F	None
Leo	18	M	Yes, for gaming
Eric	18	M	None
Mitchell	18	M	None
Martin	18	M	None
Hashana	18	F	None
Riley	18	F	None
Nicole	18	F	None
Valerie	18	F	None

Study Activities

Participants then worked in groups of three throughout the semester to complete six comparable peer-to-peer interpersonal consensus-building speaking tasks in French created by the researcher and inspired by Mroz (2012). Consensus-building activities are speaking tasks that require students to work collaboratively to come to an agreement or consensus. Typically, students are assigned opposing roles in the conversation so that they must negotiate meaning with their peers. They are therefore effective for language learning since they encourage learners to produce language and play an active role in the conversation.

The tasks created for the current study aligned with themes (e.g., technology, environmental issues, education, etc.) being discussed in the students' course at the time of the study. For each task, students were assigned opposing roles to play in the conversation and received details regarding how their role should handle the respective situations. Students then had to use this information to make an argument in favor of their role. They had 20 minutes to convince each other of their views and to come to an agreement that suited them all. Specific information about the different roles and what students negotiated during each task is presented in Table 2.

Table 2 Overview of consensus-building tasks

Task	Theme	Objective	Role 1	Role 2	Role 3
1	YouTube content creators	Come up with an idea for a new YouTube series for the social media company, *Roxane*, that you work for in Paris	A recently hired new employee	The boss	A long-time employee
2	Science & technology	Come up with an idea for a new technology that could solve a problem in society	PhD student in engineering at the *Université de Sorbonne*	The CEO of the biggest technology developer in Paris	Professor of engineering at the *Université de Sorbonne*
3	Environment	Organize a workshop that will teach locals how to protect the environment	Director of the *City Sustainability Network*	Student majoring in Ecology and Science	Community Volunteer
4	Education	Decide how budget cuts in the school will be handled	Principal	Teacher	Student liaison
5	Social media	Come up with an idea for a new type of social network	Mark Zuckerberg	An established worker at *Meta*	Intern at *Meta*
6	Sports	Work as part of the planning committee for the 2024 Paris Olympic games	President of the planning committee	Vice-President of the planning committee	Treasurer of the planning committee

Participants alternated between completing these tasks in the three different environments over a 12-week period, with 2 weeks between each session. To ensure participants' safety during the COVID-19 pandemic, participants wore masks in the classroom. During *Zoom* activities, participants worked in breakout rooms. To best mirror the classroom and VR activities, participants were instructed to keep their cameras turned on during *Zoom* tasks.

For the VR activities, *vTimeXR* was used. *vTimeXR* is a social VR application that offers over 25 different locations in which users can immerse themselves and converse with up to three friends (i.e., four total users at a time). These locations range from more traditional settings (e.g., a meeting boardroom) to more extravagant contexts (e.g., a space shuttle). To increase presence and immersion, all locations offer fully immersive 360° environments that include visual and audio effects. In this study, three different locations were used: *Terrasse de l'amour* (e.g., a Paris rooftop bar), *The Retreat* (e.g., a Japanese outdoor garden), and *The Boardroom* (e.g., a meeting room in a skyscraper) (see Fig. 2). These locations were chosen because they offered contextually relevant environments that related to the themes of participants' consensus-building activities. For example, *The Retreat*, was chosen for a consensus-building task on sustainability and the environment since it immersed participants in a convincing, naturalesque setting.

Finally, upon completing all activities, participants partook in 15-to-25-minute semi-structured interviews to discuss their experiences and give their opinions of the three learning environments. During these interviews, participants were asked a variety of questions, such as "Did you have a preference for any of the activities and learning environments?", "Do you feel like you were more successful during any of the activities?", "What were your first impressions of working with VR?", "Were you comfortable using the VR technology?", "Did you find the VR environments to be immersive?", and "Were you more at ease or relaxed during any of the activities?" All interviews were audio-recorded for further analyses.

Analysis

Participants' transcribed interviews were coded using inductive thematic analysis, which is "a method for identifying, analyzing, and reporting patterns (themes) within data" (Braun & Clarke, 2006, p. 79). Following Braun and Clarke's (2006) guidelines, five steps were taken to generate themes that were later applied to the data: (1) familiarization with the data, (2) generating initial codes, (3) searching for themes, (4) reviewing themes, and (5) defining and naming themes. Eight themes ultimately emerged from this process (see Table 3). Then, using the qualitative analysis software *MAXQDA*, all interviews were coded independently by the researcher and one research assistant. Upon comparing codes, agreement was found to be 82.92%. Any instances of disagreement were discussed until 100% agreement was reached. A total of 773 codes were applied to the data.

Fig. 2 Terrasse de l'amour, The Retreat, and The Boardroom

Findings

The frequency that each code was applied to participants' interview data is listed in Table 4.

Findings will be presented according to the three learning environments in order to directly compare how participants perceived them differently. Moreover, quotes

Table 3 Qualitative themes

Theme	Definition
Mood	When participants mention being (un)comfortable, at ease, relaxed, anxious, etc., during any point of the study
VR immersiveness & enjoyability	When participants say that VR is fun, enjoyable, entertaining, novel, etc. OR when they talk about the immersiveness of VR
VR usability	When participants mention that VR was easy/hard to use or when they talk about VR's limitations (e.g., Wi-Fi issues, etc.)
Group dynamics	When participants talk about the dynamics of their group or their interactions with the researcher
Perceptions of self/ others	Anything referring to body language, eye contact, being seen by others or seeing others, or being represented by avatars
Zoom	When participants talk about benefits and drawbacks of Zoom
Classroom	When participants talk about benefits and drawbacks of the classroom (e.g., COVID precautions, easier to communicate)
Tasks	When participants talk about the tasks or how they impacted/did not impact their performance

Table 4 Frequency of applied codes

Code	Occurrences ($n = 773$)
Mood	156
VR immersiveness & enjoyability	130
VR usability	128
Group dynamics	96
Perceptions of self/others	96
Zoom	74
Classroom	48
Tasks	45

from participant interviews will be directly given, with the aim of giving voice to the participants and capturing their unique perspectives. Pseudonyms will be used for all participants. Lastly, an emphasis will be placed on learners' perceptions of VR since it was of primary interest in the current study.

Virtual Reality

In general, participants thought that VR offered an immersive, engaging, and low-stress environment that allowed them to interact with their classmates more naturally.

Regarding immersion, participants frequently highlighted how various features of *vTimeXR* (e.g., sound effects, head tracking) contributed to the experience. For example, one participant, Samantha, mentioned:

> It felt really real because you could move around and as you moved around your environment moved around with you. The fact that you could hear the people speaking there too and there was noise, that felt really real (December 1, 2020).

Participants also noted that *vTimeXR*'s detailed, immersive scenes contributed to the task at hand, by giving them ideas for their conversations with their classmates. Specifically, Riley explained: "I felt like it [VR] did add to it [the tasks]. When we were talking about sustainability and stuff like that, I looked at the water and was like 'Oh, water!' It helped me in thinking of ideas" (April 30, 2021).

Finally, participants reported that a benefit of the fully immersive environment was that it reduced outside distractions (e.g., cellphone notifications, other people) and allowed them to better focus on speaking French. One participant, Martin, explained that this was especially important during COVID-19, saying:

> It [VR] just cut out a lot of the distractions […] I think that that really helped cause like doing it on *Zoom*, I'm just like seeing a bunch of other things on my screen right now and then in person it's easy to look away or do something on your phone. So, when you're doing the VR thing, that really helped because I couldn't do anything else. […] I could just focus on the French (November 30, 2021).

Participants also mentioned that *vTimeXR* was fun and engaging. They thought that VR was "game-like" and that being able to virtually visit new locations was exciting. For example, one participant, Nick said that "there was sort of a sense of like 'Oooo, ahh!' like everywhere you look around. It was like 'oh, this is fun!' Like it felt sort of like a game" (December 10, 2020). Another participant, Mason, noted that this made the experience more interactive, saying, "It just felt a lot more interactive […] having to put that thing [headset] on, and then choosing a different location each time" (April 30, 2021). Indeed, this ability to virtually visit different locations was frequently mentioned by participants, as they appreciated being able to "escape" their bedrooms and monotonous *Zoom* calls during the pandemic.

Participants also found that interacting in VR was less stressful than on *Zoom* and in the classroom. This was largely attributed to the use of avatars, which shielded participants from being visually seen by others and reduced visual cues (e.g., eye contact) that can heighten anxiety. One participant, Jessica, discussed how the degree to which she was seen by others in each environment impacted her anxiety, saying:

> In person it's easier to interpret body language and I think it's a little scary. I guess because you have to worry more about your whole body instead of just your top half [like on *Zoom*] or just your voice [like in VR]. In person it's more forced eye contact. You sort of have to look at them. [On] Zoom, you have other space to look at and I feel like its normal generally to not stare at the camera. Or like you can stare at them but you're not actually staring at them. That's the same for VR. Like [in] VR you don't have to care about what you look like generally, cause you're just a character. […] So, like whenever we did the VR things, I generally felt more relaxed […] [it was] easier to just talk and not worry too much about any other part of anything else (November 17, 2020).

It is important to note that participants also found it very natural to interact via avatars, despite them being cartoonish. Indeed, they viewed their classmates' avatars as extensions of themselves and appreciated that they were able to customize their avatars to look like them. One participant, Talia, explained that:

> I liked it because at least, for the most part, they [her group members] customized their avatars to look like themselves. So, I felt like it was better to see that rather than just hearing their voices and staring into space. So, I thought it was a nice addition. Especially cause their hands and mouths moved when they did so it felt more human (April 23, 2021).

Moreover, although students could not physically see each other, they felt that VR interactions were more natural than *Zoom* interactions. This was largely because students could not just turn off their cameras or microphones, which resulted in them having more natural back and forth conversations. For example, Mitchell explained:

> The VR stuff was cool, and I felt like it did improve how immersed I was. It felt like I was in the same room with someone talking to them. […] Definitely it was better than on Zoom in terms of having conversations because there's not a mute button. You can't mute yourself. And then someone talks and says, 'Oh no, you go you go, I'll get back on mute.' (April 26, 2021).

Indeed, the 360° experience that VR affords led to students experiencing a high degree of telepresence and feeling as though they were all in the same shared space together, instead of feeling disconnected on *Zoom*.

Finally, participants had mixed opinions about how easy or difficult it was to use and navigate VR. While many participants found VR easy to use, others highlighted the difficulties of this technology. These mostly centered around the set-up time required. Since students were participating in the VR sessions from home, they had to remember to charge their headsets and connect them to Wi-Fi before class. Despite reminders, students did not consistently do this, which would delay the start of class. Participants contrasted this with *Zoom* which they could easily access with no set-up. Specifically, Mason explained:

> VR – sometimes it's a little finicky to get everything set up. In case you forget to charge it – It can be a problem. […] But like, with my laptop, or I could literally use a phone, iPad, or whatever, or even like a friend's device. But if your headset breaks, or somethings wrong, it's just a lot more, you could lose a lot more points […] in class. Or just, you could miss some time (April 30, 2021).

Zoom

Regarding *Zoom*, participants reported that it was easy to use and convenient, but that they experienced extensive *Zoom* fatigue due to overuse during COVID-19, which negatively impacted their learning.

All participants mentioned that they found *Zoom* easy to use and that they had become accustomed to using it. They also frequently mentioned how *Zoom* classes were convenient since they did not have to spent time physically commuting to class. Lastly, they mentioned one of the many advantages of *Zoom* classes: being able to easily look up vocabulary in French. For example, Riley explained that this affordance of *Zoom* was useful during consensus-building activities, saying that she liked how she could "quickly look up a word on WordReference and keep going" (April 30, 2021). Many participants also mentioned that this was an advantage over VR, where they could not look up vocabulary without removing their headsets.

However, despite these benefits, participants very frequently mentioned *Zoom* fatigue and that this medium for online learning was "exhausting" (Iris, December 9, 2020), "monotonous" (Nicole, April 27, 2021), and "really isolating" (Mark, April 27, 2021). Participants further discussed how this negatively impacted their learning, with Mitchell explaining:

> I don't feel like I'm retaining information at all in pretty much all my classes […] I'm kind of worried about the future and what classes I'm going to need to look back on information from. […] I feel like I'm not learning. I'm just studying for the next test, or exam, or piece of homework, instead of learning (April 26, 2021).

Moreover, participants frequently talked about how their peer interactions were negatively impacted on *Zoom*, because students would turn their cameras and microphones off. One participant, Nick, explained the situation, saying:

> The student-to-student interactions aren't there […] most of the time, students just have their mics off and if we talk to each other we talk in the chat. And if we're not like interacting-interacting, I feel like we don't really get that sort of communication and for me that's really important. When I'm learning a new subject, I talk about it and that's how I get it cemented in my mind (December 10, 2020).

Classroom

Finally, learners felt that interacting in the classroom was natural, and many noted that COVID-19 and remote learning had made them appreciate in-person classes. Participants also frequently mentioned that for language learning specifically, they liked being able to interact with their classmates face-to-face.

Some participants also mentioned that being able to have access to all visual cues was an advantage of in-person learning. For example, Melanie explained that: "I talk with my hands a lot so I think that [being in class] also helps because you can see other body communication" (December 4, 2020). However, for others, being in person was a source of anxiety since students were fully visible to their classmates and had to maintain eye contact. Moreover, students also mentioned that the safety protocols in place for COVID-19 (e.g., masks) made it more difficult to communicate. One participant, Amanda, specifically mentioned:

> Sometimes the masks were a little intimidating. Just trying to talk over those. […] Cause if no one could understand you, it's kind of just frustrating. And then you're just like, you know, 'Never mind I'll stop talking' (November 17, 2020).

Discussion/Implications

This study examined students' perceptions of VR as a language learning environment compared to *Zoom* and a traditional classroom in the context of the COVID-19 pandemic.

Participants' interview data revealed that they enjoyed using VR for their French class, and that they found it to be an engaging, immersive, low-stress, and natural learning environment. This supports previous research which found learners to appreciate VR due to its immersive (Kaplan-Rakowski & Meseberg, 2018; Kaplan-Rakowski & Wojdynski, 2018), interesting (Chateau et al., 2019; Kaplan-Rakowski & Wojdynski, 2018), and fun qualities (Huang et al., 2021; York et al., 2021).

Moreover, aligning with previous research (Kaplan-Rakowski & Meseberg, 2018; Kaplan-Rakowski & Wojdynski, 2018), participants found the VR environments to be highly immersive, which led to them feeling as though they were truly inside the VR spaces. Participants specifically reported that *vTimeXR*'s head tracking and sound effects increased presence, which highlights the importance of considering these types of factors when choosing a VR platform to use with students.

Furthermore, while it could be argued that VR might distract students, the students in the current study reported that the high degree of immersion afforded by VR actually reduced distractions (e.g., notifications) that were present in other environments and allowed them to better focus. This complements previous research that has found that being inside a VR headset can reduce distractions for learners and, in turn, potentially benefit learning by increasing attention (Kaplan-Rakowski & Wojdynski, 2018). This finding is particularly important in the context of COVID-19, when students' attention spans are waning and *Zoom* fatigue and distractions are at an all-time high.

Finally, previous research that has argued that VR can immerse students in a contextually relevant setting was also supported (Chien et al., 2019; Parong et al., 2020). Indeed, participants frequently reported that being in the *vTimeXR* environments helped them think of new ideas and further their discussions in French since the locations related to the task topics.

Aside from immersion, learners also reported that using avatars benefited their learning in two ways. For one, participants reported being less anxious when represented by an avatar, compared to interacting with their classmates on *Zoom* or in person. This was in part because they were not being seen by their peers but also because there was a lack of potentially anxiety-inducing visual cues (e.g., eye contact). Furthermore, the use of avatars also heightened the degree of telepresence that participants experienced. Even though students' avatars were cartoonish, they were realistic enough for students to perceive them as extensions of their peers and feel as though they were immersed in the VR environment together. This benefited their peer-to-peer interactions, with participants reporting that being "together" afforded them more natural back and forth conversations and a better rapport with their classmates. As York et al. (2021) found, students thought that talking to their classmates in VR was more natural and easier than on video chat. This was largely because students could not easily turn off their camera and audio in VR.

Finally, regarding usability, participants' did not mention any discomfort, nausea, or headaches from using the VR equipment. This was surprising, as previous research has consistently found students to report these negative side effects (Kaplan-Rakowski & Meseberg, 2018; Kaplan-Rakowski & Wojdynski, 2018; York et al., 2021). This could be due to the current participants only using VR for short periods of time (i.e., around 30 minutes). They also used a VR application where they were seated instead of one that required them to walk around, since movement in VR can contribute to negative physical side effects. This reiterates the importance of being mindful about application choice and keeping VR sessions short until technology advances. However, for participants, the main drawback of VR was the set-up time that they had to put in before class. This calls attention to one of the difficulties that teachers wanting to integrate VR into their classrooms might encounter. Perhaps, it could be useful to explain to students the benefits of using VR for learning so that they are motivated to overcome these additional hurdles when preparing for class.

Conversely, participants reported that *Zoom* was much more convenient than VR. They frequently mentioned that they had become accustomed to using it and that they enjoyed being able to log into class right before it started without having to commute across campus or set up any equipment. However, aside from this main advantage, participants largely critiqued *Zoom*, saying that it was unengaging, distracting, and that peer-to-peer interactions were lacking. This is critical, as engagement and interaction are both known to foster language learning.

Concerning the classroom, the pandemic made several students appreciate in-person learning more but also presented challenges due to safety measures (e.g., masks). Moreover, for some students, classroom learning was a source of anxiety, since forced eye contact and not being hidden from their peers made them uncomfortable. This is important to note, as foreign language anxiety is detrimental to language learning and achievement (Gruber & Kaplan-Rakowski, 2020 & 2021; Kaplan-Rakowski & Wojdynski, 2018; Thrasher, 2022; York et al., 2021).

The fact that learners responded so differently to VR and *Zoom* suggests that not all online learning environments are made equal and that the affordances of each need to be considered. The current study's findings suggest that VR could offer a more engaging, authentic, and natural way for students to interact when they are unable to be physically together. Moreover, while some of students' opinions were shaped by COVID-19 (e.g., *Zoom* fatigue), other benefits of VR (e.g., lower anxiety) are applicable outside of the context of the pandemic, supporting the idea that VR has a place in language learning and teaching even when online learning is not necessarily imperative. For example, it could be beneficial to supplement an in-person language course with VR sessions that allow learners to further immerse themselves in an authentic, low-risk environment to practice the target language.

Conclusions

This study explored how language learners reacted to VR as a medium of online instruction during COVID-19. It found that learners' perceptions towards this emerging technology were largely positive, and that they felt it benefited their learning. Conversely, learners reported the opposite for *Zoom*, saying that it was unengaging and that they felt disconnected from their classmates. Lastly, although the pandemic led to some students appreciating in-person learning more, students still frequently mentioned that face-to-face learning stoked their language anxiety.

This study further unveiled the advantages of VR. However, the drawbacks of VR (e.g., cost, training time) must be stated. Despite VR becoming more popular for education and many universities investing in headsets (XR Today, 2021), not all teachers may be able to access the number of headsets necessary to use VR with their students. In these cases, teachers could use more affordable options like Google Cardboard that still allow students to view 360° media. Furthermore, teachers hoping to integrate VR into their curriculum must not underestimate the time or importance of training students to properly use the technology. Training is essential, as it reduces student frustration towards VR and helps ensure class time is used effectively. However, when used effectively, this study found that VR can offer a better solution to online learning by engaging students, reducing distractions and anxiety, and helping them build a better rapport with their classmates.

Acknowledgements Special thanks to the organizations of *Duolingo, Language Learning*, and the *National Federation of Modern Language Teachers Associations* for funding support for this research.

References

Andujar, A., & Buckner, J. (2019). The potential of 3D virtual reality (VR) for language learning: An overview. In *15th International Conference Mobile Learning*, Utrecht, The Netherlands.

Braun, V., & Clarke, V. (2006). Using thematic analysis in psychology. *Qualitative Research in Psychology, 3*(2), 77–101. https://doi.org/10.1191/1478088706qp063oa

Chateau, A., Ciekanski, M., Paris, J., & Privas-Bréauté, V. (2019). Adding virtual reality to the University self-access language centre: Brave new world or passing fad? *European Journal of Language Policy, 11*(2), 257–274. https://doi.org/10.3828/ejlp.2019.15

Chen, Y. L. (2016). The effects of virtual reality learning environment on student cognitive and linguistic development. *The Asia-Pacific Education Researcher, 25*(4), 637–646. https://doi.org/10.1007/s40299-016-0293-2

Chien, S. Y., Hwang, G. J., & Jong, S. J. (2019). Effects of peer-assessment within the context of spherical video-based virtual reality on EFL students' English-Speaking performance and learning perceptions. *Computers & Education, 146*(1), 1–17. https://doi.org/10.1016/j.compedu.2019.103751

Gruber, A., & Kaplan-Rakowski, R. (2020). User experience of public speaking practice in virtual reality. In R. Zheng (Ed.), *Cognitive and affective perspectives on immersive technology in education* (pp. 235–249). IGI Global.

Gruber, A., & Kaplan-Rakowski, R. (2021). *The impact of high-immersion virtual reality on foreign language anxiety when speaking in public*. Retrieved from: https://ssrn.com/abstract=3882215

Huang, X., Zou, D., Cheng, G., & Xie, H. (2021). A systematic review of AR and VR enhanced language learning. *Sustainability, 13*(4639), 1–28. https://doi.org/10.3390/su13094639

Kaplan-Rakowski, R., & Gruber, A. (2019). Low-immersion versus high-immersion virtual reality: Definitions, classification, and examples with a foreign language focus. In *Proceedings of the 12th international conference innovation in language learning 2019: Florence* (pp. 554-557). Pixel.

Kaplan-Rakowski, R., & Meseberg, K. (2018). Immersive media and their future. In R. M. Branch et al. (Eds.), *Educational media and technology yearbook* (Vol. 42, pp. 143–153). Springer. https://doi.org/10.1007/978-3-030-27986-8_13

Kaplan-Rakowski, R., & Wojdynski, T. (2018). Students' attitudes toward a high-immersion virtual reality assisted language learning. In P. Taalas, J. Jalkanen, L. Bradley, & S. Thouesny (Eds.), *Future-proof CALL: language learning as exploration and encounters – short papers from EUROCALL 2018* (pp. 124–129). Research-publishing.net. https://files.eric.ed.gov/fulltext/ED590663.pdf

Liaw, M.-L. (2019). EFL learners' intercultural communication in an open social virtual environment. *Educational Technology & Society, 22*(2), 38–55. https://www.j-ets.net/collection/published-issues/22_2

Mroz, A. (2012). *Nature of L2 negotiation and co-construction of meaning in a problem-based virtual learning environment: A mixed methods study.* PhD Thesis, University of Iowa.

Parmaxi, A. (2020). Virtual reality in language learning: a systematic review and implications for research and practice. *Interactive Learning Environments*, 1–13. https://doi.org/10.1080/10494820.2020.1765392

Parong, J., Pollard, K. A., Files, B. T., Oiknine, A. H., Sinatra, A. H., Moss, J. D., Passaro, A., & Khooshabeh, P. (2020). The mediating role of presence differs across types of spatial learning in immersive technologies. *Computers in Human Behavior, 107*(1), 1–10. https://doi.org/10.1016/j.chb.2020.106290

Thrasher, T. (2022). The impact of virtual reality on L2 French learners' language anxiety and oral comprehensibility: An exploratory study. *CALICO Journal, 39*(2), 219–238. https://doi.org/10.1558/cj.42198

XR Today. (2021, June 1). *Virtual reality statistics to know in 2021.* https://www.xrtoday.com/virtual-reality/virtual-reality-statistics-to-know-in-2021/

York, J., Shibata, K., Tokutake, H., & Nakayama, H. (2021). Effect of SCMC on foreign language anxiety and learning experience: A comparison of voice, video, and VR-based oral interaction. *ReCALL, 33*(1), 49–70. https://doi.org/10.1017/S0958344020000154

Part III
Reflections on Reimagining Education in an Evolving Digital Environment

Texas K-12 Teachers Technology Needs Assessment

Shelby Strawn, Michelle Starcher, Frances Mahaffey, Linda Medrano, Taylor Davis, Zohra Samji, Erin Howard, Ron Steiner, Scott Moran, Widad Kinard, Elizabeth Malin, and Tracey Smith

Background/Rationale

The current K-12 education system uses information and communication technologies, ICT, for teaching and learning to develop digital competency while preparing students for living and working in the digital age (Buabeng-Andoh, 2012; Lindqvist, 2019). Rapid advancements in ICT continually alter how individuals interact with digital information, resulting in more connection to information than previous iterations. Thus, ICT influences the job force and education systems to undergo a constant transformation to keep up with changing realities of the twenty-first century (Buabeng-Andoh, 2012; Zhong, 2017). Inevitably, leveraging technology in education is no longer a choice but a requirement for twenty-first century learning (Zhong, 2017). Although research indicates benefits of using ICT in education, ICT still lacks in transforming the current education system holistically (Claro et al., 2017; Sun & Gao, 2019; Wu et al., 2019). The challenge of ICT is further illuminated given unforeseen circumstances that impact American public education, such as the COVID-19 pandemic endured in 2020. The effects of the COVID-19 pandemic on public education were so devastating that it prompted a stringent look at information communication technologies for teaching and learning when teachers and students returned to the classroom.

S. Strawn (✉) · M. Starcher · F. Mahaffey · L. Medrano · T. Davis · Z. Samji · E. Howard
R. Steiner · S. Moran · W. Kinard · E. Malin · T. Smith
University of North Texas, Denton, TX, USA
e-mail: shelbystrawn@my.unt.edu

© The Author(s), under exclusive license to Springer Nature Switzerland AG 2023   197
D. Cockerham et al. (eds.), *Reimagining Education: Studies and Stories for Effective Learning in an Evolving Digital Environment*,
Educational Communications and Technology: Issues and Innovations,
https://doi.org/10.1007/978-3-031-25102-3_18

Understanding the Technology Needs of Teachers

ICT integration typically focuses on the technology rather than on the pedagogical and sociocultural factors that influence education (Claro et al., 2017; Sun & Gao, 2019). To transform education, technology must not only enhance traditional teaching methods (Sun & Gao, 2019) but also be used to alter the ways of teaching (Zhong, 2017). Additionally, teaching "transformation" requires innovation and institutional and pedagogical integration of ICT into teaching and learning (Wu et al., 2019). However, this type of change cannot happen without the support of school leadership.

Executive Issues

Research indicates that ICT integration is successful in some school environments but not in others, primarily because of policy factors such as ICT policy planning, leadership, support, evaluation, and cooperation (Tondeur et al., 2008). School leadership has a critical role in shaping ICT integration in schools (Anderson & Dexter, 2005; Lindqvist, 2019; Machado & Chung, 2015; Sterrett & Richardson, 2019; Sun & Gao, 2019; Whitworth & Chiu, 2015; Wu et al., 2019). Both school leaders' understanding of how ICT impacts the classroom and their vision for implementation and practices greatly impact ICT technology strategies in the classroom (Anderson & Dexter, 2005; Lindqvist, 2019; Machado & Chung, 2015; Sun & Gao, 2019).

Additionally, a study conducted by Tondeur et al. (2008) revealed that the most frequent barrier to ICT integration was access to resources. Of the 53 principals interviewed in the study, only 12 reported the availability of a comprehensive ICT plan with clear goals and a path to achieve the goals. Forty-two principals revealed they either had no plan at all or one only consisting of goals. Additionally, numerous studies stressed the importance of a shared vision and ICT policy for effective ICT integration and use (Buabeng-Andoh, 2012; Claro et al., 2017; Machado & Chung, 2015; Sterrett & Richardson, 2019; Sun & Gao, 2019; Vanderlinde et al., 2012; Whitworth & Chiu, 2015). Differing views of teachers and principals regarding the conditions of implementation make it difficult to evaluate the success or failure of ICT innovation based on current practices (Claro et al., 2017). Likewise, without a shared vision between stakeholders, it can be very difficult to implement new ICT policies and strategies (Claro et al., 2017; Tondeur et al., 2008; Machado & Chung, 2015).

Likewise, Sincar (2013) identified five challenges for technology leadership, including lack of training, resistance from the school community, resources, equity/poverty, and bureaucracy during semi-structured interviews conducted among elementary school in Turkey. Results indicated that schools lacked resources such as technological devices, support, and technical personnel for ICT integration (Sincar,

2013). This study identified that it is especially difficult for schools that serve students of poverty and in underserved communities. These students have minimal opportunities to use technology, and many of the schools do not possess the resources to mitigate the technology gaps. Principals also noted that teachers are often resistant to change and innovation, and there is a lack of in-service training opportunities for both teachers and principals. Many other research studies have noted similar challenges to ICT integration and will be discussed in more detail in the next section.

Access and Instructional Issues

Research indicates that barriers to technology exist in education for school leaders and teachers. Francom (2020) conducted a time-series survey study to investigate how teachers' perceptions of barriers to ICT integration changed over time. The study identified five categories of barriers to technology integration, including access, training and technical support, leadership support, time, and teacher beliefs based on a review of related literature. A three-section quantitative educational technology survey was administered to teachers to understand how their perceptions changed over time, with the first survey taking place 3 years before the second round. The most persistent barrier to technology integration was time.

Furthermore, effective ICT integration requires adequate time for planning quality technology supported learning experiences. It takes time to find, evaluate, and properly use technology tools and resources (Francom, 2020; Machado & Chung, 2015; Whitworth & Chiu, 2015). Time constraints due to high-stakes testing can leave teachers with little time for innovative, learner-centered ICT practices (Francom, 2020; Wu et al., 2019). To increase ICT integration, school leaders need to explore ways to provide teachers with more time to learn how to use technologies and plan for ICT use in instruction (Francom, 2020; Sterrett & Richardson, 2020). When teachers are given time to learn and practice with technology, they are more likely to integrate ICT into their teaching (Buabeng-Andoh, 2012).

In addition to time constraints, a lack of technical assistance can frustrate teachers and discourage the use of ICT in the classroom (Buabeng-Andoh, 2012; Wu et al., 2019). Research shows that effective adoption and integration of ICT depends on the availability and accessibility of resources such as hardware, software, and bandwidth (Buabeng-Andoh, 2012). If students and teachers cannot access ICT resources due to technical difficulties, they cannot use them. However, with sufficient technical support, teachers feel more competent using technology (Inan & Lowther, 2010). School leaders play an important role in providing infrastructure that supports ICT use in the classroom (Anderson & Dexter, 2005).

Moreover, teachers must have access to technology tools and resources to integrate ICT in their classroom instruction (Inan & Lowther, 2010). However, access alone is insufficient for transformative ICT use (Francom, 2020). Effective ICT integration requires changes in traditional teaching practices. High-quality professional development is a key factor for successful ICT integration (Buabeng-Andoh, 2012; Inan & Lowther, 2010; Sterrett & Richardson, 2019; Whitworth & Chiu, 2015). Studies indicate that training and support facilitates a positive interaction even when technology and resource access is lacking (Francom, 2020). However, a study by Machado and Chung (2015) revealed that there is a lack of professional development opportunities available.

Technology Use in the Classroom

How teachers use technology in the classroom is influenced by several factors, including teacher beliefs, professional development, curriculum requirements, and teachers' knowledge and skills related to ICT (O'Neal et al., 2017). McCulloch et al. (2018) analyzed the lesson plans of 43 teachers and found that, while all teachers were able to integrate technology into their instruction, only about one-third utilized technology to support students' understanding of mathematical concepts. Participants in the study primarily used technology as a tool for computation, manipulation, collaboration, assessment, and communication. When integrating technology into the classroom, teachers considered the ability of the technology to support their instructional goals, its ease of use, interactive features, and access and compatibility (McCulloch et al., 2018).

Likewise, George and Sanders (2017) evaluated the 33 technology-based tasks from 8 different subject areas to determine how teachers utilize technology for meaningful learning. They used two criteria, educational impact of technology and type of learning inherent in the pedagogical design, to judge the learning tasks and their potential to promote meaningful learning. Their analysis showed that many of the tasks used technology as a substitute for traditional learning tasks such as answering questions, taking notes, searching for information, or writing essays (George & Sanders, 2017). Of the tasks analyzed, only three tasks utilized ICT to improve the quality of learning. Other research indicates that teachers use technology to enhance traditional teaching methods, such as posting questions or preparing for assessments, rather than to redefine the learning experience (O'Neal et al., 2017).

Process

When schools began closing due to the COVID-19 pandemic in spring of 2020, many teachers found themselves needing to transition to remote learning in just a few days. The rush to find an alternative to in-school classes created an "emergency remote teaching" situation rather than a true "online education" plan (Hodges et al., 2020), which continued into the 2020–2021 academic school year.

To determine the technology needs of teachers in Texas K-12 schools, the Texas Center for Educational Technology at the University of North Texas (UNT) conducted a technology needs assessment of Texas K-12 faculty. The exploratory study asked the following questions:

1. What were the primary challenges that Texas K-12 teachers faced when teaching remotely during the COVID-19 pandemic?
2. What did teachers experience as primary technology needs when teaching remotely during the COVID-19 pandemic?
3. How will teaching experiences and changes during the pandemic impact teachers' future teaching practices?

Data were gathered through a participatory action study involving a series of focus groups in which teachers discussed their teaching experiences and needs during the 2020–2021 school year. The first focus group was composed of 12 UNT graduate students who were also K-12 faculty. Each of these participants then led a similar focus group with other K-12 schoolteachers. Sessions were recorded via Zoom, and transcripts were analyzed by three independent researchers to identify primary themes emerging from each discussion.

The study was approved by the UNT Institutional Review Board. All participants were active, full-time teachers during the 2020–2021 academic year. Collectively, the participants taught multiple age groups and grade levels from kindergarten through 12th grade. The participants represented schools from rural, urban, and suburban school districts with varying socioeconomic levels. Materials included a computer webcam with Internet access. Participants were recruited by UNT's email system to first complete a demographic survey and then participate in a focus group.

Following each focus group, a written verbatim transcription developed via Zoom's transcription service of the group's discussion was saved. Transcripts were coded by three researchers and compared for reliability. The researchers first conducted inductive coding (Thomas, 2006), in which the codes emerged naturally from the raw qualitative data. The inductive coding provided initial insights and uncovered patterns within each of the focus groups. During this process, each researcher read and explored the data for initial highlights and themes, noting patterns through in vivo analyses (Thomas, 2006). Researchers then compared insights and developed an initial codebook that reflected the identified response patterns (Creswell & Plano Clark, 2007). Afterwards, codes were organized into categories and subcategories and collated via a shared Excel document to determine potential themes.

After the initial codebook was created, the researchers met and compared notes to re-analyze the data with the intent to refine and consolidate the themes. Subcategories were rearranged or merged as needed. As themes emerged, responses that represented each theme were included in an Excel codebook.

Findings and Discussion

The respondent group for this survey was 74% female ($n = 73$, of which 54 were female). This correlates well to the published overall percent of female full- and part-time public-school teachers for the 2017–2018 academic year (US Department of Education, 2022), which shows 76% female. Similarly, the "Characteristics of Public School Teachers'" report also shows that 58% of public-school teachers held a postbaccalaureate degree (i.e., a master's, education specialist, or doctor's degree) and that is what our respondent group showed ($n = 73$, of which 43 held a postbaccalaureate degree). By ethnicity, the respondent group was 61% White, 22% Hispanic/Latino, 8% Black, and 5% Asian/Pacific Islander, which indicates more diversity than the nation (which is 79% White, 7% Hispanic/Latino, 6% Black, and 2% Asian/Pacific Islander). The experience level of the respondent group was slightly higher than that of the nation with 27% having more than 20 years of experience while the national figure was 23%.

Just under half of the respondent group taught at the high school level ($n = 73$, of which 35 taught in high school) while most of the remainder taught in elementary school (17) and middle school (13). Over half of the respondent group taught in schools where over half of the students qualified for free or reduced lunch (47 individuals or 64%), with 16 individuals at schools where over 90% of the students qualified. Not all respondents were classroom teachers, but of those who were, approximately one-third (30%) had fewer than 100 students over the course of the school day and, for the period of the survey, 60% of these students were in face-to-face classes. Regarding technology self-efficacy within the respondent group, over 90% expressed that they believed their technology skills to be adequate or that they were confident in their skills. Only 4 (5%) indicated "I have some experience but am not comfortable with new programs and applications."

When asked about the frequency of their use of desktop computers, 42% ($n = 31$) of the respondents said, "I do not have this technology," while over half (53%) said they used a desktop computer daily. Of the 31 who said they do not have access to a desktop computer, all but one indicated that they use a laptop computer daily. The sole respondent who indicated another frequency said they use a laptop more than once a week.

The main goals of this study were to determine the technology needs, challenges, and future directions of teachers in Texas K-12 schools. Results are grouped by question below:

Research Question #1. What were the primary challenges that Texas K-12 teachers faced when teaching remotely during the COVID-19 pandemic?

Most of each focus group's conversations centered on teacher challenges. Seven primary themes emerged from the teacher responses: (1) Learning new digital tools, (2) Administrative support and communication, (3) Connection, (4) Student engagement and accountability, (5) Technology issues, (6) Technology-focused and remote teaching methods, (7) Use of new digital technology tools, and (8) Parental communication. See Table 1 for information and defining quotes for each theme.

Table 1 Primary challenges noted by Texas K-12 teachers

Category	Theme	Defining characteristics	Illuminative examples
Challenges	Learning new digital tools	Teachers and students had new digital tools (both hardware and software) they needed to learn/ varying levels of understanding/gaps in knowledge when both technology skills and content competency were called into question	"I was remembering how traumatic it was at the beginning of the year to start Canvas." "Our 10th graders were already 1-to-1, so they had computers and experience. Other schools did not. We still had to learn how to conduct class on Zoom. The kids didn't know that either. A lot of kids did not learn accountability. It's not ok to be late to class." "Trying to learn all the new programs was overwhelming."
	Administrative support and communication	Administrators were changing rules, procedures, and expectations too frequently for teachers	"There is a difference between an online class versus students at home learning. It was very challenging that it wasn't an online class, where we could say here is the information, now you go do it. Not that teachers didn't want to there was no encouragement and support to do so, there was no encouragement to teach an online course." "School district requirements of instruction, there needs to be at least ten grades in the gradebook, the school did not change policy on what was required. It was just business as usual and here's a Zoom account. They didn't change how grading was done. We were also expected to teach a normal class also with students at home." "Right when we got a routine everything would get changed again." "I know it pushed way too many people over the edge. It was too much, too fast. And honestly, not nearly enough support."

(continued)

Table 1 (continued)

Category	Theme	Defining characteristics	Illuminative examples
	Connecting with students and other teachers	Establishment of relationship between teacher – student and teacher – teachers both virtually and face to face	"Feeling connected with kids [was] hard – relationships were hard, [the students] stopped having cameras on early in year. [It was] hard because relationships and interactions are what keep you going." "We didn't even have in-person kiddos. Couldn't get connected to them because had to be "here." How much can you keep track of how students are staying engaged?" "Being able to connect with kids was almost nonexistent. It's like I have never experienced not knowing how much my kids understood until they turned their project in. I chunk-thought so much more because it helped me understand how much they were getting." "The lack of student interaction affected my teaching and couldn't get their buy-in. The relationship with them didn't provide that buy in to do their work." "They just wouldn't TALK to each other."

(continued)

Table 1 (continued)

Category	Theme	Defining characteristics	Illuminative examples
	Student engagement	Distinct disconnect between students and their interaction with the school as well as overall morale; participants emphasized the difficulty level of engaging students, student collaboration, accountability, academic honesty, and student presence and performance	"[We need to] equip students with the appropriate technology for the schedule that they have or devices that they take I something that will be optimized for the student…a more individualized approach." "Some were using phones, some were using old computers. Students could not afford power cords, etc. Some of the computers were so antiquated, they could not keep up." "The cheating was there on all fronts. We saw straight A students cheat." "It was a bit of a double-edged sword in that yeah, it's good, however, are they doing the practice authentically or are they just looking at the answer and typing the answer in?" "A lot of teachers tried to just deliver in-class instruction online, and it really doesn't work that way and it does just promote cheating." "Are they manipulating us in some form or fashion (pretending to not be able to get online, etc.)? You just never know what someone is experiencing at home. I would not include them as present if they simply said they could not connect." "Was difficult to get students to do anything, even a daily check in." "I would get assignments turned in at random times. Getting all kids together in class was an issue." "I did all this extra work making videos and such and often times the kids still wouldn't do the work."

(continued)

Table 1 (continued)

Category	Theme	Defining characteristics	Illuminative examples
	Technology issues	Students would either use the technology provided, not use it, or not have enough technology available; administration used technology to say the same thing in several different avenues; lack of tech training or guidance from districts; inequal access to technology between the student and teacher groups; technology needs were often not met as reported from various participants	"[I] am a little concerned about kids' addiction to YouTube and Twitter and all of those websites they've used this year. I've never seen this before. Kids are used to being at screen and not paying attention to what we're doing." "Nobody is willing to teach the technology to the teachers." "Inequity. Inequity of what the teachers have in the classrooms. We have different models of promethean boards, some of them you can't even write on anymore. We have teachers who have laptops that are ancient versus teachers that have laptops that are newer." "This year I had to rotate between 3 classrooms. Each classroom had different types of technology." "All the issues with the kids not having internet at home."
	Tech-focused/ Remote teaching methods	New teaching methods to support student learning; teaching methods incorporated social-emotional learning activities and formative check-ins with students, which supported their learning; challenged to ensure remote instruction was presented in a way appropriate to student needs and selecting the right medium or material for the content was difficult; simultaneous remote and face-to-face instruction was the greatest concern	"Personally, [I would] like to see technology culture to change, teachers are not even at a remedial level of technology; it creates a barrier. I would like to see technology education and technology integration. The districts – I don't like the way they handle technology professional development; it is very remedial. There is more to technology than just a computer." "Had to have everything available for the kids. We had to try to get it a week ahead of time." "My biggest challenge was, I guess, converting from paper-based to more electronic-based." "I actually had a student who had a visual disability and I was asked to provide accommodations and they were virtual and I didn't know what to do, besides tell them listen. I had to be descriptive with what I was doing, but that was as far as I could go they have limited visibility and they could only see a little bit."

(continued)

Table 1 (continued)

Category	Theme	Defining characteristics	Illuminative examples
	Use of new digital technology tools	Google Classroom, Peardeck, recorded lessons, Canvas, Blackboard, Jamboards, Launchpad, Bitmoji, Zoom, quick grading, digital notebooks, Desmos, integration of different platforms (Google Classroom vs. Seesaw or Mac/iPads vs. Chromebooks) resulted in problems	I first started off as they were asynchronous and they were doing things at their own pace on their own time if they were online. And then they started incorporating the zoom meetings that were happening simultaneously at class and more of a hybrid approach. "I can teach the software, but the actual things that I'm utilizing within the virtual remote learning – I was incorporating different softwares like Peardeck. I used Nearpod – I'd never used Nearpod before. I became certified – Google certified educator one and two levels – and I had never brought in my professional development so much because I was just not really in the mindset. That Well I already teach technology. I don't need to know any more." "It was a huge learning curve for me. I was still learning things about Canvas at the end of the year. If I would have known this at the beginning of the year, it would have been much more useful." "There's so many apps...being able to pare it down and get all the parents and teachers on the same communication and the same management software [would be good]."
	Parental communication	Communication with parents during remote instruction; using different communication platforms	"[There were] problems with communication with parents, they didn't know we were doing both at the same time." "I really sincerely think the parents listened less to me [during remote instruction] than when I sent a newsletter on a piece of paper or when I went over to the parking lot and talked to them for five minutes." "[with both Google Classroom and Seesaw] I still would have to go back and forth between the two, and so, in terms of using it for parent contact, it ended up just not being very efficient – not very effective."

Learning New Digital Tools

Teachers in many focus groups reported that learning multiple new digital tools simultaneously was a challenge for both them and their students. Likewise, participants noted not only difficulty in understanding some of the tools but also gaps in technology skills and content competency for both teachers and students. "The previous year, we just used Google Classroom. [Canvas] was a large implementation of an LMS (Learning Management System) that people use in college. To get 9th graders to use it, along with a new system for grades in Canvas, was a lot. We also had to turn all of our lessons into electronic format."

Administrative Support and Communication

Multiple participants noted that administrative communication was a major setback during the 2020–2021 school year. Participants described administrators across school districts who continually and frequently changed the rules, procedures, and expectations. The uncertainty and instability resulting from these changes made it difficult for teachers to follow guidelines. Likewise, some participants noted that administrators did not always communicate changes to teachers.

Some school districts required teachers to perform additional duties and had unrealistic expectations for them. Others noted that their school districts were requiring the same level of instruction and grading as any other year. One district gave teachers a pacing guide and assessment schedule, but this was abandoned when most campuses could not keep up with the pacing.

Connecting with Students and Other Teachers

One of the biggest challenges for teachers was the lack of connectedness and relationships with students. Participants noted that maintaining student relationships throughout the year was straining and difficult. "Feeling connected with kids [was] hard – relationships were hard, [the students] stopped having cameras on early in year. [It was] hard because relationships and interactions are what keep you going." Many teachers described having to teach face-to face and virtual learners simultaneously, which disrupted connections with either group of learners. One teacher recalled, "[We] were told would NOT have to teach online and in person at the same time but that's what happened."

Teachers also commented that making connections with students, knowing how students were progressing throughout the year, and spending time with individual students was particularly challenging. When online students did not turn on their cameras or microphones, the inability to see and hear remote students impacted communication and hindered connections. The problem was compounded when a class had too many students to fit on the computer screen.

Student Engagement and Accountability

Teachers frequently commented that virtual students seemed disconnected in their interaction with the school as well as their overall morale. Participants emphasized the difficulty of keeping students engaged in class and collaborating with each other, as well as maintaining student presence and performance. As one teacher commented, "Virtual learners would simply not be present during lessons." Because of remote learner absences, teachers frequently noted the challenge of student accountability for academic honesty and completing assignments, resulting in inaccurate reflection of grades.

Technology

Participants exhibited varying levels and types of challenges with digital technology tools. Teachers debated whether technology would be appropriately used or not, and if they would have enough technology available for students throughout the year. They also noticed differences in administrative use of technology. Many administrators used multiple avenues of digital technology: emails, virtual meetings, text messages, and applications to communicate with teachers, parents, and students alike. "Information would change so frequently and be relayed through different portals that it was difficult to keep up with updates," commented one teacher.

Digital pedagogy was also considered a continuous challenge, as some teachers were more advanced in their technology skills than others. Changing instructional methods to a more technology-based and online format was a setback for some participants. The same challenge was present in student use of technology. Participants mentioned issues with device allocation for students, hotspots, Wi-Fi, and a lack of training or guidance from districts for both teachers and students. Participants across all focus groups discussed that teachers felt they were thrown into the situation of using digital technology they were unskilled in, stating, "if they can't provide us the answers, at least be sympathetic and empathetic and try to help us find a reasonable workaround to help us do our best as teachers." Teachers also mentioned that there was unequal access to technology between certain student and teacher groups. "A lot of our students didn't have devices at home, but not only that they didn't have the utilities to even provide that Internet access, so we were now providing the hotspots providing them the resources to get free Internet."

In addition, technology needs were often not met, or devices lacked needed functions. Many teachers reported using their own funds to purchase personal devices to facilitate learning.

Tech-Focused/Remote Teaching Methods

Some of the teachers interviewed, in one focus group particularly, discussed the ways remote teaching altered their instruction and teaching methods. These teachers reported their use of new teaching methods to support student learning. Converting from instruction traditionally centered on what could be done on paper to digital was a challenge for these teachers, but they recognized that the conversion to remote teaching methods allowed students to participate online when they may not have participated in person. Specific teaching methods mentioned were that of incorporating social-emotional learning activities and using formative check-ins with students, which supported their learning. However, teachers were challenged to ensure remote instruction was presented in a way appropriate to student needs, and teachers lamented that selecting the right medium or material for the content was often difficult. The logistics of simultaneous remote and face-to-face instruction was the greatest concern, making it difficult for teachers to follow-up with remote students while trying to teach the students in the classroom.

Use of New Digital Technology Tools

In all the focus groups, teachers reported the use of new digital technology tools to support student learning. These tools included Google Classroom, Pear Deck, recorded lessons, Canvas, Blackboard, Jamboards, Launchpad, Zoom, quick grading, digital notebooks, Desmos, and other applications. Google and Google Classroom were used by many, and the teachers reported both positive and negative attributes of the platforms. One benefit was that some students were more likely to participate when using chat features. However, the integration of Google apps with other platforms, such as Seesaw or Mac/iPad devices, proved problematic. Most teachers reported the use of multiple learning platforms, and many felt there were too many options which needed to be streamlined.

Although all teachers reported the use of modern technologies for instruction, some teachers and students had little knowledge of technology and were not used to learning platforms such as Google or Seesaw. Some teachers found little support from their campus or district and recruited help from family members (especially older children) or co-teachers. They lamented the fact that, in addition to needing to learn the use of technology for themselves, they were "often put in the position of being tech support for their students and families." They reported frustration that they could not always help students with technology issues, especially remotely.

Some teachers felt there was not enough tech support from either the district or campus levels. They reported that the district tech support teams did not serve students and their parents, leaving teachers to serve as tech support for families. "I got so many things that was supposed to help me, but there was no person to come and help me." Due to the remote learning situation, tech support was often offered via email or by appointment, which was inconvenient. Teachers needed help with setting up remote and in-class devices, and many felt a need for local tech staff to help with room organization for efficient use of technology and for instructional planning. Some teachers did not feel supported by technology staff and thought they were made to feel unintelligent if they had trouble, and others felt guilty for asking for support from overwhelmed technology staff. "We would get instructions and then, if it didn't work, we were too dumb to figure it out and they didn't have time."

Parental Communication

In one focus group, communication with parents was described as especially difficult during remote instruction. The teachers in this group were from two different districts, and each district was using multiple platforms and programs for parent communication. Using different platforms such as Google Classroom and Seesaw at the same time was problematic. In addition, these districts used additional programs such as School Status and Talking Points, which further confused things for teachers. Even when a campus delineated the use of platforms by grade level, teachers who served students across the grade levels felt the frustration of having to learn multiple systems to communicate with parents of different grade students.

Emotions

Challenges led to a variety of emotions among teachers.

Dissatisfaction

Teachers overall reported that they felt "overworked," "unappreciated," and "taken advantage of" during the 2020–2021 school year. As a participant stated, "I know for sure that I couldn't continuously be thrown things at the level that I was this last year and keep on keeping on for a very long time." Some felt forced to implement a new type of technology or system because the district spent money to purchase bulk devices. Teachers also discussed the sheer overwhelming feeling of having multiple responsibilities thrown at them all at once. Teachers also noted a drastic increase in workload with little return benefit. As one teacher noted "I did all this extra work making videos and such and often times the kids still wouldn't do the work," and another, "Planning for online and in person at the same time was double the work and so time consuming."

Stress

Because of the unique circumstances in the 2020–2021 academic year, teachers reported stress as a continuing emotion. Teachers cited they felt ill-prepared with technology that their districts did not have a clear technology implementation plan, or technology expectations were constantly in flux. Some districts implemented technology standards with little to no user training. Many participants stated that effects of stress and loss were still present for them, stating they felt as though their students did not receive the best of their teaching. As one participant commented, "It still weighs on me that I did not contact every single student who was on my class list, let alone every student who wasn't online in the building."

Resilience

Even amidst the challenges and negative emotions, teachers observed both teachers and students display resilience as they remained flexible and patient and continued to collaborate with the instructional team members, students, and administration. Participants discussed how they adapted to new situations, learned to navigate resources, and developed a better platform for collegial collaboration. They found students who excelled in the online learning environment, as they did not feel the pressure of in-person social issues. Overall, teachers started early to explore resources that would be more effective for teaching both virtual and face-to-face students or that might continue to support their teaching after the pandemic.

Research Question #2. What did teachers experience as primary technology needs when teaching remotely during the COVID-19 pandemic?

Teachers identified specific needs that are required to move forward in future school years for more effective teaching and learning outcomes. Needs ranged from hardware logistics, including needing more specific types of technology per teacher rather than a blanket of devices, to time constraints, team collaboration, and support from administration. See Table 2 for details.

Collaboration

Teachers widely discussed their appreciation for their campus-level IT staff, stating that their support was continually offered at an individualized, on-demand level. However, they also mentioned they like to have more proactive collaboration with technology staff members in the future. They wished to have the opportunity for collaboration with similar grade levels and subjects, stating that they felt more creative and productive when collaborating with team members. Participants were generally more open to innovative technologies because of the support they received from their colleagues.

Table 2 Future needs identified by teachers during semi-structured interviews for effective teaching and learning

Category	Theme	Defining characteristics	Illuminative examples
Needs	Collaboration	Student – student collaboration, teacher – student collaboration, teacher – tech team collaboration, teacher – parent collaboration, teacher – administration collaboration	"My campus [tech] person is a rock star, so those of you dedicated to helping us – we love you, you're a rock star!" "We were getting to give advice and guidance, you know, based on our experiences and our readings and things like that to how we wanted. To me, that was a really good because we've been trying to do that, for years, and this was the first year that we really had a seat at the table." "I don't think there's enough of an assessment of where teachers actually are, with their current technology needs and building and providing professional development that supports teachers, where they are not a generalized professional development for everybody." "Maybe we need to educate parents on 'This is what your child is doing; this is what they're learning.' Maybe we can have these parent nights where we can actually teach our parents how to use your technology so that they can reinforce on that learning at home. And if they don't have access to those technologies, I don't see why we can't check out technology. You did it for a whole year, you know, maybe we could do it for a couple of days – and then have parents and guardians and grandparents involved in their students who do learn technology."

(continued)

Table 2 (continued)

Category	Theme	Defining characteristics	Illuminative examples
	District decision-making	Administrative decisions that affected teacher instruction	"They need to consult with us – they need to consult with that fifth grade math teacher, with that secondary Spanish teacher, with the elementary music teacher." "Try to help us find a reasonable work around to help us do our best as teachers." "Why do I have to dig so deep into my pockets? The educators need to be invested in by the district." "We kept having to change and adjust to the failures and therefore having to change our expectations. A lot could have been avoided if we just had been consistent." "All my issues are with money. Games, apps, etc., were an issue. I had to pay each month. Now I need a tech stipend to take care of all apps that kids want to use. Have original Chromebook cart, so need an update on Chromebooks too." "We noticed pretty quickly that we had a wide skill set so if you were doing a webinar Google classroom, for example, you'd have a teacher that was just barely setting it up to a teacher that... wanted to do some more advanced skills. So we very quickly learned that we had to kind of, you know, differentiate that……"
	Technology hardware	Resource allocation for technology for teachers and students	"The thing I would really like is to have a classroom-issued Chromebook…there were several times that a student would either come in and they forgot theirs at home or there was an issue." "I have only two electric plugs in my whole classroom." "The only way I could avoid having skipping audio was to do a hardwire connection, but it means that I was chained to that area of the room, and so all of my materials need to be in that area of the room." "If my computer is not plugged in for longer than three minutes, it will die." "The setting up of the space with regard to all of the other stuff we had to have become a bigger problem than I would have foreseen."
	Time	Time for additional planning and instructional preparations, and training	"By the time that we, I guess, we actually want to use or learn it, it's like 'Well, how are we going to implement now, because we already moved on with our lesson?'"

District Decision-Making

Teachers in all focus groups felt that many decisions made by the district were short-sighted and unrealistic for long-term planning. Teachers were often not consulted prior to decisions that directly influenced their classroom teaching. Many participants did not feel their needs were met or that the district should implement digital pedagogy training that meets the unique needs of each teacher, grade, and subject level. Specifically, participants emphasized that a one-size-fits-all approach is not helpful for individualized teaching methodologies. Specific examples of decision-making that did not fully meet teachers' needs were lack of bandwidth and the placement of immovable technology in the classroom, resulting in hindrances in physical movement for teachers and students. As one teacher noted, "Sometimes we were told to be behind the desk; others we were told not to be. It was contrary to what I had been taught about being in the Power Zone of the classroom." Some participants commented that they would like increased autonomy to change the curriculum's scope and sequence in response to student needs. Teachers also stated that the decision of moving to a device for each student during the school year was successful for some, but unsuccessful for others.

Technology Hardware

Technology hardware was indicated as a specific need for effective teaching in the future. Teachers lacked specific technology items to meet their teaching needs. Logistical issues with using tech in the classrooms abounded, and school-issued technology devices were either not helpful or did not work consistently. Additionally, students would sometimes forget to bring Chromebooks to school, hindering their learning process. A few participants noted that charging Chromebooks or other mobile devices in the classroom while students tried to work was problematic.

Time

Teachers in one focus group described having Mondays to have time to plan and prepare their virtual and face-to-face lessons. Other participants stated that having additional time such as a weekly preparation day would be beneficial for them to prepare material for virtual and in-person instruction. Many participants cited lack of time as a factor that hindered their instructional process during the 2020–2021 school year.

Research Question #3. How will teachers' pandemic experiences impact their future teaching practices?

Participants discussed pandemic teaching strategies and tools that they would like to continue or discontinue in their instructional practices, as well as lessons learned from their experiences teaching during the 2020–2021 school year. Each of these themes is detailed in Table 3.

Aspects of Remote Learning to Continue

Streamlined grading and feedback provided by digital tools were among the highest ranked practices for teachers to continue in the future. Many participants cited the need for additional training on certain types of technology for the years ahead. "We rolled out Canvas with no training." In addition, participants generally agreed that a focus on students' social-emotional learning was a positive aspect of COVID teaching that should be continued.

Aspects of Remote Learning to Discontinue

Most teachers did not like hybrid teaching, wherein face-to-face and remote learners were taught simultaneously. With the introduction of so many new digital tools in the 2020–2021 school year, teachers expressed a desire to streamline their technology use in the future. As one teacher noted, "I will probably keep Google classroom at least some elements of it because I am super organized setting up binders at the beginning of the year is usually a big ordeal. I feel like with Google classroom is so much easier to organize those things, and as well as share my slides with them." Teachers said they want technology use to be "planned and intentional" with some anticipating a change in the teaching culture, requiring an individualized approach for technology that would be appropriate for each subject.

Lessons Learned

Teachers in all focus groups noted that the insights gained from their experiences with teaching during the COVID-19 pandemic would support them in future teaching. The lack of needed technology tools and insufficient training during the 2020–2021 school year led to a desire for a transformed approach to professional development, both regarding and due to technology. Some teachers expressed that they hope to see a change in technology teaching culture, moving from a remedial level of technology understanding to one that is more advanced. "Giving the teachers, a little bit more voice and choice as far as their [professional development] because sometimes what the district thinks they all want to learn is not what they consider effective." They understood that students' use of technology is pervasive, and that teachers need to

Table 3 Teachers' visions of future teaching practices

Category	Theme	Defining characteristics	Illuminative examples
Future/ plans	Aspects of remote learning to continue	Practices to continue for the future of teaching	"A group of us helped to design learning centers and we used the Bitmoji platform, and we embedded the links within it, and we did a center themed for every nine themes throughout the year and I still want to use that in this coming year." "We set up a Bitmoji classroom that we use for all the online lessons for the entire year…we would keep adding things to it – it would change every week – but the setup would be the same" "I like that I could create a Google form and even if it was something they were doing on paper, they could still put their answers in it and it saved me a little time from grading." "Would like training more on assignments. Would love to delve deeper. One at a time. Baby steps." "It got us out of our comfort zone and hopefully we will continue to use those new technologies we learned next year." "[I] loved being able to give immediate feedback." "I really liked that they could do group work, even outside of the classroom that they were still able to communicate with each other and work on projects together."
	Aspects of remote learning to discontinue	Practices to discontinue for the future of teaching	"I'm totally onboard with not doing hybrid thing. I came into [it] on [the] low end of using technology and I fought it for a while. It was eye opening for me to even get onboard. I found a lot of ease as I went. Using more apps, more techs in teaching and in kids' products." "I can't say that I really want to rush anything technology with four-year-olds." [For Spanish class] "I just wish that Google Translate were blocked on these students' devices." "No more Zoom for your girl. I just, I really hate it. I'm just, I like to be up and around in it, so I can actively monitor what you're doing so, yes Zoom is definitely the first thing I'm going to throw in trash."

(continued)

Table 3 (continued)

Category	Theme	Defining characteristics	Illuminative examples
	Lessons learned	Lessons from the school year that will remain with the participant in the future	"'I feel like I need to spend more time…[on] digital citizenship, responsible technology use… it's knowing when to draw the line and what's too much and what is school use and what is personal use and all those kind of things. I think we need to, like, really teach that better. I need to teach that better – from the get go." "I wish I would have known that students were going to be dropping in and out, I would have altered some assignments." "Teachers who were doing things they never though they could do. And were being empowered by that." "So, um, I wish I had known the permanence of the situation, because I think I was in denial, for at least a month or so. I would have developed better systems from the start, like from an accountability standpoint as a teacher in regards to a lot of different metrics whether that's like student engagement to attendance in general." "I was happy to learn I could make connections with students online. The feedback I got was so positive. The breakout rooms…I did that at the beginning. I used that so students could build their own relationships with each other. They were able to connect. A nice surprise was grading. With Canvas, the system does it for me. I would say the chat box was to ease into the school year. When I started using PearDeck, they would interact without having to reveal their identity. They could express a lot. They knew that I genuinely cared about them."

take an active role in guiding that use. "We still need the professional development… it's not just technology you have to have the development with it in tandem and it has to be continuous, it has to be different for different teachers so just like you differentiate for your students, you have to differentiate for teacher."

Teachers also noted that they did not anticipate how many students would be dropping in and out of class throughout the school year due to COVID. If they had known, they would have altered assignments and prepared more pre-recorded lessons. Teachers expressed pride in the way they and their students handled an unprecedented year and showed a newfound regard for the importance of relationships and social-emotional learning. "It was a great learning experience and, overall, we had a great year, you know, students overall were very positive every day and it wasn't anything that I regret going into."

Conclusion

The sudden shift to online learning during the COVID-19 pandemic appears to have exacerbated problems with ICT integration and amplified the negative impact on both teachers and students. Respondents generally felt confident in their own abilities to use technology for personal use, but expressed concerns about broader school issues such as infrastructure and the implementation of technology in the educational setting.

Teachers indicated high utilization of a broad array of technology tools, but were frustrated by outdated hardware, unreliable network and Internet access, and inconsistent support and training. As one English teacher commented, "I need more purposeful technology training instead of a million tools thrown at me all at once." Similarly, an elementary school teacher suggested that there were either "...not enough devices for each student or devices were out of date and didn't work well." This is in line with Machado and Chung (2015), who found a lack of professional development opportunities for teachers.

Respondents expressed concerns that some technology platforms were implemented as short-term remedies (i.e., during the pandemic) but would not be adequate in the long term. As a high school science teacher suggested, "The push for Chromebooks for teachers is disconcerting. They are not as powerful and great as districts make them out to be." Respondents also broached other subjects, including academic dishonesty, student apathy, concerns about student's home environment as it relates to technology, and student burnout, but the broader themes focused on availability, reliability, and accessibility of hardware and bandwidth; training and technical support for teachers and students; more dedicated time to implement and integrate technology in all aspects of education; and the number of different tools provided and with limited or poor training and implementation planning. In line with the finding of Tondeur et al. (2008) that the most frequent barrier to ICT integration is access to resources. The challenges and needs described by participants in this study also reinforce the findings of Francom (2020), Machado and Chung (2015), and Whitworth and Chiu (2015), who all note that effective ICT integration requires adequate time for planning quality technology-supported learning experiences.

However, the sudden move to online learning did not allow administrators or teachers time to reflect and plan before integrating ICT expectations into the school environment. Based on the feedback shared by participants in this study, the time to plan for potential future emergencies is now. The current infusion of technology into all aspects of society emphasizes that the use of technology in education is no longer a choice. Instead, educational technology resources and understanding are essential for educating students to become responsible citizens who can function in the twenty-first century (Zhong, 2017).

The optimism displayed by teachers who participated in the Texas Technology Needs Assessment illuminates their resilience during the challenges encountered during remote teaching. The courage and fortitude these teachers exhibited as they worked to provide quality education for all students not only guides decisions and directions for future educational needs, but also suggests that students can face their educational future with confidence and hope.

References

Anderson, R. E., & Dexter, S. (2005). School technology leadership: An empirical investigation of prevalence and effect. *Educational Administration Quarterly, 41*(1), 49–82.

Buabeng-Andoh, C. (2012). Factors influencing teachers' adoption and integration of information and communication technology into teaching: A review of the literature. *International Journal of Education and Development using Information and Communication Technology, 8*(1), 136–155.

Claro, M., Nussbaum, M., Lopez, X., & Contardo, V. (2017). Differences in views of school principals and teachers regarding technology integration. *Educational Technology & Society, 20*(3), 42–53.

Creswell, J., & Plano Clark, V. (2007). Designing and conducting mixed methods research. Sage. *Organizational Research Methods, 12*(4), 801–804.

Francom, G. M. (2020). Barriers to technology integration: A time-series survey study. *Journal of Research on Technology in Education, 52*(1), 1–16.

George, A., & Sanders, M. (2017). Evaluating the potential of teacher-designed technology-based tasks for meaningful learning: Identifying needs for professional development. *Education and Information Technologies, 22*, 2871–2895.

Hodges, C., Moore, S., Lockee, B., Trust, T., & Bond, A. (2020). The difference between emergency remote teaching and online learning. *Educause Review, 27*.

Inan, F. A., & Lowther, D. L. (2010). Factors affecting technology integration in K-12 classrooms: A path model. *Educational Technology Research and Development, 58*, 137–154.

Lindqvist, M. H. (2019). School leaders' practices for innovative use of digital technologies in schools. *British Journal of Educational Technology, 50*(3), 1226–1240.

Machado, L. J., & Chung, C. J. (2015). Integrating technology: The principals' role and effect. *International Education Studies, 8*(5), 43–53.

McCulloch, A. W., Hollebrands, K., Lee, H., Harrison, T., & Mutlu, A. (2018). Factors that influence secondary mathematics teachers' integration of technology in mathematics lessons. *Computers & Education, 123*, 26–40.

O'Neal, L. J., Gipson, P., & Cotton, S. R. (2017). Elementary school teachers' beliefs about the role of technology in 21st-century teaching and learning. *Computers in the Schools, 34*(3), 192–206.

Sincar, M. (2013). Challenges school principals facing in the context of technology leadership. *Educational Sciences: Theory & Practice, 13*(2), 1273–1284.

Sterrett, W. L., & Richardson, J. W. (2019). The change-ready leadership of technology-savvy superintendents. *Journal of Educational Administration, 57*(3), 227–242.

Sterrett, W., & Richardson, J. W. (2020). Supporting professional development through digital principal leadership. *Journal of Organizational & Educational Leadership, 5*(2), Article 4.

Sun, Y., & Gao, F. (2019). Exploring the roles of school leaders and teachers in a school-wide adoption of flipped classroom: School dynamics and institutional cultures. *British Journal of Educational Technology, 50*(3), 1241–1259.

Thomas, D. R. (2006). A general inductive approach for analyzing qualitative evaluation data. *American Journal of Evaluation, 27*(2), 237–246. https://doi.org/10.1177/1098214005283748

Tondeur, J., van Keer, H., van Braak, J., & Valcke, M. (2008). ICT integration in the classroom: Challenging the potential of a school policy. *Computers & Education, 51*, 212–223.

Vanderlinde, R., van Braak, J., & Dexter, S. (2012). ICT policy planning in a context of curriculum reform: Disentanglement of ICT policy domains and artifacts. *Computers & Education, 58*, 1339–1350.

Whitworth, B. A., & Chiu, J. L. (2015). Professional development and teacher change: The missing leadership link. *Journal of Science Teacher Education, 26*, 121–137.

Wu, B., Yu, X., & Hu, Y. (2019). How does principal e-leadership affect ICT transformation across different school stages in K-12 education: Perspectives from teachers in Shanghai. *British Journal of Educational Technology, 50*(3), 1210–1225.

Zhong, L. (2017). Indicators of digital leadership in the context of K-12 education. *Journal of Educational Technology Development and Exchange, 10*(1), 27–40.

Universal Design for Learning Access: Faculty-Centered Community Design

Chelsey M. Bahlmann Bollinger, Liz Chenevey, Juhong Christie Liu, Jessica Lantz, Dayna Henry, B. J. Bryson, and Raven King

Introduction & Background

How might we create learning spaces that welcome all students to engage in their best efforts of learning whether in the physical classroom or online spaces? Students with diverse racial, gender, and socioeconomic identities, especially in predominantly white institutions, can experience a learning disconnect from the presentation of course materials, language used in a learning environment, and to approaches of learning assessment (Gonzales et al., 2021). During the COVID-19 pandemic, students faced an insurmountable barrier with the sudden pivot to remote learning. They experienced difficulties accessing learning and had to continuously adjust mentally and cognitively to the pandemic life (Carey et al., 2020). These barriers hindered students' attainment of learning objectives while also depriving them of the sense of belonging in the classroom (Zamora et al., 2022).

With the abrupt transition to online learning, inclusivity for all learners through online formats has become unexpectedly and explicitly visible. The needs for Universal Design for Learning (UDL) have increased, which includes factors beyond accommodations, such as learning access to content, with various (or lack of) computer hardware or software, reliance on limited data plans of phones, unevenly distributed network connection, and the ever-growing concerns of disparity in socioeconomic status (Whitacre & Higgins, 2021). Inclusive language used in

C. M. Bahlmann Bollinger (✉) · L. Chenevey · J. C. Liu · J. Lantz · D. Henry · B. J. Bryson · R. King
James Madison University, Harrisonburg, VA, USA
e-mail: bahlmacm@jmu.edu; chenevet@jmu.edu; liujc@jmu.edu; lantzjl@jmu.edu; henryds@jmu.edu; brysonbj@jmu.edu; kingrd@jmu.edu

© The Author(s), under exclusive license to Springer Nature Switzerland AG 2023
D. Cockerham et al. (eds.), *Reimagining Education: Studies and Stories for Effective Learning in an Evolving Digital Environment*, Educational Communications and Technology: Issues and Innovations, https://doi.org/10.1007/978-3-031-25102-3_18

written, verbal, and media formats in both in-person and online classes needs to take intersectionality into consideration.

When students enter a learning environment, their intersecting identities of race, gender, gender expression, ability status, or economic background do not disappear; yet their identities should not impact the classroom experience for them or others. LGBTQ+ and BIPOC students are entitled to learning experiences in which they do not have to constantly translate gender and racial identity or expression. Adelson et al. (2021) propose that societal norms play crucial roles in the sense of belonging perceived by LGBTQ youth. For example, LGBTQ students feel excluded in classrooms when teachers use non inclusive language (Sava et al., 2021). Therefore, inclusive language can heal "identity concealment and rejection anticipation" (Adelson et al., 2021, p. 805). Research indicates students appreciate the use of inclusive language in the classroom (Linley et al., 2016). Writing scholars advocate for the use of the singular *they,* especially when the gender of the person is unknown, or the gender is not relevant to the context, such as with hypothetical characters for a scenario or case study to use in class or on an exam (LaScotte, 2016). Other examples of inclusive language in course materials include:

- Using gender and identity diverse examples that are relevant to your course. Pay attention to whether examples are always cisgender men or straight couples.
- Use general rather than gendered terms such as "children" instead of "boys and girls" and "partner" rather than "husband and wife."
- Use gender neutral titles such as "students" or use the person's full name if you don't know their title (Wyrick, 2021).

In learning environments, it is best to ask students privately (i.e., in office hours or on a survey) about their pronouns and not force everyone to publicly state them (Goldberg et al., 2019; Wyrick, 2021). Given these considerations, faculty may wish to enhance their teaching of discipline-specific content with inclusive language and build positive learning spaces. We argue that Universal Design for Learning (UDL) may proactively provide a set of strategies for inclusive pedagogy that minimizes barriers to learning access (Burgstahler, 2015).

While faculty may strive to produce positive learning spaces, they may also need to overcome challenges and adapt in developing UDL awareness, conceptualization, and action in course redesign by learning new strategies, languages, techniques, and technologies (Lomellini & Lowenthal, 2022; Olivier & Potvin, 2021). There is a need to better understand technology functions for learning access and connect UDL with design, inclusive pedagogy, and selection of technologies across all modalities (Lomellini & Lowenthal, 2022). Facing these challenges, one higher education institution piloted a collaboratively designed professional development opportunity for faculty. This Learning Access through Universal Design (LAUD) initiative formed an in-person and online professional learning community. This chapter will present the stories of the co-design, development, and pilot of this program. The authors also provide recommendations for emerging technologies and instructional design practices related to empowering faculty adoption of UDL in their course design and teaching.

Rationale and Related Literature

UDL & Limitations of UDL

Universal Design (UD) is about principles and practices to minimize barriers for all people in their living, societal, and learning environments. UD promotes an expanded goal to make products, spaces, and interactivity welcoming and useful to groups that are diverse with respect to many dimensions, including gender, race, ethnicity, age, socioeconomic status, ability, veteran status, disability, and learning abilities. UD has more recently emerged as a paradigm to address diversity and equity in the design of a broad range of educational applications, including educational hardware and software, on-site and online instruction, and student services (Burgstahler, 2022).

Universal Design for Learning (UDL) is about access to learning for all learners. These UDL practices are closely related to accessibility accommodations in educational institutions (Lowenthal et al., 2020; Rao & Tanners, 2011). Unlike legal compliance for accommodations, UDL can more broadly and inclusively enable learning access with minimal use of assistive means (Burgstahler, 2015) through three overarching guidelines to provide *multiple means of representation, action, expression, and engagement* (Center for Applied Special Technology, CAST, 2018). While compliance and accommodation have played a significant role in education, UDL, with digital and online alternatives, has gained attention because of its flexibility and equitable reach to more diverse student populations (Burgstahler, 2015).

"A key premise of Universal Design for Learning (UDL) is that a curriculum should include alternatives to make it accessible and applicable to students with different backgrounds, learning preferences, abilities, and disabilities and to minimize the need for assistive technology" (Burgstahler & Cory, 2010, p. 37). Although UDL is not necessarily achieved solely by using technologies, the guiding principles of UDL for generating multiple means of instructional representation, action and expression, and engagement of learning connect the implementation of UDL to technology affordances. The appropriate selection and use of technology can lighten the load of UDL practices (Hitchcock et al., 2002; Rao et al., 2021).

While there is promise in the use of UDL in classrooms, it is not without its limitations. The development of alternatives for various students can be a roadblock for faculty who may be resistant due to lack of clarity in the descriptions and the amount of time required to alter their course design and create intentional alternatives (Lachheb et al., 2021). There is also a misconception that UDL is used solely as an intervention or an accommodation rather than as a method to benefit all (Fornauf & Erickson, 2020).

With varied awareness and education, the process of creating UDL-based content can be a collaboration between instructional design, technology selection and customization, support services, and instructors. UDL practices are usually not a one-shot type of implementation and can evolve along with emerging social, historical, cognitive, and technological changes. There are many factors that can affect the design and implementation of inclusive pedagogy including: alignment with UDL principles, advancement of learning sciences, transformation in educational perceptions, instructors' perspectives, and the evolving dynamics of learners.

Inclusive pedagogy provides a framework that aims to ensure learner accessibility regardless of their backgrounds, focusing on building a sense of belonging for each learner, scaffolding the learning process with respect to each student's unique strengths, and rejecting deficit models of education (Florian & Black-Hawkins, 2011; Sanger, 2020; Spratt & Florian, 2015). While some researchers refer to inclusive pedagogies solely in the context of "special education" and for differently abled learners (Spratt & Florian, 2015), others have expanded its use to include the learning needs of students from varying racial, gendered, and socio-economic contexts (Sanger, 2020). Evidently, educational inequities exist across intersectional contexts, and there is an increasing need to be proactive in engaging with these in our pedagogies; transforming teaching in explicitly socially just ways (Fornauf & Erickson, 2020; Fornauf & Mascio, 2021; Podlucká, 2020; Waitoller & Thorius, 2016). As inclusive pedagogy aims to "shift pedagogical thinking" to an approach that works for *all* learners, as opposed to accommodations added for some (Florian & Black-Hawkins, 2011), there is an opportunity to use this framework in these intersectional contexts. It is here that the authors found value in utilizing these frameworks in tandem, using UDL as the design tool with which to enact a process of inclusive pedagogy that addressed Diversity, Equity, Inclusion, Justice, and Accessibility (DEIJA) in the learning environment.

Faculty Community of Practice

Faculty members teaching in colleges and universities have expertise within their respective discipline and have built experiences in their disciplinary-situated teaching. To update ever-changing pedagogies with societal expectations and changing student populations, however, lifelong learning is needed for faculty members to embrace evolving teaching methods and construct learning environments that promote a sense of belonging for all students.

Adult learning mostly takes place through experiences (Kolb, 2014). Working adults gain concrete experiences in actual contexts, through peer collaborations, and apply learning content with active experimentations. This has been proven in literature and systematic reviews (see, for example, Morris, 2020). Faculty members seeking to gain knowledge on innovative and inclusive teaching practices pursue these passions and paths with experiential learning events such as workshops, which are usually designed to provide new information, how-tos, and hands-on learning (Steinert, 2010). While these workshops can provide a focused topic within an efficient block of time, the one-time experiences may not be contextualized enough for broader application (Steinert, 2010). Increasingly, faculty professional development providers find formal and informal networking and shared resources may flexibly sustain knowledge renewal (Stark & Smith, 2016).

Wenger's community of practice (CoP) (Wenger, 2010) has been adopted to sustain experiential learning for faculty in real-world contexts with proper guidance, mediation, and support through a networked body of shared interest and resources (de Carvalho-Filho et al., 2020; Stark & Smith, 2016). The three major building blocks of a CoP intended to sustain networked learning and development for faculty members in their collective and individual teaching contexts include: (1) a collective understanding of the goal of CoP, joint knowledge base, and building process; (2) mutual engagement and peer learning; and (3) shared repertoire of resources and artifacts (e.g., languages, tips, and tools used to improve teaching). These core building blocks might enable faculty members to apply Universal Design for Learning (UDL) to their courses. Since members in a CoP are building, contributing, and experimenting based on a common goal, we used the following strategies in designing the LAUD project: (1) selecting and convening a core group of members with shared interests based on clearly articulated common goals and identified essentials of the knowledge base; (2) making the starting point doable and flexible so team members can locate where and how to contribute with their respective competencies; (3) communicating with care, intention, and invitation to new ideas, with a central facilitation point to ensure smooth project management from multiple directions (de Carvalho-Filho et al., 2020).

Process

LAUD Project

The Learning Access through Universal Design (LAUD) project in this chapter took place in a large doctoral education university on the east coast of the United States. With the increasing attention to diversity, equity, inclusion, justice, and accessibility (DEIJA) in learning environments, leaders in this university pinpointed a practical lens to making learning accessible to all learners.

After the pandemic forced remote learning, the discrepancy in socio-economic status, racial, gender, and cultural representation equity and related technology availability became more visible (Whitacre & Higgins, 2021). Social justice movements, ignited by historical and continual disenfranchisement and harm, like the murder of George Floyd, drove marginalized populations of students to simultaneously engage in the pursuit of social equity, marching for civic engagement, and fulfillment of academic work. As a result, the LAUD project was initiated in early Summer 2021 with the core goal of incorporating social justice in learning environments for student learning access. Campus DEIJA leaders held meetings with key campus stakeholders and instructional designers to identify the initial steps of embracing DEIJA for teaching and learning activities, resources, and support. With a pilot in one academic college, Universal Design for Learning practices were identified as the entry point to the multi-faceted and multi-dimensional DEIJA implementation (Fig. 1).

Conceptual Framework

The societal attention to DEIJA in learning environments consists of the historical context to build an inclusive learning environment. Ensuring that each learner enters physical and virtual classrooms with a sense of belonging requires systemic transformation through faculty buy-in, adoption, and experimenting with inclusive teaching methods.

This conceptualization of the LAUD initiative took a faculty centered and networked collaborative approach of *learning by doing* in context. The collaborative experiments relied on UDL and inclusive teaching literature and up to date UDL best practices. In a community of practice, informed by practical instructional design principles, the faculty collaboratively designed, developed, piloted, and evaluated a two-phase LAUD initiative with three interactive building blocks (Fig. 1).

Collaborative Design with Rapid Prototyping

The quick turn-around of UDL educative models expects close and efficient collaboration between instructional designers and faculty collaborators who had more experience in DEIJA and related teaching settings. Therefore, collaborative design and development with rapid prototyping were adopted with a module-by-module approach. Rapid prototyping "involves the development of a working model of an instructional product that is used early in a project to assist in the analysis, design, development, and evaluation of an instructional innovation" (Jones & Richey, 2000, p. 63). In the practical context of this project with multiple collaborative constituents, a modified rapid prototyping of design was adopted to optimize the diverse expertise and evolving technology affordances (Fig. 2).

When designing and developing multiple representations of instructional materials, UDL of courses, curriculum, and learning environments can bring attention to issues of technology capabilities, technology infrastructure, interoperability of access to digital content, project management, and workload in generating

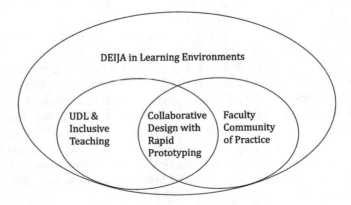

Fig. 1 Learning Access through Universal Design (LAUD) development framework

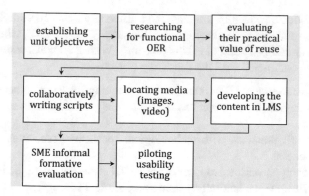

Fig. 2 Collaborative design with rapid prototyping in developing LAUD initiative

accessible formats. While many scholars like Burgstahler advocate that UDL is based on and beyond accessibility, there are practical technological means to comply with and fulfill actionable steps in UDL for instruction. In a recent systematic review and position paper publication, Lowenthal et al. (2020) detailed the auditory and visual content development to optimize UDL. However, instructors getting to use the technologies smoothly will need to learn (or research) these functions, collaborating with instructional designers, and putting the design to development and then teaching. These are no small commitments. After a case study of converting a course to a UDL-complied online course, Rao and Tanners (2011) have concluded that "integrating UD components into online courses can be a time-consuming process" and needs highly coordinated collaborations between teaching faculty, instructional designers, education, and academic technology support.

Given the uncertainty, limited time, and limited resources in the first summer after the pandemic, an initial group composed of faculty members with disciplinary expertise and DEI training in social work, health sciences, and kinesiology, instructional design personnel with working knowledge of UDL, and existing resources from the campus Office of Disability Services (ODS) launched the collaborative design in the early summer of 2021 and targeted for the initial pilot in August 2021. The goal of the initial stage was to present a product of practical value to pilot with teaching faculty in the College of Health and Behavioral Studies (CHBS).

A collaborative design with rapid prototyping approach was adopted to fold analysis, design, development, and formative evaluation within a short time for key objectives. In this initiative, the rapid prototyping included establishing unit objectives, researching for functional open educational resources (OER), evaluating their practical value of reuse, collaboratively writing scripts, locating media, developing institution-specific introduction of the initiative, developing the content in learning management system (LMS), subject matter expert (SME) informal formative evaluation, and usability testing (Fig. 2).

Part of the LAUD initiative consisted of four self-paced asynchronous modules in a learning management system (LMS). The LAUD LMS modules started with a video introduction narrated by speakers of diverse representations of race, gender, discipline, leadership, faculty, students, and university staff. To comply with UDL principles, the video was reviewed by the University Office of Disability Services (ODS) experts and provided closed captioning. With 2 months, three of the four modules were completed with the following objectives:

- Develop awareness of UDL integration in teaching for learning access.
- Apply essential UDL practices to optimize learning access with online alternatives.
- Identify UDL practices with technologies, space, and resources for inclusive learning access.
- Connect campus partners on actionable UDL integration (e.g., learning with online environments, laboratory, fieldwork, clinical settings).
- Build inclusive learning access and a sense of student belonging into teaching practices.

The collaborative rapid prototype design and development approach continued through fall 2021 and early spring of 2022, along with hybrid interactive professional learning community presentations, explorations, and consultations. These resulted in four modules co-developed in the LMS (Table 1).

To assist faculty to be able to apply UDL in their teaching, the team also co-designed and developed four, 2-hour synchronous hybrid professional learning community interactive sessions in fall 2021 and spring 2022 (Table 2). These sessions received in-depth questions from faculty participants. The instructional designers provided customized consultations as follow-up. These questions and consultations also became grounding evidence for future development and revision of the LAUD Initiative.

Table 1 Learning Access through Universal Design (LAUD) initiative asynchronous content structure

Asynchronous modules
Welcome Video and Introduction to Learning Objectives of the Initiative
Module 1 – UDL Principles, Importance, and Examples
Module 2 – UDL Essentials for Course Syllabi
Module 3 – UDL Basics for Class Climate
Module 4 – UDL Essentials for Learning Assessment

Table 2 LAUD initiative hybrid interactive sessions

Hybrid sessions
Advancing UDL I: Making the Semester Easier through Learning Access Considerations (Fall 2021)
Advancing UDL II: Making Exams Accessible to ALL Students (Fall 2021)
Advancing UDL III: Fun Tools for UDL checking (Spring 2022)
Advancing UDL IV: UDL for Digital Presentations (Spring 2022)

Collaborative Reflections/Cases/Stories

This CoP in asynchronous and hybrid modalities supported faculty with existing skill sets related to UDL, ranging from educators with high levels of expertise on UDL to novices who were motivated to begin their professional journey towards creating more equitable and inclusive learning environments for their students. This range of expertise was also present in the faculty who developed and facilitated the learning. The programming was collaboratively developed by pairs or small groups of faculty within the CoP and offered in a variety of formats, ranging from synchronous presentation and discussion-based workshops in a hybrid format, self-paced asynchronous learning modules, and one-on-one and small group consultations. Each mode of training was designed with care and attention to the needs of the community, with the goal of collective learning in a supportive and responsive environment. This section includes reflections and stories from the development of various programming elements in the CoP.

Inclusive Design with Interoperabilty

Inclusive design needs to take into consideration of UDL affordances offered by technology interoperabilty. The collaborators of this project gradually realized this through the development of modules. For instance, faculty leaders in the community collaboratively developed a self-paced asynchronous module in the learning management system focused on comprehensive assessment strategies of "UDL-oriented Learning Assessment."

The process of developing the module began by collaboratively creating an outline for content. The module content was sourced from previous workshops and resources related to learning assessment, current research on UDL and assessment, and practical strategies provided by team members. In the writing, team members first had discussions about similar cases and provided companion solutions, such as proper use of rubrics. At the initial stage, the authors split up the topics for writing, while also planning interactive elements and media which were added later. The authors worked together to develop a writing style that was conversational and less technical to aid participants in understanding the dense content. Once the script was formed, other colleagues created the interactive elements using h5p.com and edited the content to the LMS course. H5P stands for HTML5 interactive objects, which allows a creator to develop interactive presentations, videos, quizzes, or games without using HTML5 codes (h5p.org). Extensive time was then spent with usability testing to ensure each element in the module was fully accessible before sharing it with the CoP. One caveat in developing this module was the disconnect between accessibility checking of LMS-default layout and external content embedded in LMS.

We realized that the designed interactivity could not be easily realized into the LMS as they were written. And using a third-party plug-in to embed the content was not readable by the default LMS screen reader. Therefore, the instructional media developer and one of the senior instructional designers redesigned the interactivity according to the LMS affordance and conducted substantial technical research to hand-code the HTML behind the WYSIWYG (What You See Is What You Get) LMS pages. These trade-offs took time but generated UD-friendly content.

Collaborative Media Development

When learners access the "Learning Access Through Universal Design" (LAUD) asynchronous content, the page that welcomes them is a professionally produced and edited video introducing the value of implementing UDL for student learning. The video showcases 11 members with diverse representations of the campus community, including administrators, faculty, and students, with diverse and intersectional identities. They share or reflect on personal stories and have hopes for a more inclusive campus. This video project included the coordination of speakers, script writing, planning and production of the video, as well as post-production (see Table 3).

This video, along with most of the 2021 LAUD asynchronous modules, was created during the summer, when many faculty and stakeholders were not on contract and students were not on campus. The LAUD initiative leaders worked diligently to schedule the video interviews, which involved finding people willing and able to come on campus during the second summer impacted by the pandemic, as well as busy administrator schedules. This logistical challenge was solved by team collaboration and advocacy across campus, including faculty members from two major colleges, the key departments from Libraries, Instructional Design (ID) for asynchronous site design and development, Media Production Services (MPS) for planning and production, and Communication and Outreach for editing the script. MPS provided the resources and capacity to film and edit the video. Once the video was ready to be shared on the LAUD LMS course, the leaders collaborated on editing and proofreading a transcript file and enabling accurate closed captioning for accessibility.

Table 3 Collaborative media development process

Pre-production	Project leaders reached out to MPS for video production.
	Project leaders determined the purpose and composition of the video.
	Project leaders identified diverse campus representations.
	Scripts were collaboratively written and revised for publicity.
	MPS scheduled participants to attend filming sessions in the Studio.
Production	Participants attended filming sessions and made use of teleprompter to record their personal stories and hopes.
Post-production	MPS and ID edited the composition of the video and published it to LMS.
	MPS and ID edited transcript files to ensure accurate closed captioning.
	ID published video and embedded into the LAUD LMS course.

Supporting Hybrid Workshops with Consultations

As part of larger college-wide DEIJA initiatives, the College of Health and Behavioral Studies instituted a professional learning community for faculty and staff to learn about and engage with issues of diversity, equity, and inclusion. Sessions were scheduled across the academic year and members of the college were expected to attend three to fulfill DEI professional development credits. This initiative provided an opportunity for the LAUD project to tap into an existing structure to provide hybrid sessions on UDL and inclusive pedagogies where participants could dive deeper into the content presented in the LMS course. We designed and developed four course design and UDL techniques sessions, offered in a hybrid format, addressing various UDL topics (Table 2). Colleagues from multiple disciplinary areas collaboratively developed and presented the workshops. Each presenter developed the pieces they felt most confident in sharing, therefore reducing the individual workload with the support of expert colleagues. Presenters worked asynchronously to develop the agenda, content, and slides, which were presented in a hybrid modality to support equity and inclusivity for participants. These hybrid sessions were scaffolded according to the asynchronous content to "advance UDL." After the sessions, presenters followed up with participants to provide answers to questions that needed more research before answering or offer individual consultation.

Throughout the CoP, faculty leaders provided consultations for members of the community who desired focused follow-up support from their colleagues with expertise in a one-on-one or small group setting. These consultation requests commonly arose from specific and in-depth questions asked during the hybrid programming. For example, there was a concern for captions being distracting on a digital presentation within a Zoom meeting. The instructional designers followed up with literature and best practices to explain how to effectively use captioning.

Discussion and Implications

UDL practices can evolve along with emerging social, historical, cognitive, and technological changes and updates. Factors to consider include alignment of UDL principles, advancement of learning sciences, systematic transformation in educational perceptions, instructors' perspectives, and the evolving dynamics of learners.

Historic Transitions

The pandemic introduced a requirement for instructional technology skills for everyone involved in teaching, educating, and supporting instruction and learning. How did this fully online mode shift the views of UDL with online and in-person teaching and learning activities? For example, Zoom could be set to automatically record a virtual class, which could meet the needs of multiple formats of the course presentations and after-class access to course content. However, there were fairness and ethical concerns when sharing these recordings. The live transcription function of Zoom could facilitate the search for time stamped excerpts of video clips. However, the preservation of these accessible recordings increased the cloud storage quota and cost for the subscribing institution. Some campus or college DEIJA initiatives recognizing faculty efforts in actionable strategies such as UDL also set good examples of investment in faculty development to make learning environments inclusive. The evolving phases of module-by-module collaborative design showed faculty how UDL may require up-front investment of time but pays off. The flexibility of the asynchronous LAUD LMS site means it can be accessed by faculty when it is convenient for them. The availability of consultations also provided customized "on-demand" help.

Simplicity as Key

Multiple modalities of access to learning required close and intense collaboration between instructors, instructional designers, and technology support. One course can easily create a substantial amount of workload (Rao & Tanners, 2011). With rising accessible tools like Zoom recording transcript reuse, Canvas Immersive Reader, and UDL course site in LMS, an intentionally designed template and workflow with companion job aids can ease the process. For instance, to ensure that the LAUD asynchronous self-paced course was accessible, the design team had multiple cycles of reviewing the selected video for captioning, adding alt text for images, conducting accessibility checking, and making the navigation of the segment usable and user friendly on standard computer monitors and mobile device screens.

UDL for Learning Access

The awareness to teach faculty about existing UDL features in physical and virtual learning spaces is critical for implementation. For example, presenting an instructional session with expository images can reach all students when meaningful alt text is built into the presentations and with the right color contrast. Sharing the presentation with students with alternative online options ahead of and after class sessions will ensure accessibility for all students. After the presentation is generated, it can be reused in subsequent semesters. Faculty developers, instructional designers, campus resources, and technical support, as well as valuing this work in tenure/promotion guidelines, can escalate these UDL updates.

Conclusions

This chapter reflects the basic steps of piloting a UD initiative to not only raise awareness of the impact that UDL can have on an inclusive learning environment but also equip faculty with methods, tools, and resources to enable inclusive learning experiences for students. Using a collaborative faculty-centered design, development, and implementation, the voices, expertise, and experiences of faculty collaborators from multiple disciplines were evidenced in selecting pragmatic UDL-driven pedagogical approaches and tools. While still in its initial stage of development, the stories and cases from the project have revealed that clearly identifying goals and objectives for this type of interdisciplinary integration is the key to project management, design, development, and connection with various campus stakeholders. These initial inclusive steps provided a community of diverse identities to co-build a socially just learning environment in the larger societal context, raised awareness of faculty to build day-to-day teaching practices with UDL considerations, and facilitated the inclusion building with multiple means, representations, and methods. The combination of asynchronous self-paced training, interactive synchronous hybrid professional learning community, and follow-up consultations was supported with evaluations and leadership support as the project continues to evolve to newer phases. Implications are also valuable to cross-unit and interdisciplinary collaborations, as well as integration of system-wide technologies at evaluating their accessibility features and interoperability.

Acknowledgements The authors acknowledge the support from James Madison University, and the sponsorship from Online Virginia Network (OVN).

References

Adelson, S. L., Reid, G., Miller, A. M., & Sandfort, T. G. (2021). Health justice for LGBT youths: Combining public health and human rights. *Journal of the American Academy of Child and Adolescent Psychiatry, 60*(7), 804–807. https://doi.org/10.1016/j.jaac.2021.02.021

Burgstahler, S., & Cory, R. (2010). *Universal design in higher education: From principles to practice*. Harvard Education Press.

Burgstahler, S. (2015). Preface. In S. Burgstahler (Ed.), *Universal design in higher education: Promising practices*. University of Washington. www.uw.edu/doit/UDHE-promisingpractices/preface.html.

Burgstahler, S. (2022). *Universal design as a framework for diversity, equity, and inclusion initiatives in higher education*. https://www.washington.edu/doit/universal-design-framework-diversity-equity-and-inclusion-initiatives-higher-education

Carey, L. B., Sadera, W. A., & Cai, Q. (2020). Creating a community of practice for educators forced to transition to remote teaching. In R. E. Ferdig, E. Baumgartner, R. Hartshorne, R. Kaplan-Rakowski, & C. Mouza (Eds.), *Teaching, technology, and teacher education during the COVID-19 pandemic: Stories from the field* (pp. 251–256). Association for the Advancement of Computing in Education (AACE).

Center for Applied Special Technology. (2018). *Universal design for learning guidelines version 2.2.* UDL Guidelines. http://udlguidelines.cast.org

de Carvalho-Filho, M. A., Tio, R. A., & Steinert, Y. (2020). Twelve tips for implementing a community of practice for faculty development. *Medical Teacher, 42*(2), 143–149. https://doi.org/1 0.1080/0142159X.2018.1552782

Florian, L., & Black-Hawkins, K. (2011). Exploring inclusive pedagogy. *British Educational Research Journal, 37*(5), 813–828. https://doi.org/10.1080/01411926.2010.501096

Fornauf, B. S., & Erickson, J. D. (2020). Toward an inclusive pedagogy through universal design for learning in higher education: A review of the literature. *Journal of Postsecondary Education and Disability, 33*(2), 183–199. https://files.eric.ed.gov/fulltext/EJ1273677.pdf

Fornauf, B. S., & Mascio, B. (2021). Extending DisCrit: A case of universal design for learning and equity in a rural teacher residency. *Race Ethnicity and Education, 24*(5), 671–686. https://doi.org/10.1080/13613324.2021.1918409

Goldberg, A. E., Beemyn, G., & Smith, J. Z. (2019). What is needed, what is valued: Trans students' perspectives on trans-inclusive policies and practices in higher education. *Journal of Educational & Psychological Consultation, 29*(1), 27–67. https://doi.org/10.1080/1047441 2.2018.1480376

Gonzales, E., Gordon, S., Whetung, C., Connaught, G., Collazo, J., & Hinton, J. (2021). Acknowledging systemic discrimination in the context of a pandemic: Advancing an anti-racist and anti-ageist movement. *Journal of Gerontological Social Work, 64*(3), 223–237. https://doi.org/10.1080/01634372.2020.1870604

Hitchcock, C., Meyer, A., Rose, D., & Jackson, R. (2002). Providing new access to the general curriculum: Universal design for learning. *Teaching Exceptional Children, 35*(2), 8–17. https://doi.org/10.1177/004005990203500201

Jones, T. S., & Richey, R. C. (2000). Rapid prototyping methodology in action: A developmental study. *Educational Technology Research and Development, 48*(2), 63–80. https://doi.org/10.1007/BF02313401

Kolb, D. A. (2014). *Experiential learning: Experience as the source of learning and development.* FT Press.

Lachheb, A., Abramenka-Lachheb, V., & Huber, L. (2021). Challenges and opportunities in adhering to UDL principles to design online courses. *The Journal of Applied Instructional Design, 10*(1) https://edtechbooks.org/jaid:10_1/challenges_and_oppor

LaScotte, D. K. (2016). Singular they: An empirical study of generic pronoun use. *American Speech, 91*(1), 62–80. https://doi.org/10.1215/00031283-3509469

Linley, J. L., Nguyen, D., Brazelton, G. B., Becker, B., Renn, K., & Woodford, M. (2016). Faculty as sources of support for LGBTQ college students. *College Teaching, 64*(2), 55–63. https://doi.org/10.1080/87567555.2015.1078275

Lomellini, A., & Lowenthal, P. R. (2022). Inclusive online courses: Universal design for learning strategies that impact faculty buy-in. In J. E. Stefaniak & R. M. Reese (Eds.), *The instructional design trainer's guide* (pp. 101–111). Routledge.

Lowenthal, P. R., Humphrey, M., Conley, Q., Dunlap, J. C., Greear, K., Lowenthal, A., & Giacumo, L. A. (2020). Creating accessible and inclusive online learning: Moving beyond compliance and broadening the discussion. *Quarterly Review of Distance Education, 21*(2), 1–21. https://www.infoagepub.com/quarterly-review-of-distance-education.html

Morris, T. H. (2020). Experiential learning–a systematic review and revision of Kolb's model. *Interactive Learning Environments, 28*(8), 1064–1077. https://doi.org/10.1080/1049482 0.2019.1570279

Olivier, E., & Potvin, M. C. (2021). Faculty development: Reaching every college student with universal design for learning. *Journal of Formative Design in Learning, 5*(2), 106–115. https://doi.org/10.1007/s41686-021-00061-x

Podlucká, D. (2020). Transformative anti-ableist pedagogy for social justice: Charting a critical agenda for inclusive education. *Outlines: Critical Practice Studies, 21*(1), 69–97. https://doi.org/10.7146/ocps.v21i1.118234

Rao, K., & Tanners, A. (2011). Curb cuts in cyberspace: Universal instructional design for online courses. *Journal of Postsecondary Education and Disability, 24*(3), 211–229. https://files.eric.ed.gov/fulltext/EJ966125.pdf

Rao, K., Torres, C., & Smith, S. J. (2021). Digital tools and UDL-based instructional strategies to support students with disabilities online. *Journal of Special Education Technology, 36*(2), 105–112. https://doi.org/10.3390/su14106177

Sanger, C. S. (2020). Inclusive pedagogy and universal design approaches for diverse learning environments. In C. S. Sanger & N. W. Gleason (Eds.), *Diversity and inclusion in global higher education* (pp. 31–71). Palgrave Macmillan. https://doi.org/10.1007/978-981-15-1628-3_2

Sava, L. M., Earnshaw, V. A., Menino, D. D., Perrotti, J., & Reisner, S. L. (2021). LGBTQ student health: A mixed-methods study of unmet needs in Massachusetts schools. *Journal of School Health, 91*(11), 894–905. https://doi.org/10.1111/josh.13082

Spratt, J., & Florian, L. (2015). Inclusive pedagogy: From learning to action. Supporting each individual in the context of 'everybody'. *Teaching and Teacher Education, 49*, 89–96. https://doi.org/10.1016/j.tate.2015.03.006

Stark, A. M., & Smith, G. A. (2016). Communities of practice as agents of future faculty development. *The Journal of Faculty Development, 30*(2), 59–67. https://www.magnapubs.com/product/leadership/faculty-support/journal-of-faculty-development/

Steinert, Y. (2010). Faculty development: From workshops to communities of practice. *Medical Teacher, 32*(5), 425–428. https://doi.org/10.3109/01421591003677897

Waitoller, F. R., & Thorius, K. A. (2016). Cross-pollinating culturally sustaining pedagogy and universal design for learning: Toward an inclusive pedagogy that accounts for dis/ability. *Harvard Educational Review, 86*, 366–389. https://doi.org/10.17763/1943-5045-86.3.366

Wenger, E. (2010). Communities of practice and social learning systems: The career of a concept. In C. Blackmore (Ed.), *Social learning systems and communities of practice* (pp. 179–198). Springer. https://doi.org/10.1007/978-1-84996-133-2_11

Whitacre, B., & Higgins, A. (2021). Do hotspots improve student performance? Evidence from a small-scale randomized controlled trial. *First Monday, 26*(7). https://doi.org/10.5210/fm.v26i7.11467

Wyrick, A. J. (2021). Contemporary issues in terminology: Using gender-inclusive language to create affirming spaces. In M. E. Kite, K. A. Case, & W. R. Williams (Eds.), *Navigating difficult moments in teaching diversity and social justice* (pp. 179–194). American Psychological Association. https://doi.org/10.1037/0000216-013

Zamora, A. N., August, E., Fossee, E., & Anderson, O. S. (2022). Impact of transitioning to remote learning on student learning interactions and sense of belonging among public health graduate students. *Pedagogy in Health Promotion*. Advance Online Publication. https://doi.org/10.1177/23733799221101539

Game-Based Learning Design Optimized for Cognitive Load

Anita Knox

Introduction

There has been a growing interest in the use of technology for learning. It is affordable and makes education accessible beyond the walls of a traditional classroom. This is logical since technological advancements change the way we live, work, and experience entertainment. This technology that has infiltrated our daily lives should and does change the way that we learn (Shaffer et al., 2005). Technology continues to evolve and offer innovative opportunities for educational use, requiring educators to rethink and innovate the instructional design strategy.

Game-based learning exemplifies the influence current technology has on learning. Personal computer processing power, affordable high-speed Internet, and an array of affordable development tools offer the ability to marry the enjoyment of games with pedagogical outcomes. Games can be created as easily as dragging and dropping audio, visuals, animations, and interactive elements, no longer requiring expensive outsourcing. This brings up the need to take a closer look at how game mechanics and design can influence the learning experience. More specifically, how information is processed during gameplay, and how this can be used to design better learning. Cohesive integration of game components and learning outcomes has the potential to foster learning; however, poor design can increase cognitive load and do more harm than good (Huang, 2011; Lee et al., 2020; Qian & Clark, 2016).

In general, learning with technology can strain the working memory (Sweller, 2020). Just like other digital mediums, the visual, audio, and interactions in gameplay might succeed in motivation; however, it may also overload the working

A. Knox (✉)
University of North Texas, Denton, TX, USA
e-mail: AnitaKnox@my.unt.edu

memory, which impedes learning (Huang, 2011). Currently, the small body of research lacks in showing how game-based learning affects cognitive load. Further study is needed to understand the impact and identify efficient design techniques (Chang et al., 2017; Huang, 2011). Even with this gap in research, it is proposed that game-based learning can minimize cognitive load. The logic behind this is that game design aligns with Sweller's (2020) principles for optimal design in educational technology. These principles included worked examples, split-attention, modality, transient, redundancy, expertise reversal and element interactivity, and working memory depletion (Sweller, 2020).

This chapter will first look at game-based learning, investigate cognitive load theory, and then discuss how game mechanics and design align with the principles outlined by Sweller (2020).

Game-Based Learning

Game-based learning is the combination of gameplay and learning theory to enhance the overall learning experience (Roodt & Ryklief, 2019). More specifically, educational computer games integrate the interactive components, challenging activities, and clear goals of gameplay with pedagogical outcomes (Chang et al., 2017). Mundane, challenging, or even well-received educational content can leverage the engaging storyline and competitive activities that make video games so popular. Game-based learning may include a two- or three-dimensional space that will engage learners and motivate a high level of interaction (Chang et al., 2017). Game mechanics can be adapted to teach specific subjects (Chang et al., 2017), as well as provide real-world experiences (Schrader & Bastiaens, 2012).

Activities experienced in a game environment can influence knowledge acquisition, skill development, social interaction, collaborative thinking, and encourage problem-solving (Qian & Clark, 2016; Shaffer et al., 2005; Yang, 2012). Demonstrated benefits of video gameplay, like improved working memory, can be harnessed for learning (Lee et al., 2020; Mitre-Hernandez et al., 2021). In addition, game-based learning can improve flow, or the ability to concentrate without disruption from outside distractions (Chang et al., 2017).

Cognitive Load

When information is taken in, it is processed in the working memory and transferred to long-term memory for storage. Over time, this information becomes part of a large repository of domain-specific information, which is how expert skills are developed (Sweller, 2020). Although there are capacity limits on novel information, there are no capacity limits on domain-specific information, since it is processed differently (Sweller, 2020). When this information is needed, it transfers back to the working memory for use (Sweller, 2020). The working memory is sensitive to complex information which influences the ability to transfer and achieve that long-term storage (Sweller, 2016). Cognitive load can happen when the amount of information taken in exceeds an individual's working memory capacity (Chang et al., 2017; Huang, 2011).

Cognitive load research is still evolving, progressing from generalizations to more specific categorizations of intrinsic, extraneous, and germane. Intrinsic load refers to demands placed when completing a task and could vary based on the actual task and the learner's experience level with that task (Lee et al., 2020). The extraneous load comes from the physical learning environment or distractions in the environment that split attention between learning materials and an unrelated source (Lee et al., 2020). In addition, unnecessary elements in learning materials are distracting and increase the extraneous cognitive load (Chang et al., 2017). Germane load is the actual mental effort exerted during schema development for long-term storage (Lee et al., 2020).

The current body of research does not fully support game-based learning as a desirable option for cognitive load. Typically, environments that promote exploration, interaction, and manipulation have a higher cognitive load (Alexiou & Schippers, 2018). Elements like three-dimensional animation influence user engagement but also increase cognitive load (Chang et al., 2017). The dynamic nature of game mechanics might succeed in accomplishing engagement, but it may also be overloading the working memory, which impedes learning (Huang, 2011). For example, the intense focus required to succeed in serious games for learning or even multiplayer online role games exposes learners to a higher level of cognitive demand (Huang, 2011). This level of intensity and complexity of gameplay has shown to increase cognitive load, since these storylines aid in an emotional engagement between characters and learners (Alexiou & Schippers, 2018). Heightened emotion can negatively influence extraneous load, with dynamic interactions and simulations causing higher intrinsic load (Lee et al., 2020).

Schrader and Bastiaens (2012) compared a highly immersive educational game to a less immersive environment using narrated and animated on-screen text. The level of immersion in delivery was used to create varying levels of virtual presence for the eighth-grade participants. It was found that higher immersion created more strain on the working memory. One point discussed was the additional cognitive demand required to learn how to work the game. In contrast, Chang et al. (2018) compared the level of flow between game-based learning and materials accessed on a website. Flow is achieved when an experience is enjoyable enough to hold a learner's attention, even with distractions. Game-based learning was shown to weakly enhance extraneous cognitive load, but largely enhance germane load, with no significant difference for intrinsic load. One reason for this difference may be related to categorizing findings. Chang et al. (2018) reported load based on categorization; however, Schrader and Bastiaens (2012) did not have the same measurement tools for the cognitive load categories and took the position that all categories should be addressed to support optimal cognitive load.

Research in game-based learning finds some agreement on the effect design has on cognitive load. The design of educational games must consider limitations in cognitive processing to reduce load and promote transfer (Huang, 2011). Design consideration should be given to the environment and complexity of tasks to reduce cognitive demands (Schrader & Bastiaens, 2012). Game mechanics and learning alignment are necessary to reduce load and facilitate learning (Kalmpourtzis & Romero, 2020). Game mechanics refers to what the game can do, and learning objectives are what we want learners to be able to do after completion (Kalmpourtzis & Romero, 2020).

Principles for Optimizing Cognitive Load

Optimal design of educational games can be fostered by addressing principles of the cognitive load theory. Huang (2011) surmised this theory as a construct that includes mental load based on tasks, learner performance, and the effort exerted in the working memory to process information. The cognitive load theory is a framework for interactions between instructional design, learning processes, and cognitive load (Lee et al., 2020). It is concerned with the presentation of information and can be applied to instruction to improve that presentation (Sweller, 2020). This can be used as a resource to provide instructional design principles for computer-based learning to achieve desired outcomes (Chen et al., 2017).

Based on the constructs of the cognitive load theory, Sweller (2020) identified principles that can be applied to educational technology to minimize the load. These principles include worked examples, split-attention, modality, transient, redundancy, expertise reversal and element interactivity, and working memory depletion. In some instances, by nature, game-based learning aligns with Sweller's (2020) principles; however, thoughtful design can address these principles to lower load and promote learning.

Worked Examples

Problem-solving requires simultaneous processing of multiple elements, which spends a high amount of working memory load; however, prior knowledge requires less processing effort (Sweller, 2020). Worked examples help novice learners problem solve as someone with prior knowledge, which is with reduced working memory load (Sweller, 2020).

Classroom worked examples were exemplified by ter Vrugte et al. (2017) who studied the use of fading. The game and content were identical with the only difference of one group having faded worked examples in game challenges and the other group having none. Fading was described as displaying a full worked example, then a partial worked example, with less of the example showing until it was gone (ter Vrugte et al., 2017). This method allowed learners to adapt to problems before progressing to more difficult problems. Findings showed faded worked examples integrated into gameplay improved proportional reasoning skills, as well as accuracy. This indicates that students who had worked examples were more able to apply knowledge, as well as identify the appropriate solution for solving problems (ter Vrugte et al., 2017).

A broader context of worked examples can be experienced with simulations. Novice learners can interact in a real-world scenario to address training for situations that might otherwise be left to a textbook. Students gain hands-on virtual experience (Shaffer et al., 2005) and practice, which assist with long-term retention (Yang, 2012). This is exemplified by Tsai et al. (2015) who developed a training simulation for disaster prevention. It was found that current disaster training incorporated more traditional theoretical educational methods, which lacked actual skill development for disaster preparedness. Learning goals were combined with game mechanics to provide opportunities to practice and explore techniques in a safe environment. Interaction with the game evolved tangible skills for strategy and manipulation of resources (Tsai et al., 2015). The game environment provided opportunities for trial and error, where students can grow from mistakes without fear of loss (Yang, 2012).

Split Attention

Split attention is separating multiple sources of information that have a relationship. This requires the learner to take on the extra task of integrating information. For example, when presenting a diagram, text or callouts should be incorporated with the diagram, instead of positioned separately (Sweller, 2020). Multiple sources of information should be smoothly integrated and occur simultaneously (Sweller, 2020).

Game mechanics add a context that unifies visual, audio, and tactile elements. Organically incorporating communicative elements into the game will create a cohesive flow (Van Eck, 2010). For example, visual elements like status bars serve as a guide through the experience within the context of the theme (Van Eck, 2010). The learner is not forced to lose focus on the learning information; however, extra support is integrated into the environment if needed.

Components like the narrative are depicted in characters, settings, and game elements; this is combined with audio to tell a story that unifies learning elements and game interactions (Van Eck, 2010). The game narrative adds a real-life context to gameplay, creating a simulation to facilitate knowledge development for use outside of the game (Alexiou & Schippers, 2018). This can reinforce skills through game interaction, and game environments can provide contexts beyond pedagogy to further aid processing (Alexiou & Schippers, 2018). A single-player design tends to involve the learner in the narrative, whereas a multi-player design allows gameplay to dictate the narrative (Van Eck, 2010). Learning activities should be problem-based and applied within the context of the narrative (Van Eck, 2010).

Modality Effect

Modality effect, like split attention, addresses the presentation of complementary elements. In technology, it is not always possible to visually create relationships with information. Delivering complimentary information in different modes, like visuals on a screen that are coordinated with audio, can create that relationship (Sweller, 2020). The working memory increases efficiency when dual modularity is applied (Sweller, 2020).

Game-based learning uses a higher modality than traditional learning and even other technologies, by incorporating the multimodal mechanics of video games. Texts are delivered through a combination of graphics, animations, sounds, and written words (Lee & Ke, 2019). Gameplay promotes information to transform into learning by the way these multiple intake methods are incorporated (Plass et al., 2015). This experience is complimented with interactive challenges to reinforce concepts. The ability to interact with a dynamically changing environment fosters a relationship between game mechanics and learning information.

Challenges directly incorporate multimodal auditory and visual cues with an opportunity to engage in practice, problem-solve and apply information. They trigger curiosity, which leads to exploration, which leads to learning (Mosiane & Brown, 2020). They can be thought of as competitions played individually or against other learners. Design can be as simple as offering a limited selection of choices, coordinated with corrective feedback (Plass et al., 2015). Ranging to a more complex design where decisions made in gameplay determine the level of difficulty (Plass et al., 2015). In aligning with pedagogy, challenges can be directly mapped to learning outcomes and used as a method to measure achievement.

Redundancy Effect

Redundancy refers to unnecessary information, or clutter which includes repeating information, and busy visuals. This can be overwhelming and take more effort to process (Sweller, 2020). Redundant information will interfere with learning by becoming more important than non-redundant information (Sweller, 2020). Reducing complexity will reduce working memory load and promote the acquisition of new knowledge (Sweller, 2020).

Multiple components of the game environment can add complexity and require simultaneous processing with key learning elements (Schrader & Bastiaens, 2012). Gameplay offers opportunities to reduce the need for repeating information. Learning components and related activities can fluctuate between structured activities when necessary to unstructured, allowing opportunities to experiment and make discoveries (Alexiou & Schippers, 2018).

Redundancy can be reduced with timely and relative feedback (Mosiane & Brown, 2020; ter Vrugte et al., 2017). Feedback can be used to reduce uncertainty, assist in adjusting strategies, identify status and progress made, maintain alignment with learning objectives (Alexiou & Schippers, 2018), and track progress in reaching goals (Mosiane & Brown, 2020). It helps learners identify mistakes, recognize correct actions, and guide the journey to foster knowledge transfer (Goldberg & Cannon-Bowers, 2015).

This can be built in by incorporating feedback with clues or tips when triggered by the learner. Game interaction will gradually adapt the experience to knowledge and eliminate redundancy (ter Vrugte et al., 2017). It is important to note that external feedback can increase cognitive load, so it is recommended to incorporate it into the environment (Alexiou & Schippers, 2018).

Transient Information

Holding large chunks of information for long periods, while trying to assimilate with permanent information is difficult for the working memory to perform (Sweller, 2020). The goal is to convert transient information into permanent information. Sweller (2020) suggests transient information can be addressed by eliminating lengthy chunks of information; this will make it easier to process current and previous relationships.

Aligning content, activities, and overall game mechanics will automatically initiate some level of chunking (Van Eck, 2010). Instead of a specific mechanic, chunking can be simulated with the way game mechanics are used together and integrated with learning information. As previously discussed in worked problems, the level of fade applied to worked problems is based on game progress (ter Vrugte et al., 2017). In this case, chunking is applied based on performance or skill level. Leveling is discussed in more detail under expertise reversal and element interactivity. This can address transient information by designating that start and end point within the game as it associates with learning content chunking (Van Eck, 2010). Information can be broken out into logical start and end points, which may include a book chapter, learning module, or lesson. Information chunking within each level should relate new and prior knowledge, which can be accomplished through the use of challenges.

In addition to chunking information further, challenges present a break from processing new information and a way to practice what was presented. This offers a way to reinforce new information by constructing knowledge in a realistic context (Alexiou & Schippers, 2018). This not only benefits the construction of new knowledge but can also be used to enhance existing skills (Alexiou & Schippers, 2018). The challenge is followed by immediate feedback based on performance. This would end the cycle for this chunk of information and promote the next steps based on the type of feedback provided.

Expertise Reversal and Element Interactivity

Expert learners require less information for processing. Presenting information to the granularity a novice might require is less effective and could do more harm than good (Sweller, 2020). This requires a balance based on the skill level of the intended audience. An easy task may bore experienced learners, and a difficult task may frustrate novice learners. The level of difficulty should align with the learner (Chang et al., 2017).

Game mechanics should include some form of leveling, which is triggered by the skill required by a player to progress in the game (Mitre-Hernandez et al., 2021). Activities in gameplay gradually incorporate more complex tasks which will accommodate various experience levels and promote scaffolding (Alexiou & Schippers, 2018). Scaffolding occurs when a learner is guided to achieve a task that was previously beyond their capability (Plass et al., 2015). This approach will build knowledge as an understanding, which is formed during interaction with the game environment (Alexiou & Schippers, 2018). Information can be presented, mastered, and then fade into more challenging concepts (Plass et al., 2015). For example, components such as new player tutorials are present when needed but fade to allow players to focus on game activities. Game mechanics can be designed to assess one level to determine mastery and then identify the next level and challenges that the learner should encounter (Plass et al., 2015).

Mitre-Hernandez et al. (2021) discussed two approaches to leveling. Manual leveling would allow players to determine difficulty. This would allow learners to personalize the difficulty of the game based on their skills and experience (Alexiou & Schippers, 2018). This can be approached similarly to video games, where interaction starts at a comfortable level and gradually becomes more challenging (Mitre-Hernandez et al., 2021). Manual leveling presents a solution to addressing expert learners; however, there are also some challenges. For example, learners may not know which level they belong at, which requires playing a level (Mitre-Hernandez et al., 2021). Offering leveling guidance can help learners quickly adjust and mitigate any potential losses.

Another option is automated or adaptive leveling, which allows the game to dynamically adjust based on learner interaction (Mitre-Hernandez et al., 2021). There is some indication that this approach is more successful in achieving learning outcomes than manual leveling (Mitre-Hernandez et al., 2021). Mitre-Hernandez et al. (2021) used eye tracking to study pupil dilation to determine how difficult or easy a task was during gameplay. This is based on how the pupils become dilated as the level of mental effort increases. When a lower effort was experienced, the game dynamically adjusted to more challenging concepts. A significant correlation was found between the diameter of the pupil and the level of difficulty. Game performance aligned with findings, meaning leveling slowed when players perceived something as difficult. Highlighting an opportunity to use player performance to determine success or failure at a level and identify when it is necessary to progress in the game (Mitre-Hernandez et al., 2021). An automated design can also include positive and negative feedback loops to adjust leveling accordingly (Alexiou &

Schippers, 2018). This progression through levels provides immediate feedback which can guide the learner, maintain engagement, and promote scaffolding (Chang et al., 2017).

Working Memory Depletion

The working memory becomes depleted in long interactions with new information and needs resting periods to recover (Sweller, 2020). Working memory capacity is greater when information is spaced out (Sweller, 2020). Similar to chunking for transient information, game design can incorporate appropriate spacing of information, accompanied by opportunities to practice. Knowledge can transfer through repeated practice of a skill or higher-level application like problem-solving (Plass et al., 2015).

Previous research identified segmenting, sequencing, and prior training as a counter to the decline experienced by higher load (Lee et al., 2020). Exemplified by Lee et al. (2020) who integrated a pausing effect into the game, this effect simulates chunking to reduce a flood of challenging information. Pauses can be used to relax the working memory, reflect on information, or give extra time for processing. Lee et al. (2020) studied this in a medical simulation game, where critical patient care was required, with the experimental group being given opportunities to pause. Findings indicated cognitive load was reduced during gameplay pauses, with significant improvement found in overall performance. Since pauses were voluntary, the success of this technique requires self-regulation from the learner; however, this technique can be thoughtfully integrated into the game design for planned breaks or lighter activities dispersed throughout exhaustive concepts.

Discussion

This chapter identified game mechanics that align with the principles for designing educational technology from Sweller (2020). In an effort to exemplify how design can minimize cognitive load, some topics like split attention and transient information give some thought into how mechanics can work together. More consideration should be given to how components relate to each other. The design should make sense and have a purpose. The use of mechanics for the sake of using can contribute to clutter and do more harm than good. A successful learning game does not need to include everything but should include the most appropriate elements to achieve desired learning goals.

The type of learning content was not discussed here. There is still some debate as to what content is best suited for a game-based learning intervention. There is some belief that educational games are not effective with traditional instruction, like math (Lee & Ke, 2019). Games create iconic relationships, which aid in adding context and skill development. Lee and Ke (2019) point out that although iconic relationships might not teach the actual math calculation, they will teach how to determine which calculation should be used to problem-solve a situation. The ability to analyze a situation and determine the best course of action is a higher-level thinking task and the ultimate goal of teaching the calculation. In this context, the use of game-based learning depends on desired learning outcomes.

Game-based learning technology has evolved more than research (Hirumi et al., 2010). More specifically, there are varying perspectives on how learning games elicit transfer, highlighting opportunities for further study (Bunch et al., 2016; Kuipers et al., 2017). For example, gameplay offers an opportunity to create a real-world learning context, which has shown to promote transfer; however, there is not enough research to confirm or deny it (Kuipers et al., 2017).

Conclusion

Innovative technology will continue to influence education, which highlights the need to continue innovating the design of instructional materials. There is still a great deal of research needed on game-based learning, and how it influences cognitive load. Researchers do agree that design matters, yet research lacks on how to design game-based learning for optimal load (Chang et al., 2017; Huang, 2011). Educational games are met with skepticism by scholars because of a lack of theoretical understanding of how game design, mechanics, and pedagogical integration can influence knowledge development (Alexiou & Schippers, 2018).

This chapter attempts to add an innovative perspective by aligning what is known about game-based learning design and Sweller's (2020) principles for optimizing load in educational technology. Research would benefit from studying Sweller's (2020) principles in a game-based learning experience to add to the body of work and establish design standards. Sound design decisions, alignment with learning outcomes, and fully integrated mechanics can contribute to an impactful learning experience while taking advantage of the enjoyment, motivation, and engagement that game-based learning provides.

References

Alexiou, A., & Schippers, M. C. (2018). Digital game elements, user experience and learning: A conceptual framework. *Education and Information Technologies, 23*, 2545–2567. https://doi. org/10.1007/s10639-018-9730-6

Bunch, J. C., Robinson, J. S., Edwards, M. C., & Antonenko, P. D. (2016). The effect of a serious digital game on students' ability to transfer knowledge in secondary agricultural education: An exploratory study. *Journal of Human Sciences and Extension, 4*(2). https://www.jhseonline. com/article/view/698

Chang, C. C., Liang, C., Chou, P. N., & Lin, G. Y. (2017). Is game-based learning better in flow experience and various types of cognitive load than non-game-based learning? Perspective from multimedia and media richness. *Computers in Human Behavior, 71*, 218–227. https://doi.org/10.1016/j.chb.2017.01.031

Chang, C. C., Warden, C. A., Liang, C., & Lin, G. Y. (2018). Effects of digital game-based learning on achievement, flow and overall cognitive load. *Australasian Journal of Educational Technology, 34*(4). https://doi.org/10.14742/ajet.2961

Chen, O., Woolcott, G., & Sweller, J. (2017). Using cognitive load theory to structure computer-based learning including MOOCs. *Journal of Computer Assisted Learning, 33*, 293–305. https://doi.org/10.1111/jcal.12188

Goldberg, B., & Cannon-Bowers, J. (2015). Feedback source modality effects on training outcomes in a serious game: Pedagogical agents make a difference. *Computers in Human Behavior, 52*, 1–11. https://doi.org/10.1016/j.chb.2015.05.008

Hirumi, A., Appelman, B., Rieber, L., & Van Eck, R. (2010). Preparing instructional designers for game-based learning: Part 1. *TechTrends, 54*(3), 27–37. https://doi.org/10.1007/s11528-010-0400-9

Huang, W. H. (2011). Evaluating learners' motivational and cognitive processing in an online game-based learning environment. *Computers in Human Behavior, 27*(2), 694–704. https://doi.org/10.1016/j.chb.2010.07.021

Kalmpourtzis, G., & Romero, M. (2020). Constructive alignment of learning mechanics and game mechanics in serious game design in higher education. *International Journal of Serious Games, 7*(4), 75–88. https://doi.org/10.17083/ijsg.v7i4.361

Kuipers, D. A., Terlouw, G., Wartena, B. O., van't Veer, J., Prins, J. T., & Pierie, J. P. (2017). The role of transfer in designing games and simulations for health: Systematic review. *JMIR Serious Games, 5*(4). https://doi.org/10.2196/games.7880

Lee, J. Y., Donkers, J., Jarodzka, H., Sellenraad, G., & van Merriënboer, J. J. (2020). Different effects of pausing on cognitive load in a medical simulation game. *Computers in Human Behavior, 110*, 106385. https://doi.org/10.1016/j.chb.2020.106385

Lee, S., & Ke, F. (2019). The format of problem representation for in-game learning supports. *Journal of Computer Assisted Learning, 35*, 390–406. https://doi.org/10.1111/jcal.12345

Mitre-Hernandez, H., Carrillo, R. C., & Lara-Alvarez, C. (2021). Pupillary responses for cognitive load measurement to classify difficulty levels in an educational video game: Empirical study. *JMIR Serious Games, 9*(1). https://doi.org/10.2196/21620

Mosiane, S., & Brown, I. (2020). Factors influencing online game-based learning effectiveness. *The Electronic Journal of Information Systems Evaluation, 23*(1), 79–95. https://doi.org/10.34190/EJISE.20.23.1.006

Plass, J. L., Homer, B. D., & Kinzer, C. K. (2015). Foundations of game-based learning. *Educational Psychologist, 50*(4), 258–283. https://doi.org/10.1080/00461520.2015.1122533

Qian, M., & Clark, K. R. (2016). Game-based learning and 21st century skills: A review of recent research. *Computers in Human Behavior, 63*, 50–58. https://doi.org/10.1016/j.chb.2016.05.023

Roodt, S., & Ryklief, Y. (2019). Using digital game-based learning to improve the academic efficiency of vocational education students. *International Journal of Game-Based Learning, 9*(4), 45–69. https://doi.org/10.4018/IJGBL.2019100104

Schrader, C., & Bastiaens, T. J. (2012). The influence of virtual presence: Effects on experienced cognitive load and learning outcomes in educational computer games. *Computers in Human Behavior, 28*(2), 648e658. https://doi.org/10.1016/j.chb.2011.11.011

Shaffer, D. W., Squire, K. R., Halverson, R., & Gee, J. P. (2005). Video games and the future of learning. *Phi Delta Kappan, 87*(2), 105–111.

Sweller, J. (2020). Cognitive load theory and educational technology. *Educational Technology Research and Development, 68*, 1–16. https://doi.org/10.1007/s11423-019-09701-3

Sweller, J. (2016). Cognitive load theory: What we learn and how we learn. *Learning, Design, and Technology*, 1–7. https://doi.org/10.1007/978-3-319-17727-4_50-1

ter Vrugte, J., de Jong, T., Vandercruysse, S., Wouters, P., van Oostendorp, H., & Elen, J. (2017). Computer game-based mathematics education: Embedded faded worked examples facilitate knowledge acquisition. *Learning and Instruction, 50*, 44–53. https://doi.org/10.1016/j.learninstruc.2016.11.007

Tsai, M., Wen, M., Chang, Y., & Kang, S. (2015). Game-based education for disaster prevention. *AI & SOCIETY, 30*, 463–475. https://doi.org/10.1007/s00146-014-0562-7

Van Eck, R. (Ed.). (2010). *Gaming and cognition: Theories and practice from the learning sciences: Theories and practice from the learning sciences*. IGI Global.

Yang, Y. C. (2012). Building virtual cities, inspiring intelligent citizens: Digital games for developing students' problem solving and learning motivation. *Computers & Education, 59*(2), 365–377. https://doi.org/10.1016/j.compedu.2012.01.012

Privacy Literacy and Library Instruction

Brittany Musgrave Rivera and Kimberly S. Grotewold

Background/Rationale

In the United States, the global COVID-19 pandemic shifted important societal functions, such as education, to online environments. Suddenly, learners at all levels were required to engage with online technologies, including video-conferencing and learning management systems. Privacy concerns as simple as whether students should be required to have their cameras on during instruction in online classroom environments (e.g., Zoom) became topics of debate and discussion. School and academic librarians have a long history of facilitating students' development of information literacy, which has branched out to include media and digital literacy in many contexts. Is it time for librarians to more actively embrace PL as another area in which they lead the way in promoting learners' knowledge and agency? This chapter provides an overview of instructional standards, current research literature, and sample curricula available to address PL in K-12 and higher education. It also offers recommendations for how librarians can extend their roles as PL instructors and advocates at their schools and institutions.

B. M. Rivera (✉)
University of North Texas, Denton, TX, USA
e-mail: BrittanyRivera@my.unt.edu

K. S. Grotewold
University of North Texas, Denton, TX, USA

Texas A&M University-San Antonio, San Antonio, TX, USA
e-mail: KimberlyGrotewold@my.unt.edu; Kimberly.Grotewold@tamusa.edu

Process

A review of the privacy literacy literature and professional organization websites was conducted in December 2021. Because of time constraints and our perceptions that COVID was presenting new challenges to librarians working in both K-12 and higher education, our focus was more conceptual and directed toward thinking about understanding privacy throughout the learner's lifespan. Our initial work suggested that while there is increasing concern about online privacy and a growing interest in ways to improve students' understanding of and power over how their personal data is collected and used, there is limited consensus on ways to best engage learners around these issues. K-12 school librarians, academic librarians, and other agencies have become involved in privacy awareness and empowerment to varying degrees, but particularly in the U.S., cohesive and widely used curricula are limited (Egelman et al., 2016; Hartman-Caverly & Chisholm, 2020, 2021). Particularly in higher education, because academic librarians' roles tend to be specialized, the emerging work is rightly geared toward librarian professional development and training (American Library Association, 2021; Hinchliffe & Jones, 2022; Institute of Museum & Library Services, 2019).

Findings

Privacy Literacy in K-12 Education

Initial research suggests a lack of formal instruction on the topic of PL. While an argument is made that it is necessary for digital citizens of all ages and should be included in library instruction, it is currently not a standard practice in K-12 schools (Wissinger, 2017). Questions remain concerning where instruction about online privacy fits in the curriculum and who should be responsible for its instruction.

An effort to address these concerns was made in 2016 by Common Sense Education, the education division of Common Sense, in partnership with the National Association of Media Literacy Education (NAMLE) and Media Literacy Now. Together, these organizations have developed a policy referred to as Common Sense Kids Action (Starrett, 2016). This policy called for a committee to be formed, composed of educators, parents, and researchers to "develop best practices, resources, and models for instruction in digital citizenship, internet safety, and media literacy," (Starrett, 2016, para. 3). Additionally, this group would work towards passing a legislation that would require school districts to review their own policies regarding the areas of impact.

This was not the only effort made by Common Sense. In 2021, the organization proposed legislation to further protect children's online privacy. According to their Privacy Matters for Kids: Proposals for Legislative and Regulatory Reform document, Common Sense emphasized the importance of actionable efforts towards protecting children's privacy online, when they are still developing their own PL (Common Sense Media, 2021). The proposed legislation has the potential to bridge the gap between when a child is still developing PL and when they are older and fully capable of making informed decisions regarding their online privacy (Common Sense Media, 2021).

Hartman-Caverly and Chisholm (2020) echoed the idea of people developing autonomy over time. In their work, they described "concentric zones'" governing a person's digital existence (p. 307). In a similar fashion as Common Sense Education, Hartman-Caverly and Chisholm (2020) explained that these concentric zones start with the person at a young age and grow out as they learn and develop the necessary skills to make informed decisions regarding their online privacy (p. 307). Parental role should also be considered. How can parents help support efforts for PL at home? According to Culatta (2021), it is the responsibility of both the parents and educators in students' lives to develop a "digital culture at home and at school" (p. 38). One primary method for accomplishing this at home and at school is by modeling digital citizenship, which includes ethical privacy practices (Culatta, 2021).

The digital divide is another contributing factor to the lack of PL. According to Sanders and Scanlon (2021), looking into the issue of the digital divide highlights the needs for digital literacy instruction. They continued by stating, "Educating and training both individuals and library and information (LIS) professionals are crucial components in the digital divide in order to provide information congruent with ever changing technology and points of access," (Sanders & Scanlon, 2021, p. 131). Addressing PL means also addressing digital equity. Individuals who fall on the "have-not" side of the divide lack proper exposure and education. According to Real et al. (2014), the concept of "digital inclusion" is useful in emphasizing "the importance of ensuring individuals have access to digital technologies as well as the means to learn how to use them," (p. 8). Also worth noting is that scholars such as Hagendorff (2018) have raised concerns about the term PL itself and how it frames central concepts. Inherent in most approaches to PL instruction is the idea that technology users who engage in privacy-risking online behaviors, such as banking on a public access computer, are either uninformed or are making poor decisions. Hagendorff (2018) pushed back against these assumptions by pointing out that marginalized people often do not have the luxury of making privacy-protecting choices. A computer at the public library may be their only option for managing their finances.

Roles for K-12 Librarians

For K-12 librarians, it is important that their "efforts to defend youth privacy must delicately balance protecting and empowering youth while allowing them to gradually develop autonomy and resilience" (Future Privacy Forum, 2021, header section). One of those strategies includes digital literacy and citizenship. The idea of digital literacy, and by extension PL, is to "empower young people to take control of their privacy and promote … responsible engagement online" (Park & Vance, 2021, Digital Literacy and Citizenship section). In a K-12 environment, that happens in the library or media center with the campus librarian at the helm of instruction.

To support librarians as the leaders of PL instruction on their campuses, professional development opportunities should be provided to them and their staff members. There are resources available on professional websites such as the American Library Association (ALA). One resource provided is the NYC Digital Safety program. This program was created by the public library branches of New York City in conjunction with the Mayor's Office of the Chief Technology Officer as an effort to provide PL training and resources to library staff (NYC Digital Safety, 2018). The following modules are included in the NYC Digital Safety (2018) training:

- Introduction to Digital Safety
- Internet Technologies and the Information Flow
- Who Collects Data; connecting Securely
- Securing Accounts and Devices
- Preventing Tracking
- Avoiding Scams and Malware; minimizing your Digital Footprint
- Privacy and Security in the Library (Modules section)

The professional development opportunities provided by NYC Digital Safety will allow librarians and their staff to prepare themselves for protecting patron privacy and helping patrons to begin developing their own PL.

According to the International Society for Technology in Education (ISTE) standards for educators, including librarians, Standards 2.3 c and 2.3 d state that educators are expected to help students learn how to function safely in an online environment (ISTE, 2022a). This includes knowing what information is safe to share and managing personal online identity and data privacy (ISTE, 2022a). Specifically addressing librarian expectations, the ALA developed the Library Bill of Rights. The Library Bill of Rights is a published list of policies intended to guide librarians during their career. Number seven on the list states that libraries and their librarians are responsible for educating users about privacy and maintaining patron privacy (ALA, 2019). It is clearly stated by multiple sources that addressing PL falls under the purview of librarians. With that being said, the question that still needs to be addressed is what resources presently exist to support this expectation.

Roles for Academic Librarians

ACRL Framework for Information Literacy

The Association of College and Research Libraries (ACRL, 2015) Framework for Information Literacy for Higher Education is organized around six conceptual frames:

- Authority is Constructed and Contextual
- Information Creation as a Process
- Information Has Value
- Research as Inquiry
- Scholarship as Conversation
- Searching as Strategic Exploration (p. 5)

The Framework document describes the frames as threshold concepts and lists specific learner Knowledge Practices and Dispositions under each. Learners who demonstrate most or all the Knowledge Practices and Dispositions are on their way toward mastering the overarching conceptual construct. The word privacy only appears once in the Framework within the Information Has Value frame. The document states, "Learners who are developing their information literacy abilities make informed choices regarding their online actions in full awareness of issues related to privacy and the commodification of personal information" (p. 17). This frame clearly advocates for learners to recognize the worth of their own personal data. It also calls for acknowledgement that personal data can be collected and judged in ways that cause a disadvantage to particular socio-demographic groups, thereby creating a situation in which their information is used against them and exacerbating their marginalization.

If learners are positioned as both consumers and creators of information, then other frames are also relevant to PL. The Authority is Constructed and Contextual frame implies that information literate learners evaluate the credentials and the underlying purposes of information producers (ACRL, 2015). Because online information can be manipulated, users must increasingly apply a critical lens to assess the accuracy of information presented and the authenticity of authorship details. They also need to recognize that information they share online can be vulnerable to distortion or exploitation. Finally, under the frame of Information Creation as a Process, the prevalence and expansion of online information distribution platforms has led to varying processes concerning how facts, data, and knowledge are disseminated for public consumption (ACRL, 2015). With most of these processes happening online, there can be greater risk for interception, information tampering, or amplification of ideas that have not been fully verified.

Learning Analytics, Librarians, and Privacy

The Educause Horizon Action Plan: Privacy (2021) set a future goal for higher education students, "As informed and engaged stakeholders, students understand how and why their institutions use academic and personal data" (McCormack et al., 2021, p. 4). The COVID-19 pandemic resulted in higher education institutions' increased reliance on their learning management system (LMS) platforms as the primary mechanism for continuing to provide instructional content and educational experiences for their students when campuses were closed. At the institution of one of the chapter authors, prior to the pandemic, some faculty used the LMS very minimally, primarily for recording attendance and grades. Moving the bulk of educational content and class meeting space online arguably reduced students' privacy and control over their data. At least in physical, on-campus classrooms, assuming the absence of classroom cameras and recording systems, students' behaviors could be considered more private, or less documented than what has become possible through the learning analytics features embedded in typical LMS platforms (Hagendorff, 2018).

The shift of courses to increased engagement with the LMS platform has generally persisted despite class meetings returning to campus. LMS platforms and other online university portals are equipped to collect a constant flow of user data in ways that are often not obvious to students or faculty. Increased deployment of application program interfaces (APIs) extends the capacity for collecting students' information beyond the now porous boundaries of the LMS presenting more opportunities for triangulation, classification, and re-identification of private data (Jones et al., 2020). This rise of LMS centrality, big data, and learning analytics means that the roles of academic librarians have room to expand.

Particularly at large research universities, academic librarians are supporters and collaborators in faculty research efforts and are often expected to have knowledge of the rules of responsible conduct of research with human subjects. These rules include stipulations regarding user confidentiality and stringent privacy protection for any data collected (CITI Program, 2021). While students are prompted at some point during their LMS usage to read and agree to the privacy policies of the LMS provider, their review and understanding of the relevant statements is questionable. A study by the Pew Research Center in 2019 found that while 81% of United States adults are asked on a monthly basis or more frequently to agree to company-associated privacy terms and conditions, 36% of those responding reported that they never read the policies (Auxier et al., 2019, pp. 5, 37).

Because the data collected through the LMS is arguably used for course and program improvement, quality assurance, and other purposes designed to connect students to resources at their point of need, university administration and service providers tend to dismiss such practices as not qualifying as research with human subjects. Therefore, the prevailing attitude is that such data is not subject to the same rigorous protections. Academic librarians can serve to increase students' awareness of privacy statements and terms of use agreements and can engage in campus conversations around who has access to the LMS data collected and for what purposes.

New Roles: Risks and Challenges

Taking on the role of a shield against comprehensive data collection can place academic librarians in an ethical quandary. As noted by Jones et al. (2020), academic librarians have historically faced continuing pressures to provide evidence that their libraries are adding value to their institutions, both in terms of supporting research capacity and student success. Jones et al. (2020) have also reviewed library learning analytics studies which are increasingly pulling in student data from other campus systems in efforts to demonstrate connections between library services and student success. A central tension arises between the librarians' need to better understand and communicate the library's value, and the ethical role of helping students and other stakeholders protect their own privacy.

While academic librarians may be familiar with basic ethics related to user privacy, such as the responsibility to protect user checkout records, they may be less informed about more current issues related to interconnectivity of data across digital environments. Utilization of APIs and other technological tools to connect multiple data points about users across systems can serve to render previously de-identified user data identifiable again, thereby violating privacy in ways that may have been unanticipated (Hagendorff, 2018; Jones et al., 2020; O'Neil, 2016). Universities of significant size may be able to address the knowledge gap by hiring technical and data management librarians; however, all academic librarians would benefit from education and professional development aimed at building awareness of the intersections among emerging technologies, learning analytics in libraries, and user privacy.

In 2019, the Institute of Museum and Library Services (IMLS) awarded nearly $250,000 of grant funding to a three-year project proposed by Lisa Janicke Hinchliffe of the University of Illinois at Urbana-Champaign Libraries and Kyle Jones from Indiana University-Indianapolis to train academic library staff on issues of data privacy and ethics (IMLS, 2019). So far, their project entitled Prioritizing Privacy: Data Ethics Training for Library Professionals has facilitated a free online professional development course on privacy for two cohorts of 50 participants each (with additional offerings planned) and has released a source book under an open license for use by other librarians (Hinchliffe & Jones, 2022). Academic librarians can use the resources shared on the project website, workshops being offered, and the research publications coming out of the project to first build their own knowledge on issues related to privacy online and then develop activities and programs for their own institutions. The creation of adaptable modular curricula aimed toward college-level learners which academic librarians could embed into their current information literacy instructional programs would provide significant utility. Additional activities and programs targeting higher education faculty and staff who work outside libraries would also be helpful because members of these groups may have limited understanding of data ethics depending on their disciplines and professional backgrounds.

Existing K-12 Privacy Literacy Curricula

At present there is not a national mandate for digital citizenship to be included in public school curriculums. For the states that choose to include digital standards in their state standards, there are several resources available to support that endeavor, at no cost to the school system. One such resource is the ALA Training and Programming webpage (ALA, 2021). On this page, the ALA provides programming resources for academic, public, and school librarians. Each of the described curricula provides instruction on various areas of digital citizenship, including PL.

Common Sense Education

Common Sense Education provides free digital citizenship instruction materials for educators to utilize in their schools. On their website, users can select their grade level and then the subsection of digital citizenship they want to provide instruction on. Regarding PL, there is an abundance of lessons and support materials available for librarians to access and incorporate into their programs. The curriculum addresses "the issue of privacy from two angles: data privacy and privacy as it relates to students' digital footprints and reputations" (James et al., 2021, p.32). The lessons provided are meant to build on each other from one grade level to the next. Examples of PL topics included in the curriculum are:

- importance of password strength
- identifying private information
- identifying and avoiding clickbait
- identifying appropriate websites
- preventing phishing attacks
- data collection algorithms (Common Sense Education, 2019, Digital Citizenship Curriculum section)

Common Sense Education also provides an alignment chart representing the English Language Arts Common Core (ELA), American Association of School Librarians (AASL), International Society for Technology in Education (ISTE), and Core SEL Competencies (CASEL) (Common Sense Education, 2020, Standards Alignment section).

Be Internet Awesome

In 2017, Google developed a free curriculum named Be Internet Awesome. This curriculum "gives educators the tools and methods they need to teach digital safety fundamentals" (Google, 2021, For Educators section). In 2021, ISTE awarded Be Internet Awesome the Seal of Alignment. According to their website, the Seal of Alignment is awarded for products that are in alignment with their standards and lets users know they are utilizing a high-quality product or program (ISTE, 2022b). Additionally, Be Internet Awesome leverages a gamification feature titled Interland. Interland facilitates interactive, engaging, and fun lessons in a game setting (Google, 2021, For Kids section). According to Google engineer and developer of Be Internet

Awesome, Diwanji (2017), it is the responsibility of the adults – parents, teachers, librarians, etc. – present in the lives of young Internet users to have the necessary tools to guide and educate students on proper online etiquette, including PL (para. 1–2). This thought was a driving force behind developing Be Internet Awesome.

Ignition: Digital Literacy

Ignition: Digital Literacy curriculum is available for free to K-12 educators, though it is specifically intended for sixth grade through ninth grade students. Learning objectives are clearly stated and of the seven listed, digital privacy is included. Their curriculum for digital privacy includes discussion on digital footprints and identity theft (EVERFI, 2022, Lesson 2 section). According to EVERFI's (2022) Ignition: Digital Literacy curriculum, "students learn what it means to have a digital footprint and ways to safeguard their privacy and security online" (Safety and Privacy section). A unique feature of this curriculum is that it is presently available in English, French, and Spanish (EVERFI, 2022, Course Details section). This allows the curriculum to reach a larger scope of participants and potentially support efforts to address digital inclusion.

Empire State Information Fluency Continuum

According to a letter published by the School Library Systems Association (SLSA), the original efforts to develop a digital citizenship curriculum were started in 2009 by New York City librarians (SLSA, 2019). The present effort is titled Empire State Information Fluency Continuum, a progression of skills and standards arranged by grade level; this curriculum includes a dedicated section to pre-kindergarten educators. Areas addressed in the curriculum include all areas of responsible use and follow the Inquiry Learning Cycle (SLSA, 2019). The digital citizenship part of the curriculum is addressed and led by the New York City School Library System, with the material coordinated with the Empire State Information Fluency Continuum and Common Sense Education (New York City School Library System, 2021).

Privacy Literacy Curricula for Higher Education

Existing curricula for PL development for college students are insufficient. Searching the online instructional materials repository MERLOT (https://merlot. org/merlot/) for curriculum on PL and related topics targeting a higher education or adult professional audience yielded 468 results. These results covered an array of resource types, ranging from course syllabi, whole courses, individual video lectures to open access, or OER books and articles. Of the full course resources, the common discipline areas represented were information science, public policy, engineering, research ethics, media arts and sciences, and health systems (Merlot, 2022). The complete courses tended to be affiliated with large universities that offer open educational initiatives, including MIT Opencourseware and Open Michigan. Many of the course materials were created in 2012 or earlier, suggesting the possibility that some of their content may be outdated. While discipline-specific PL content offers value to the students studying those subjects, the potential negative effects of possessing limited knowledge concerning information privacy extend beyond the boundaries of computer science, information science, and related disciplines. Understanding how one's personal data is collected and used in various ways should be a fundamental right afforded to all students, not just those majoring in specific subjects. More general Internet searching revealed instances of other freely available privacy literacy curricula, but again, easily adoptable resources were limited. This section features a few examples.

Teaching Privacy Curriculum

Teaching Privacy was an early curriculum developed by researchers at the University of California, Berkeley, beginning in 2014. A review of existing privacy-oriented instructional materials at the time found them to be discipline-specific for computer science, law, and ethics. This led Egelman et al. (2016) to build a freely available program that was geared toward the more general high school or college-age Internet user. The curriculum is organized around ten fundamental principles which are the content modules: "You're Leaving Footprints; There's no Anonymity; Information is Valuable; Someone Could Listen; Sharing Releases Control; Search is Improving; Online is Real; Identity Isn't Guaranteed; You Can't Escape; and Privacy Requires Work" (pp. 592–593). Initial assessment of the program by its creators demonstrated participants' statistically significant gains in their desire for "transparency and control" concerning usage of their personal data (p. 595). In 2019, new modules were added to the curriculum to reflect technological advances (more sophisticated APIs and algorithms) which allow for cross-platform collection and aggregation of personal data and increased likelihood of user identification (Bernd, 2019). In addition to the student-focused materials, Egelman et al.'s (2016) complementary project, TROPE, provided instructor support resources for implementing the modules.

Surveillance Self-Defense Guide

The Surveillance Self-Defense Guide is a resource geared primarily toward individual use, although in its Privacy for Students section, it asserts: "While there are many steps you can take to protect your privacy on your own, the real protection comes when we protect each others' privacy as a group" (Electronic Frontier Foundation, 2020, Privacy as a Team Sport section). In other words, if we engage with others online or in situations that can be monitored, and those others are not mindful of how they are sharing information, we can still be tracked. This concept arose in at least one other existing curriculum and instruction example. (Hartman-Caverly & Chisholm, 2020, p. 316; see their assessment survey that asks participants if they learned something they "want to share with their friends or family.") The Surveillance Self Defense Guide explains various terms and tools (e.g., encryption, virtual private network [VPN], open source) and offers instructions on how to install and use specific software applications. It also provides recommendations for different user populations (e.g., students, researchers, LGBTQ) and for specific situations (e.g., attending a protest) with regard to avoiding data surveillance (https:// ssd.eff.org/en). The Surveillance Self Defense Guide appears to have been actively updated between 2015 and 2020, so it lacks content from the past 2 years, which may affect its usability.

Data Detox Kit

Tactical Tech's Data Detox Kit (2021) is a digital literacy toolkit covering a variety of privacy-related topics. It offers content related to identifying misinformation, deception, and automated content online and includes information and exercises to help users identify deep fake videos, copycat URLs, and posts generated by bots. The resource highlights the three areas of privacy, security, and well-being, with the inclusion of the latter suggesting a link between online technology usage, polarizing information online, and mental health. Additional privacy-oriented recommendations are presented, such as how to curate and manage one's online identity and how to delete location data from smartphones. One section of the kit, Data Detox X Youth, is geared specifically toward 11–16-year-olds, while the rest of the site assumes a more adult audience. The site was last updated in September 2021, so its content is relatively current.

Academic Librarian-Facilitated Instruction

Hartman-Caverly and Chisholm (2020, 2021); see also Chisholm & Hartman-Caverly, 2020, 2022) have made important, current contributions to understanding privacy in the context of academic libraries. Their work has provided an account of established and emerging definitions of privacy, explained goals and critiques of privacy literacy instructional practices, and introduced a new learner-centered model for improved learner agency. Hartman-Caverly and Chisholm's (2020) *Six Private I's Privacy Conceptual Model* is represented by a diagram in the shape of an eye and "depicts concentric zones of agency over one's presence in the world, from identity, to intellect, to bodily and contextual integrity, to intimacy, to autonomous interaction with and isolation from others" (p. 307). The authors conducted PL workshops in collaboration with the first-year experience program at their regional campus of a large R1 university.

Hartman-Caverly and Chisolm's workshops involved a series of individual and small group active engagement exercises and large-group reflection opportunities designed to have students examine their own online behaviors in relation to privacy and to consider implications of various behaviors, not just to themselves, but to others and to society more broadly. Through workshop exit surveys, they found that participating students self-reported very high measures of agreement with statements related to their increased knowledge of personal data impacts and strategies for evaluating personal privacy preferences and developing corresponding data practices (Hartman-Caverly & Chisholm, 2020). In the time since these workshops, the librarians have convened librarians from other colleges and universities to discuss strategies for building students' personal data awareness and agency around privacy; they have offered a course on the privacy literacy on the Library Juice Academy professional learning platform; and they have written about privacy in relation to the COVID-19 pandemic and mental health (Chisholm & Hartman-Caverly, 2020, 2022).

Discussion, Implications, and Conclusions

During the past decade, an expanding percentage of the public's everyday activities have been conducted online. This trend has infiltrated education and has been turbocharged by the pandemic. Librarians have long been recognized as advocates for the free pursuit of ideas and information; consequently, they are natural leaders in scholarly and professional practices connected to privacy. K-12 school and academic librarians in instructional and faculty collaboration roles can be especially instrumental in fostering improved understanding among their stakeholder communities: students, educators, administrative staff, etc. The following will be important elements for moving PL work forward in educational settings:

- Additional high-quality, adaptable PL curricula
- Increased opportunities for librarians' professional development
- Librarians' engagement in campus- and system level partnerships with instructional technology specialists, subject-area instructors, discipline leads, and others
- Collaboration among K-12 and academic instructional librarians to identify and bridge gaps in learners' continuum of knowledge related to privacy.

School and academic librarians' understanding of the PL instructional role seems to be increasing as increasing numbers of scholarly articles and professional development activities are available, but the need is still great.

Looking ahead in K-12 and academic librarianship, PL should not fall entirely on the librarian's shoulders. According to ISTE standards, education leaders, like librarians, are responsible for ensuring that PL efforts are in place in their institutions, while all educators, including classroom educators, are responsible for ensuring the development of their students' or patrons' PL (ISTE, 2022a, c). Available resources, such as the ALA field guides and the NYC Digital Safety program, provide a start for training library staff and education professionals (ALA, 2021; NYC Digital Safety, 2018). However, in line with the need for PL instruction to become standardized in K-12 and more broadly applied higher education settings, PL-related professional development is also needed to fully address the concerns regarding PL in education environments. As educational technologies advance with heightened capacities for pulling user data in from multiple, disparate sources and these systems are empowered with more decision-making functions, it will become even more critical for K-12 and higher education librarians to develop their own knowledge and find ways to share their expertise with others.

References

American Library Association. (2019). *Library bill of rights.* https://www.ala.org/advocacy/intfreedom/librarybill

American Library Association. (2021). *Training & programming.* https://www.ala.org/advocacy/privacy/training

Association of College and Research Libraries. (2015). *Framework for information literacy for higher education.* https://www.ala.org/acrl/sites/ala.org.acrl/files/content/issues/infolit/framework1.pdf

Auxier, B., Rainie, L., Anderson, M., Perrin, A., Kumar, M., & Turner, E. (2019). *Americans and privacy: Concerned, confused and feeling lack of control over their personal information* [report]. (pp. 1–63). Pew Research Center. https://www.pewresearch.org/internet/2019/11/15/americans-and-privacy-concerned-confused-and-feeling-lack-of-control-over-their-personal-information/

Bernd, J. (2019). *New addition: Programming for privacy!* Teaching Privacy. https://teachingprivacy.org/new-addition-programming-for-privacy/

Chisholm, A. E., & Hartman-Caverly, S. (2020). *Privacy literacy reboot.* https://scholarsphere.psu.edu/resources/508a8440-a7ab-45dc-9e64-9737efccf294

Chisholm, A. E., & Hartman-Caverly, S. (2022). Privacy literacy: From doomscrolling to digital wellness. *Libraries and the Academy, 22*(1), 53–79. https://preprint.press.jhu.edu/portal/sites/ajm/files/chisholm.pdf

CITI Program. (2021). *Human subjects research (HSR).* https://about.citiprogram.org/series/human-subjects-research-hsr/

Common Sense Education. (2019). *Digital citizenship curriculum.* https://www.commonsense.org/education/digital-citizenship/curriculum?topic=privacy%2D%2Dsecurity&grades=3,4,5,k,1,2,6,7,8,12,11,10,9

Common Sense Education. (2020). *Digital citizenship curriculum standards alignment.* https://www.commonsense.org/education/new-digital-citizenship-standards-alignment-2019

Common Sense Media. (2021). *Privacy matters for kids.* https://www.commonsensemedia.org/sites/default/files/featured-content/files/2021_privacy_one_pager_leave_behind.pdf

Culatta, R. (2021). *Digital for good: Raising kids to thrive in an online world.* Harvard Business Review Press.

Diwanji, P. (2017). *"Be internet awesome": Helping kids make smart decisions online*. The Keyword. https://www.blog.google/technology/families/be-internet-awesome-helping-kids-make-smart-decisions-online/

Egelman, S., Bernd, J., Friedland, G., & Garcia, D. (2016). The teaching privacy curriculum. In *Proceedings of the 47th ACM technical symposium on computing science education* (pp. 591–596). https://doi.org/10.1145/2839509.2844619

Electronic Frontier Foundation. (2020). *Privacy for students*. Surveillance Self-defense. https://ssd.eff.org/en/module/privacy-students

EVERFI. (2022). *Ignition: Digital literacy curriculum for wellness and safety*. https://everfi.com/courses/k-12/digital-literacy-wellness-safety/

Future Privacy Forum. (2021). *Youth privacy & data protection 101* [infographic]. https://student-privacycompass.org/wp-content/uploads/2021/04/FPF-Youth-Privacy-Infographic-1.png

Google. (2021). *Be internet awesome*. Google. https://beinternetawesome.withgoogle.com/en_us/educators

Hagendorff, T. (2018). Privacy literacy and its problems. *Journal of Information Ethics, 27*(2), 127–145.

Hartman-Caverly, S., & Chisholm, A. E. (2020). Privacy literacy instruction practices in academic libraries: Past, present, and possibilities. *IFLA Journal, 46*(4), 305–327. https://doi.org/10.1177/0340035220956804

Hartman-Caverly, S., & Chisholm, A. E. (2021). Transforming privacy literacy instruction. In *LOEX 2021 proceedings* (pp. 1–8). https://doi.org/10.26207/417p-p335

Hinchliffe, L., & Jones, K. M. (2022). *Prioritizing privacy: Data ethics training for library professionals*. https://prioritizingprivacy.org/

Institute of Museum and Library Services. (2019). *University of Illinois at Urbana-Champaign (University of Illinois, University Library) project proposal* (grant application RE-18-19-0014-19).

International Society for Technology in Education. (2022a). *ISTE standards: Educators*. International Society for Technology in Education. https://www.iste.org/standards/iste-standards-for-teachers

International Society for Technology in Education. (2022b). *Seal of alignment*. https://www.iste.org/standards/iste-seal-of-alignment

International Society for Technology in Education. (2022c). *ISTE standards: Education leaders*. https://www.iste.org/standards/iste-standards-for-education-leaders

James, C., Weinstein, E., & Mendoza, K. (2021). *Teaching digital citizens in today's world: Research and insights behind the common sense K–12 digital citizenship curriculum*. (version 2). Common Sense Media.

Jones, K. M. L., Briney, K. A., Goben, A., Salo, D., Asher, A., & Perry, M. R. (2020). A comprehensive primer to library learning analytics practices, initiatives, and privacy issues. *College & Research Libraries, 81*(3), 570–591. https://doi.org/10.5860/crl.81.3.570

McCormack, M., Brooks, D. C., & Reeves, J. (2021). *2021 Educause horizon action plan: Privacy* (pp. 1–10). https://library.educause.edu/resources/2021/10/2021-educause-horizon-action-plan-privacy

Merlot. (2022). *Community portals*. https://merlot.org/merlot/communities.htm?type=0

New York City School Library System. (2021). *Digital citizenship: Digital citizenship*. https://nycdoe.libguides.com/digitalcitizenship

NYC Digital Safety. (2018). *Digital privacy & security in the library*. https://nycdigitalsafety.org/

O'Neil, C. (2016). *Weapons of math destruction: How big data increases inequality and threatens democracy*. Broadway Books.

Park, J. & Vance, A. (2021). *Youth privacy and data protection 101*. Privacy Compass. https://studentprivacycompass.org/youth-privacy-and-data-protection-101/

Real, B., Bertot, J. C., & Jaeger, P. T. (2014). Rural public libraries and Digital inclusion: Issues and challenges. *Information Technology and Libraries (Online), 33*(1), 6–24. https://www.proquest.com/docview/1512388143/fulltext/B698BC8F33154449PQ/1?accountid=7113

Sanders, C. K., & Scanlon, E. (2021). The digital divide is a human rights issue: Advancing social inclusion through social work advocacy. *Journal of Human Rights and Social Work, 6*, 130–143. https://doi.org/10.1007/s41134-020-00147-9

School Library Systems Association. (2019). *Information fluency continuum.* https://slsa-nys.lib-guides.com/ifc/home

Starrett, J. R. (2016). *Model policy for digital citizenship and media literacy in public schools.* https://www.commonsensemedia.org/kids-action/articles/model-policy-for-digital-citizenship-and-media-literacy-in-public-schools

Tactical Tech. (2021). *Data detox kit: Homepage.* https://datadetoxkit.org/en/home

Wissinger, C. L. (2017). Privacy literacy: From theory to practice. *Communications in Information Literacy, 11*(2), 378–389. https://eric.ed.gov/?id=EJ1166461

Instructional Disobedience in Flipped Higher Education Classrooms: An Exploration

Katie Goeman, Morane Stevens, and Jan Elen

Introduction

Due to the COVID-19 pandemic, many instructors in higher education have been forced to address their instructional course design capacities, redesign practices, and swiftly change the nature of student learning activities. This has led to fast innovations and digitalization, where the "smart university" gained momentum (Stracke et al., 2017). Nevertheless, the disruptive character of these imposed changes has also sparked attention about somnolent issues that significantly challenge the strengths and opportunities of online and blended learning environments (e.g., Tawfik et al., 2021).

This chapter focuses on one of these issues, namely "instructional disobedience" demonstrated by learners within formal learning environments. The term was first coined by Jan Elen during the EARLI 2013 conference (Elen, 2013); nonetheless, some authors (implicitly) referred to the phenomenon in earlier contributions (see Elen, 2020).

The occurrence of instructional disobedience is characterized by divergent behavior in terms of usage of human- or technology-mediated instructional interventions. These interventions are conceived by the educator as being effective for reaching predefined learning goals within a specific context. They are designed and developed by means of a particular ID (Instructional Design) and made explicit using learning tasks and materials in particular learning spaces. Instructional disobedience reveals a mis- or nonalignment between the intended (as stipulated by design) and the achieved learning behavior (as displayed by a learner). Consistent

K. Goeman (✉) · M. Stevens · J. Elen
Katholieke Universiteit Leuven, Leuven, Belgium
e-mail: katie.goeman@kuleuven.be; morane.stevens@kuleuven.be; jan.elen@kuleuven.be

© The Author(s), under exclusive license to Springer Nature Switzerland AG 2023   267
D. Cockerham et al. (eds.), *Reimagining Education: Studies and Stories for Effective Learning in an Evolving Digital Environment*,
Educational Communications and Technology: Issues and Innovations,
https://doi.org/10.1007/978-3-031-25102-3_22

with the view of Elen (2020), two types of instructional disobedience are discerned, namely: (1) quantitative disobedience or "when students do not or only partially use the learning opportunities provided by elements of the learning environment," and (2) qualitative disobedience or "when students do interact with the elements of the learning environment but not as intended by the designer" (p. 2025). Additionally, instructional disobedience may occur as a result of a conscious decision by a learner (*active* or *proactive instructional disobedience*) or may be caused by negligence, an inadequate ID and/or a maladjusted embedment of a learning environment in a wider context (*passive instructional disobedience*).

Instructional disobedience may not only affect student learning but also lead to serious consequences from an instructor's point of view. Stott (2016), for example, was confronted with negative course and instructor assessments. Moreover, when a substantial proportion of a student group does not abide by a design, the impact may be amplified from an individual to an aggregated level. This in turn may question the principles upon which the environment was designed. Addressing instructional disobedience is, therefore, one of the great challenges of instructional designers and educators, as well as those in search of design principles or a theory of design for learning (Goodyear & Dimitriadis, 2013). Besides the early accounts of Elen (2013, 2016) and a few references to "non-submissive" or "non-compliant" students (Goodyear, 2000; Jonassen et al., 2000), it seems that more detailed research is necessary. In this regard, Stöhr et al. (2020) make a call for sound theoretical frameworks, while Rasheed et al. (2020) posit that "flipped classroom researchers should refocus their attention on investigating and providing additional interventions to dysfunctional behavior" (p. 851).

The current study examines instructional disobedience against the backdrop of self-regulated learning in the "flipped" or "inverted" classroom. Self-regulated learning refers to "active and volitional behaviors on the part of individuals to achieve in their learning" (Barnard-Brak et al., 2010, p. 62). It encompasses planning, monitoring, assessing, and adjusting one's learning progress, as well as being motivated to learn (Panadero, 2017). A flipped classroom is considered an instructional strategy for effective higher education which incorporates student-centered, independent, and collaborative learning techniques (Bredow et al., 2021; Kim et al., 2014; Thai et al., 2017).

This contribution presents the findings derived from a review of the literature conducted by three researchers. The following questions are addressed: (1) what is the nature of instructional disobedience in relation to a flipped classroom design?, (2) what impact does instructional disobedience have in a flipped classroom?, and (3) what solutions are proposed in flipped classroom literature to handle instructional disobedience? Data derived from secondary sources are considered reliable and all originated from publications with recognized authority, a guiding principle for desk research according to Moore (2006).

This work is informed by generic contemporary research on flipped classrooms, exemplified by reports on student behavior during the pandemic. The results might be of interest to instructional designers, instructors acting as designers, or educational design researchers. The findings of the study might help to optimize the ID of flipped classrooms by acknowledging instructional disobedience and its relation with engagement and course outcomes.

The Effectiveness of Flipped Classrooms

A flipped classroom differs from a traditional classroom because it "flips" the typical structure of a course (or course unit) in terms of the types of learning activities and the learning spaces in which they take place (Long et al., 2016). The flipped classroom model distinguishes between pre-, during, and post-class activities, or in-class and out-of-class activities (Bäcklund & Hugo, 2018; Baytiyeh, 2017; Zuber, 2016). In particular, the presentation of concepts (traditionally delivered through in-class lectures) takes place outside the classroom – often online, whereas classroom time is used for (inter)active and collaborative learning activities that focus on processing these concepts (Peterson, 2016; Song et al., 2017).

Research at a Spanish university before and during the COVID-19 crisis considers the flipped classroom as a catalyst for the modernization of education and as a future proof approach to have students acquire twenty-first-century skills (Latorre-Cosculluela et al., 2022). According to Brewer and Movahedazarhouligh (2018), flipped classrooms allow instructors to better accommodate group and independent study, and it helps students develop conceptual understanding and "procedural fluency." These authors further point out that a flipped classroom evokes deep learning, thanks to four key elements (p. 413): (1) an opportunity for students to gain exposure to content prior to class, (2) an incentive for students to prepare for class, (3) a mechanism to assess student understanding, and (4) in-class activities that focus on higher-level cognitive activities. Similarly, a review conducted by Oudbier et al. (2022) mentions that a flipped classroom "prevents procrastination by completing the study material of the pre-study before the in-class activities" and "enables the student to develop his self-directing learning readiness" (p. 6).

Instructional Disobedience in Flipped Classrooms

The above mentioned strengths also seem to be a flipped classroom's Achilles' heel. In order to achieve academic success in a flipped classroom, students should remain involved during the entire instructional process (Wang, 2017). Flipped classrooms heavily lean upon students' self-regulated learning during pre- and post-class learning activities (Long et al., 2016) and strongly addresses the learners' motivation (Oudbier et al., 2022). Nevertheless, some studies report overtly about non-compliance in this regard. In the following paragraphs, this phenomenon is illustrated.

Issues with Participation in Pre-class Learning Tasks

First of all, students may simply refuse to carry out learning tasks. Oudbier et al. (2022) and Chen et al. (2014) mention refusal to prepare and learners' disengagement. A similar observation is voiced by Lo and Hew (2017): "The major problems of using flipped classroom approach include teachers' considerable workload of creating flipped learning materials, and students' disengagement in the out-of-class learning. In fact, the previous reviews report that some students did not familiarize with this new learning approach and skipped the pre-class activities." (p. 2). Elvers et al. (2003) report that students postpone learning tasks or carry out learning tasks only by virtue of deadlines.

Students who do not complete preparatory work find themselves lost in class which has an unfavorable impact on the group dynamics during in-class activities (Billings, 2016; Clark, 2015). Unpublished observations from Goeman (2022) regarding students' out-of-class participation in a flipped research methodology classroom indicate that a group is affected significantly when a substantial proportion of a student group does not abide by the course design.

Issues with Tool Use

Secondly, as McCarthy (2016) observes, instructional disobedience in a flipped classroom might be demonstrated by students' (lack of) usage of online tools. Wong et al. (2019) state in their review about online learning environments:

One of these challenges is ensuring learners act according to the prompts or use the tools provided. Online learning environments are highly autonomous, and learners decide on their own whether or not to act upon the prompt or to use the tools provided (p. 369).

Lust et al. (2011) observed tool use differences, indicating that not every student profits from the opportunities provided in a blended learning environment. Three distinct profiles are discerned: no-users, incoherent users (those who use a selection of tools), and intensive users (those who use all of the available tools extensively). While the performance on a course of no-users is significantly different from the other student groups, no significant differences were found between incoherent and intensive users. Plausibly, incoherent users have a lesser need for certain tools to support their learning and are, therefore, "self-regulating" their tool use adequately. The authors relate their findings to a relevant question in ID, namely "how much student control, and for whom?" In the same line of reasoning, Luo et al. (2019) posited that a high level of student agency in the flipped classroom does not automatically improve students' performance and learning experience. They discovered that a low level of student agency resulted in better learning outcomes. In addition, students favored a more teacher-centered approach, especially during in-class activities.

Other flipped classroom studies regarding the processing of particular media or learning aids, such as videos, show various occurrences of instructional disobedience. Recent research from Walsh and Rísquez (2020) documents the opposite:

flipped classroom materials may be accessed by different clusters of students in distinct ways; however, but without any further manifestation of instructional disobedience. Wood et al. (2021) examined students' usage of available digital resources and observed that they pick resources based on what they feel best suits their needs. Additionally, students' choice of resources also depends on their beliefs about learning. These results imply that pre-class videos might be pushed aside by students when they believe that another resource. For example, a textbook might better fit their learning purposes. Witton (2021), in turn, revealed that the way in which lecture recordings are structured, which affects how students use them. This study finds that students are less likely to engage with traditional lecture capture content and content that has a long average session length. So, even when students are willing to engage with video materials, they may still not do so because of the way they are structured. These results are corroborated by Long et al. (2016).

Additionally, Zhang et al. (2021) report that during campus closures, students switched their planning and goal setting strategies for completing learning tasks; however, these changes did not impact the time of completion nor the outcomes, suggesting that the learning environment was sufficiently adapted to students' self-regulated learning behavior (Zhang et al., 2021).

The Sources of Instructional Disobedience

A series of affective, (meta)cognitive and motivational factors, as well as contextual characteristics, might result in instructional disobedience.

First, in various respects, the formal learning environment itself can be the source of instructional disobedience. On the one hand, it might be poorly designed, causing a misalignment between the (sequence of the) learning tasks and the pre-established goals. In case the student notices the misalignment and prefers to select a different approach in order to reach the goals—for instance, by neglecting elements of the learning environment—such defiant behavior is a positive, proactive kind of instructional disobedience. On the other hand, the learning environment might have a structural deficit in one or more of its elements, causing confusion or a lack of understanding among learners about their functionality or operationality. As a consequence, students possibly ignore or only partially use (a) certain element(s). The latter types of instructional disobedience may be classified as passive.

Secondly, students themselves can be the source of instructional disobedience. From a social-cognitive perspective of motivation, the learners' perceived value of a learning task in relation to the learning activities and learning goals determines whether and how they will interact with the different components of the learning environment. Learners' goal orientation, either mastery or performance oriented, also impacts their actual behavior (Lust et al., 2013). It seems plausible that instructional designers assume that all students wish to achieve the pre-established goals (as opposed to merely obtaining a "pass"). However, the anticipated student motivation and the actual motivation might differ, which may result in instructional disobedience. In addition, if the (ID elements of) learning environments are judged by students as being uncompelling or are considered as being less valuable than their rooted learning experiences, which will preclude their engagement. In this regard, Oudbier et al. (2022) draws attention to the value students still place on direct instruction. Like educators, learners have to adjust their conceptions of teaching and learning (Lo & Hew, 2017). Gopalan et al. (2021) found that students who were already familiar with the flipped classroom approach prior to the pandemic were able to adapt more swiftly to fully online education than those without previous experience. As flipped classrooms integrate much asynchronous online content, students might bear a "culture shock" when it comes to personal time management (Leeds, 2014). Cheng et al. (2019) suggested that a "reverse novelty effect" occurs with students "that are unaccustomed to pedagogy requiring active participation in classrooms" (p. 815).

Finally, with respect to students' self-regulation abilities, misconceptions about (elements of the) learning environment may also arise, which can affect (the monitoring of) their learning activities (Butler & Cartier, 2004). This might impede (correct) execution of learning tasks and usage of materials in (a) particular learning space(s). These types of instructional disobedience are deemed active.

The COVID-19 pandemic has shown that instructional disobedience may occur as a result of intertwining personal and contextual factors. In the case of home-based learning, the partition between the formal and informal learning environment is blurred. This is to a certain extent comparable with the reality of student learning in a flipped classroom, as the latter concentrates to a large extent on out-of-class activities. Given these (exceptional) circumstances, it is plausible that the actual context in which learning takes place deviates from the context for which the learning environment is designed. Logically, if inaccurate assumptions about the actual context are made, this may lead to an ill-fitted learning environment.

Students might dedicate less time to learning tasks due to other time-consuming obligations (e.g., taking a PCR test). Possibly, they re-assess the importance of (specific elements of) the learning environment and select others as means to study (e.g., rather than attending a lecture on-campus, watching its recording at double speed). In this regard, the initial suitability of learning tools is plausibly affected due to its non-availability in informal environments (e.g., the inclusion of virtual reality applications and accessory simulations on campus, but not available in distance education mode). Lastly, also concerns about health, depressed feelings, isolation, and so forth may jeopardize students' motivation and affect their achieved learning behavior. Such mis- or nonalignment classifies amongst the passive types of instructional disobedience.

Addressing Instructional Disobedience in Flipped Classrooms

Precluding (the negative impact of) instructional disobedience may not be avoided in all circumstances. Generally, given the limitations of ID, it is unfeasible to tailor a learning environment entirely to individual characteristics of all learners. Perhaps it is not even desirable to clear all instantiations of instructional disobedience. Notwithstanding, it is assumed that a couple of measures foster learners' usage of human- or technology-mediated instructional interventions as designed, while taking into account the difficulties with online self-regulated learning. Three propositions for ID might address instructional disobedience in flipped classrooms:

(1) To establish a lean, transparent, and structured instructional design Obviously, a close alignment between learning goals on the one hand and the different elements of the formal environment on the other hand, is essential to avoid instructional disobedience. Furthermore, a lean environment – one that contains only *need-to-have* elements, rather than also being loaded with *nice-to-have elements* – may reduce instructional disobedience. A series of studies have put forward evidence-based frameworks in this regard. For example, the seven recommendations of Quigley et al. (2018) might be applied when designing pre- and post-class learning activities.

It is also beyond question that being transparent about the *how*, *why* and *when* of each of the different elements of the flipped classroom is crucial for its effectiveness, as it supports students' self-regulation. Basically, this implies that a learner understands and accepts the pre-established goals, sees the functionality of the different elements (how can it aid the learner to reach the goals), and is able to use the elements as expected (see Gropper, 2015). In Latorre-Cosculluela et al. (2022), reference is made to students being informed upfront about the mechanics of flipped classrooms. In this way, it might help learners to know how much they will have to invest in order to be successful, what equipment they will need, and what contextual features may facilitate the usage of the designed interventions. Cunningham and Bergström (2020) emphasize the value of a clear structure and the usage of non-transient resources.

(2) To ensure flexibility, while controlling learners' completion of learning tasks and usage of tools Based on Luo et al. (2019), it seems justified to distribute agency between instructors and students when designing and implementing a flipped classroom.

In their account of a quasi-experimental study in the area of foreign language learning, Çakıroğlu and Öztürk's (2021) relate particular self-regulated learning strategies to either out-of-class (online) sessions or in-class (face-to-face) sessions. Next to this, a system indicates learner engagement progress, as well as problems. Educators offer help when students do not actively engage or do not finish pre-class activities. Latorre-Cosculluela et al. (2022) emphasize the role of instructors as supervisors of students' completion of learning tasks and as guides for students' self-regulation development in general. Cunningham and Bergström (2020) recommend to use mandatory engagement tasks and to require from students that they attend synchronous parts of a flipped classroom. A recent study in a medical educational setting (Zheng & Zhang, 2020) reports that self-regulated learning strategies involving peers or help-seeking are beneficial. In Michinov et al. (2011), one finds practical solutions for tutoring online activities and for stimulating participation in online learning environments. Viberg et al. (2020) describe a comprehensive open source system to counter freeriding behavior. The self-reflection part of the system is developed to have students give regular consideration to their individual progress towards the learning objectives of a course. From his side, an educator is able to monitor their progress and intervene, if deemed necessary.

(3) To integrate elements of adaptivity, in accordance with learners' self-regulated learning abilities Some authors propose instructional interventions which ensure more adaptivity in a blended course, hence, flipped classrooms (e.g., Van Laer & Elen, 2017; Lin, 2019). In general, data are collected in order to discern self-regulated learning profiles among students (e.g., Vanslambrouck et al., 2019), which in turn lead to targeted interventions (e.g., Broadbent et al., 2020). Online tools such as pedagogical agents, learning analytics, data visualization, and integrated support systems could be used to this end (Triquet et al., 2017; Wong et al., 2019).

A study in the midst of the pandemic by Clark et al. (2020) shows that implementing adaptive learning software for pre-class preparation in a flipped classroom has positive effects on students' perceived learning gain, motivation, and sense of responsibility. More recently, Lau (2021) describes a program-wide instructional intervention with four distinct phases. The ID includes pre-, in-, and post-class learning activities that accord with the learners' developmental stages of self-regulated learning behavior. The interventions focus on mastery-oriented evaluation, next to adaptive solutions regarding the nature of tasks, teacher support, and student autonomy.

Conclusions and Suggestions for Further Research

The authors' reflections on reimagining education in an evolving digital environment focus on a specific type of engagement, i.e., instructional disobedience. Instructional disobedience implies that students do not comply with the ID, which leads to an incongruence between students' actions in pursuance of pre-established learning goals and educators' expectations. Ultimately, a learner shows agency and is not or not as intended toward using elements of the formal learning environment. Instructional disobedience is not a totally new given; however, it is more manifest in learning environments based on a flipped classroom design.

Literature about flipped classrooms before and during the pandemic show that they have its merits for contemporary higher education, resilient to sudden changes (e.g., switching to full online mode of teaching) (Divjak et al., 2022). Notwithstanding, a flipped classroom challenges students particularly in terms of self-regulation for the out-of-class learning activities, and it seems that its design might never be a 100% resistant to instructional disobedience—even when substantiated by research evidence. Nevertheless, rather than penalizing non-compliant learning behavior, we believe that its occurrence should prompt scholars to reflect more profoundly about design elements that might have been missed.

As bikers or pedestrians may create over time the so-called "elephant paths," these are intended or unintended alternative trails to the regular road to reach a destination in a more convenient manner; one might try to understand problematic issues with participation in pre-class learning tasks or tool use. The "elephant paths" of successful, yet disobedient students indicate that not all elements of the learning environment might be necessary and/or functional. As elephant trails often become paved roads, likewise, initial non-compliant student behavior might steer innovative design and development. In sum, it is important to integrate observations about instructional disobedience in the loop of continuous quality improvement of flipped higher education classes.

As detailed above, this review attempts to take a first step toward resolving the lack of a framework in the literature. The contribution describes and illustrates instructional disobedience's nature and impact in higher education flipped classrooms and investigates some possible solutions to deal with it. As a result, it might give impetus to further considerations regarding students' actual learning behavior and appropriate flipped classroom designs.

Reeves and Lin (2020) expressed the need for more studies that are guided by socially responsible questions which "seek to make a difference in the lives of learners" (p. 1999). We believe that future research about flipped higher education classrooms needs to take students' compliance and disobedience into account. It will contribute to our understanding of quality teaching and learning in contexts of higher education. Among others, it seems that learner control and instructional knowledge (re)appear to the forefront as research topics. It is important that forthcoming studies focus on students' behavior "in environment" (Veletsianos et al., 2022), meaning that a series of ecological aspects of the students' learning situation and the flipped learning environment are considered, not neglected. In light of this, a highly valuable direction for future research is to conduct educational design research and collaborate closely with practitioners in higher education (McKenney & Reeves, 2019). Given the above considerations and applied to Reeves' and Lin's reasoning, such an endeavor might be expressed as follows:

1. What is the problem? (instructional disobedience in relation to outcomes)
2. How can we solve it? (responsive flipped classroom ecology)
3. What new knowledge can be derived from the solution? (principles for instructional design)

This study has only explored the phenomenon of instructional disobedience. As relevant data are highly dispersed and often "hidden" in (personal) reflections of scholars or practitioners, the research team was forced to look with an open visor to a wide series of contributions. Future investigations need to further classify, synthesize, and critically compare scientific accounts of instructional disobedience. Therefore, this chapter would like to include an unpretentious call to adopt "instructional disobedience" as a key term in future publications so that it becomes possible to conduct systematic reviews of studies.

To conclude, it is plausible that authors have been reluctant to report overtly on instructional disobedience. On the same note, we express our hope that more contributions about instructional disobedience will appear, as it is part of the ongoing quest for a better understanding of how to design, develop, and assess learning environments. Therefore, we also call on the research community to describe instances of instructional disobedience.

References

Bäcklund, J., & Hugo, M. (2018). The paradox of the flipped classroom: One method, many intentions. *Problems of Education in the 21st Century, 76*(4), 451–464. https://doi.org/10.33225/pec/18.76.451

Barnard-Brak, L., Paton, V. O., & Lan, W. Y. (2010). Profiles in self-regulated learning in the online learning environment. *The International Review of Research in Open and Distance Learning, 11*(1), 61–80. https://doi.org/10.19173/irrodl.v11i1.769

Baytiyeh, H. (2017). The flipped classroom model: When technology enhances professional skills. *International Journal of Information and Learning Technology, 34*(1), 51–62. https://doi.org/10.1108/IJILT-07-2016-0025

Billings, D. M. (2016). 'Flipping' the classroom. *American Journal of Nursing, 116*(9), 52–56. https://doi.org/10.1097/01.NAJ.0000494696.86240.35

Bredow, C. A., Roehling, P. V., Knorp, A. J., & Sweet, A. M. (2021). To flip or not to flip? A meta-analysis of the efficacy of flipped learning in higher education. *Review of Educational Research, 91*(6), 878–918. https://doi.org/10.3102/2F00346543211019122

Brewer, R., & Movahedazarhouligh, S. (2018). Successful stories and conflicts: A literature review on the effectiveness of flipped learning in higher education. *Journal of Computer Assisted Learning, 34*(4), 409–416. https://doi.org/10.1111/jcal.12250

Broadbent, J., Panadero, E., Lodge, J. M., & Barba, P. D. (2020). Technologies to enhance self-regulated learning in online and computer-mediated learning environments. In I. M. Bishop, E. Boling, J. Elen, & V. Svihla (Eds.), *Handbook of research in educational communications and technology* (pp. 37–52). Springer. https://doi.org/10.1007/978-3-030-36119-8_3

Butler, D. L., & Cartier, S. C. (2004). Promoting effective task interpretation as an important work habit: Key to successful teaching and learning. *Teachers College Record, 106*(9), 1729–1758. https://doi.org/10.1111/j.1467-9620.2004.00403.x

Çakıroğlu, Ü., & Öztürk, M. (2021). Cultivating self-regulated learning in flipped EFL courses: A model for course design. *European Journal of Open, Distance and E-Learning, 23*(2), 20–36. https://doi.org/10.2478/eurodl-2020-0008

Chen, W., Kinshuk, Y., & Chen, N.-S. (2014). Is FLIP enough? Or should we use the FLIPPED model instead? *Computers and Education, 79*, 16–27. https://doi.org/10.1016/j.compedu.2014.07.004

Cheng, L., Ritzhaupt, A. D., & Antonenko, P. (2019). Effects of the flipped classroom instructional strategy on students' learning outcomes: A meta-analysis. *Educational Technology Research and Development, 67*, 793–824. https://doi.org/10.1007/s11423-018-9633-7

Clark, K. R. (2015). The effects of the flipped model of instruction on student engagement and performance in the secondary mathematics classroom. *Journal of Educators Online, 12*(1), 91–115. https://www.thejeo.com/archive/2015_12_1/clark

Clark, R. M., Kaw, A. K., & Gomes, R. B. (2020). Adaptive learning: Helpful to the flipped classroom in the online environment of COVID? *Computer Applications in Engineering Education, 30*(2), 517–531. https://doi.org/10.1002/cae.22470

Cunningham, U., & Bergström, A. (2020). Reimagining learning in a language education course thrust online: Social Constructivism in times of social isolation. In R. E. Ferdig, E. Baumgartner,

R. Hartshorne, R. Kaplan-Rakowski, & C. Mouza (Eds.), *Teaching, technology, and teacher education during the covid-19 pandemic: Stories from the field* (pp. 449–456). Association for the Advancement of Computing in Education (AACE).

Divjak, B., Rienties, B., Iniesto, F., Vondra, P., & Žižak, M. (2022). Flipped classrooms in higher education during the COVID-19 pandemic: Findings and future research recommendations. *International Journal of Educational Technology in Higher Education, 19*(1), 9–9. https://doi.org/10.1186/s41239-021-00316-4

Elen, J. (2013). "Instructional disobedience": Challenging instructional design research. In *Book of abstracts and extended summaries 15th biennial conference EARLI 2013 "responsible teaching and sustainable learning"* (p. 804). Technische Universität München.

Elen, J. (2016). Reflections on the future of instructional design research. In J. Spector, D. Ifenthaler, D. Sampson, & P. Isaias (Eds.), *Competencies in teaching, learning and educational leadership in the digital age* (pp. 1–14). Springer. https://doi.org/10.1007/978-3-319-30295-9_1

Elen, J. (2020). "Instructional disobedience": A largely neglected phenomenon deserving more systematic research attention. *Educational Technology Research and Development, 68*(5), 2021–2032. https://doi.org/10.1007/s11423-020-09776-3

Elvers, G. C., Polzella, D. J., & Graetz, K. (2003). Procrastination in online courses: Performance and attitudinal differences. *Teaching of Psychology, 30*(2), 159–162. https://doi.org/10.1207/2FS15328023TOP3002_13

Goeman, K. (2022). *Course assessment report "Data analysis"*. [Unpublished manuscript].

Goodyear, P. (2000). Environments for lifelong learning: Ergonomics, architecture and educational design. In J. Spector & T. Anderson (Eds.), *Integrated and holistic perspectives on learning, instruction and technology* (pp. 1–18). Springer. https://doi.org/10.1007/0-306-47584-7_1

Goodyear, P., & Dimitriadis, Y. (2013). In medias res: Reframing design for learning. *Research in Learning Technology, 21*, 1–13. https://doi.org/10.3402/rlt.v21i0.19909

Gopalan, C., Sinan, O., Butts-Wilmsmeyer, C., Dickney, P., Serrano, C., Bracey, G., Bartels, L., Locke, S., & Fickas, J. (2021). Flipped teaching eased the transition of students to online learning during the COVID-19 pandemic. *The FASEB Journal, 35*(1). https://doi.org/10.1096/fasebj.2021.35.S1.04659

Gropper, J. L. (2015). Inclusive instructional design: Creating a "learner" version of instructional design that fosters active learner engagement. *Educational Technology, 55*(3), 3–13. http://www.jstor.org/stable/44430366

Jonassen, D. H., Hernandez-Serrano, J., & Choi, I. (2000). Integrating constructivism and learning technologies. In J. M. Spector & T. M. Anderson (Eds.), *Integrated and holistic perspectives on learning, instruction and technology* (pp. 103–128). Springer. https://doi.org/10.1007/0-306-47584-7_7

Kim, M. K., Kim, S. M., Khera, O., & Getman, J. (2014). The experience of three flipped classrooms in an urban university: An exploration of design principles. *The Internet and Higher Education, 22*, 37–50. https://doi.org/10.1016/j.iheduc.2014.04.003

Latorre-Cosculluela, C., Suárez, C., Quiroga, S., Anzano-Oto, S., Lira-Rodríguez, E., & Salamanca-Villate, A. (2022). Facilitating self-efficacy in university students: An interactive approach with flipped classroom. *Higher Education Research & Development, 4*(5), 1603–1617. https://doi.org/10.1080/07294360.2021.1937067

Lau, K. L. (2021). Integrating e-learning into self-regulated learning instruction: A holistic flipped classroom design of a classical Chinese reading intervention program. In M. Rodrigo, S. Iyer, & A. Mitrovic (Eds.), *Proceedings of the 29th international conference on computers in education* (pp. 503–509). Asia-Pacific Society for Computers in Education. https://icce2021.apsce.net/proceedings/volume1/

Leeds, B. (2014). Temporal experiences of e-learning by distance learners. *Education + Training, 56*(2/3), 179–189. https://doi.org/10.1108/ET-11-2012-0114

Lin, Y. (2019). Impacts of a flipped classroom with a smart learning diagnosis system on students' learning performance, perception, and problem solving ability in a software engineering course. *Computers in Human Behavior, 95*, 187–196. https://doi.org/10.1016/j.chb.2018.11.036

Lo, C. K., & Hew, K. F. (2017). A critical review of flipped classroom challenges in K-12 education: Possible solutions and recommendations for future research. *RPTEL, 12*(4). https://doi.org/10.1186/s41039-016-0044-2

Long, T., Logan, J., & Waugh, M. (2016). Students' perceptions of the value of using videos as a pre-class learning experience in the flipped classroom. *TechTrends, 60*(3), 245–252. https://doi.org/10.1007/s11528-016-0045-4

Luo, H., Yang, T., Xue, J., & Zuo, M. (2019). Impact of student agency on learning performance and learning experience in a flipped classroom. *British Journal of Educational Technology, 50*(2), 819–831. https://doi.org/10.1111/bjet.12604

Lust, G., Vandewaetere, M., Ceulemans, E., Elen, J., & Clarebout, G. (2011). Tool-use in a blended undergraduate course: In search of user profiles. *Computers & Education, 57*(3), 2135–2144. https://doi.org/10.1016/j.compedu.2011.05.010

Lust, G., Elen, J., & Clarebout, G. (2013). Students' tool-use within a web enhanced course: Explanatory mechanisms of students' tool-use pattern. *Computers in Human Behavior, 29*(5), 2013–2021. https://doi.org/10.1016/j.chb.2013.03.014

McCarthy, J. (2016). Reflections on a flipped classroom in first year higher education. *Issues in Educational Research, 26*(2), 332–350. http://www.iier.org.au/iier26/mccarthy-j.html

McKenney, S., & Reeves, T. C. (2019). *Conducting educational design research* (2nd ed.). Routledge.

Michinov, N., Brunot, S., Le Bohec, O., Juhel, J., & Delaval, M. (2011). Procrastination, participation, and performance in online learning environments. *Computers & Education, 56*(1), 243–252. https://doi.org/10.1016/j.compedu.2010.07.025

Moore, N. (2006). Desk research. In *How to do research: A practical guide to designing and managing research projects* (pp. 106–111). Facet.

Oudbier, J., Spaai, G., Timmermans, K., & Boerboom, T. (2022). Enhancing the effectiveness of flipped classrooms in health science education: A state-of-the-art review. *BMC Medical Education, 22*(34), 1–15. https://doi.org/10.1186/s12909-021-03052-5

Panadero, E. (2017). A review of self-regulated learning: Six models and four directions for research. *Frontiers in Psychology, 8*(422), 1–28. https://doi.org/10.3389/fpsyg.2017.00422

Peterson, D. J. (2016). The flipped classroom improves student achievement and course satisfaction in a statistics course. *Teaching of Psychology, 43*(1), 10–15. https://doi.org/10.1177/0098628315620063

Quigley, A., Muijs, D., & Stringer, E. (2018). *Guidance report: Metacognition and self-regulated learning.* Education Endowment Foundation. https://educationendowmentfoundation.org.uk/education-evidence/guidance-reports/metacognition

Rasheed, R. A., Kamsin, A., Abdullah, N. A., Kakudi, H. A., Ali, A. S., Musa, A. S., & Yahaya, A. S. (2020). Self-regulated learning in flipped classrooms: A systematic literature review. *International Journal of Information and Education Technology, 10*(11), 848–853. https://doi.org/10.18178/ijiet.2020.10.11.1469

Reeves, T. C., & Lin, L. (2020). The research we have is not the research we need. *Educational Technology Research and Development, 68*, 1991–2001. https://doi.org/10.1007/s11423-020-09811-3

Song, Y., Jong, M. S. Y., Chang, M., & Chen, W. (2017). Guest editorial: "HOW" to design, implement and evaluate the flipped classroom? – A synthesis. *Journal of Educational Technology & Society, 20*(1), 180–183. https://www.proquest.com/scholarly-journals/how-design-implement-evaluate-flipped-classroom/docview/2147735131/se-2

Stöhr, C., Demazière, C., & Adawi, T. (2020). The polarizing effect of the online flipped classroom. *Computers & Education, 147*, 103789. https://doi.org/10.1016/j.compedu.2019.103789

Stott, P. (2016). The perils of a lack of student engagement: Reflections of a "lonely, brave, and rather exposed" online instructor. *British Journal of Educational Technology, 47*(1), 51–64. https://doi.org/10.1111/bjet.12215

Stracke, C., Shanks, M., & Tveiten, O. (2017). *Smart universities: Education's digital future.* Logos Verlag. https://doi.org/10.5281/zenodo.1204290

Tawfik, A., Shepherd, C., Gatewood, J., & Gish-Lieberman, J. (2021). First and second order barriers to teaching in k-12 online learning. *TechTrends, 65*(6), 925–938. https://doi.org/10.1007/s11528-021-00648-y

Thai, N., De Wever, B., & Valcke, M. (2017). The impact of a flipped classroom design on learning performance in higher education: Looking for the best "blend" of lectures and guiding questions with feedback. *Computers & Education, 107*, 113–126. https://doi.org/10.1016/j.compedu.2017.01.003

Triquet, K., Peeters, J., & Lombaerts, K. (2017). *Self-regulated learning online: Benefits, empirical foundations, multi-level, and multi-modal promotion & evaluation thereof for teacher professional development.* Teach-UP. http://teachup.eun.org/outputs

Van Laer, S., & Elen, J. (2017). In search of attributes that support self-regulation in blended learning environments. *Education and Information Technologies, 22*, 1395–1454. https://doi.org/10.1007/s10639-016-9505-x

Vanslambrouck, S., Zhu, C., Pynoo, B., Lombaerts, K., Tondeur, J., & Scherer, R. (2019). A latent profile analysis of adult students' online self-regulation in blended learning environments. *Computers in Human Behavior, 99*, 126–136. https://doi.org/10.1016/j.chb.2019.05.021

Veletsianos, G., Childs, E., Cox, R., Cordua-von Specht, I., Grundy, S., Hughes, J., Karleen, D., & Willson, A. (2022). Person in environment: Focusing on the ecological aspects of online and distance learning. *Distance Education, 43*(2), 318–324. https://doi.org/10.1080/0158791 9.2022.2064827

Viberg, O., Mavroudi, A., Fernaeus, Y., Bogdan, C., & Laaksolahti, J. (2020). Reducing free riding: CLASS – A system for collaborative learning assessment. In R. Gennari, P. Vittorini, F. De la Prieta, T. Di Mascio, M. Temperini, R. Siveira, & D. Carranza (Eds.), *Methodologies and intelligent systems for technology enhanced learning* (pp. 132–138). Springer. https://doi.org/10.1007/978-3-030-23884-1_17

Walsh, J. N., & Rísquez, A. (2020). Using cluster analysis to explore the engagement with a flipped classroom of native and non-native English-speaking management students. *The International Journal of Management Education, 18*(2), 100381. https://doi.org/10.1016/j.ijme.2020.100381

Wang, F. H. (2017). An exploration of online behaviour engagement and achievement in flipped classroom supported by learning management system. *Computers & Education, 114*, 79–91. https://doi.org/10.1016/j.compedu.2017.06.012

Witton, G. (2021). Exploring dissonance in the use of (lecture) capture technologies: Institutional approaches and the realities of student engagement. *Interactive Learning Environments, 5*(1), 1–12. https://doi.org/10.1080/10494820.2021.1905002

Wong, J., Baars, M., Davis, D., van der Zee, M. T., Houben, G. J. P., & Paas, F. (2019). Supporting self-regulated learning in online learning environments and MOOCs: A systematic review. *International Journal of Human-Computer Interaction, 35*(4–5), 356. https://doi.org/10.108 0/10447318.2018.1543084

Wood, A. K., Bailey, T. N., Galloway, R. K., Hardy, J. A., Sangwin, C. J., & Docherty, P. J. (2021). Lecture capture as an element of the digital resource landscape: A qualitative study of flipped and non–flipped classrooms. *Technology, Pedagogy and Education, 30*(3), 443–458. https://doi.org/10.1080/1475939X.2021.1917449

Zhang, T., Taub, M., & Chen, Z. (2021). Measuring the impact of COVID-19 induced campus closure on student self-regulated learning in physics online learning modules. *ACM International Conference Proceeding Series*, 110–120. https://doi.org/10.1145/3448139.3448150

Zheng, B., & Zhang, Y. (2020). Self-regulated learning: The effect on medical student learning outcomes in a flipped classroom environment. *BMC Medical Education, 20*(100), 100. https://doi.org/10.1186/s12909-020-02023-6

Zuber, W. J. (2016). The flipped classroom: A review of the literature. *Industrial and Commercial Training, 48*(2), 97–103. https://doi.org/10.1108/ICT-05-2015-0039

Reimagining the Future of Special Education Technology

Dave L. Edyburn

Introduction

The field of special education technology is focused on applications of technology that serve to augment, bypass, or compensate for a disability (Edyburn, 2013). Within this discipline are three specialty areas: assistive technologies, instructional technologies, and/or universal design for learning.

Historically, any technology used by a person with a disability has been thought of as *assistive technology*. Federal law defines an assistive technology device as follows:

> …any item. piece of equipment, or product system, whether acquired commercially, off the shelf, modified, or customized, that is used to increase, maintain, or improve the functional capabilities of a child with a disability. (20 USC § 1401(1)(A))

Some experts have argued that the definition of assistive technology is so broad that it could include anything (Edyburn, 2004). In fact, that is a simple way to think about it: Assistive technology is *anything* that improves the functional performance of an individual with a disability. Because of the potential assistive technology holds for individuals with disabilities, federal law requires that assistive technology be considered when planning the Individualized Education Plan (IEP) for every student with a disability.

Instructional, or educational technologies, are those technologies used in schools to promote learning (Roblyer & Hughes, 2019). For students with disabilities who have difficulty learning, specialized instructional technologies may feature detailed feedback and error analysis, branching, simplified language, and personalized learning. It is

D. L. Edyburn (✉)
University of Wisconsin-Milwaukee, Milwaukee, WI, USA
e-mail: edyburn@uwm.edu

© The Author(s), under exclusive license to Springer Nature Switzerland AG 2023
D. Cockerham et al. (eds.), *Reimagining Education: Studies
and Stories for Effective Learning in an Evolving Digital Environment*,
Educational Communications and Technology: Issues and Innovations,
https://doi.org/10.1007/978-3-031-25102-3_23

often difficult to discern in advance whether or not an instructional technology will be effective for a student with disability in achieving a given instructional objective. However, the inability to learn academic content in the same way, or at the same pace as peers, is a key characteristic of a disability and therefore should be considered when selecting instructional technologies to support diverse learners (Edyburn, 2019).

Universal design for learning (UDL) is an approach to instructional design that embeds supports for learners before they are needed (Meyer et al., 2014). That is, learners may use a slider to adjust the font size to enlarge the text to a comfortable reading level, turn on closed captions to make audio information accessible, or use text to speech tools to foster comprehension of text that could not be read independently. The value of UDL is that these design features not only help students with disabilities but also have the potential to help many students in the general classroom.

For the foreseeable future, it is appropriate that educators focus on these three types of technologies that are well-known within special education. However, there are larger trends and issues impacting the world around us that have profound implications for the future of education in general and special education technology specifically. The purpose of this chapter is to re-imagine the future of educational technology applications for individuals with disabilities, a population that represents 10–14% of school-aged children (National Center for Education Statistics, 2021).

Process

Technologists often focus on the latest advances being made in research labs or new entries in the commercial marketplace by making it a priority to stay-up-to-date with the latest technology trends and issues (Future Today Institute, 2022; Pelletier et al., 2022). However, just knowing about new technologies is not enough for educational leaders because there is little guidance about how or when a new technology trend will emerge into a force that has significant impact.

Futurists often describe three types of change and the types of impact that is produced (Burrus, 1994, 2011). *Incremental change* is predictable, involves little risk, and enthuses a high degree of confidence that the scenario will become a reality. A second type of change occurs when two different trends come together in ways that accelerate the effect of the change. Seeing relationships that foster *convergence change* requires a bit of vision and creativity, because the ability to connect dots is not readily apparent to everyone, yet. However, research has shown that when a business harnesses *disruptive change* technologies, it is not necessarily the first or the one with the best technology that achieves market dominance (Christensen, 2013). Rather disruptive organizations prosper because the rules of the game changed while others were still playing by the old rules. Analyzing change using these three techniques from the work of futurists can provide educational technology leaders and educators with keen insight about planning for the future of education during a period of rapid change.

To connect the dots between factors that could significantly alter the future of special education, two sets of variables are worth considering. Table 1 illustrates 13

Table 1 Pandemic influenced trends and issues impacting the future of special education

Trend & issue	Description
Accountability	Emphasis on monitoring student attendance, engagement, and achievement of grade level learning standards. Accountability measures can be targeted at multiple levels: Classroom, school, district, and/or state. Accountability initiatives were often modified in favor of flexibility given the unprecedented nature of the pandemic
Assessment	During the pandemic, high-stakes assessments were often suspended. As a result, little normative information is available concerning student achievement. Formative assessment will continue to be important while new initiatives are created for benchmarking student achievement and are re-instituted or re-designed
Classroom demographics	American classrooms are more diverse than ever before. Educational systems will be challenged to diversify its teaching staff
Effective practice	Recent research has focused on high leverage practices. That is, research-based practices that have been demonstrated to increase student achievement. Now that such practices have been identified, how do pre service and in-service teachers learn to implement these practices in their classroom during and after the pandemic?
Engaged learning	Pedagogy continues to shift from teacher-centered classrooms to a focus on learning engagement. During the pandemic, concern about student engagement became a critical concern. Engagement is essential for learning
Equity	The pandemic revealed many structural inequities that disproportionately impacted students of color, students with disabilities, English language learners, and students living in poverty and their families. Federal American Recovery Plan funds have been distributed to assist educational leaders in addressing structural inequities
Learning loss	What can be done to reduce/eliminate the learning deficits caused by the pandemic? At this point, while initial research studies are emerging, little is known about the long-term impact of learning loss
Mental health	As the pandemic impacts its third school year (2019–2020, 2020–2021, 2021–2022), mental health has become a critical issue for children and families, as well as teachers. Some schools have developed new initiatives to integrate social emotional learning (SEL) into the curriculum
Remote learning	The pandemic required schools to pivot from face-to-face learning to remote instruction. While many teachers, students, and parents were required to learn new skills in order to connect, remote learning is likely to continue post-pandemic as a form of flexibility
Space utilization	During the initial phase of the pandemic, schools were empty. Later, in initial efforts to reopen schools and socially distance, some schools adopted a block schedule where students would attend two days a week (e.g., M & T or R & F) and participate in remote Learning two other days. Similar to the questions raised by business, are there better ways to utilize space?
Teacher pipeline	Enrollment in teacher education programs is down 5–10% which signals we are not preparing enough future teachers to meet current demands – Much less to fill existing teacher shortages. Predictably, a teacher shortage crisis is on the horizon
Teacher shortages	School districts have always faced a shortage of special education teachers. However, teacher shortages in all disciplines, and at all levels, have significantly increased during the pandemic such that certified special education personnel are not available for every classroom
Workforce readiness	Questions continue to be raised about whether K-12 students completing are workforce ready. Increased technology use in the workplace challenges educators to ensure students have the necessary knowledge and skills for 21st college and careers.

trends and issues selected by the author that have received renewed attention during the pandemic and likely have the potential to impact the foreseeable future of education and the provision of special education. Similarly, Table 2 summarizes 13 technology trends and issues that are the routine focus of technology developers and start-up companies and are of interest to educational technology specialists interested in emerging technologies. Readers are encouraged to browse both tables and consider whether or not they have a general awareness with each issue. Ideally, readers will have a cursory understanding of each item, which individually, are likely to be unremarkable at this point. It should be noted that many other topics could be added to these lists. The topics have been selected by the author to illustrate a predictive process that will be described in detail in the next section.

The next section examines the potential convergence of these trends in light of Burrus' (1994, 2011) three types of change in order to understand the influences on the education of students with disabilities in inclusive settings. The goal is to provide the tools necessary to assist educational technology leaders and educators to answer the question: Is it possible to discern the difference between technologies that will produce incremental, and perhaps inconsequential, change with technologies that will produce profoundly disruptive effects in order to plan for the future of inclusive education?

Findings

Burrus (1994) contends that new futures are created from a mix of technological innovations and new rules that change the nature of the game. He uses the metaphor of a card game to illustrate what happens when the game is played by the conventional rules (the future will be similar to life as it is today). However, he periodically introduces new cards and new rules into the game, injecting the appropriate level of chaos that real change brings. (Perhaps you have noticed how hard it is to win a game when you don't know the rules?)

Focusing exclusively on trends may point to predictable change, but new rules and tools can fundamentally alter the ways systems work. Pausing for a moment, isn't this what education experienced during the pandemic? The need to pivot from classroom-based instruction to remote learning? The need to change from paper-based learning materials to digital learning materials? The need for learners to become less dependent on teachers and more self-directed? While educators have debated these issues for decades, did we ever anticipate that such profound changes would be implemented in every school district across the country in a matter of weeks during Spring 2020?

Using the information presented in Tables 1 and 2, I believe it is possible to engage the educational community in a process of recognizing trends in education and technology that may have a significant impact on the future of inclusive education. In the sections that follow, I model the process of selecting a trend from each

Table 2 Technology trends and issues with the potential to impact inclusive education

Trend & issue	Description
1–1	For many years, schools longed to provide each student with a computer (known as a 1–1 program). The pivot to remote learning during the pandemic made this goal a reality as many schools sent students home with a Chromebook. Yet, many teachers, students, and families were unprepared for online learning. Now that the basic infrastructure is in place, what does the future of 1–1 learning look like?
Apps	As smartphones have become ubiquitous, apps have become a necessary tool for mobile professionals. However, in the educational space, apps often have a single function and do not talk to each other or share data. As a result, teachers are required to sign-in and manage many different apps. How will apps of the future be different?
Cloud computing	A key design principle of many cloud computing applications is that they allow users to sign in from multiple devices (i.e., smartphone, tablet, laptop, desktop) to use apps or software and access their data. The backbone that makes this workflow possible is known as cloud storage. What are the implications of cloud computing for the future of education?
Data	It is increasingly possible to collect a wide variety of data explicitly from users (e.g., name, preferences) as well as extract data from their behaviors (e.g., time to respond, correct/incorrect). Online learning may afford additional data such as the user's image, voice, and IP address. At the present time, there are few protections of user data and limited opportunities to opt out. As companies seek to monetize this data, what rights do students/parents have about how student data will be used?
Digital curricula	The pandemic accelerated the adoption of digital curricula. Yet, many learning materials are not much more than scanned PDFs of print material. And, there have been many instances where digital curricula were inaccessible to students who utilized assistive technologies. As schools adopt more commercial digital curricula, what instructional design principles should be put in place to ensure that learning materials are not only accessible, but effective, in producing learning outcomes in diverse students?
Immersive environments	Augmented reality (AR), virtual reality (VR), and mixed reality (MR) are all forms of immersive learning environments. The recent announcement about the Metaverse has renewed attention about the future of this sector of educational technology. To the extent that immersive learning environments are effective in promoting learning, to what extent will these new technologies be adopted and used in schools?
Learning analytics	Given the exponential increase in data collected by software and apps, learning analytics involve statistical methods to make sense of the data. Writing an equation that determines whether or not a student has demonstrated sufficient understanding of an instructional topic is extremely challenging. However, advances in learning analytics will be essential to achieving the promise of personalized learning. At the present time, little is known about what learning analytics can tell us about learning during the pandemic
Learning management systems	Learning management systems (LMS) are designed to facilitate online teaching and learning. In the K-12 space, Google classroom and Moodle are the most common LMS and blackboard the most common LMS in higher education. How might the current generation of LMS evolve in the future to enhance personalized learning and effectively use learning analytics?

(continued)

Table 2 (continued)

Trend & issue	Description
Machine learning	Machine learning (ML) involves statistical analysis to make sense of patterns in extremely large data sets. At the present time, insufficient data is available at the classroom or school level to apply ML. However, when data is aggregated through a LMS with hundreds of thousands of students, interesting problems can be posed. How might ML be applied in post-pandemic education?
Online learning	Prior to the pandemic, online learning was primarily the domain of higher education and specialized advanced placement classes in high schools. The pandemic accelerated online learning into K-12 education with many unanswered questions about its appropriateness for young children. In the future, how will schools deploy online learning effectively?
Personalized learning	Understanding that one-size-does-not-fit all, curriculum developers are increasingly designing learning systems that afford multiple pathways to achieving learning objectives. Whereas individualized instruction was once the purview of special education, personalized learning is viewed as desirable for every student. What advances might be expected in the personalized learning space if remote learning continues or in a return to classroom-based instruction?
Privacy	The increased prevalence of data collection has raised a number of questions and concerns about privacy. While there are several federal laws designed to protect minors, there are few agreed upon student privacy standards. As school districts implement more digital curricula products, what needs to be done so that student privacy is protected?
Security	The pandemic revealed a number of security flaws in educational software and school district server maintenance practices. As a result, student and teacher data has been compromised. As schools become much more dependent on technology-based instruction, what investments need to be made in security systems and user practices to prevent unauthorized access of student data?

of the tables and then use the information to frame a description of a scenario concerning a future that re-imagines education for students with disabilities.

Incremental Change Scenarios

If we anticipate that change will occur slowly and incrementally, then the future will simply evolve from where we are today. Leaders and educators who plan for the future of technology by focusing on a single trend may take action found in the following scenarios.

Scenario #1

Trend Learning Loss

The Future Policymaker and educators have become concerned about evidence that suggests that most students failed to achieve a full grade of academic achievement during the pandemic. Significant questions are raised about the long-term impact of these lost opportunities.

Implications Students with disabilities have been identified as one of several groups that have been inordinately impacted by learning loss during the pandemic. Federal funding allocated through the American Recovery Plan has specifically targeted learning loss as a priority to be addressed through new state and local programs. Schools could choose to use these funds to implement summer school programs or purchase new digital learning materials designed to close the achievement gap.

Scenario #2

Trend Security

The Future As twenty-first century teaching and learning becomes more digital, data breaches will continue to become increasingly common as more student data is collected and stored online.

Implications During the pandemic, ransomware attacks against schools increased dramatically (Cybersecurity and Infrastructure Security Agency, 2020). As a result, schools will need to devote an increasing percentage of their technology budget to enhancing security training and services. (Yet, these expenditures become a significant cost of doing business and yet have no direct relationship to student achievement.) The technical requirements of this work will require external contracts as the expertise is too expensive to employ local personnel. Some security protocols will make it difficult or impossible for some students with cognitive disabilities to independently log-on. Students who use alternative input devices because physical disabilities prevent them from using the standard keyboard and mouse are likely dependent on someone else to sign-in for them.

Scenarios 1 and 2 represent logical and conservative actions to utilize technology in a way that improves education in the future. Each scenario represents incremental change that may be resisted by some, but will be, in general, supported by many as a means to plan for the future by adopting emerging technology tools. There is little risk for an educational leader to adopt technology addressing incremental change because the actions appear logical and obvious. The seductive nature of incremental change is that it appears we are preparing for a future that looks similar to the world we know today. Readers are encouraged to expand on any of the trends listed in Tables 1 and 2, or identify a trend not listed, to create their own incremental change scenario that may describe the future of special education.

Convergence Change Scenarios

A more challenging task involving incremental change relates to the impact of the convergence of multiple trends. Whereas there can be an element of predictability in this process, the convergence of trends has the potential to significantly impact the daily operation of inclusive education. Consider the following scenarios that illustrate the process of combining trends in ways that are not initially obvious (or, perhaps not deemed desirable by the status quo) and simultaneously accelerate the need for change.

Scenario #3

Trend Teacher Shortages + Online Learning

The Future The pandemic accelerated a trend in educators retiring or leaving the classroom. Teacher shortages are now common in most communities beyond the historical shortages of special education teachers. Given a shortage of qualified teachers, schools could invest in new online learning systems that provide direct instruction for students with access to online tutors as needed thereby reducing the number of teachers needed.

Implications School districts have purchased many types of digital curricula products that feature content aligned with standards, pre- and post-test assessment, and guided instructional learning modules. The scale-up of online teaching in K-12 during the pandemic has created a new infrastructure that could be significantly expanded again as a response to the shortage of qualified teachers. While some may view a change of replacing teachers with online instruction as undesirable, it may be necessary to address the teacher shortage, and these changes could become more attractive if bundled with childcare, academic and social enrichment opportunities to address society's needs for safe places for children during the work day. Parents of children with special education needs are often concerned about whether or not this scenario will help or hinder their child's progress.

Scenario #4

Trend Mental Health + Apps

The Future Emerging evidence suggests that the need for mental health services has increased exponentially during the pandemic. As a result, schools are likely to expand their implementation of social emotional learning (SEL) curricula and technology tools like apps. Well-designed mental health apps could provide early warning indicators to professionals to ensure that students receive the support services they need.

Implications Schools will be expected to expand mental health services to students and expand SEL curricula to focus on prevention. UDL principles could be helpful in the design of app-based services with students receiving digital passes to in-school mental health services. Daily mental health check-ins could become a routine part of homeroom. Expanding mental health services for all students could be beneficial to many students with disabilities. Consideration will need to be made concerning the accessibility of apps.

The pandemic revealed that innovation can scale at a significant speed. And yet, as we seek to transition from life in a pandemic to living with viruses as part of an endemic, many experts believe that online learning will continue to be used widely. Many communities are now engaged in lively debates about what it means to return to "normal" or what a "new normal" should look like. For example, consider how some school districts have discontinued the concept of a snow day by simply declaring that a given day with excessive snow or ice will be a remote learning day rather than an in-person learning day. However, the key point here is that the convergence of trends is a complex matter, beyond the control of any one individual or organization. Now that almost all families have experienced online learning, there is considerable opinion and influence about what may come next. As a result, there is a need to examine each scenario and decide whether or not it is a viable description of the future and determine whether or not an organization should take action to move in that direction, or wait until more evidence is available to connect the dots.

Disruptive Change Scenarios

Individually, any one of the previous scenarios could affect the future of education (positively or negatively). However, when the trends and scenarios become bundled, they can produce powerful disruptive change scenarios. In this final section, I outline some disruptive change scenarios that I believe have the potential to emerge from the current chaos of post-pandemic education:

Scenario #5

Trend Equity + Accountability + Learning Loss + Machine Learning + Learning Analytics

The Future The pandemic revealed a number of structural inequities concerning learning and achievement for many groups of students, including students with disabilities. To address these shortcomings, new accountability efforts could be implemented along with the use of machine learning and learning analytics to analyze student data in order to monitor student engagement and progress.

Implications The expanded use of digital curricula affords new opportunities for data collection, analysis, and reporting. Schools that are concerned about equity could use learning analytics to provide more personalized instruction and create data dashboards to provide public accountability about progress towards various goals. Because this scenario would probably place more emphasis on technology as a solution for closing the achievement gap, less emphasis may be given to teacher professional development. With the improvement of machine learning, the role of the teacher could be significantly altered and diminished as other adults are employed in schools to manage students.

Scenario #6

Trend Remote Learning + Space Utilization + Immersive Environments + Personalized Learning

The Future In the future, schooling could reflect the scheduling found in flexible office environments. That is, students and families would create a schedule that would involve some in-school time and some remote learning time reflective of personalized learning systems. Because not all students would be in a school building at the same time, space utilization will become a major opportunity for schools to create learning centers around the community, including under-utilized space in office buildings. This could mean that physical education is no longer conducted at school but at a local fitness center under the direction of a personalized trainer. Immersive environments could be created in schools or in office buildings to use the most advanced augmented and virtual reality tools to engage students in deep learning, accelerate learning outcomes, and decrease learning time. Such immersive learning centers could also be used by businesses to support advanced workforce development investments in their employees.

Implications The impact of COVID-19 has been disruptive to many societal institutions, including education. The pandemic exposed the critical role of schools not only in preparing the future workforce but also for providing children with safe environments while parents were working. Given the need for life-long education, disruptive applications of technology could provide critical flexibility for children and adults in personalizing learning processes and outcomes. Public schools that were built for the initiation of compulsory education in the 1800s are ripe for the re-imagination of the future of schooling where technology, personalization, and flexibility are characteristics of life in the twenty-first century.

Discussion

Educators are often so focused on their day-to-day work that there is little time for considering the emerging trends and issues happening around us. Trend analysis is a basic technique futurists use in order to develop scenarios that are helpful in planning for the future. Educational technology leaders and educators can use the information provided in Tables 1 and 2 to generate their own scenarios and evaluate the viability of such futures and the potential change on the horizon. While focusing on incremental change scenarios may allow some risk-averse leaders (Lovallo et al., 2020) to feel like they are helping an organization move into the future, risk-takers will aggressively focus on understanding trends that will lead to disruptive change. For those willing to take great risks, there is the potential for great reward.

The special educational needs of individuals with disabilities require considerable effort and technologies to assist them in maximizing their potential. However, there are many secondary benefits to society when some specialized technologies (i.e., screen magnification, text to speech, word prediction) are implemented as inclusive technologies, providing benefits for everyone (Edyburn, 2019). As a result, it is important to think about the needs of diverse individuals when planning for the future of education.

Conclusions

In conclusion, the author acknowledges that he does not have any special insight about the future of education. On the other hand, understanding how existing trends and issues can converge does provide a powerful tool for creating scenarios describing how the future might be different than today. Clearly, the pandemic significantly accelerated investments in technology, infrastructure, and innovation that set the stage for a future where education could look very different than current educational practice. Furthermore, trends in automation and machine learning have critical consequences for the employability of individuals with disabilities who currently work in jobs that are clearly targeted for elimination (Chai et al., 2016). As a result, it is essential that educators and leaders reflect on how the pandemic impacted education and begin re-imagining the future of schooling.

References

Burrus, D. (1994). *Technotrends: How to use technology to go beyond your competition*. Harper – Business.

Burrus, D. (2011). *Flash foresight*. Harper Business.

Chai, M., Manyika, J., & Miremadi, M. (2016). Where machines could replace humans–And where they can't yet. *McKinsey Quarterly*. https://www.mckinsey.com/business-functions/mckinsey-digital/our-insights/where-machines-could-replace-humans-and-where-they-cant-yet

Christensen, C. M. (2013). *The innovator's dilemma: When new technologies cause great firms to fail*. Harvard Business Review Press.

Cybersecurity and Infrastructure Security Agency. (2020). *Cyber actors target K-12 distance learning education to cause disruptions and steal data (alert AA20–345A)*. https://www.cisa.gov/uscert/ncas/alerts/aa20-345a

Edyburn, D. L. (2004). Assisted learning: How assistive technologies developed for people with disabilities will affect learning for everyone. *Threshold, 2*(2), 22–25.

Edyburn, D. L. (2013). Critical issues in advancing the special education technology evidence-base. *Exceptional Children, 80*(1), 7–24. https://doi.org/10.1177/001440291308000107

Edyburn, D. L. (2019). *Inclusive technologies: Tools for helping diverse learners achieve academic success* (2nd ed.). Bridgepoint Education, Inc.

Future Today Institute. (2022). *2022 tech trends report*. https://futuretodayinstitute.com/trends/

Lovallo, D., Koller, T., Uhlaner, R., & Kahneman, D. (2020). Your company is too risk-averse. *Harvard Business Review, 98*(2), 104–111.

Meyer, A., Rose, D. H., & Gordon, D. T. (2014). *Universal design for learning: Theory and practice*. CAST Professional Publishing.

National Center for Education Statistics. (2021). *Students with disabilities*. https://nces.ed.gov/programs/coe/indicator/cgg

Pelletier, K., McCormack, M., Reeves, J., Robert, J., & Arbino, N. (2022). *2022 EDUCAUSE horizon report: Teaching and learning edition*. https://library.educause.edu/resources/2022/4/2022-educause-horizon-report-teaching-and-learning-edition

Roblyer, M. D., & Hughes, J. E. (2019). *Integrating educational technology into teaching* (8th ed.). Pearson.

Reimagining Higher Education Pedagogy: Building an Active Understanding of the Research Process

Deborah Cockerham

Background/Rationale

Traditional higher education pedagogies such as lectures often situate students as recipients of knowledge (Akbar, 2016). Yet knowledge itself may not adequately prepare students to confront the complexity and uncertainty of global challenges in our rapidly changing society. Individuals who are prepared to face such challenges must be able to recognize problems, address potential ambiguity and dissonance, and work together to solve common concerns (UNESCO International Commission on the Futures of Education 2015, pp. 51–60). Learners must also navigate the plethora of knowledge and resources available digitally as they prioritize, analyze, and synthesize information for decision-making and problem-solving (Shim & Walczak, 2012).

A transformative approach to higher education pedagogies may be needed to support the development of teaching practices that meet the demands of our increasingly complex and globally connected world (Lotz-Sisitka et al., 2015). Instructional pedagogies that involve students in actively determining and investigating relevant problems can increase learner knowledge while simultaneously building on students' personal experiences and supporting the development and practice of twenty-first century core competencies: communication, collaboration, critical-thinking, and creativity (UNESCO, 2015; World Economic Forum, 2016). In addition, higher education that is grounded in experience can engage students and support internalization of key theoretical concepts (Jickling, 2009). As educators prepare and implement their curriculums, they must reflect upon the purpose and impact of each

D. Cockerham (✉)
University of North Texas, Denton, TX, USA
e-mail: deborah.cockerham@unt.edu

© The Author(s), under exclusive license to Springer Nature Switzerland AG 2023
D. Cockerham et al. (eds.), *Reimagining Education: Studies and Stories for Effective Learning in an Evolving Digital Environment*,
Educational Communications and Technology: Issues and Innovations,
https://doi.org/10.1007/978-3-031-25102-3_24

instructional action, interaction, and expectation for students and their academic foundations (Garuba, 2015).

The goal of this chapter is to consider how higher education pedagogies might be reimagined to support doctoral students and faculty in addressing the challenges of our rapidly changing world. The chapter will begin by examining recent literature that considers the impact of higher education instructional pedagogies upon the learner's development of knowledge, skills, and capacity for addressing current challenges and needs. Following this, we will discuss instructional pedagogies in doctoral education as related to the goal of building research scholars. We next describe an experiential research course in which doctoral students build an active understanding of the research process by designing and conducting original research. The chapter concludes with a brief discussion that considers how the integration of higher education instructional pedagogies, applied research, and community connections can build student agency and empower students to address future challenges for the good of society.

Impact of Higher Education Pedagogies Upon Learning

Instructional profiles from the Approach to Teaching Inventory (Prosser & Trigwell, 1999) group higher education pedagogies into two basic categories: an information transmission/teacher-focused approach (ITTF) and a conceptual change/student-focused approach (CCSF) (Stes & Van Petegem, 2014). In ITTF, the primary instructional goal is to transmit information. Content is often delivered through lectures or demonstrations, and progress is measured through visible outcomes (e.g., tests) in which students reproduce the conveyed information. Students are not generally included as active participants in an ITTF teaching and learning process (Prosser & Trigwell, 2014).

In contrast, CCSF goals focus on actively using new information and experiences to deepen students' understanding or ability to use knowledge. As students interact with information, they adjust their prior conceptions and build an active understanding of course content (Prosser & Trigwell, 2014). CCSF methods may be centered in experiential opportunities or collaborative work within the community, or may include activities such as student discussions and breakout rooms, student-initiated projects, game-based learning, or problem-solving activities. ITTF ("lecture methods") and CCSF ("active" or "experiential learning") methods are generally considered as the primary instructional approaches in higher education and will be recognized as such throughout this chapter.

Lecture Versus Active Learning

Since the early twentieth century, education experts have espoused the idea that classroom learning is incomplete without integrated experience (Dewey, 1938; McCrary & Jones, 2008), and that student development of problem solving and critical thinking skills depends upon the infusion of factual knowledge with skills practice (Collins et al., 2018). Lectures currently predominate as the primary instructional mode in higher education. Recent analyses (Stains et al., 2018) suggest that higher education science, technology, engineering, and math (STEM) instructors deliver approximately 82% of their instruction through lectures with few or no opportunities for student interaction (e.g., clicker questions with group work).

While lectures may be effective in some situations, instructional methods that support active learning generally appear to result in stronger STEM outcomes than lectures (Yik et al., 2022; Wieman, 2014). In a 2014 study comparing lecture and active learning methods, 850 students who had been taught by lecture for half a semester were taught for a week either by experienced, motivated professors using a lecture-based approach or by inexperienced postdoctoral fellows who had students predict, engage in relevant discussions and arguments, solve problems, and evaluate their personal understanding (Deslauriers et al., 2011). Following a week of instruction in these conditions, researchers found that student engagement doubled among the active learning group, which was taught by the inexperienced postdoctoral fellows, but remained consistent among the lecture group, taught by the experienced professors. Additionally, students in the active learning condition scored an average post-test score of 74%, compared with a score of 41% for students in the lecture-based condition.

In like manner, Ge et al. (2015) found positive results when conducting an intervention study comparing student self-efficacy and collaborative problem-solving skills. Before and after implementing instruction through technology-enhanced active learning methods, data was collected through class observations, instructor interviews, and surveys administered to 92 students from a total of 5 university science courses. Findings showed significantly higher student self-efficacy scores with the active learning approach, but no significant differences in perceived student motivation for problem solving. Three of the five instructors appreciated the technology affordances and support for abstract learning and noted that the technology-enhanced active learning inspired ideas for additional active learning methods. Researchers noted large discrepancies between professors who maximized their applications of technology, using digital tools for group work and collaborative activities, and those who used the technology only to support their lectures.

Active learning in STEM courses has also been shown to reduce academic gaps in underrepresented undergraduate students (Theobald et al., 2020). A meta-analysis conducted by 33 researchers began with a search of 1659 research studies on active versus passive learning. After limiting the sample to 397 studies from two analyses, researchers compared study exam scores and failure rates for almost 54,000 students from minority races, ethnicities, or lower socioeconomic status who were enrolled in undergraduate active learning classrooms or lecture-based STEM classes (Theobald et al., 2020). For the study, researchers defined traditional learning as "continuous exposition by the instructor with involvement by the students limited to occasional questions" and active learning as "any approach that engages students in the learning process through in-class activities, with an emphasis on higher order thinking and group work" (Theobald et al., 2020). Results showed a 33% lower achievement gap on exams and a 45% lower failure rate in active learning than in traditional lecture classes. Based on these results, researchers suggested that the achievement gap could be narrowed through a comprehensive shift to active learning instruction in higher education, along with an emphasis on research-based educational strategies and little to no instruction through traditional lecturing formats.

In addition, a large meta-analysis of 225 studies investigated the effects of active learning instructional methods versus lecture-based approaches on learning performance (Freeman et al., 2014). In this study, researchers posed the instructional methods question, "In the STEM classroom, should we ask, or should we tell?" Findings showed that students taught by lecture-based approaches were 1.5 times more likely to fail than those who were taught with active learning approaches. Researchers concluded that an "ask, don't tell" instructional approach based on the constructivist theory can strengthen learning outcomes and that an active learning approach is an empirically validated approach to teaching (Freeman et al., 2014).

Active learning designs based on the constructivist theory were also investigated by Oliver & McLoughlin (2001, cited in McLoughlin, 2002), who suggested that active learning opportunities incorporate relevant experiences, support student agency, embed learning in social experience, provide insight into multiple perspectives, and afford student leadership and self-awareness in building understanding.

When integrating active learning into the higher educational learning environment, instructors and designers must consider the ability of technology to incorporate interactive and authentic learning opportunities that encourage student agency and collaboration (Parker et al., 2013). Thaiposri and Wannapiroon's (2015) assessment of an online inquiry-based learning experience that was implemented in the courses of five university professors suggested that digital resources and communication tools enhanced student learning. In addition to improving academic performance, the students involved in the inquiry-based approach showed stronger critical thinking skills than those in lecture-based instructional methods (Thaiposri & Wannapiroon, 2015).

The Online Learning Environment Survey (OLES, Trinidad et al., 2005) incorporates themes from four established learning environment surveys as it assesses relevance in an active online learning environment through eight scales:

- Teacher support
- Student interaction and collaboration
- Personal relevance
- Authenticity
- Student autonomy
- Equity
- Technology usage
- Asynchronicity

These elements can work together to build an active, student-focused online learning environment in higher education.

Instructional Needs in Doctoral Education

Although much of the research comparing higher education pedagogy examines instructional approaches for undergraduate students, instructional methods within graduate programs must also address student learning needs. Research-centered doctoral degrees such as the Doctor of Philosophy degree (PhD) aim to develop scholars who contribute to current knowledge through original research and scholarly work (Association of American Universities, 1998). As PhD students prepare for future careers as researchers, teachers, and scholars, they not only need to learn information that is known and established in the field but must also understand how to create effective questions and design investigations for discovering evidence that contributes to scholarly knowledge (Walker et al., 2009, p. 4). Many students need guidance in moving beyond an educational mindset in which learning is directed and the goal is to be a good "course-taker" (Lovitts, 2005). Attainment of the skills and confidence needed not only to engage in autonomous learning but also to collaborate with other researchers and the community requires both practice and mentoring (Hannah & Arreguin, 2017).

Walker et al. (2009, pp. 89–91) views the PhD trajectory as a type of apprenticeship in which one-to-one education is essential to development of a solid foundation in the discipline. For PhD students, interacting with experienced researchers and engaging in learning activities that support cultivation of creativity, critical thinking, and communication skills are essential to future success. Such pursuits foster independent thinking and initiative, encourage collaborative work, and lead to the formation of solid research questions (Lovitts, 2005).

Although the integration of knowledge and skills has been linked with the development of basic research skills such as problem solving, creativity, and critical thinking skills (Dewey, 1938; McCrary & Jones, 2008; Collins et al., 2018), assignments in research methods courses often focus on literature reviews and dissertation proposals (Rickly & Cook, 2017). Such assignments provide specific skill training but present no opportunities to design studies and actively experience or understand the complete research process. Critiques of relevant research publications, another common assignment, can support a basic understanding of how to conduct research, but research publications tend to be neatly packaged and do not reveal the complex, unpredictable, "messy" nature of most research, nor do they convey the need to narrow the research focus as the problem is clarified and questions emerge (Grant-Davie et al., 2017).

In like manner, research statistics courses may provide a solid grounding in formulas and statistical tests but often do not clearly demonstrate the relationship between research questions, methods, and data analysis. The integration of these three areas is important for building the critical thinking skills needed to interpret and communicate the data (Albers, 2017). Experiential learning and practice that includes targeted feedback can help students understand the need to think beyond research hypotheses and find the practical story within the data, which often contributes more to the body of knowledge than the data itself (Sanscartier, 2020).

This literature review has highlighted two primary concepts:

1. An instructional pedagogy grounded in active learning opportunities has consistently been seen to improve student outcomes in higher education. Active learning can support student agency, build leadership skills, and encourage self-confidence.
2. Research skills are not innate. As PhD students work to develop their research capacities, they need opportunities to learn and practice skills that will benefit their future work as researchers and scholars.

The overview below describes a PhD course that integrated these two concepts by incorporating active learning into a doctoral level research course.

Active Learning in an Experiential Research Course

The rapid move from physical classrooms to online learning during the COVID-19 pandemic presented researchers and graduate students with abundant opportunities to investigate the effectiveness of online education. Yet many students who expressed high interest in examining timely and relevant issues lacked research experience and, consequently, considered themselves unprepared to initiate or conduct research studies independently. To encourage PhD students to take the lead in designing and conducting research studies, an online PhD course grounded in experience was initiated in one large university's educational technology program. The course overview below describes how a pedagogical approach in which graduate students actively experience the unpredictable, disorderly nature of the complete research process can help future scholars build confidence and conduct quality research studies in the evolving digital environment.

Course Overview

Course Goals and Introduction

Promotion for the course began with the question: "How is COVID-19 impacting our technology usage?" Students were invited to enroll in an online research course in which they would take the lead in designing and conducting a research study and preparing a manuscript suitable for publication. The main goals of the course were for students to develop an active understanding of the research process, to complete a research study, to articulate it in a research manuscript, and to develop confidence in their own research skills.

Course Structure

The course structure took an hour-glass shape. Students were first presented with the overarching goal (conduct a complete research study). This goal was then separated into its primary components: literature review, methods, results and analysis, discussion/conclusion, and abstract. Finally, the "big picture" re-emerged as each student connected the components to prepare the final course product, a manuscript articulating the research. The dates and sequencing of assignments were flexible, allowing students to work on individual components as their research evolved. Students also learned to manage the various tasks as they worked on overlapping components. For example, students worked simultaneously to attain Institutional Review Board (IRB) approval, write the literature review, and determine appropriate journals for submission. The solid but flexible course structure provided a strong scaffolding within which students could explore and deepen their understanding of the research gestalt.

Within this structure, the online learning environment was carefully designed with a repository of resources and models to enrich understanding of the research process. Each of the six learning modules, presented asynchronously through Canvas learning management systems, focused on a specific component of a traditional research manuscript. Information in each module described the purpose of the specific manuscript component and provided pointers and examples for preparing the specified portion of the manuscript. In addition, a list of publications and tools offered suggestions on effective research writing and linked to examples of quality published manuscripts. Students learned strategies that could support effective searches for quality literature online.

Mentoring

While the course was asynchronous, mentoring was crucial to its success. Before the semester began, each enrolled student met one-to-one with the instructor to discuss the student's research ideas and interests and identify the issue to be studied. These early meetings allowed time for the student to refine the research focus and questions before preparing an IRB submission. The instructor asked clarifying questions to help the student develop targeted research questions and consider important details of the investigation process but allowed the student to make the final decisions in study approach.

Students were at all levels of their PhD trajectories, from first semester doctoral students to doctoral candidates in their final semester of course work. The small class size (12 students) allowed time for the instructor to meet with students in regular one-to-one meetings throughout the semester. Students briefed the instructor and received study guidance and support according to their individual needs. The instructor also provided detailed feedback on each learning assignment (manuscript component) and encouraged students to edit the assignments before they assembled components for the final manuscript.

In addition to instructional mentoring, peer mentoring evolved through the Discussion Board. As students posted their project ideas, described relevant publications, and shared potential journals, they discovered common interests and learned from each other. Some students chose to collaborate on the research with a partner rather than independently. Those who chose this option received additional peer support.

Student Challenges

Students often began the research process with an idealized vision of how the research would work and who their participants would be. However, as in most investigations, the research process did not always proceed according to plan. A first challenge for many students was receiving approval to recruit participants through either an online or place-based institution. As students quickly learned, businesses and public school districts could be slow to respond, and social media groups were not always willing to allow researchers to post the recruitment messages.

Additional challenges emerged as data collection began. Individuals who were expected to participate in the study did not always agree to be a part, and others who did agree only partially completed the data collection. Survey questions were sometimes interpreted incorrectly. Demographic questions didn't provide enough information. Situations such as these quickly introduced students to the unpredictable, sometimes chaotic, nature of research that is typical even when the project is carefully designed.

Yet as students worked through their issues and concerns, they learned valuable insights, gaining critical thinking and communication skills that could support their leadership in future research. The online learning environment provided a stable scaffolding that supported student agency, active learning, and internalization of the research process through experience and practice. By the end of the semester, students had prepared all components of a research manuscript and assembled them in sequence to complete the final write-up.

Discussion: Developing Confidence and Skills Through Active Learning

Critical elements of an active online learning experience were integrated into the research course through core course components:

- Opportunities for PhD student mentoring
- Collaborations with the community
- Student-initiated learning experiences

- Technology integration
- Communication of research

Each of these components is supported by one or more scales of the Online Learning Environment Survey ([OLES], Trinidad et al., 2005), which provide a framework for discussing the active experiential learning opportunity.

Opportunities for PhD Student Mentoring

OLES Scales: Teacher/Peer Support and Collaboration; Equity

In line with the theories of Walker et al. (2009), the course afforded various opportunities for student mentoring. Most participating students had never completed an IRB submission, so they received guidance on accessing the system and preparing an IRB. Both instructor feedback and peer responses offered encouragement and suggestions that kept students moving towards their goals. For example, a student who had only secured two participants by the middle of the semester was concerned that she would not be able to complete the study. The instructor encouraged her to complete her analysis with the participants she had for the purpose of the class and to focus on additional participants after the semester ended. In so doing, the student articulated the methods and prepared a solid research manuscript that she adapted after gaining other participants.

Peer mentoring was an invaluable resource for students. Responses to discussion postings broadened the perspectives and added insights that boosted the understanding of all involved. Students who collaborated with a partner displayed additional confidence in their decisions and plans.

Community Collaborations

OLES Scale: Authentic Learning

Student research goals were often related to issues that they had observed or experienced in their personal place-based or online communities during the pandemic. As they recruited individuals and clarified the data collection process with participants from their schools, workplaces, community organizations, or social media groups, even students who were at first hesitant to reach out improved their communication skills. The community connections situated students' theoretical knowledge amidst practical needs, enriching their understanding through personal application of learning, as seen in Hannah and Arreguin (2017).

Student-Led Learning Experiences

OLES Scales: Student Autonomy and Personal Relevance

Students were encouraged to assess relevant issues and develop investigations of personal interest. While one-to-one mentoring with the instructor helped students to shape and narrow the research focus and to determine methods that would accurately target the issues, achievement of the course goals required student agency and self-directed, autonomous learning. Students sometimes expressed confusion or surprise when they experienced unforeseen circumstances, difficulties in implementation, or incomplete data, but navigating through these situations helped them better understand the research and realize the value of perseverance even when research is difficult. This aligns with Rickly and Cook's (2017) proposition that hands-on experience builds understanding when working through research that does not proceed according to plan.

Technology Integration

OLES Scales: Technology as a Tool to Access Information; Asynchronicity

The research course was grounded in inquiry and supported by technological tools. Videoconferencing tools allowed students to communicate directly with the university IRB team in the online introductory class session, supporting the student IRB submissions. Both videoconferencing tools and social media sites enabled students to communicate with participants. In addition, online survey platforms, research repositories, social media, writing tools, and a variety of online resources facilitated students in accessing information and collecting data.

The asynchronous nature of the online course required student agency and allowed students to independently develop and implement their research studies. Sharing ideas and insights through online discussion postings allowed time for students to reflect before responding. Technology was integral to both the online course design and student data collection and enabled connections throughout the research and learning experience.

Communicating the Research

OLES Scale: Technology as a Tool to Communicate with Others

Designing and conducting a research study is only of value if the findings are disseminated to support growth and build the scholarly body of knowledge. PhD students must develop the skills to clearly articulate their research (Rickly & Cook,

2017), which requires both knowledge of the scholarly writing approach and time spent in practice. The research course provided models and examples to help in learning the standard research manuscript format and visualize the importance of well-aligned study components. It also supported students in chunking the writing so that practice in articulating the research background, process, and findings continued throughout the semester. Thorough feedback was provided for all aspects of the writing. For students, articulating the research often created "ah-ha!" moments that solidified understanding of the research and supported confidence in their own research skills.

Course Outcomes

Dewey's (1938) "learn by doing" theory suggests that student participation in authentic experiences can deepen learning. In line with this theory, the active involvement of the PhD students in authentic research experiences allowed them to internalize the many steps that go into designing and conducting a research study. As they assimilated the elements into a complete research studies, students linked academic knowledge with practical experience, enhanced understanding, and increased confidence in their own research skills. Students noted how envisioning the complete process supported their research growth. As one student commented, "Working on dozens of projects at once, as many of us did this semester, is extremely overwhelming, and having a chance to connect the dots and make some of this work as meaningful as it can be is truly worth a lot."

Students also observed how the opportunity to select their own topic and lead their own investigation made the research more meaningful and applicable towards their future research goals. Designing and conducting a research study in a single semester can be a daunting task, but the focus on active learning, relevance, and authenticity can nurture research skills and build confidence for leading future research studies.

Conclusion

Higher education that transforms students into scholars must be centered in instructional practices in which students take an active role. As they work to develop scholarly research skills, students must experience the complete research process, navigating the uncertainties, ambiguity, and potential failures that are encountered in authentic research experiences (Rickly & Cook, 2017). Students need more than knowledge to address the complex, rapidly changing world. Active learning experiences in which students make complex decisions, solve multidimensional problems, deal with unpredictable outcomes, and apply academic theories to practical situations can promote growth of the essential critical thinking skills that underlie effective research.

When learning experiences foster the development of research skills, both students and instructors can benefit. Teaching that supports students in actively understanding and improving research skills can boost student confidence and encourage students to begin molding their own scholarly identities (Walker et al., 2009). As instructors guide students to build an active understanding of the research process, they empower tomorrow's scholars to address the uncertain and complex global issues of the future.

References

Akbar, M. (2016). Digital technology shaping teaching practices in higher education. *Frontiers in ICT, 3*, 1. https://doi.org/10.3389/fict.2016.00001

Albers, M. J. (2017). Quantitative data analysis—In the graduate curriculum. *Journal of Technical Writing and Communication, 47*(2), 215–233. https://doi.org/10.1177/0047281617692067

Association of American Universities. (1998). *Committee on graduate education report and recommendations*. Association of American Universities. https://www.aau.edu/key-issues/aau-committee-graduate-education-report-and-recommendations

Collins, A., Brown, J. S., & Newman, S. E. (2018). Cognitive apprenticeship: Teaching the crafts of reading, writing, and mathematics. In *Knowing, learning, and instruction* (pp. 453–494). Routledge.

Deslauriers, L., Schelew, E., & Wieman, C. (2011). Improved learning in a large-enrollment physics class. *Science, 332*(6031), 862–864. https://doi.org/10.1126/science.1201783

Dewey, J. (1938). *The theory of inquiry*. Holt, Rinehart & Winston.

Freeman, S., Eddy, S. L., McDonough, M., Smith, M. K., Okoroafor, N., Jordt, H., & Wenderoth, M. P. (2014). Active learning increases student performance in science, engineering, and mathematics. *Proceedings of the National Academy of Sciences, 111*(23), 8410–8415. https://www.pnas.org/doi/abs/10.1073/pnas.1319030111

Garuba, H. (2015). *Towards an African curriculum*. Getting Ahead. Supplement to the Mail and Guardian Newspaper. http://mg.co.za/article/2015-04-17-what-is-an-african-curriculum/

Ge, X., Yang, Y. J., Liao, L., & Wolfe, E. G. (2015). Perceived affordances of a technology-enhanced active learning classroom in promoting collaborative problem solving. In *E-learning systems, environments and approaches* (pp. 305–322). Springer.

Grant-Davie, K., Matheson, B., & James Stephens, E. (2017). Helping doctoral students establish long-term identities as technical communication scholars. *Journal of Technical Writing and Communication, 47*(2), 151–171. https://doi.org/10.1177/0047281617692071

Hannah, M. A., & Arreguin, A. (2017). Cultivating conditions for access: A case for "case-making" in graduate student preparation for interdisciplinary research. *Journal of Technical Writing and Communication, 47*(2), 172–193. https://doi.org/10.1177/0047281617692070

Jickling, B. (2009). Environmental education research: To what ends? *Environmental Education Research, 15*(2), 209–216. https://doi.org/10.1080/13504620902770345

Lotz-Sisitka, H., Wals, A. E., Kronlid, D., & McGarry, D. (2015). Transformative, transgressive social learning: Rethinking higher education pedagogy in times of systemic global dysfunction. *Current Opinion in Environmental Sustainability, 16*, 73–80. https://doi.org/10.1016/j.cosust.2015.07.018

Lovitts, B. E. (2005). Being a good course-taker is not enough: A theoretical perspective on the transition to independent research. *Studies in Higher Education, 30*(2), 137–154. https://doi.org/10.1080/03075070500043093

McCrary, S. W., & Jones, M. P. (2008). Build it and they will learn: Enhancing experiential learning opportunities in the statics classroom. In *Annual international conference of associated schools of construction*. http://ascpro0.ascweb.org/archives/cd/2008/paper/CEUE283002008.pdf

McLoughlin, C. (2002). Learner support in distance and networked learning environments: Ten dimensions for successful design. *Distance Education, 23*(2), 149–162. https://doi.org/10.1080/0158791022000009178

Oliver, R., & McLoughlin, C. (2001). Using networking tools to support online learning. In F. Lockwood (Ed.), *Innovation in open and distance learning: Successful development of online and E-web-based learning* (pp. 160–171). Routledge.

Parker, J., Maor, D., & Herrington, J. (2013). Authentic online learning: Aligning learner needs, pedagogy and technology. *Issues in Educational Research, 23*(2), 227–241. https://search.informit.org/doi/abs/10.3316/ielapa.354613892620670

Prosser, M., & Trigwell, K. (1999). Relational perspectives on higher education teaching and learning in the sciences. *Studies in Science Education, 33*(1), 31–60. https://doi.org/10.1080/03057269908560135

Prosser, M., & Trigwell, K. (2014). Qualitative variation in approaches to university teaching and learning in large first-year classes. *Higher Education, 67*(6), 783–795. https://doi.org/10.1007/s10734-013-9690-0

Rickly, R., & Cook, K. C. (2017). Failing forward: Training graduate students for research—An introduction to the special issue. *Journal of Technical Writing and Communication, 47*(2), 119–129. https://doi.org/10.1177/0047281617692074

Sanscartier, M. D. (2020). The craft attitude: Navigating mess in mixed methods research. *Journal of Mixed Methods Research, 14*(1), 47–62. https://doi.org/10.1177/1558689818816248

Shim, W. J., & Walczak, K. (2012). The impact of faculty teaching practices on the development of students' critical thinking skills. *International Journal of Teaching and Learning in Higher Education, 24*(1), 16–30. https://eric.ed.gov/?id=EJ977179

Stains, M., Harshman, J., Barker, M. K., Chasteen, S. V., Cole, R., DeChenne-Peters, S. E., Eagan, M. K., Jr., Esson, J. M., Knight, J. K., et al. (2018). Anatomy of STEM teaching in north American universities. *Science, 359*(6383), 1468–1470. https://www.science.org/doi/abs/10.1126/science.aap8892.

Stes, A., & Van Petegem, P. (2014). Profiling approaches to teaching in higher education: A cluster-analytic study. *Studies in Higher Education, 39*(4), 644–658. https://doi.org/10.1080/03075079.2012.729032

Theobald, E. J., Hill, M. J., Tran, E., Agrawal, S., Arroyo, E. N., Behling, S., et al. (2020). Active learning narrows achievement gaps for underrepresented students in undergraduate science, technology, engineering, and math. *Proceedings of the National Academy of Sciences, 117*(12), 6476–6483. https://www.pnas.org/doi/abs/10.1073/pnas.1916903117.

Thaiposri, P., & Wannapiroon, P. (2015). Enhancing students' critical thinking skills through teaching and learning by inquiry-based learning activities using social network and cloud computing. *Procedia-Social and Behavioral Sciences, 174*, 2137–2144. https://doi.org/10.1016/j.sbspro.2015.02.013

Trinidad, S., Aldridge, J., & Fraser, B. (2005). Development, validation and use of the online learning environment survey. *Australasian Journal of Educational Technology, 21*(1). https://doi.org/10.14742/ajet.1343

UNESCO International Commission on the Futures of Education. (2015). *Reimagining our futures together: A new social contract for the future of education*. UNESCO. https://reliefweb.int/report/world/reimagining-our-futures-together-new-social-contract-education

Walker, G. E., Golde, C. M., Jones, L., Bueschel, A. C., & Hutchings, P. (2009). *The formation of scholars: Rethinking doctoral education for the twenty-first century*. Wiley.

Wieman, C. E. (2014). Large-scale comparison of science teaching methods sends clear message. *Proceedings of the National Academy of Sciences, 111*(23), 8319–8320. https://doi.org/10.1073/pnas.1407304111

World Economic Forum. (2016). *New vision for education: Fostering social and emotional learning through technology*. World Economic Forum. https://www.weforum.org/reports/new-vision-for-education-fostering-social-and-emotional-learning-through-technology

Yik, B. J., Raker, J. R., Apkarian, N., Stains, M., Henderson, C., Dancy, M. H., & Johnson, E. (2022). Evaluating the impact of malleable factors on percent time lecturing in gateway chemistry, mathematics, and physics courses. *International Journal of STEM Education, 9*(1), 1–23. https://doi.org/10.1186/s40594-022-00333-3

Index

© Association for Educational Communications and Technology (AECT) 2023
D. Cockerham et al. (eds.), *Reimagining Education: Studies and Stories for Effective Learning in an Evolving Digital Environment*, Educational Communications and Technology: Issues and Innovations, https://doi.org/10.1007/978-3-031-25102-3

Printed in the United States
by Baker & Taylor Publisher Services